CompTIA EXAM SY0-701
SECURITY+™
Study Supplement

MARK "SHUE" SCHUMACHER

Lowry Global Media LLC

Shue's, CompTIA Security+, Exam SY0-701, Study Supplement

Copyright © by Lowry Global Media LLC

All rights reserved. This book, including its cover (front, back, and spine), may not be copied or reproduced, partially or totally, by any means, including but not limited to digital or analog methods, without the written permission of Lowry Global Media LLC; exceptions are granted for brief excerpts used in published reviews.

```
Permission is granted to copy, distribute and/or modify the Wikipedia® content
(interior content) under the terms of the GNU Free Documentation License, Version 1.3
or any later version published by the Free Software Foundation; with no Invariant
Sections, no Front-Cover Texts, and no Back-Cover Texts.
```

Wikipedia® content from http://en.wikipedia.org/, retreived in September of 2023, main content of this book, is presented as made available under the Creative Commons Attribution-ShareAlike License, (http://en.wikipedia.org/wiki/Wikipedia:Text_of_Creative_Commons_Attribution-ShareAlike_3.0_Unported_License; and also where applicable, is made available under the GNU Free Documentation License (http://www.gnu.org/copyleft/fdl.html).
The intention is to comply with the "Wikipedia: Reusing Wikipedia content" guidance as described here, http://en.wikipedia.org/wiki/Wikipedia:Reusing_Wikipedia_content.
Use of Wikipedia® content does not imply endorsement from Wikipedia® or from the authors of the Wikipedia® content.
Wikipedia® content may or may not have been modified by Lowry Global Media LLC.

Wikipedia® is a registered trademark of the Wikimedia Foundation, Inc., a non-profit organization.

CompTIA® is a registered trademark of the CompTIA, Inc.

Disclaimer
This book is not affiliated with or endorsed by CompTIA, Inc., or any representatives thereof.

ISBN: 978-1-950961-72-6

Contents

Introduction

Information Security – 1
Encryption – 22
Computer Security – 26
Network Security – 55
Honeytoken – 56
Physical Security – 57
Social Engineering – 72
Malware – 76
Security Testing – 85
Cryptography – 87
Electronic Authentication – 102
Public Key Infrastructure – 110
Certificate Authority – 116
Vulnerability – 124
Computer Network – 131
Cloud Computing – 149
Cloud Computing Security – 161
Computer Access Control – 171
Data Backup – 175
IT Risk Management – 184

Introduction

At a minimum, you need to be able to speak the language Security; when Security comes up in conversation you need to be able to speak intelligently on the subject (this is the bare minimum). Aditionally, when in planning meetings (you know there are going to be a LOT of these) you need to be able to compare and contrast different approaches and implementations of Security.

This is the book to get you where you need to be. Just 199 pages, in an easy to read format, so you can get up to speed.

This book contains the perfect balance of subject matter and depth to provide you with the additional perspective you need to broaden your experience so you can speak the language of security and get ready for the Security+ exam.

Open source software is created by the community we belong to; IT professionals that want to do more and contribute. Just like open source software, this book has been created from open sources; a compilation of information for your benefit to help you speak the language of security and get ready for the Security+ exam.

Enjoy,

Mark "Shue" Schumacher
President
Lowry Global Media LLC

Information Security

Information security, sometimes shortened to **InfoSec**,[1] is the practice of protecting information by mitigating information risks. It is part of information risk management.[2][3] It typically involves preventing or reducing the probability of unauthorized or inappropriate access to data or the unlawful use, disclosure, disruption, deletion, corruption, modification, inspection, recording, or devaluation of information.[4] It also involves actions intended to reduce the adverse impacts of such incidents. Protected information may take any form, e.g., electronic or physical, tangible (e.g., paperwork), or intangible (e.g., knowledge).[5][6] Information security's primary focus is the balanced protection of data confidentiality, integrity, and availability (also known as the CIA triad) while maintaining a focus on efficient policy implementation, all without hampering organization productivity.[7] This is largely achieved through a structured risk management process that involves:

- Identifying information and related assets, plus potential threats, vulnerabilities, and impacts;
- Evaluating the risks
- Deciding how to address or treat the risks, i.e., to avoid, mitigate, share, or accept them
- Where risk mitigation is required, selecting or designing appropriate security controls and implementing them
- Monitoring the activities and making adjustments as necessary to address any issues, changes, or improvement opportunities[8]

To standardize this discipline, academics and professionals collaborate to offer guidance, policies, and industry standards on passwords, antivirus software, firewalls, encryption software, legal liability, security awareness and training, and so forth.[9] This standardization may be further driven by a wide variety of laws and regulations that affect how data is accessed, processed, stored, transferred, and destroyed.[10] However, the implementation of any standards and guidance within an entity may have limited effect if a culture of continual improvement is not adopted.[11]

Definition

Information Security Attributes: or qualities, i.e., Confidentiality, Integrity and Availability (CIA). Information Systems are composed in three main portions, hardware, software and communications with the purpose to help identify and apply information security industry standards, as mechanisms of protection and prevention, at three levels or layers: physical, personal and organizational. Essentially, procedures or policies are implemented to tell administrators, users and operators how to use products to ensure information security within the organizations.[12]

Various definitions of information security are suggested below, summarized from different sources:

1. "Preservation of confidentiality, integrity and availability of information. Note: In addition, other properties, such as authenticity, accountability, non-repudiation and reliability can also be involved." (ISO/IEC 27000:2018)[13]

2. "The protection of information and information systems from unauthorized access, use, disclosure, disruption, modification, or destruction in order to provide confidentiality, integrity, and availability." (CNSS, 2010)[14]
3. "Ensures that only authorized users (confidentiality) have access to accurate and complete information (integrity) when required (availability)." (ISACA, 2008)[15]
4. "Information Security is the process of protecting the intellectual property of an organization." (Pipkin, 2000)[16]
5. "...information security is a risk management discipline, whose job is to manage the cost of information risk to the business." (McDermott and Geer, 2001)[17]
6. "A well-informed sense of assurance that information risks and controls are in balance." (Anderson, J., 2003)[18]
7. "Information security is the protection of information and minimizes the risk of exposing information to unauthorized parties." (Venter and Eloff, 2003)[19]
8. "Information Security is a multidisciplinary area of study and professional activity which is concerned with the development and implementation of security mechanisms of all available types (technical, organizational, human-oriented and legal) in order to keep information in all its locations (within and outside the organization's perimeter) and, consequently, information systems, where information is created, processed, stored, transmitted and destroyed, free from threats.[20] Threats to information and information systems may be categorized and a corresponding security goal may be defined for each category of threats.[21] A set of security goals, identified as a result of a threat analysis, should be revised periodically to ensure its adequacy and conformance with the evolving environment.[22] The currently relevant set of security goals may include: *confidentiality, integrity, availability, privacy, authenticity & trustworthiness, non-repudiation, accountability and auditability.*" (Cherdantseva and Hilton, 2013)[12]
9. Information and information resource security using telecommunication system or devices means protecting information, information systems or books from unauthorized access, damage, theft, or destruction (Kurose and Ross, 2010).[23]

Overview

At the core of information security is information assurance, the act of maintaining the confidentiality, integrity, and availability (CIA) of information, ensuring that information is not compromised in any way when critical issues arise.[24] These issues include but are not limited to natural disasters, computer/server malfunction, and physical theft. While paper-based business operations are still prevalent, requiring their own set of information security practices, enterprise digital initiatives are increasingly being emphasized,[25][26] with information assurance now typically being dealt with by information technology (IT) security specialists. These specialists apply information security to technology (most often some form of computer system). It is worthwhile to note that a computer does not necessarily mean a home desktop.[27] A computer is any device with a processor and some memory. Such devices can range from non-networked standalone devices as simple as calculators, to networked mobile computing devices such as smartphones and tablet computers.[28] IT security specialists are almost always found in any major enterprise/establishment due to the nature and value of the data within larger businesses.[29] They are responsible for keeping all of the technology within the company secure from malicious cyber attacks that often attempt to acquire critical private information or gain control of the internal systems.[30][31]

The field of information security has grown and evolved significantly in recent years.[32] It offers many areas for specialization, including securing networks and allied infrastructure, securing applications and databases, security testing, information systems auditing, business continuity planning, electronic record discovery, and digital forensics. Information security professionals are very stable in their employment.[33] As of 2013 more than 80 percent of professionals had no change in employer or employment over a period of a year, and the number of professionals is projected to continuously grow more than 11 percent annually from 2014 to 2019.[34]

Threats

Information security threats come in many different forms.[35][36] Some of the most common threats today are software attacks, theft of intellectual property, theft of identity, theft of equipment or information, sabotage, and information extortion.[37][38] Viruses,[39] worms, phishing attacks, and Trojan horses are a few common examples of software attacks. The theft of intellectual property has also been an extensive issue for many businesses in the information technology (IT) field.[40] Identity theft is the attempt to act as someone else usually to obtain that person's personal information or to take advantage of their access to vital information through social engineering.[41][42] Theft of equipment or information is becoming more prevalent today due to the fact that most devices today are mobile,[43] are prone to theft and have also become far more desirable as the amount of data capacity increases. Sabotage usually consists of the destruction of an organization's website in an attempt to cause loss of confidence on the part of its customers.[44] Information extortion consists of theft of a company's property or information as an attempt to receive a payment in exchange for returning the information or property back to its owner, as with ransomware.[45] There are many ways to help protect yourself from some of these attacks but one of the most functional precautions is conduct periodical user awareness.[46] The number one threat to any organisation are users or internal employees, they are also called insider threats.[47]

Governments, military, corporations, financial institutions, hospitals, non-profit organisations, and private businesses amass a great deal of confidential information about their employees, customers, products, research, and financial status.[48] Should confidential information about a business's customers or finances or new product line fall into the hands of a competitor or a black hat hacker, a business and its customers could suffer widespread, irreparable financial loss, as well as damage to the company's reputation.[49] From a business perspective, information security must be balanced against cost; the Gordon-Loeb Model provides a mathematical economic approach for addressing this concern.[50]

For the individual, information security has a significant effect on privacy, which is viewed very differently in various cultures.[51]

Responses to threats

Possible responses to a security threat or risk are:[52]

- reduce/mitigate – implement safeguards and countermeasures to eliminate vulnerabilities or block threats
- assign/transfer – place the cost of the threat onto another entity or organization such as purchasing insurance or outsourcing

- accept – evaluate if the cost of the countermeasure outweighs the possible cost of loss due to the threat[53]

History

Since the early days of communication, diplomats and military commanders understood that it was necessary to provide some mechanism to protect the confidentiality of correspondence and to have some means of detecting tampering.[54] Julius Caesar is credited with the invention of the Caesar cipher c. 50 B.C., which was created in order to prevent his secret messages from being read should a message fall into the wrong hands.[55] However, for the most part protection was achieved through the application of procedural handling controls.[56][57] Sensitive information was marked up to indicate that it should be protected and transported by trusted persons, guarded and stored in a secure environment or strong box.[58] As postal services expanded, governments created official organizations to intercept, decipher, read, and reseal letters (e.g., the U.K.'s Secret Office, founded in 1653[59]).

In the mid-nineteenth century more complex classification systems were developed to allow governments to manage their information according to the degree of sensitivity.[60] For example, the British Government codified this, to some extent, with the publication of the Official Secrets Act in 1889.[61] Section 1 of the law concerned espionage and unlawful disclosures of information, while Section 2 dealt with breaches of official trust.[62] A public interest defense was soon added to defend disclosures in the interest of the state.[63] A similar law was passed in India in 1889, The Indian Official Secrets Act, which was associated with the British colonial era and used to crack down on newspapers that opposed the Raj's policies.[64] A newer version was passed in 1923 that extended to all matters of confidential or secret information for governance.[65] By the time of the First World War, multi-tier classification systems were used to communicate information to and from various fronts, which encouraged greater use of code making and breaking sections in diplomatic and military headquarters.[66] Encoding became more sophisticated between the wars as machines were employed to scramble and unscramble information.[67]

The establishment of computer security inaugurated the history of information security. The need for such appeared during World War II.[68] The volume of information shared by the Allied countries during the Second World War necessitated formal alignment of classification systems and procedural controls.[69] An arcane range of markings evolved to indicate who could handle documents (usually officers rather than enlisted troops) and where they should be stored as increasingly complex safes and storage facilities were developed.[70] The Enigma Machine, which was employed by the Germans to encrypt the data of warfare and was successfully decrypted by Alan Turing, can be regarded as a striking example of creating and using secured information.[71] Procedures evolved to ensure documents were destroyed properly, and it was the failure to follow these procedures which led to some of the greatest intelligence coups of the war (e.g., the capture of U-570[71]).

Various Mainframe computers were connected online during the Cold War to complete more sophisticated tasks, in a communication process easier than mailing magnetic tapes back and forth by computer centers. As such, the Advanced Research Projects Agency (ARPA), of the United States Department of Defense, started researching the feasibility of a networked system of communication to trade information within the United States Armed Forces. In 1968, the ARPANET project was formulated by Dr. Larry Roberts, which would later evolve into what is known as the internet.[72]

In 1973, important elements of ARPANET security were found by internet pioneer Robert Metcalfe to have many flaws such as the: "vulnerability of password structure and formats; lack of safety procedures for dial-up connections; and nonexistent user identification and authorizations", aside from the lack of controls and safeguards to keep data safe from unauthorized access. Hackers had effortless access to ARPANET, as phone numbers were known by the public.[73] Due to these problems, coupled with the constant violation of computer security, as well as the exponential increase in the number of hosts and users of the system, "network security" was often alluded to as "network insecurity".[73]

The end of the twentieth century and the early years of the twenty-first century saw rapid advancements in telecommunications, computing hardware and software, and data encryption.[74] The availability of smaller, more powerful, and less expensive computing equipment made electronic data processing within the reach of small business and home users.[75] The establishment of Transfer Control Protocol/Internetwork Protocol (TCP/IP) in the early 1980s enabled different types of computers to communicate.[76] These computers quickly became interconnected through the internet.[77]

The rapid growth and widespread use of electronic data processing and electronic business conducted through the internet, along with numerous occurrences of international terrorism, fueled the need for better methods of protecting the computers and the information they store, process, and transmit.[78] The academic disciplines of computer security and information assurance emerged along with numerous professional organizations, all sharing the common goals of ensuring the security and reliability of information systems.

Basic principles

Key concepts

The CIA triad of confidentiality, integrity, and availability is at the heart of information security.[79] (The members of the classic InfoSec triad—confidentiality, integrity, and availability—are interchangeably referred to in the literature as security attributes, properties, security goals, fundamental aspects, information criteria, critical information characteristics and basic building blocks.)[80] However, debate continues about whether or not this CIA triad is sufficient to address rapidly changing technology and business requirements, with recommendations to consider expanding on the intersections between availability and confidentiality, as well as the relationship between security and privacy.[24] Other principles such as "accountability" have sometimes been proposed; it has been pointed out that issues such as non-repudiation do not fit well within the three core concepts.[81]

The triad seems to have first been mentioned in a NIST publication in 1977.[82]

In 1992 and revised in 2002, the OECD's *Guidelines for the Security of Information Systems and Networks*[83] proposed the nine generally accepted principles: awareness, responsibility, response, ethics, democracy, risk assessment, security design and implementation, security management, and reassessment.[84] Building upon those, in 2004 the NIST's *Engineering Principles for Information Technology Security*[81] proposed 33 principles. From each of these derived guidelines and practices.

In 1998, Donn Parker proposed an alternative model for the classic CIA triad that he called the six atomic elements of information. The elements are confidentiality, possession, integrity, authenticity, availability, and utility. The merits of the Parkerian Hexad are a subject of debate amongst security professionals.[85]

In 2011, The Open Group published the information security management standard O-ISM3.[86] This standard proposed an operational definition of the key concepts of security, with elements called "security objectives", related to access control (9), availability (3), data quality (1), compliance, and technical (4). In 2009, DoD Software Protection Initiative Archived 2016-09-25 at the Wayback Machine released the Three Tenets of Cybersecurity Archived 2020-05-10 at the Wayback Machine which are System Susceptibility, Access to the Flaw, and Capability to Exploit the Flaw.[87][88][89] Neither of these models are widely adopted.

Confidentiality

In information security, confidentiality "is the property, that information is not made available or disclosed to unauthorized individuals, entities, or processes."[90] While similar to "privacy," the two words are not interchangeable. Rather, confidentiality is a component of privacy that implements to protect our data from unauthorized viewers.[91] Examples of confidentiality of electronic data being compromised include laptop theft, password theft, or sensitive emails being sent to the incorrect individuals.[92]

Integrity

In IT security, data integrity means maintaining and assuring the accuracy and completeness of data over its entire lifecycle.[93] This means that data cannot be modified in an unauthorized or undetected manner.[94] This is not the same thing as referential integrity in databases, although it can be viewed as a special case of consistency as understood in the classic ACID model of transaction processing.[95] Information security systems typically incorporate controls to ensure their own integrity, in particular protecting the kernel or core functions against both deliberate and accidental threats.[96] Multi-purpose and multi-user computer systems aim to compartmentalize the data and processing such that no user or process can adversely impact another: the controls may not succeed however, as we see in incidents such as malware infections, hacks, data theft, fraud, and privacy breaches.[97]

More broadly, integrity is an information security principle that involves human/social, process, and commercial integrity, as well as data integrity. As such it touches on aspects such as credibility, consistency, truthfulness, completeness, accuracy, timeliness, and assurance.[98]

Availability

For any information system to serve its purpose, the information must be available when it is needed.[99] This means the computing systems used to store and process the information, the security controls used to protect it, and the communication channels used to access it must be functioning correctly.[100] High availability systems aim to remain available at all times, preventing service disruptions due to power outages, hardware failures, and system upgrades.[101] Ensuring availability also involves preventing denial-of-service attacks, such as a flood of incoming messages to the target system, essentially forcing it to shut down.[102]

In the realm of information security, availability can often be viewed as one of the most important parts of a successful information security program. Ultimately end-users need to be able to perform job functions; by ensuring availability an organization is able to perform to the standards that an organization's stakeholders expect.[103] This can involve topics such as proxy configurations, outside web access, the ability to access shared drives and the ability to send emails.[104] Executives oftentimes do not understand the technical side of information security and look at availability as an easy fix, but this often requires collaboration from many different organizational teams, such as network operations, development operations, incident response, and policy/change management.[105] A successful information security team involves many different key roles to mesh and align for the CIA triad to be provided effectively.[106]

Non-repudiation

In law, non-repudiation implies one's intention to fulfill their obligations to a contract. It also implies that one party of a transaction cannot deny having received a transaction, nor can the other party deny having sent a transaction.[107]

It is important to note that while technology such as cryptographic systems can assist in non-repudiation efforts, the concept is at its core a legal concept transcending the realm of technology.[108] It is not, for instance, sufficient to show that the message matches a digital signature signed with the sender's private key, and thus only the sender could have sent the message, and nobody else could have altered it in transit (data integrity).[109] The alleged sender could in return demonstrate that the digital signature algorithm is vulnerable or flawed, or allege or prove that his signing key has been compromised.[110] The fault for these violations may or may not lie with the sender, and such assertions may or may not relieve the sender of liability, but the assertion would invalidate the claim that the signature necessarily proves authenticity and integrity. As such, the sender may repudiate the message (because authenticity and integrity are pre-requisites for non-repudiation).[111]

Risk management

Broadly speaking, risk is the likelihood that something bad will happen that causes harm to an informational asset (or the loss of the asset).[112] A vulnerability is a weakness that could be used to endanger or cause harm to an informational asset. A threat is anything (man-made or act of nature) that has the potential to cause harm.[113] The likelihood that a threat will use a vulnerability to cause harm creates a risk. When a threat does use a vulnerability to inflict harm, it has an impact.[114] In the context of information security, the impact is a loss of availability, integrity, and confidentiality, and possibly other losses (lost income, loss of life, loss of real property).[115]

The *Certified Information Systems Auditor (CISA) Review Manual 2006* defines **risk management** as "the process of identifying vulnerabilities and threats to the information resources used by an organization in achieving business objectives, and deciding what countermeasures,[116] if any, to take in reducing risk to an acceptable level, based on the value of the information resource to the organization."[117]

There are two things in this definition that may need some clarification. First, the *process* of risk management is an ongoing, iterative process. It must be repeated indefinitely. The business environment is constantly changing and new threats and vulnerabilities emerge every day.[118] Second, the choice of countermeasures (controls) used to manage risks must strike a balance between productivity, cost, effectiveness of the countermeasure, and the value of the informational asset being protected.[119] Furthermore, these processes have limitations as security breaches are generally rare and emerge in a specific context which may not be easily duplicated.[120] Thus, any process and countermeasure should itself be evaluated for vulnerabilities.[121] It is not possible to identify all risks, nor is it possible to eliminate all risk. The remaining risk is called "residual risk.[122]"

A risk assessment is carried out by a team of people who have knowledge of specific areas of the business.[123] Membership of the team may vary over time as different parts of the business are assessed.[124] The assessment may use a subjective qualitative analysis based on informed opinion, or where reliable dollar figures and historical information is available, the analysis may use quantitative analysis.

Research has shown that the most vulnerable point in most information systems is the human user, operator, designer, or other human.[125] The ISO/IEC 27002:2005 Code of practice for information security management recommends the following be examined during a risk assessment:

- security policy,
- organization of information security,
- asset management,
- human resources security,
- physical and environmental security,
- communications and operations management,
- access control,
- information systems acquisition, development, and maintenance,
- information security incident management,
- business continuity management
- regulatory compliance.

In broad terms, the risk management process consists of:[126][127]

1. Identification of assets and estimating their value. Include: people, buildings, hardware, software, data (electronic, print, other), supplies.[128]
2. Conduct a threat assessment. Include: Acts of nature, acts of war, accidents, malicious acts originating from inside or outside the organization.[129]
3. Conduct a vulnerability assessment, and for each vulnerability, calculate the probability that it will be exploited. Evaluate policies, procedures, standards, training, physical security, quality control, technical security.[130]
4. Calculate the impact that each threat would have on each asset. Use qualitative analysis or quantitative analysis.[131]
5. Identify, select and implement appropriate controls. Provide a proportional response. Consider productivity, cost effectiveness, and value of the asset.[132]
6. Evaluate the effectiveness of the control measures. Ensure the controls provide the required cost effective protection without discernible loss of productivity.[133]

For any given risk, management can choose to accept the risk based upon the relative low value of the asset, the relative low frequency of occurrence, and the relative low impact on the business.[134] Or, leadership may choose to mitigate the risk by selecting and implementing appropriate control measures to reduce the risk. In some cases, the risk can be transferred to another business by buying insurance or outsourcing to another business.[135] The reality of some risks may be disputed. In such cases leadership may choose to deny the risk.[136]

Security controls

Selecting and implementing proper security controls will initially help an organization bring down risk to acceptable levels.[137] Control selection should follow and should be based on the risk assessment.[138] Controls can vary in nature, but fundamentally they are ways of protecting the confidentiality, integrity or availability of information. ISO/IEC 27001 has defined controls in different areas.[139] Organizations can implement additional controls according to requirement of the organization.[140] ISO/IEC 27002 offers a guideline for organizational information security standards.[141]

Administrative

Administrative controls (also called procedural controls) consist of approved written policies, procedures, standards, and guidelines. Administrative controls form the framework for running the business and managing people.[142] They inform people on how the business is to be run and how day-to-day operations are to be conducted. Laws and regulations created by government bodies are also a type of administrative control because they inform the business.[143] Some industry sectors have policies, procedures, standards, and guidelines that must be followed – the Payment Card Industry Data Security Standard[144] (PCI DSS) required by Visa and MasterCard is such an example. Other examples of administrative controls include the corporate security policy, password policy, hiring policies, and disciplinary policies.[145]

Administrative controls form the basis for the selection and implementation of logical and physical controls. Logical and physical controls are manifestations of administrative controls, which are of paramount importance.[142]

Logical

Logical controls (also called technical controls) use software and data to monitor and control access to information and computing systems. Passwords, network and host-based firewalls, network intrusion detection systems, access control lists, and data encryption are examples of logical controls.[146]

An important logical control that is frequently overlooked is the principle of least privilege, which requires that an individual, program or system process not be granted any more access privileges than are necessary to perform the task.[147] A blatant example of the failure to adhere to the principle of least privilege is logging into Windows as user Administrator to read email and surf the web. Violations of this principle can also occur when an individual collects additional access privileges over time.[148] This happens when employees' job duties change, employees are promoted to a new position, or employees are transferred to another department.[149] The access privileges required by their new duties are frequently added onto their already existing access privileges, which may no longer be necessary or appropriate.[150]

Physical

Physical controls monitor and control the environment of the work place and computing facilities.[151] They also monitor and control access to and from such facilities and include doors, locks, heating and air conditioning, smoke and fire alarms, fire suppression systems, cameras, barricades, fencing, security guards, cable locks, etc. Separating the network and workplace into functional areas are also physical controls.[152]

An important physical control that is frequently overlooked is separation of duties, which ensures that an individual can not complete a critical task by himself.[153] For example, an employee who submits a request for reimbursement should not also be able to authorize payment or print the check.[154] An applications programmer should not also be the server administrator or the database administrator; these roles and responsibilities must be separated from one another.[155]

Defense in depth

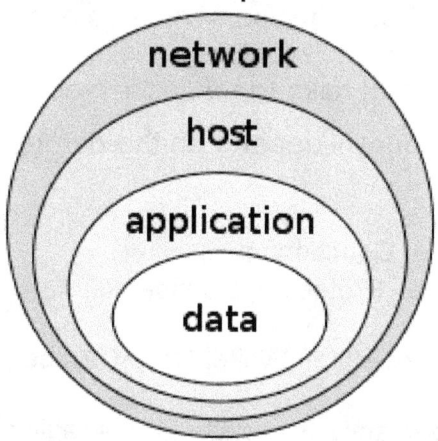

The onion model of defense in depth

Information security must protect information throughout its lifespan, from the initial creation of the information on through to the final disposal of the information.[156] The information must be protected while in motion and while at rest. During its lifetime, information may pass through many different information processing systems and through many different parts of information processing systems.[157] There are many different ways the information and information systems can be threatened. To fully protect the information during its lifetime, each component of the information processing system must have its own protection mechanisms.[158] The building up, layering on, and overlapping of security measures is called "defense in depth."[159] In contrast to a metal chain, which is famously only as strong as its weakest link, the defense in depth strategy aims at a structure where, should one defensive measure fail, other measures will continue to provide protection.[160]

Recall the earlier discussion about administrative controls, logical controls, and physical controls. The three types of controls can be used to form the basis upon which to build a defense in depth strategy.[142] With this approach, defense in depth can be conceptualized as three distinct layers or planes laid one on top of the other.[161] Additional insight into defense in depth can be gained by thinking of it as forming the layers of an onion, with data at the core of the onion, people the next outer layer of the onion, and network security, host-based security, and application security forming the outermost layers of the onion.[162] Both perspectives are equally valid, and each provides valuable insight into the implementation of a good defense in depth strategy.[163]

Classification

An important aspect of information security and risk management is recognizing the value of information and defining appropriate procedures and protection requirements for the information.[164] Not all information is equal and so not all information requires the same degree of protection.[165] This requires information to be assigned a security classification.[166] The first step in information classification is to identify a member of senior management as the owner of the particular information to be classified. Next, develop a classification policy.[167] The policy should describe the different classification labels, define the criteria for information to be assigned a particular label, and list the required security controls for each classification.[168]

Some factors that influence which classification information should be assigned include how much value that information has to the organization, how old the information is and whether or not the information has become obsolete.[169] Laws and other regulatory requirements are also important considerations when classifying information.[170] The Information Systems Audit and Control Association (ISACA) and its *Business Model for Information Security* also serves as a tool for security professionals to examine security from a systems perspective, creating an environment where security can be managed holistically, allowing actual risks to be addressed.[171]

The type of information security classification labels selected and used will depend on the nature of the organization, with examples being:[168]

- In the business sector, labels such as: Public, Sensitive, Private, Confidential.
- In the government sector, labels such as: Unclassified, Unofficial, Protected, Confidential, Secret, Top Secret, and their non-English equivalents.[172]
- In cross-sectoral formations, the Traffic Light Protocol, which consists of: White, Green, Amber, and Red.
- In the personal sector, one label such as Financial. This includes activities related to managing money, such as online banking.[173]

All employees in the organization, as well as business partners, must be trained on the classification schema and understand the required security controls and handling procedures for each classification.[174] The classification of a particular information asset that has been assigned should be reviewed periodically to ensure the classification is still appropriate for the information and to ensure the security controls required by the classification are in place and are followed in their right procedures.[175]

Access control

Access to protected information must be restricted to people who are authorized to access the information.[176] The computer programs, and in many cases the computers that process the information, must also be authorized.[177] This requires that mechanisms be in place to control the access to protected information.[177] The sophistication of the access control mechanisms should be in parity with the value of the information being protected; the more sensitive or valuable the information the stronger the control mechanisms need to be.[178] The foundation on which access control mechanisms are built start with identification and authentication.[179]

Access control is generally considered in three steps: identification, authentication, and authorization.[180][92]

Identification

Identification is an assertion of who someone is or what something is. If a person makes the statement "Hello, my name is John Doe" they are making a claim of who they are.[181] However, their claim may or may not be true. Before John Doe can be granted access to protected information it will be necessary to verify that the person claiming to be John Doe really is John Doe.[182] Typically the claim is in the form of a username. By entering that username you are claiming "I am the person the username belongs to".[183]

Authentication

Authentication is the act of verifying a claim of identity. When John Doe goes into a bank to make a withdrawal, he tells the bank teller he is John Doe, a claim of identity.[184] The bank teller asks to see a photo ID, so he hands the teller his driver's license.[185] The bank teller checks the license to make sure it has John Doe printed on it and compares the photograph on the license against the person claiming to be John Doe.[186] If the photo and name match the person, then the teller has authenticated that John Doe is who he claimed to be. Similarly, by entering the correct password, the user is providing evidence that he/she is the person the username belongs to.[187]

There are three different types of information that can be used for authentication:[188][189]

- Something you know: things such as a PIN, a password, or your mother's maiden name[190][191]
- Something you have: a driver's license or a magnetic swipe card[192][193]
- Something you are: biometrics, including palm prints, fingerprints, voice prints, and retina (eye) scans[194]

Strong authentication requires providing more than one type of authentication information (two-factor authentication).[195] The username is the most common form of identification on computer systems today and the password is the most common form of authentication.[196] Usernames and passwords have served their purpose, but they are increasingly inadequate.[197] Usernames and passwords are slowly being replaced or supplemented with more sophisticated authentication mechanisms such as Time-based One-time Password algorithms.[198]

Authorization

After a person, program or computer has successfully been identified and authenticated then it must be determined what informational resources they are permitted to access and what actions they will be allowed to perform (run, view, create, delete, or change).[199] This is called authorization. Authorization to access information and other computing services begins with administrative policies and procedures.[200] The policies prescribe what information and computing services can be accessed, by whom, and under what conditions. The access control mechanisms are then configured to enforce these policies.[201] Different computing systems are equipped with different kinds of access control mechanisms. Some may even offer a choice of different access control mechanisms.[202] The access control mechanism a system offers will be based upon one of three approaches to access control, or it may be derived from a combination of the three approaches.[92]

The non-discretionary approach consolidates all access control under a centralized administration.[203] The access to information and other resources is usually based on the individuals function (role) in the organization or the tasks the individual must perform.[204][205] The discretionary approach gives the creator or owner of the information resource the ability to control access to those resources.[203] In the mandatory access control approach, access is granted or denied basing upon the security classification assigned to the information resource.[176]

Examples of common access control mechanisms in use today include role-based access control, available in many advanced database management systems; simple file permissions provided in the UNIX and Windows operating systems;[206] Group Policy Objects provided in Windows network systems; and Kerberos, RADIUS, TACACS, and the simple access lists used in many firewalls and routers.[207]

To be effective, policies and other security controls must be enforceable and upheld. Effective policies ensure that people are held accountable for their actions.[208] The U.S. Treasury's guidelines for systems processing sensitive or proprietary information, for example, states that all failed and successful authentication and access attempts must be logged, and all access to information must leave some type of audit trail.[209]

Also, the need-to-know principle needs to be in effect when talking about access control. This principle gives access rights to a person to perform their job functions.[210] This principle is used in the government when dealing with difference clearances.[211] Even though two employees in different departments have a top-secret clearance, they must have a need-to-know in order for information to be exchanged. Within the need-to-know principle, network administrators grant the employee the least amount of privilege to prevent employees from accessing more than what they are supposed to.[212] Need-to-know helps to enforce the confidentiality-integrity-availability triad. Need-to-know directly impacts the confidential area of the triad.[213]

Cryptography

Information security uses cryptography to transform usable information into a form that renders it unusable by anyone other than an authorized user; this process is called encryption.[214] Information that has been encrypted (rendered unusable) can be transformed back into its original usable form by an authorized user who possesses the cryptographic key, through the process of decryption.[215] Cryptography is used in information security to protect information from unauthorized or accidental disclosure while the information is in transit (either electronically or physically) and while information is in storage.[92]

Cryptography provides information security with other useful applications as well, including improved authentication methods, message digests, digital signatures, non-repudiation, and encrypted network communications.[216] Older, less secure applications such as Telnet and File Transfer Protocol (FTP) are slowly being replaced with more secure applications such as Secure Shell (SSH) that use encrypted network communications.[217] Wireless communications can be encrypted using protocols such as WPA/WPA2 or the older (and less secure) WEP. Wired communications (such as ITU-T G.hn) are secured using AES for encryption and X.1035 for authentication and key exchange.[218] Software applications such as GnuPG or PGP can be used to encrypt data files and email.[219]

Cryptography can introduce security problems when it is not implemented correctly.[220] Cryptographic solutions need to be implemented using industry-accepted solutions that have undergone rigorous peer review by independent experts in cryptography.[221] The length and strength of the encryption key is also an important consideration.[222] A key that is weak or too short will produce weak encryption.[222] The keys used for encryption and decryption must be protected with the same degree of rigor as any other confidential information.[223] They must be protected from unauthorized disclosure and destruction, and they must be available when needed.[224] Public key infrastructure (PKI) solutions address many of the problems that surround key management.[92]

Process

The terms "reasonable and prudent person", "due care", and "due diligence" have been used in the fields of finance, securities, and law for many years. In recent years these terms have found their way into the fields of computing and information security.[127] U.S. Federal Sentencing Guidelines now make it possible to hold corporate officers liable for failing to exercise due care and due diligence in the management of their information systems.[225]

In the business world, stockholders, customers, business partners, and governments have the expectation that corporate officers will run the business in accordance with accepted business practices and in compliance with laws and other regulatory requirements. This is often described as the "reasonable and prudent person" rule. A prudent person takes due care to ensure that everything necessary is done to operate the business by sound business principles and in a legal, ethical manner. A prudent person is also diligent (mindful, attentive, ongoing) in their due care of the business.

In the field of information security, Harris[226] offers the following definitions of due care and due diligence:

"Due care are steps that are taken to show that a company has taken responsibility for the activities that take place within the corporation and has taken the necessary steps to help protect the company, its resources, and employees[227]*."* And, [Due diligence are the] *"continual activities that make sure the protection mechanisms are continually maintained and operational."*[228]

Attention should be made to two important points in these definitions.[229][230] First, in due care, steps are taken to show; this means that the steps can be verified, measured, or even produce tangible artifacts.[231][232] Second, in due diligence, there are continual activities; this means that people are actually doing things to monitor and maintain the protection mechanisms, and these activities are ongoing.[233]

Organizations have a responsibility with practicing duty of care when applying information security. The Duty of Care Risk Analysis Standard (DoCRA)[234] provides principles and practices for evaluating risk.[235] It considers all parties that could be affected by those risks.[236] DoCRA helps evaluate safeguards if they are appropriate in protecting others from harm while presenting a reasonable burden.[237] With increased data breach litigation, companies must balance security controls, compliance, and its mission.[238]

Security governance

The Software Engineering Institute at Carnegie Mellon University, in a publication titled *Governing for Enterprise Security (GES) Implementation Guide*, defines characteristics of effective security governance. These include:[239]

- An enterprise-wide issue
- Leaders are accountable
- Viewed as a business requirement
- Risk-based
- Roles, responsibilities, and segregation of duties defined
- Addressed and enforced in policy
- Adequate resources committed
- Staff aware and trained
- A development life cycle requirement
- Planned, managed, measurable, and measured
- Reviewed and audited

Incident response plans

An incident response plan (IRP) is a group of policies that dictate an organizations reaction to a cyber attack. Once an security breach has been identified, for example by Network Intrusion Detection System (NIDS) or Host-Based Intrusion Detection System (HIDS) (if configured to do so), the plan is initiated.[240] It is important to note that there can be legal implications to a data breach. Knowing local and federal laws is critical.[241] Every plan is unique to the needs of the organization, and it can involve skill sets that are not part of an IT team.[242] For example, a lawyer may be included in the response plan to help navigate legal implications to a data breach.

As mentioned above every plan is unique but most plans will include the following:[243]

Preparation

Good preparation includes the development of an Incident Response Team (IRT).[244] Skills need to be used by this team would be, penetration testing, computer forensics, network security, etc.[245] This team should also keep track of trends in cybersecurity and modern attack strategies.[246] A training program for end users is important as well as most modern attack strategies target users on the network.[243]

Identification

This part of the incident response plan identifies if there was a security event.[247] When an end user reports information or an admin notices irregularities, an investigation is launched. An incident log is a crucial part of this step.[248] All of the members of the team should be updating this log to ensure that information flows as fast as possible.[249] If it has been identified that a security breach has occurred the next step should be activated.[250]

Containment

In this phase, the IRT works to isolate the areas that the breach took place to limit the scope of the security event.[251] During this phase it is important to preserve information forensically so it can be analyzed later in the process.[252] Containment could be as simple as physically containing a server room or as complex as segmenting a network to not allow the spread of a virus.[253]

Eradication

This is where the threat that was identified is removed from the affected systems.[254] This could include deleting malicious files, terminating compromised accounts, or deleting other components.[255][256] Some events do not require this step, however it is important to fully understand the event before moving to this step.[257] This will help to ensure that the threat is completely removed.[253]

Recovery

This stage is where the systems are restored back to original operation.[258] This stage could include the recovery of data, changing user access information, or updating firewall rules or policies to prevent a breach in the future.[259][260] Without executing this step, the system could still be vulnerable to future security threats.[253]

Lessons Learned

In this step information that has been gathered during this process is used to make future decisions on security.[261] This step is crucial to the ensure that future events are prevented. Using this information to further train admins is critical to the process.[262] This step can also be used to process information that is distributed from other entities who have experienced a security event.[263]

Change management

Change management is a formal process for directing and controlling alterations to the information processing environment.[264][265] This includes alterations to desktop computers, the network, servers, and software.[266] The objectives of change management are to reduce the risks posed by changes to the information processing environment and improve the stability and reliability of the processing environment as changes are made.[267] It is not the objective of change management to prevent or hinder necessary changes from being implemented.[268][269]

Any change to the information processing environment introduces an element of risk.[270] Even apparently simple changes can have unexpected effects.[271] One of management's many responsibilities is the management of risk.[272][273] Change management is a tool for managing the risks introduced by changes to the information processing environment.[274] Part of the change management process ensures that changes are not implemented at inopportune times when they may disrupt critical business processes or interfere with other changes being implemented.[275]

Not every change needs to be managed.[276][277] Some kinds of changes are a part of the everyday routine of information processing and adhere to a predefined procedure, which reduces the overall level of risk to the processing environment.[278] Creating a new user account or deploying a new desktop computer are examples of changes that do not generally require change management.[279] However, relocating user file shares, or upgrading the Email server pose a much higher level of risk to the processing environment and are not a normal everyday activity.[280] The critical first steps in change management are (a) defining change (and communicating that definition) and (b) defining the scope of the change system.[281]

Change management is usually overseen by a change review board composed of representatives from key business areas,[282] security, networking, systems administrators, database administration, application developers, desktop support, and the help desk.[283] The tasks of the change review board can be facilitated with the use of automated work flow application.[284] The responsibility of the change review board is to ensure the organization's documented change management procedures are followed.[285] The change management process is as follows[286]

- **Request:** Anyone can request a change.[287][288] The person making the change request may or may not be the same person that performs the analysis or implements the change.[289][290] When a request for change is received, it may undergo a preliminary review to determine if the requested change is compatible with the organizations business model and practices, and to determine the amount of resources needed to implement the change.[291]
- **Approve:** Management runs the business and controls the allocation of resources therefore, management must approve requests for changes and assign a priority for every change.[292] Management might choose to reject a change request if the change is not compatible with the business model, industry standards or best practices.[293][294] Management might also choose to reject a change request if the change requires more resources than can be allocated for the change.[295]
- **Plan:** Planning a change involves discovering the scope and impact of the proposed change; analyzing the complexity of the change; allocation of resources and, developing, testing, and documenting both implementation and back-out plans.[296] Need to define the criteria on which a decision to back out will be made.[297]
- **Test:** Every change must be tested in a safe test environment, which closely reflects the actual production environment, before the change is applied to the production environment.[298] The backout plan must also be tested.[299]
- **Schedule:** Part of the change review board's responsibility is to assist in the scheduling of changes by reviewing the proposed implementation date for potential conflicts with other scheduled changes or critical business activities.[300]
- **Communicate:** Once a change has been scheduled it must be communicated.[301] The communication is to give others the opportunity to remind the change review board about other changes or critical business activities that might have been overlooked when scheduling the change.[302] The communication also serves to make the help desk and users aware that a change is about to occur.[303] Another responsibility of the change review board is to ensure that

scheduled changes have been properly communicated to those who will be affected by the change or otherwise have an interest in the change.[304][305]
- **Implement:** At the appointed date and time, the changes must be implemented.[306][307] Part of the planning process was to develop an implementation plan, testing plan and, a back out plan.[308][309] If the implementation of the change should fail or, the post implementation testing fails or, other "drop dead" criteria have been met, the back out plan should be implemented.[310]
- **Document:** All changes must be documented.[311][312] The documentation includes the initial request for change, its approval, the priority assigned to it, the implementation,[313] testing and back out plans, the results of the change review board critique, the date/time the change was implemented,[314] who implemented it, and whether the change was implemented successfully, failed or postponed.[315][316]
- **Post-change review:** The change review board should hold a post-implementation review of changes.[317] It is particularly important to review failed and backed out changes. The review board should try to understand the problems that were encountered, and look for areas for improvement.[317]

Change management procedures that are simple to follow and easy to use can greatly reduce the overall risks created when changes are made to the information processing environment.[318] Good change management procedures improve the overall quality and success of changes as they are implemented.[319] This is accomplished through planning, peer review, documentation, and communication.[320]

ISO/IEC 20000, The Visible OPS Handbook: Implementing ITIL in 4 Practical and Auditable Steps[321] (Full book summary),[322] and ITIL all provide valuable guidance on implementing an efficient and effective change management program information security.[323]

Business continuity

Business continuity management (BCM) concerns arrangements aiming to protect an organization's critical business functions from interruption due to incidents, or at least minimize the effects.[324][325] BCM is essential to any organization to keep technology and business in line with current threats to the continuation of business as usual.[326] The BCM should be included in an organizations risk analysis plan to ensure that all of the necessary business functions have what they need to keep going in the event of any type of threat to any business function.[327]

It encompasses:

- Analysis of requirements, e.g., identifying critical business functions, dependencies and potential failure points, potential threats and hence incidents or risks of concern to the organization;[328][329]
- Specification, e.g., maximum tolerable outage periods; recovery point objectives (maximum acceptable periods of data loss);[330]
- Architecture and design, e.g., an appropriate combination of approaches including resilience (e.g. engineering IT systems and processes for high availability,[331] avoiding or preventing situations that might interrupt the business), incident and emergency management (e.g., evacuating premises, calling the emergency services, triage/situation[332] assessment and invoking recovery plans), recovery (e.g., rebuilding) and contingency management (generic capabilities to deal positively with whatever occurs using whatever resources are available);[333]
- Implementation, e.g., configuring and scheduling backups, data transfers, etc., duplicating and strengthening critical elements; contracting with service and equipment suppliers;
- Testing, e.g., business continuity exercises of various types, costs and assurance levels;[334]

- Management, e.g., defining strategies, setting objectives and goals; planning and directing the work; allocating funds, people and other resources; prioritization relative to other activities; team building, leadership, control, motivation and coordination with other business functions and activities[335] (e.g., IT, facilities, human resources, risk management, information risk and security, operations); monitoring the situation, checking and updating the arrangements when things change; maturing the approach through continuous improvement, learning and appropriate investment;
- Assurance, e.g., testing against specified requirements; measuring, analyzing, and reporting key parameters; conducting additional tests, reviews and audits for greater confidence that the arrangements will go to plan if invoked.[336]

Whereas BCM takes a broad approach to minimizing disaster-related risks by reducing both the probability and the severity of incidents, a disaster recovery plan (DRP) focuses specifically on resuming business operations as quickly as possible after a disaster.[337] A disaster recovery plan, invoked soon after a disaster occurs, lays out the steps necessary to recover critical information and communications technology (ICT) infrastructure.[338] Disaster recovery planning includes establishing a planning group, performing risk assessment, establishing priorities, developing recovery strategies, preparing inventories and documentation of the plan, developing verification criteria and procedure, and lastly implementing the plan.[339]

Laws and regulations

Below is a partial listing of governmental laws and regulations in various parts of the world that have, had, or will have, a significant effect on data processing and information security.[340][341] Important industry sector regulations have also been included when they have a significant impact on information security.[340]

- The UK Data Protection Act 1998 makes new provisions for the regulation of the processing of information relating to individuals, including the obtaining, holding, use or disclosure of such information.[342][343] The European Union Data Protection Directive (EUDPD) requires that all E.U. members adopt national regulations to standardize the protection of data privacy for citizens throughout the E.U.[344][345]
- The Computer Misuse Act 1990 is an Act of the U.K. Parliament making computer crime (e.g., hacking) a criminal offense.[346] The act has become a model upon which several other countries,[347] including Canada and the Republic of Ireland, have drawn inspiration from when subsequently drafting their own information security laws.[348][349]
- The E.U.'s Data Retention Directive (annulled) required internet service providers and phone companies to keep data on every electronic message sent and phone call made for between six months and two years.[350]
- The Family Educational Rights and Privacy Act (FERPA) (20 U.S.C. § 1232 g; 34 CFR Part 99) is a U.S. Federal law that protects the privacy of student education records.[351] The law applies to all schools that receive funds under an applicable program of the U.S. Department of Education.[352] Generally, schools must have written permission from the parent or eligible student[352][353] in order to release any information from a student's education record.[354]
- The Federal Financial Institutions Examination Council's (FFIEC) security guidelines for auditors specifies requirements for online banking security.[355]
- The Health Insurance Portability and Accountability Act (HIPAA) of 1996 requires the adoption of national standards for electronic health care transactions and national identifiers for providers, health insurance plans, and employers.[356] Additionally, it requires health care providers, insurance providers and employers to safeguard the security and privacy of health data.[357]

- The Gramm–Leach–Bliley Act of 1999 (GLBA), also known as the Financial Services Modernization Act of 1999, protects the privacy and security of private financial information that financial institutions collect, hold, and process.[358]
- Section 404 of the Sarbanes–Oxley Act of 2002 (SOX) requires publicly traded companies to assess the effectiveness of their internal controls for financial reporting in annual reports they submit at the end of each fiscal year.[359] Chief information officers are responsible for the security, accuracy, and the reliability of the systems that manage and report the financial data.[360] The act also requires publicly traded companies to engage with independent auditors who must attest to, and report on, the validity of their assessments.[361]
- The Payment Card Industry Data Security Standard (PCI DSS) establishes comprehensive requirements for enhancing payment account data security.[362] It was developed by the founding payment brands of the PCI Security Standards Council — including American Express, Discover Financial Services, JCB, MasterCard Worldwide,[363] and Visa International — to help facilitate the broad adoption of consistent data security measures on a global basis.[364] The PCI DSS is a multifaceted security standard that includes requirements for security management, policies, procedures, network architecture, software design, and other critical protective measures.[365]
- State security breach notification laws (California and many others) require businesses, nonprofits, and state institutions to notify consumers when unencrypted "personal information" may have been compromised, lost, or stolen.[366]
- The Personal Information Protection and Electronics Document Act (PIPEDA) of Canada supports and promotes electronic commerce by protecting personal information that is collected, used or disclosed in certain circumstances,[367][368] by providing for the use of electronic means to communicate or record information or transactions and by amending the Canada Evidence Act, the Statutory Instruments Act and the Statute Revision Act.[369][370][371]
- Greece's Hellenic Authority for Communication Security and Privacy (ADAE) (Law 165/2011) establishes and describes the minimum information security controls that should be deployed by every company which provides electronic communication networks and/or services in Greece in order to protect customers' confidentiality.[372] These include both managerial and technical controls (e.g., log records should be stored for two years).[373]
- Greece's Hellenic Authority for Communication Security and Privacy (ADAE) (Law 205/2013) concentrates around the protection of the integrity and availability of the services and data offered by Greek telecommunication companies.[374] The law forces these and other related companies to build, deploy, and test appropriate business continuity plans and redundant infrastructures.[375]

The US Department of Defense (DoD) issued DoD Directive 8570 in 2004, supplemented by DoD Directive 8140, requiring all DoD employees and all DoD contract personnel involved in information assurance roles and activities to earn and maintain various industry Information Technology (IT) certifications in an effort to ensure that all DoD personnel involved in network infrastructure defense have minimum levels of IT industry recognized knowledge, skills and abilities (KSA). Andersson and Reimers (2019) report these certifications range from CompTIA's A+ and Security+ through the ICS2.org's CISSP, etc.. [376]

Culture

Describing more than simply how security aware employees are, information security culture is the ideas, customs, and social behaviors of an organization that impact information security in both positive and negative ways.[377] Cultural concepts can help different segments of the organization work effectively or work against effectiveness towards information security within an organization. The way employees think and feel about security and the actions they take can have a big impact on information security in organizations. Roer & Petric (2017) identify seven core dimensions of information security culture in organizations:[378]

- Attitudes: Employees' feelings and emotions about the various activities that pertain to the organizational security of information.[379]
- Behaviors: Actual or intended activities and risk-taking actions of employees that have direct or indirect impact on information security.
- Cognition: Employees' awareness, verifiable knowledge, and beliefs regarding practices, activities, and self-efficacy relation that are related to information security.
- Communication: Ways employees communicate with each other, sense of belonging, support for security issues, and incident reporting.
- Compliance: Adherence to organizational security policies, awareness of the existence of such policies and the ability to recall the substance of such policies.
- Norms: Perceptions of security-related organizational conduct and practices that are informally deemed either normal or deviant by employees and their peers, e.g. hidden expectations regarding security behaviors and unwritten rules regarding uses of information-communication technologies.
- Responsibilities: Employees' understanding of the roles and responsibilities they have as a critical factor in sustaining or endangering the security of information, and thereby the organization.

Andersson and Reimers (2014) found that employees often do not see themselves as part of the organization Information Security "effort" and often take actions that ignore organizational information security best interests.[380] Research shows information security culture needs to be improved continuously. In *Information Security Culture from Analysis to Change*, authors commented, "It's a never ending process, a cycle of evaluation and change or maintenance." To manage the information security culture, five steps should be taken: pre-evaluation, strategic planning, operative planning, implementation, and post-evaluation.[381]

- Pre-Evaluation: to identify the awareness of information security within employees and to analyze current security policy
- Strategic Planning: to come up a better awareness-program, we need to set clear targets. Clustering people is helpful to achieve it
- Operative Planning: create a good security culture based on internal communication, management buy-in, security awareness, and training programs
- Implementation: should feature commitment of management, communication with organizational members, courses for all organizational members, and commitment of the employees[381]
- Post-evaluation: to better gauge the effectiveness of the prior steps and build on continuous improvement

Sources of standards

The International Organization for Standardization (ISO) is an international standards organization organized as a consortium of national standards institutions from 167 countries, coordinated through a secretariat in Geneva, Switzerland. ISO is the world's largest developer of international standards. The International Electrotechnical Commission (IEC) is an international standards organization that deals with electrotechnology and cooperates closely with ISO. ISO/IEC 15443: "Information technology – Security techniques – A framework for IT security assurance", ISO/IEC 27002: "Information technology – Security techniques – Code of practice for information security management", ISO/IEC 20000: "Information technology – Service management", and ISO/IEC 27001: "Information technology – Security techniques – Information security management systems – Requirements" are of particular interest to information security professionals.

The US National Institute of Standards and Technology (NIST) is a non-regulatory federal agency within the U.S. Department of Commerce. The NIST Computer Security Division develops standards, metrics, tests, and validation programs as well as publishes standards and guidelines to increase secure IT planning, implementation, management, and operation. NIST is also the custodian of the U.S. Federal Information Processing Standard publications (FIPS).

The Internet Society is a professional membership society with more than 100 organizations and over 20,000 individual members in over 180 countries. It provides leadership in addressing issues that confront the future of the internet, and it is the organizational home for the groups responsible for internet infrastructure standards, including the Internet Engineering Task Force (IETF) and the Internet Architecture Board (IAB). The ISOC hosts the Requests for Comments (RFCs) which includes the Official Internet Protocol Standards and the RFC-2196 Site Security Handbook.

The Information Security Forum (ISF) is a global nonprofit organization of several hundred leading organizations in financial services, manufacturing, telecommunications, consumer goods, government, and other areas. It undertakes research into information security practices and offers advice in its biannual Standard of Good Practice and more detailed advisories for members.

The Institute of Information Security Professionals (IISP) is an independent, non-profit body governed by its members, with the principal objective of advancing the professionalism of information security practitioners and thereby the professionalism of the industry as a whole. The institute developed the IISP Skills Framework. This framework describes the range of competencies expected of information security and information assurance professionals in the effective performance of their roles. It was developed through collaboration between both private and public sector organizations, world-renowned academics, and security leaders.[382]

The German Federal Office for Information Security (in German *Bundesamt für Sicherheit in der Informationstechnik (BSI)*) BSI-Standards 100–1 to 100-4 are a set of recommendations including "methods, processes, procedures, approaches and measures relating to information security".[383] The BSI-Standard 100-2 *IT-Grundschutz Methodology* describes how information security management can be implemented and operated. The standard includes a very specific guide, the IT Baseline Protection Catalogs (also known as IT-Grundschutz Catalogs). Before 2005, the catalogs were formerly known as "IT Baseline Protection Manual". The Catalogs are a collection of documents useful for detecting and combating security-relevant weak points in the IT environment (IT cluster). The collection encompasses as of September 2013 over 4,400 pages with the introduction and catalogs. The IT-Grundschutz approach is aligned with to the ISO/IEC 2700x family.

The European Telecommunications Standards Institute standardized a catalog of information security indicators, headed by the Industrial Specification Group (ISG) ISI.

Encryption

In cryptography, **encryption** is the process of encoding information. This process converts the original representation of the information, known as plaintext, into an alternative form known as ciphertext. Ideally, only authorized parties can decipher a ciphertext back to plaintext and access the original information. Encryption does not itself prevent interference but denies the intelligible content to a would-be interceptor.

For technical reasons, an encryption scheme usually uses a pseudo-random encryption key generated by an algorithm. It is possible to decrypt the message without possessing the key but, for a well-designed encryption scheme, considerable computational resources and skills are required. An authorized recipient can easily decrypt the message with the key provided by the originator to recipients but not to unauthorized users.

Historically, various forms of encryption have been used to aid in cryptography. Early encryption techniques were often used in military messaging. Since then, new techniques have emerged and become commonplace in all areas of modern computing.[1] Modern encryption schemes use the concepts of public-key and symmetric-key.[1] Modern encryption techniques ensure security because modern computers are inefficient at cracking the encryption.

History

Ancient

One of the earliest forms of encryption is symbol replacement, which was first found in the tomb of Khnumhotep II, who lived in 1900 BC Egypt. Symbol replacement encryption is "non-standard," which means that the symbols require a cipher or key to understand. This type of early encryption was used throughout Ancient Greece and Rome for military purposes.[2] One of the most famous military encryption developments was the Caesar Cipher, which was a system in which a letter in normal text is shifted down a fixed number of positions down the alphabet to get the encoded letter. A message encoded with this type of encryption could be decoded with the fixed number on the Caesar Cipher.[3]

Around 800 AD, Arab mathematician Al-Kindi developed the technique of frequency analysis – which was an attempt to systematically crack Caesar ciphers.[2] This technique looked at the frequency of letters in the encrypted message to determine the appropriate shift. This technique was rendered ineffective after the creation of the polyalphabetic cipher by Leon Battista Alberti in 1465, which incorporated different sets of languages. In order for frequency analysis to be useful, the person trying to decrypt the message would need to know which language the sender chose.[2]

19th–20th century

Around 1790, Thomas Jefferson theorized a cipher to encode and decode messages in order to provide a more secure way of military correspondence. The cipher, known today as the Wheel Cipher or the Jefferson Disk, although never actually built, was theorized as a spool that could jumble an English message up to 36 characters. The message could be decrypted by plugging in the jumbled message to a receiver with an identical cipher.[4]

A similar device to the Jefferson Disk, the M-94, was developed in 1917 independently by US Army Major Joseph Mauborne. This device was used in U.S. military communications until 1942.[5]

In World War II, the Axis powers used a more advanced version of the M-94 called the Enigma Machine. The Enigma Machine was more complex because unlike the Jefferson Wheel and the M-94, each day the jumble of letters switched to a completely new combination. Each day's combination was only known by the Axis, so many thought the only way to break the code would be to try over 17,000 combinations within 24 hours.[6] The Allies used computing power to severely limit the number of reasonable combinations they needed to check every day, leading to the breaking of the Enigma Machine.

Modern

Today, encryption is used in the transfer of communication over the Internet for security and commerce.[1] As computing power continues to increase, computer encryption is constantly evolving to prevent eavesdropping attacks.[7] With one of the first "modern" cipher suites, DES, utilizing a 56-bit key with 72,057,594,037,927,936 possibilities being able to be cracked in 22 hours and 15 minutes by EFF's DES cracker in 1999, which used a brute-force method of cracking. Modern encryption standards often use stronger key sizes often 256, like AES(256-bit mode), TwoFish, ChaCha20-Poly1305, Serpent(configurable up to 512-bit). Cipher suites utilizing a 128-bit or higher key, like AES, will not be able to be brute-forced due to the total amount of keys of 3.4028237e+38 possibilities. The most likely option for cracking ciphers with high key size is to find vulnerabilities in the cipher itself, like inherent biases and backdoors. For example, RC4, a stream cipher, was cracked due to inherent biases and vulnerabilities in the cipher.

Encryption in cryptography

In the context of cryptography, encryption serves as a mechanism to ensure confidentiality.[1] Since data may be visible on the Internet, sensitive information such as passwords and personal communication may be exposed to potential interceptors.[1] The process of encrypting and decrypting messages involves keys. The two main types of keys in cryptographic systems are symmetric-key and public-key (also known as asymmetric-key).[8][9]

Many complex cryptographic algorithms often use simple modular arithmetic in their implementations.[10]

Types

In symmetric-key schemes,[11] the encryption and decryption keys are the same. Communicating parties must have the same key in order to achieve secure communication. The German Enigma Machine utilized a new symmetric-key each day for encoding and decoding messages.

In public-key encryption schemes, the encryption key is published for anyone to use and encrypt messages. However, only the receiving party has access to the decryption key that enables messages to be read.[12] Public-key encryption was first described in a secret document in 1973;[13] beforehand, all encryption schemes were symmetric-key (also called private-key).[14]:478 Although published subsequently, the work of Diffie and Hellman was published in a journal with a large readership, and the value of the methodology was explicitly described.[15] The method became known as the Diffie-Hellman key exchange.

RSA (Rivest–Shamir–Adleman) is another notable public-key cryptosystem. Created in 1978, it is still used today for applications involving digital signatures.[16] Using number theory, the RSA algorithm selects two prime numbers, which help generate both the encryption and decryption keys.[17]

A publicly available public-key encryption application called Pretty Good Privacy (PGP) was written in 1991 by Phil Zimmermann, and distributed free of charge with source code. PGP was purchased by Symantec in 2010 and is regularly updated.[18]

Uses

Encryption has long been used by militaries and governments to facilitate secret communication. It is now commonly used in protecting information within many kinds of civilian systems. For example, the Computer Security Institute reported that in 2007, 71% of companies surveyed utilized encryption for some of their data in transit, and 53% utilized encryption for some of their data in storage.[19] Encryption can be used to protect data "at rest", such as information stored on computers and storage devices (e.g. USB flash drives). In recent years, there have been numerous reports of confidential data, such as customers' personal records, being exposed through loss or theft of laptops or backup drives; encrypting such files at rest helps protect them if physical security measures fail.[20][21][22] Digital rights management systems, which prevent unauthorized use or reproduction of copyrighted material and protect software against reverse engineering, is another somewhat different example of using encryption on data at rest.[23]

Encryption is also used to protect data in transit, for example data being transferred via networks (e.g. the Internet, e-commerce), mobile telephones, wireless microphones, wireless intercom systems, Bluetooth devices and bank automatic teller machines. There have been numerous reports of data in transit being intercepted in recent years.[24] Data should also be encrypted when transmitted across networks in order to protect against eavesdropping of network traffic by unauthorized users.[25]

Data erasure

Conventional methods for permanently deleting data from a storage device involve overwriting the device's whole content with zeros, ones, or other patterns – a process which can take a significant amount of time, depending on the capacity and the type of storage medium. Cryptography offers a way of making the erasure almost instantaneous. This method is called crypto-shredding. An example implementation of this method can be found on iOS devices, where the cryptographic key is kept in a dedicated 'effaceable storage'.[26] Because the key is stored on the same device, this setup on its own does not offer full privacy or security protection if an unauthorized person gains physical access to the device.

Limitations

Encryption is used in the 21st century to protect digital data and information systems. As computing power increased over the years, encryption technology has only become more advanced and secure. However, this advancement in technology has also exposed a potential limitation of today's encryption methods.

The length of the encryption key is an indicator of the strength of the encryption method.[27] For example, the original encryption key, DES (Data Encryption Standard), was 56 bits, meaning it had 2^{56} combination possibilities. With today's computing power, a 56-bit key is no longer secure, being vulnerable to brute force attacks.[28]

Quantum computing utilizes properties of quantum mechanics in order to process large amounts of data simultaneously. Quantum computing has been found to achieve computing speeds thousands of times faster than today's supercomputers.[29] This computing power presents a challenge to today's encryption technology. For example, RSA encryption utilizes the multiplication of very large prime numbers to create a semiprime number for its public key. Decoding this key without its private key requires this semiprime number to be factored, which can take a very long time to do with modern computers. It would take a supercomputer anywhere between weeks to months to factor in this key. However, quantum computing can use quantum algorithms to factor this semiprime number in the same amount of time it takes for normal computers to generate it. This would make all data protected by current public-key encryption vulnerable to quantum computing attacks.[30] Other encryption techniques like elliptic curve cryptography and symmetric key encryption are also vulnerable to quantum computing.

While quantum computing could be a threat to encryption security in the future, quantum computing as it currently stands is still very limited. Quantum computing currently is not commercially available, cannot handle large amounts of code, and only exists as computational devices, not computers.[31] Furthermore, quantum computing advancements will be able to be utilized in favor of encryption as well. The National Security Agency (NSA) is currently preparing post-quantum encryption standards for the future.[32] Quantum encryption promises a level of security that will be able to counter the threat of quantum computing.[31]

Attacks and countermeasures

Encryption is an important tool but is not sufficient alone to ensure the security or privacy of sensitive information throughout its lifetime. Most applications of encryption protect information only at rest or in transit, leaving sensitive data in clear text and potentially vulnerable to improper disclosure during processing, such as by a cloud service for example. Homomorphic encryption and secure multi-party computation are emerging techniques to compute on encrypted data; these techniques are general and Turing complete but incur high computational and/or communication costs.

In response to encryption of data at rest, cyber-adversaries have developed new types of attacks. These more recent threats to encryption of data at rest include cryptographic attacks,[33] stolen ciphertext attacks,[34] attacks on encryption keys,[35] insider attacks, data corruption or integrity attacks,[36] data destruction attacks, and ransomware attacks. Data fragmentation[37] and active defense[38] data protection technologies attempt to counter some of these attacks, by distributing, moving, or mutating ciphertext so it is more difficult to identify, steal, corrupt, or destroy.[39]

The debate around encryption

The question of balancing the need for national security with the right to privacy has been debated for years, since encryption has become critical in today's digital society. The modern encryption debate[40] started around the '90 when US government tried to ban cryptography because, according to them, it would threaten national security. The debate is polarized around two opposing views. Those who see strong encryption as a problem making it easier for criminals to hide their illegal acts online and others who argue that encryption keep digital communications safe. The debate heated up in 2014, when Big Tech like Apple and Google set encryption by default in their devices. This was the start of a series of controversies that puts governments, companies and internet users at stake.

Integrity protection of ciphertexts

Encryption, by itself, can protect the confidentiality of messages, but other techniques are still needed to protect the integrity and authenticity of a message; for example, verification of a message authentication code (MAC) or a digital signature usually done by a hashing algorithm or a PGP signature. Authenticated encryption algorithms are designed to provide both encryption and integrity protection together. Standards for cryptographic software and hardware to perform encryption are widely available, but successfully using encryption to ensure security may be a challenging problem. A single error in system design or execution can allow successful attacks. Sometimes an adversary can obtain unencrypted information without directly undoing the encryption. See for example traffic analysis, TEMPEST, or Trojan horse.[41]

Integrity protection mechanisms such as MACs and digital signatures must be applied to the ciphertext when it is first created, typically on the same device used to compose the message, to protect a message end-to-end along its full transmission path; otherwise, any node between the sender and the encryption agent could potentially tamper with it. Encrypting at the time of creation is only secure if the encryption device itself has correct keys and has not been tampered with. If an endpoint device has been configured to trust a root certificate that an attacker controls, for example, then the attacker can both inspect and tamper with encrypted data by performing a man-in-the-middle attack anywhere along the message's path. The common practice of TLS interception by network operators represents a controlled and institutionally sanctioned form of such an attack, but countries have also attempted to employ such attacks as a form of control and censorship.[42]

Ciphertext length and padding

Even when encryption correctly hides a message's content and it cannot be tampered with at rest or in transit, a message's *length* is a form of metadata that can still leak sensitive information about the message. For example, the well-known CRIME and BREACH attacks against HTTPS were side-channel attacks that relied on information leakage via the length of encrypted content.[43] Traffic analysis is a broad class of techniques that often employs message lengths to infer sensitive implementation about traffic flows by aggregating information about a large number of messages.

Padding a message's payload before encrypting it can help obscure the cleartext's true length, at the cost of increasing the ciphertext's size and introducing or increasing bandwidth overhead. Messages may be padded randomly or deterministically, with each approach having different tradeoffs.[44]

Computer Security

Computer security, **cyber security**, **digital security** or **information technology security** (**IT security**) is the protection of computer systems and networks from attacks by malicious actors that may result in unauthorized information disclosure, theft of, or damage to hardware, software, or data, as well as from the disruption or misdirection of the services they provide.[1][2]

The field is significant due to the expanded reliance on computer systems, the Internet,[3] and wireless network standards such as Bluetooth and Wi-Fi. Also, due to the growth of smart devices, including smartphones, televisions, and the various devices that constitute the Internet of things (IoT). Cybersecurity is one of the most significant challenges of the contemporary world, due to both the complexity of information systems and the societies they support. Security is of especially high importance for systems that govern large-scale systems with far-reaching physical effects, such as power distribution, elections, and finance.[4][5]

History

Since the Internet's arrival and with the digital transformation initiated in recent years, the notion of cybersecurity has become a familiar subject in both our professional and personal lives. Cybersecurity and cyber threats have been consistently present for the last 60 years of technological change. In the 1970s and 1980s, computer security was mainly limited to academia until the conception of the Internet, where, with increased connectivity, computer viruses and network intrusions began to take off. After the spread of viruses in the 1990s, the 2000s marked the institutionalization of cyber threats and cybersecurity.

The April 1967 session organized by Willis Ware at the Spring Joint Computer Conference, and the later publication of the Ware Report, were foundational moments in the history of the field of computer security.[6] Ware's work straddled the intersection of material, cultural, political, and social concerns.[6]

A 1977 NIST publication[7] introduced the *CIA triad* of confidentiality, integrity, and availability as a clear and simple way to describe key security goals.[8] While still relevant, many more elaborate frameworks have since been proposed.[9][10]

However, in the 1970s and 1980s, there were no grave computer threats because computers and the internet were still developing, and security threats were easily identifiable. More often, threats came from malicious insiders who gained unauthorized access to sensitive documents and files. Although malware and network breaches existed during the early years, they did not use them for financial gain. By the second half of the 1970s, established computer firms like IBM started offering commercial access control systems and computer security software products.[11]

One of the earliest examples of an attack on a computer network was the computer worm Creeper written by Bob Thomas at BBN, which propagated through the ARPANET in 1971. The program was purely experimental in nature and carried no malicious payload. A later program, Reaper, was created by Ray Tomlinson in 1972 and used to destroy Creeper.

Between September 1986 and June 1987, a group of German hackers performed the first documented case of cyber espionage. The group hacked into American defense contractors, universities, and military base networks and sold gathered information to the Soviet KGB. The group was led by Markus Hess, who was arrested on 29 June, 1987. He was convicted of espionage (along with two co-conspirators) on 15 Feb 1990.

In 1988, one of the first computer worms, called the Morris worm, was distributed via the Internet. It gained significant mainstream media attention.

In 1993, Netscape started developing the protocol SSL, shortly after the National Center for Supercomputing Applications (NCSA) launched Mosaic 1.0, the first web browser, in 1993. Netscape had SSL version 1.0 ready in 1994, but it was never released to the public due to many serious security vulnerabilities. These weaknesses included replay attacks and a vulnerability that allowed hackers to alter unencrypted communications sent by users. However, in February 1995, Netscape launched Version 2.0.

The National Security Agency (NSA) is responsible for the protection of U.S. information systems and also for collecting foreign intelligence.[12]

The agency analyzes commonly used software in order to find security flaws, which it reserves for offensive purposes against competitors of the United States. The agency seldom takes defensive action by reporting the flaws to software producers so that they can eliminate them.[13]

NSA contractors created and sold *click-and-shoot* attack tools to US agencies and close allies, but eventually, the tools made their way to foreign adversaries. In 2016, NSAs own hacking tools were hacked, and they have been used by Russia and North Korea. NSA's employees and contractors have been recruited at high salaries by adversaries, anxious to compete in cyberwarfare. In 2007, the United States and Israel began exploiting security flaws in the Microsoft Windows operating system to attack and damage equipment used in Iran to refine nuclear materials. Iran responded by heavily investing in their own cyberwarfare capability, which it began using against the United States.[13]

Vulnerabilities and attacks

A vulnerability is a weakness in design, implementation, operation, or internal control. Most of the vulnerabilities that have been discovered are documented in the Common Vulnerabilities and Exposures (CVE) database.[14] An *exploitable* vulnerability is one for which at least one working attack or *exploit* exists.[15] Vulnerabilities can be researched, reverse-engineered, hunted, or exploited using automated tools or customized scripts.[16][17] To secure a computer system, it is important to understand the attacks that can be made against it, and these threats can typically be classified into one of these categories below:

Backdoor

A backdoor in a computer system, a cryptosystem, or an algorithm, is any secret method of bypassing normal authentication or security controls. They may exist for many reasons, including original design or poor configuration. They may have been added by an authorized party to allow some legitimate access, or by an attacker for malicious reasons; but regardless of the motives for their existence, they create a vulnerability. Backdoors can be very hard to detect, and backdoors are usually discovered by someone who has access to the application source code or intimate knowledge of the operating system of the computer.

Denial-of-service attack

Denial of service attacks (DoS) are designed to make a machine or network resource unavailable to its intended users.[18] Attackers can deny service to individual victims, such as by deliberately entering a wrong password enough consecutive times to cause the victim's account to be locked, or they may overload the capabilities of a machine or network and block all users at once. While a network attack from a single IP address can be blocked by adding a new firewall rule, many forms of Distributed denial of service (DDoS) attacks are possible, where the attack comes from a large number of points – and defending is much more difficult. Such attacks can originate from the zombie computers of a botnet or from a range of other possible techniques, including distributed reflective denial of service (DRDoS), where innocent systems are fooled into sending traffic to the victim. With such attacks, the amplification factor makes the attack easier for the attacker because they have to use little bandwidth themselves.

Direct-access attacks

An unauthorized user gaining physical access to a computer is most likely able to directly copy data from it. They may also compromise security by making operating system modifications, installing software worms, keyloggers, covert listening devices or using wireless microphones. Even when the system is protected by standard security measures, these may be bypassed by booting another operating system or tool from a CD-ROM or other bootable media. Disk encryption and Trusted Platform Module are designed to prevent these attacks.

Eavesdropping

Eavesdropping is the act of surreptitiously listening to a private computer conversation (communication), typically between hosts on a network. For instance, programs such as Carnivore and NarusInSight have been used by the Federal Bureau of Investigation (FBI) and NSA to eavesdrop on the systems of internet service providers. Even machines that operate as a closed system (i.e., with no contact with the outside world) can be eavesdropped upon by monitoring the faint electromagnetic transmissions generated by the hardware. TEMPEST is a specification by the NSA referring to these attacks.

Multi-vector, polymorphic attacks

Surfacing in 2017, a new class of multi-vector,[19] polymorphic[20] cyber threats combined several types of attacks and changed form to avoid cybersecurity controls as they spread.

Phishing

Phishing is the attempt of acquiring sensitive information such as usernames, passwords, and credit card details directly from users by deceiving the users.[21] Phishing is typically carried out by email spoofing or instant messaging, and it often directs users to enter details at a fake website whose look and feel are almost identical to the legitimate one. The fake website often asks for personal information, such as login details and passwords. This information can then be used to gain access to the individual's real account on the real website. Preying on a victim's trust, phishing can be classified as a form of social engineering. Attackers are using creative ways to gain access to real accounts. A common scam is for attackers to send fake electronic invoices[22] to individuals showing that they recently purchased music, apps, or others, and instructing them to click on a link if the purchases were not authorized. A more strategic type of phishing is spear-phishing which leverages personal or organization-specific details to make the attacker appear like a trusted source. Spear-phishing attacks target specific individuals, rather than the broad net cast by phishing attempts.[23]

Privilege escalation

Privilege escalation describes a situation where an attacker with some level of restricted access is able to, without authorization, elevate their privileges or access level. For example, a standard computer user may be able to exploit a vulnerability in the system to gain access to restricted data; or even become *root* and have full unrestricted access to a system.

Reverse engineering

Reverse engineering is the process by which a man-made object is deconstructed to reveal its designs, code, and architecture, or to extract knowledge from the object; similar to scientific research, the only difference being that scientific research is about a natural phenomenon.[24]:3

Side-channel attack

Any computational system affects its environment in some form. This effect it has on its environment includes a wide range of criteria, which can range from electromagnetic radiation to residual effect on RAM cells which as a consequence make a Cold boot attack possible, to hardware implementation faults that allow for access and or guessing of other values that normally should be inaccessible. In Side-channel attack scenarios, the attacker would gather such information about a system or network to guess its internal state and as a result access the information which is assumed by the victim to be secure.

Social engineering

Social engineering, in the context of computer security, aims to convince a user to disclose secrets such as passwords, card numbers, etc. or grant physical access by, for example, impersonating a senior executive, bank, a contractor, or a customer.[25] This generally involves exploiting people's trust, and relying on their cognitive biases. A common scam involves emails sent to accounting and finance department personnel, impersonating their CEO and urgently requesting some action. In early 2016, the FBI reported that such business email compromise (BEC) scams had cost US businesses more than $2 billion in about two years.[26]

In May 2016, the Milwaukee Bucks NBA team was the victim of this type of cyber scam with a perpetrator impersonating the team's president Peter Feigin, resulting in the handover of all the team's employees' 2015 W-2 tax forms.[27]

Spoofing

Spoofing is an act of masquerading as a valid entity through the falsification of data (such as an IP address or username), in order to gain access to information or resources that one is otherwise unauthorized to obtain.[28][29] There are several types of spoofing, including:

- Email spoofing, is where an attacker forges the sending (*From*, or source) address of an email.
- IP address spoofing, where an attacker alters the source IP address in a network packet to hide their identity or impersonate another computing system.
- MAC spoofing, where an attacker modifies the Media Access Control (MAC) address of their network interface controller to obscure their identity, or to pose as another.
- Biometric spoofing, where an attacker produces a fake biometric sample to pose as another user.[30]
- Address Resolution Protocol (ARP) spoofing, where an attacker sends spoofed address resolution protocol onto a local area network to associate their Media Access Control address with a different host's IP address. This causes data to be sent to the attacker rather than the intended host.

In 2018, the cybersecurity firm Trellix published research on the life-threatening risk of spoofing in the healthcare industry.[31]

Tampering

Tampering describes a malicious modification or alteration of data. An intentional but unauthorized act resulting in the modification of a system, components of systems, its intended behavior, or data. So-called Evil Maid attacks and security services planting of surveillance capability into routers are examples.[32]

Malware

Malicious software (malware) installed on a computer can leak any information, such as personal information, business information and passwords, can give control of the system to the attacker, and can corrupt or delete data permanently.[33]

HTML smuggling

HTML files can carry payloads concealed as benign, inert data in order to defeat content filters. These payloads can be reconstructed on the other side of the filter.[34]

Information security culture

Employee behavior can have a big impact on information security in organizations. Cultural concepts can help different segments of the organization work effectively or work against effectiveness toward information security within an organization. Information security culture is the "...totality of patterns of behavior in an organization that contributes to the protection of information of all kinds."[35]

Andersson and Reimers (2014) found that employees often do not see themselves as part of their organization's information security effort and often take actions that impede organizational changes.[36] Indeed, the Verizon Data Breach Investigations Report 2020, which examined 3,950 security breaches, discovered 30% of cybersecurity incidents involved internal actors within a company.[37] Research shows information security culture needs to be improved continuously. In "Information Security Culture from Analysis to Change", authors commented, "It's a never-ending process, a cycle of evaluation and change or maintenance." To manage the information security culture, five steps should be taken: pre-evaluation, strategic planning, operative planning, implementation, and post-evaluation.[38]

- Pre-evaluation: To identify the awareness of information security within employees and to analyze the current security policies.
- Strategic planning: To come up with a better awareness program, clear targets need to be set. Assembling a team of skilled professionals is helpful to achieve it.
- Operative planning: A good security culture can be established based on internal communication, management buy-in, security awareness and a training program.[38]
- Implementation: Four stages should be used to implement the information security culture. They are:
    1. Commitment of the management
    2. Communication with organizational members
    3. Courses for all organizational members
    4. Commitment of the employees[38]

- Post-evaluation: To assess the success of the planning and implementation, and to identify unresolved areas of concern.

Systems at risk

The growth in the number of computer systems and the increasing reliance upon them by individuals, businesses, industries, and governments means that there are an increasing number of systems at risk.

Financial systems

The computer systems of financial regulators and financial institutions like the U.S. Securities and Exchange Commission, SWIFT, investment banks, and commercial banks are prominent hacking targets for cybercriminals interested in manipulating markets and making illicit gains.[39] Websites and apps that accept or store credit card numbers, brokerage accounts, and bank account information are also prominent hacking targets, because of the potential for immediate financial gain from transferring money, making purchases, or selling the information on the black market.[40] In-store payment systems and ATMs have also been tampered with in order to gather customer account data and PINs.

The UCLA Internet Report: Surveying the Digital Future (2000) found that the privacy of personal data created barriers to online sales and that more than nine out of 10 internet users were somewhat or very concerned about credit card security.[41]

The most common web technologies for improving security between browsers and websites are named SSL (Secure Sockets Layer), and its successor TLS (Transport Layer Security), identity management and authentication services, and domain name services allow companies and consumers to engage in secure communications and commerce. Several versions of SSL and TLS are commonly used today in applications such as web browsing, e-mail, internet faxing, instant messaging, and VoIP (voice-over-IP). There are various interoperable implementations of these technologies, including at least one implementation that is open source. Open source allows anyone to view the application's source code, and look for and report vulnerabilities.

The credit card companies Visa and MasterCard cooperated to develop the secure EMV chip which is embedded in credit cards. Further developments include the Chip Authentication Program where banks give customers hand-held card readers to perform online secure transactions. Other developments in this arena include the development of technology such as Instant Issuance which has enabled shopping mall kiosks acting on behalf of banks to issue on-the-spot credit cards to interested customers.

Utilities and industrial equipment

Computers control functions at many utilities, including coordination of telecommunications, the power grid, nuclear power plants, and valve opening and closing in water and gas networks. The Internet is a potential attack vector for such machines if connected, but the Stuxnet worm demonstrated that even equipment controlled by computers not connected to the Internet can be vulnerable. In 2014, the Computer Emergency Readiness Team, a division of the Department of Homeland Security, investigated 79 hacking incidents at energy companies.[42]

Aviation

The aviation industry is very reliant on a series of complex systems which could be attacked.[43] A simple power outage at one airport can cause repercussions worldwide,[44] much of the system relies on radio transmissions which could be disrupted,[45] and controlling aircraft over oceans is especially dangerous because radar surveillance only extends 175 to 225 miles offshore.[46] There is also potential for attack from within an aircraft.[47]

In Europe, with the (Pan-European Network Service)[48] and NewPENS,[49] and in the US with the NextGen program,[50] air navigation service providers are moving to create their own dedicated networks.

Many modern passports are now biometric passports, containing an embedded microchip that stores a digitized photograph and personal information such as name, gender, and date of birth. In addition, more countries[which?] are introducing facial recognition technology to reduce identity-related fraud. The introduction of the ePassport has assisted border officials in verifying the identity of the passport holder, thus allowing for quick passenger processing.[51] Plans are under way in the US, the UK, and Australia to introduce SmartGate kiosks with both retina and fingerprint recognition technology.[52] The airline industry is moving from the use of traditional paper tickets towards the use of electronic tickets (e-tickets). These have been made possible by advances in online credit card transactions in partnership with the airlines. Long-distance bus companies[which?] are also switching over to e-ticketing transactions today.

The consequences of a successful attack range from loss of confidentiality to loss of system integrity, air traffic control outages, loss of aircraft, and even loss of life.

Consumer devices

Desktop computers and laptops are commonly targeted to gather passwords or financial account information or to construct a botnet to attack another target. Smartphones, tablet computers, smart watches, and other mobile devices such as quantified self devices like activity trackers have sensors such as cameras, microphones, GPS receivers, compasses, and accelerometers which could be exploited, and may collect personal information, including sensitive health information. WiFi, Bluetooth, and cell phone networks on any of these devices could be used as attack vectors, and sensors might be remotely activated after a successful breach.[53]

The increasing number of home automation devices such as the Nest thermostat are also potential targets.[53]

Healthcare

Today many health-care providers and health insurance companies use the internet to provide enhanced products and services, for example through use of tele-health to potentially offer better quality and access to healthcare, or fitness trackers to lower insurance premiums.

The health care company Humana partners with WebMD, Oracle Corporation, EDS and Microsoft to enable its members to access their health care records, as well as to provide an overview of health care plans.[54] Patient records are increasingly being placed on secure in-house networks, alleviating the need for extra storage space.[55]

Large corporations

Large corporations are common targets. In many cases attacks are aimed at financial gain through identity theft and involve data breaches. Examples include the loss of millions of clients' credit card and financial details by Home Depot,[56] Staples,[57] Target Corporation,[58] and Equifax.[59]

Medical records have been targeted in general identify theft, health insurance fraud, and impersonating patients to obtain prescription drugs for recreational purposes or resale.[60] Although cyber threats continue to increase, 62% of all organizations did not increase security training for their business in 2015.[61]

Not all attacks are financially motivated, however: security firm HBGary Federal had a serious series of attacks in 2011 from hacktivist group Anonymous in retaliation for the firm's CEO claiming to have infiltrated their group,[62][63] and Sony Pictures was hacked in 2014 with the apparent dual motive of embarrassing the company through data leaks and crippling the company by wiping workstations and servers.[64][65]

Automobiles

Vehicles are increasingly computerized, with engine timing, cruise control, anti-lock brakes, seat belt tensioners, door locks, airbags and advanced driver-assistance systems on many models. Additionally, connected cars may use WiFi and Bluetooth to communicate with onboard consumer devices and the cell phone network.[66] Self-driving cars are expected to be even more complex. All of these systems carry some security risks, and such issues have gained wide attention.[67][68][69]

Simple examples of risk include a malicious compact disc being used as an attack vector,[70] and the car's onboard microphones being used for eavesdropping. However, if access is gained to a car's internal controller area network, the danger is much greater[66] – and in a widely publicized 2015 test, hackers remotely carjacked a vehicle from 10 miles away and drove it into a ditch.[71][72]

Manufacturers are reacting in numerous ways, with Tesla in 2016 pushing out some security fixes *over the air* into its cars' computer systems.[73] In the area of autonomous vehicles, in September 2016 the United States Department of Transportation announced some initial safety standards, and called for states to come up with uniform policies.[74][75][76]

Additionally, e-Drivers' licenses are being developed using the same technology. For example, Mexico's licensing authority (ICV) has used a smart card platform to issue the first e-Drivers' licenses to the city of Monterrey, in the state of Nuevo León.[77]

Shipping

Shipping companies[78] have adopted RFID (Radio Frequency Identification) technology as an efficient, digitally secure, tracking device. Unlike a barcode, RFID can be read up to 20 feet away. RFID is used by FedEx[79] and UPS.[80]

Government

Government and military computer systems are commonly attacked by activists[81][82][83] and foreign powers.[84][85][86][87] Local and regional government infrastructure such as traffic light controls, police and intelligence agency communications, personnel records, as well as student records.[88]

The FBI, CIA, and Pentagon, all utilize secure controlled access technology for any of their buildings. However, the use of this form of technology is spreading into the entrepreneurial world. More and more companies are taking advantage of the development of digitally secure controlled access technology. GE's ACUVision, for example, offers a single panel platform for access control, alarm monitoring and digital recording.[89]

Internet of things and physical vulnerabilities

The Internet of things (IoT) is the network of physical objects such as devices, vehicles, and buildings that are embedded with electronics, software, sensors, and network connectivity that enables them to collect and exchange data.[90] Concerns have been raised that this is being developed without appropriate consideration of the security challenges involved.[91][92]

While the IoT creates opportunities for more direct integration of the physical world into computer-based systems,[93][94] it also provides opportunities for misuse. In particular, as the Internet of Things spreads widely, cyberattacks are likely to become an increasingly physical (rather than simply virtual) threat.[95] If a front door's lock is connected to the Internet, and can be locked/unlocked from a phone, then a criminal could enter the home at the press of a button from a stolen or hacked phone. People could stand to lose much more than their credit card numbers in a world controlled by IoT-enabled devices. Thieves have also used electronic means to circumvent non-Internet-connected hotel door locks.[96]

An attack that targets physical infrastructure and/or human lives is sometimes referred to as a cyber-kinetic attack. As IoT devices and appliances gain currency, cyber-kinetic attacks can become pervasive and significantly damaging.

Medical systems

Medical devices have either been successfully attacked or had potentially deadly vulnerabilities demonstrated, including both in-hospital diagnostic equipment[97] and implanted devices including pacemakers[98] and insulin pumps.[99] There are many reports of hospitals and hospital organizations getting hacked, including ransomware attacks,[100][101][102][103] Windows XP exploits,[104][105] viruses,[106][107] and data breaches of sensitive data stored on hospital servers.[108][101][109][110] On 28 December 2016 the US Food and Drug Administration released its recommendations for how medical device manufacturers should maintain the security of Internet-connected devices – but no structure for enforcement.[111][112]

Energy sector

In distributed generation systems, the risk of a cyber attack is real, according to *Daily Energy Insider*. An attack could cause a loss of power in a large area for a long period of time, and such an attack could have just as severe consequences as a natural disaster. The District of Columbia is considering creating a Distributed Energy Resources (DER) Authority within the city, with the goal being for customers to have more insight into their own energy use and giving the local electric utility, Pepco, the chance to better estimate energy demand. The D.C. proposal, however, would "allow third-party vendors to create numerous points of energy distribution, which could potentially create more opportunities for cyber attackers to threaten the electric grid."[113]

Telecommunications

Perhaps the most widely known digitally secure telecommunication device is the SIM (Subscriber Identity Module) card, a device that is embedded in most of the world's cellular devices before any service can be obtained. The SIM card is just the beginning of this digitally secure environment.

The Smart Card Web Servers draft standard (SCWS) defines the interfaces to an HTTP server in a smart card.[114] Tests are being conducted to secure OTA ("over-the-air") payment and credit card information from and to a mobile phone. Combination SIM/DVD devices are being developed through Smart Video Card technology which embeds a DVD-compliant optical disc into the card body of a regular SIM card.

Other telecommunication developments involving digital security include mobile signatures, which use the embedded SIM card to generate a legally binding electronic signature.

Impact of security breaches

Serious financial damage has been caused by security breaches, but because there is no standard model for estimating the cost of an incident, the only data available is that which is made public by the organizations involved. "Several computer security consulting firms produce estimates of total worldwide losses attributable to virus and worm attacks and to hostile digital acts in general. The 2003 loss estimates by these firms range from $13 billion (worms and viruses only) to $226 billion (for all forms of covert attacks). The reliability of these estimates is often challenged; the underlying methodology is basically anecdotal."[115]

However, reasonable estimates of the financial cost of security breaches can actually help organizations make rational investment decisions. According to the classic Gordon-Loeb Model analyzing the optimal investment level in information security, one can conclude that the amount a firm spends to protect information should generally be only a small fraction of the expected loss (i.e., the expected value of the loss resulting from a cyber/information security breach).[116]

Attacker motivation

As with physical security, the motivations for breaches of computer security vary between attackers. Some are thrill-seekers or vandals, some are activists, others are criminals looking for financial gain. State-sponsored attackers are now common and well resourced but started with amateurs such as Markus Hess who hacked for the KGB, as recounted by Clifford Stoll in *The Cuckoo's Egg*.

Additionally, recent attacker motivations can be traced back to extremist organizations seeking to gain political advantage or disrupt social agendas.[117] The growth of the internet, mobile technologies, and inexpensive computing devices have led to a rise in capabilities but also to the risk to environments that are deemed as vital to operations. All critical targeted environments are susceptible to compromise and this has led to a series of proactive studies on how to migrate the risk by taking into consideration motivations by these types of actors. Several stark differences exist between the hacker motivation and that of nation state actors seeking to attack based on an ideological preference.[118]

A standard part of threat modeling for any particular system is to identify what might motivate an attack on that system, and who might be motivated to breach it. The level and detail of precautions will vary depending on the system to be secured. A home personal computer, bank, and classified military network face very different threats, even when the underlying technologies in use are similar.[119]

Computer protection (countermeasures)

In computer security, a countermeasure is an action, device, procedure or technique that reduces a threat, a vulnerability, or an attack by eliminating or preventing it, by minimizing the harm it can cause, or by discovering and reporting it so that corrective action can be taken.[120][121][122]

Some common countermeasures are listed in the following sections:

Security by design

Security by design, or alternately secure by design, means that the software has been designed from the ground up to be secure. In this case, security is considered a main feature.

Some of the techniques in this approach include:

- The principle of least privilege, where each part of the system has only the privileges that are needed for its function. That way, even if an attacker gains access to that part, they only have limited access to the whole system.
- Automated theorem proving to prove the correctness of crucial software subsystems.
- Code reviews and unit testing, approaches to make modules more secure where formal correctness proofs are not possible.
- Defense in depth, where the design is such that more than one subsystem needs to be violated to compromise the integrity of the system and the information it holds.
- Default secure settings, and design to *fail secure* rather than *fail insecure* (see fail-safe for the equivalent in safety engineering). Ideally, a secure system should require a deliberate, conscious, knowledgeable and free decision on the part of legitimate authorities in order to make it insecure.
- Audit trails track system activity so that when a security breach occurs, the mechanism and extent of the breach can be determined. Storing audit trails remotely, where they can only be appended to, can keep intruders from covering their tracks.
- Full disclosure of all vulnerabilities, to ensure that the *window of vulnerability* is kept as short as possible when bugs are discovered.

Security architecture

The Open Security Architecture organization defines IT security architecture as "the design artifacts that describe how the security controls (security countermeasures) are positioned, and how they relate to the overall information technology architecture. These controls serve the purpose to maintain the system's quality attributes: confidentiality, integrity, availability, accountability and assurance services".[123]

Techopedia defines security architecture as "a unified security design that addresses the necessities and potential risks involved in a certain scenario or environment. It also specifies when and where to apply security controls. The design process is generally reproducible." The key attributes of security architecture are:[124]

- the relationship of different components and how they depend on each other.
- determination of controls based on risk assessment, good practices, finances, and legal matters.
- the standardization of controls.

Practicing security architecture provides the right foundation to systematically address business, IT and security concerns in an organization.

Security measures

A state of computer security is the conceptual ideal, attained by the use of the three processes: threat prevention, detection, and response. These processes are based on various policies and system components, which include the following:

- User account access controls and cryptography can protect systems files and data, respectively.
- Firewalls are by far the most common prevention systems from a network security perspective as they can (if properly configured) shield access to internal network services, and block certain kinds of attacks through packet filtering. Firewalls can be both hardware and software-based.
- Intrusion Detection System (IDS) products are designed to detect network attacks in-progress and assist in post-attack forensics, while audit trails and logs serve a similar function for individual systems.
- *Response* is necessarily defined by the assessed security requirements of an individual system and may cover the range from simple upgrade of protections to notification of legal authorities, counter-attacks, and the like. In some special cases, the complete destruction of the compromised system is favored, as it may happen that not all the compromised resources are detected.
- Cyber security awareness training to cope with cyber threats and attacks. [125]
- Forward web proxy solutions can prevent the client to visit malicious web pages and inspect the content before downloading to the client machines.

Today, computer security consists mainly of preventive measures, like firewalls or an exit procedure. A firewall can be defined as a way of filtering network data between a host or a network and another network, such as the Internet, and can be implemented as software running on the machine, hooking into the network stack (or, in the case of most UNIX-based operating systems such as Linux, built into the operating system kernel) to provide real-time filtering and blocking. Another implementation is a so-called *physical firewall*, which consists of a separate machine filtering network traffic. Firewalls are common amongst machines that are permanently connected to the Internet.

Some organizations are turning to big data platforms, such as Apache Hadoop, to extend data accessibility and machine learning to detect advanced persistent threats.[126]

However, relatively few organizations maintain computer systems with effective detection systems, and fewer still have organized response mechanisms in place. As a result, as Reuters pointed out in 2010: "Companies for the first time report they are losing more through electronic theft of data than physical stealing of assets".[127] The primary obstacle to effective eradication of cybercrime could be traced to excessive reliance on firewalls and other automated detection systems. Yet it is basic evidence gathering by using packet capture appliances that puts criminals behind bars.

In order to ensure adequate security, the confidentiality, integrity and availability of a network, better known as the CIA triad, must be protected and is considered the foundation to information security.[128] To achieve those objectives, administrative, physical and technical security measures should be employed. The amount of security afforded to an asset can only be determined when its value is known.[129]

Vulnerability management

Vulnerability management is the cycle of identifying, remediating or mitigating vulnerabilities,[130] especially in software and firmware. Vulnerability management is integral to computer security and network security.

Vulnerabilities can be discovered with a vulnerability scanner, which analyzes a computer system in search of known vulnerabilities,[131] such as open ports, insecure software configuration, and susceptibility to malware. In order for these tools to be effective, they must be kept up to date with every new update the vendor release. Typically, these updates will scan for the new vulnerabilities that were introduced recently.

Beyond vulnerability scanning, many organizations contract outside security auditors to run regular penetration tests against their systems to identify vulnerabilities. In some sectors, this is a contractual requirement.[132]

Reducing vulnerabilities

While formal verification of the correctness of computer systems is possible,[133][134] it is not yet common. Operating systems formally verified include seL4,[135] and SYSGO's PikeOS[136][137] – but these make up a very small percentage of the market.

Two factor authentication is a method for mitigating unauthorized access to a system or sensitive information. It requires *something you know*; a password or PIN, and *something you have*; a card, dongle, cellphone, or another piece of hardware. This increases security as an unauthorized person needs both of these to gain access.

Social engineering and direct computer access (physical) attacks can only be prevented by non-computer means, which can be difficult to enforce, relative to the sensitivity of the information. Training is often involved to help mitigate this risk, but even in highly disciplined environments (e.g. military organizations), social engineering attacks can still be difficult to foresee and prevent.

Inoculation, derived from inoculation theory, seeks to prevent social engineering and other fraudulent tricks or traps by instilling a resistance to persuasion attempts through exposure to similar or related attempts.[138]

It is possible to reduce an attacker's chances by keeping systems up to date with security patches and updates, using a security scanner[definition needed] and/or hiring people with expertise in security, though none of these guarantee the prevention of an attack. The effects of data loss/damage can be reduced by careful backing up and insurance.

Hardware protection mechanisms

While hardware may be a source of insecurity, such as with microchip vulnerabilities maliciously introduced during the manufacturing process,[139][140] hardware-based or assisted computer security also offers an alternative to software-only computer security. Using devices and methods such as dongles, trusted platform modules, intrusion-aware cases, drive locks, disabling USB ports, and mobile-enabled access may be considered more secure due to the physical access (or sophisticated backdoor access) required in order to be compromised. Each of these is covered in more detail below.

- USB dongles are typically used in software licensing schemes to unlock software capabilities, but they can also be seen as a way to prevent unauthorized access to a computer or other device's software. The dongle, or key, essentially creates a secure encrypted tunnel between the software application and the key. The principle is that an encryption scheme on the dongle, such as Advanced Encryption Standard (AES) provides a stronger measure of security since it is harder to hack and replicate the dongle than to simply copy the native software to another machine and use it. Another security application for dongles is to use them for accessing web-based content such as cloud software or Virtual Private Networks (VPNs).[141] In addition, a USB dongle can be configured to lock or unlock a computer.[142]
- Trusted platform modules (TPMs) secure devices by integrating cryptographic capabilities onto access devices, through the use of microprocessors, or so-called computers-on-a-chip. TPMs used in conjunction with server-side software offer a way to detect and authenticate hardware devices, preventing unauthorized network and data access.[143]
- Computer case intrusion detection refers to a device, typically a push-button switch, which detects when a computer case is opened. The firmware or BIOS is programmed to show an alert to the operator when the computer is booted up the next time.
- Drive locks are essentially software tools to encrypt hard drives, making them inaccessible to thieves.[144] Tools exist specifically for encrypting external drives as well.[145]
- Disabling USB ports is a security option for preventing unauthorized and malicious access to an otherwise secure computer. Infected USB dongles connected to a network from a computer inside the firewall are considered by the magazine Network World as the most common hardware threat facing computer networks.
- Disconnecting or disabling peripheral devices (like camera, GPS, removable storage etc.), that are not in use.[146]
- Mobile-enabled access devices are growing in popularity due to the ubiquitous nature of cell phones. Built-in capabilities such as Bluetooth, the newer Bluetooth low energy (LE), near-field communication (NFC) on non-iOS devices and biometric validation such as thumbprint readers, as well as QR code reader software designed for mobile devices, offer new, secure ways for mobile phones to

connect to access control systems. These control systems provide computer security and can also be used for controlling access to secure buildings.[147]
- IOMMUs allow for hardware-based sandboxing of components in mobile and desktop computers by utilizing direct memory access protections.[148][149]
- Physical Unclonable Functions (PUFs) can be used as a digital fingerprint or a unique identifier to integrated circuits and hardware, providing users the ability to secure the hardware supply chains going into their systems.[150][151]

Secure operating systems

One use of the term *computer security* refers to technology that is used to implement secure operating systems. In the 1980s, the United States Department of Defense (DoD) used the "Orange Book"[152] standards, but the current international standard ISO/IEC 15408, Common Criteria defines a number of progressively more stringent Evaluation Assurance Levels. Many common operating systems meet the EAL4 standard of being "Methodically Designed, Tested and Reviewed", but the formal verification required for the highest levels means that they are uncommon. An example of an EAL6 ("Semiformally Verified Design and Tested") system is INTEGRITY-178B, which is used in the Airbus A380[153] and several military jets.[154]

Secure coding

In software engineering, secure coding aims to guard against the accidental introduction of security vulnerabilities. It is also possible to create software designed from the ground up to be secure. Such systems are *secure by design*. Beyond this, formal verification aims to prove the correctness of the algorithms underlying a system;[155] important for cryptographic protocols for example.

Capabilities and access control lists

Within computer systems, two of the main security models capable of enforcing privilege separation are access control lists (ACLs) and role-based access control (RBAC).

An access-control list (ACL), with respect to a computer file system, is a list of permissions associated with an object. An ACL specifies which users or system processes are granted access to objects, as well as what operations are allowed on given objects.

Role-based access control is an approach to restricting system access to authorized users,[156][157][158] used by the majority of enterprises with more than 500 employees,[159] and can implement mandatory access control (MAC) or discretionary access control (DAC).

A further approach, capability-based security has been mostly restricted to research operating systems. Capabilities can, however, also be implemented at the language level, leading to a style of programming that is essentially a refinement of standard object-oriented design. An open-source project in the area is the E language.

End user security training

The end-user is widely recognized as the weakest link in the security chain[160] and it is estimated that more than 90% of security incidents and breaches involve some kind of human error.[161][162] Among the most commonly recorded forms of errors and misjudgment are poor password management, sending emails containing sensitive data and attachments to the wrong recipient, the inability to recognize misleading URLs and to identify fake websites and dangerous email attachments. A common mistake that users make is saving their user id/password in their browsers to make it easier to log in to banking sites. This is a gift to attackers who have obtained access to a machine by some means. The risk may be mitigated by the use of two-factor authentication.[163]

As the human component of cyber risk is particularly relevant in determining the global cyber risk[164] an organization is facing, security awareness training, at all levels, not only provides formal compliance with regulatory and industry mandates but is considered essential[165] in reducing cyber risk and protecting individuals and companies from the great majority of cyber threats.

The focus on the end-user represents a profound cultural change for many security practitioners, who have traditionally approached cybersecurity exclusively from a technical perspective, and moves along the lines suggested by major security centers[166] to develop a culture of cyber awareness within the organization, recognizing that a security-aware user provides an important line of defense against cyber attacks.

Digital hygiene

Related to end-user training, **digital hygiene** or **cyber hygiene** is a fundamental principle relating to information security and, as the analogy with personal hygiene shows, is the equivalent of establishing simple routine measures to minimize the risks from cyber threats. The assumption is that good cyber hygiene practices can give networked users another layer of protection, reducing the risk that one vulnerable node will be used to either mount attacks or compromise another node or network, especially from common cyberattacks.[167] Cyber hygiene should also not be mistaken for proactive cyber defence, a military term.[168]

As opposed to a purely technology-based defense against threats, cyber hygiene mostly regards routine measures that are technically simple to implement and mostly dependent on discipline[169] or education.[170] It can be thought of as an abstract list of tips or measures that have been demonstrated as having a positive effect on personal and/or collective digital security. As such, these measures can be performed by laypeople, not just security experts.

Cyber hygiene relates to personal hygiene as computer viruses relate to biological viruses (or pathogens). However, while the term *computer virus* was coined almost simultaneously with the creation of the first working computer viruses,[171] the term *cyber hygiene* is a much later invention, perhaps as late as 2000[172] by Internet pioneer Vint Cerf. It has since been adopted by the Congress[173] and Senate of the United States,[174] the FBI,[175] EU institutions[167] and heads of state.[168]

Response to breaches

Responding to attempted security breaches is often very difficult for a variety of reasons, including:

- Identifying attackers is difficult, as they may operate through proxies, temporary anonymous dial-up accounts, wireless connections, and other anonymizing procedures which make back-tracing difficult – and are often located in another jurisdiction. If they successfully breach security, they have also often gained enough administrative access to enable them to delete logs to cover their tracks.

- The sheer number of attempted attacks, often by automated vulnerability scanners and computer worms, is so large that organizations cannot spend time pursuing each.
- Law enforcement officers often lack the skills, interest or budget to pursue attackers. In addition, the identification of attackers across a network may require logs from various points in the network and in many countries, which may be difficult or time-consuming to obtain.

Where an attack succeeds and a breach occurs, many jurisdictions now have in place mandatory security breach notification laws.

Types of security and privacy

- Access control
- Anti-keyloggers
- Anti-malware
- Anti-spyware
- Anti-subversion software
- Anti-tamper software
- Anti-theft
- Antivirus software
- Cryptographic software
- Computer-aided dispatch (CAD)
- Firewall
- Intrusion detection system (IDS)
- Intrusion prevention system (IPS)
- Log management software
- Parental control
- Records management
- Sandbox
- Security information management
- Security information and event management (SIEM)
- Software and operating system updating
- Vulnerability Management

Computer security incident management

Computer security incident management is an organized approach to addressing and managing the aftermath of a computer security incident or compromise with the goal of preventing a breach or thwarting a cyberattack. An incident that is not identified and managed at the time of intrusion typically escalates to a more damaging event such as a data breach or system failure. The intended outcome of a computer security incident response plan is to contain the incident, limit damage and assist recovery to business as usual. Responding to compromises quickly can mitigate exploited vulnerabilities, restore services and processes and minimize losses.[176] Incident response planning allows an organization to establish a series of best practices to stop an intrusion before it causes damage. Typical incident response plans contain a set of written instructions that outline the organization's response to a cyberattack. Without a documented plan in place, an organization may not success'ully detect an intrusion or compromise and stakeholders may not understand their roles,'processes and procedures during an escalation, slowing the organization's response and resolution.

There are four key components of a computer security incident response plan:

1. Preparation: Preparing stakeholders on the procedures for handling computer security incidents or compromises
2. Detection and analysis: Identifying and investigating suspicious activity to confirm a security incident, prioritizing the response based on impact and coordinating notification of the incident
3. Containment, eradication and recovery: Isolating affected systems to prevent escalation and limit impact, pinpointing the genesis of the incident, removing malware, affected systems and bad actors from the environment and restoring systems and data when a threat no longer remains
4. Post incident activity: Post mortem analysis of the incident, its root cause and the organization's response with the intent of improving the incident response plan and future response efforts.[177]

Notable attacks and breaches

Some illustrative examples of different types of computer security breaches are given below.

Robert Morris and the first computer worm

In 1988, 60,000 computers were connected to the Internet, and most were mainframes, minicomputers and professional workstations. On 2 November 1988, many started to slow down, because they were running a malicious code that demanded processor time and that spread itself to other computers – the first internet computer worm.[178] The software was traced back to 23-year-old Cornell University graduate student Robert Tappan Morris who said "he wanted to count how many machines were connected to the Internet".[178]

Rome Laboratory

In 1994, over a hundred intrusions were made by unidentified crackers into the Rome Laboratory, the US Air Force's main command and research facility. Using trojan horses, hackers were able to obtain unrestricted access to Rome's networking systems and remove traces of their activities. The intruders were able to obtain classified files, such as air tasking order systems data and furthermore able to penetrate connected networks of National Aeronautics and Space Administration's Goddard Space Flight Center, Wright-Patterson Air Force Base, some Defense contractors, and other private sector organizations, by posing as a trusted Rome center user.[179]

TJX customer credit card details

In early 2007, American apparel and home goods company TJX announced that it was the victim of an unauthorized computer systems intrusion[180] and that the hackers had accessed a system that stored data on credit card, debit card, check, and merchandise return transactions.[181]

Stuxnet attack

In 2010, the computer worm known as Stuxnet reportedly ruined almost one-fifth of Iran's nuclear centrifuges.[182] It did so by disrupting industrial programmable logic controllers (PLCs) in a targeted attack. This is generally believed to have been launched by Israel and the United States to disrupt Iran's nuclear program[183][184][185][186] – although neither has publicly admitted this.

Global surveillance disclosures

In early 2013, documents provided by Edward Snowden were published by *The Washington Post* and *The Guardian*[187][188] exposing the massive scale of NSA global surveillance. There were also indications that the NSA may have inserted a backdoor in a NIST standard for encryption.[189] This standard was later withdrawn due to widespread criticism.[190] The NSA additionally were revealed to have tapped the links between Google's data centers.[191]

Target and Home Depot breaches

A Ukrainian hacker known as Rescator broke into Target Corporation computers in 2013, stealing roughly 40 million credit cards,[192] and then Home Depot computers in 2014, stealing between 53 and 56 million credit card numbers.[193] Warnings were delivered at both corporations, but ignored; physical security breaches using self checkout machines are believed to have played a large role. "The malware utilized is absolutely unsophisticated and uninteresting," says Jim Walter, director of threat intelligence operations at security technology company McAfee – meaning that the heists could have easily been stopped by existing antivirus software had administrators responded to the warnings. The size of the thefts has resulted in major attention from state and Federal United States authorities and the investigation is ongoing.

Office of Personnel Management data breach

In April 2015, the Office of Personnel Management discovered it had been hacked more than a year earlier in a data breach, resulting in the theft of approximately 21.5 million personnel records handled by the office.[194] The Office of Personnel Management hack has been described by federal officials as among the largest breaches of government data in the history of the United States.[195] Data targeted in the breach included personally identifiable information such as Social Security numbers, names, dates and places of birth, addresses, and fingerprints of current and former government employees as well as anyone who had undergone a government background check.[196][197] It is believed the hack was perpetrated by Chinese hackers.[198]

Ashley Madison breach

In July 2015, a hacker group is known as The Impact Team successfully breached the extramarital relationship website Ashley Madison, created by Avid Life Media. The group claimed that they had taken not only company data but user data as well. After the breach, The Impact Team dumped emails from the company's CEO, to prove their point, and threatened to dump customer data unless the website was taken down permanently.[199] When Avid Life Media did not take the site offline the group released two more compressed files, one 9.7GB and the second 20GB. After the second data dump, Avid Life Media CEO Noel Biderman resigned; but the website remained to function.

Colonial Pipeline ransomware attack

In June 2021, the cyber attack took down the largest fuel pipeline in the U.S. and led to shortages across the East Coast.[200]

Legal issues and global regulation

International legal issues of cyber attacks are complicated in nature. There is no global base of common rules to judge, and eventually punish, cybercrimes and cybercriminals – and where security firms or agencies do locate the cybercriminal behind the creation of a particular piece of malware or form of cyber attack, often the local authorities cannot take action due to lack of laws under which to prosecute.[201][202] Proving attribution for cybercrimes and cyberattacks is also a major problem for all law enforcement agencies. "Computer viruses switch from one country to another, from one jurisdiction to another – moving around the world, using the fact that we don't have the capability to globally police operations like this. So the Internet is as if someone [had] given free plane tickets to all the online criminals of the world."[201] The use of techniques such as dynamic DNS, fast flux and bullet proof servers add to the difficulty of investigation and enforcement.

Role of government

The role of the government is to make regulations to force companies and organizations to protect their systems, infrastructure and information from any cyberattacks, but also to protect its own national infrastructure such as the national power-grid.[203]

The government's regulatory role in cyberspace is complicated. For some, cyberspace was seen as a virtual space that was to remain free of government intervention, as can be seen in many of today's libertarian blockchain and bitcoin discussions.[204]

Many government officials and experts think that the government should do more and that there is a crucial need for improved regulation, mainly due to the failure of the private sector to solve efficiently the cybersecurity problem. R. Clarke said during a panel discussion at the RSA Security Conference in San Francisco, he believes that the "industry only responds when you threaten regulation. If the industry doesn't respond (to the threat), you have to follow through."[205] On the other hand, executives from the private sector agree that improvements are necessary, but think that government intervention would affect their ability to innovate efficiently. Daniel R. McCarthy analyzed this public-private partnership in cybersecurity and reflected on the role of cybersecurity in the broader constitution of political order.[206]

On 22 May 2020, the UN Security Council held its second ever informal meeting on cybersecurity to focus on cyber challenges to international peace. According to UN Secretary-General António Guterres, new technologies are too often used to violate rights.[207]

International actions

Many different teams and organizations exist, including:

- The Forum of Incident Response and Security Teams (FIRST) is the global association of CSIRTs.[208] The US-

- CERT, AT&T, Apple, Cisco, McAfee, Microsoft are all members of this international team.[209]
- The Council of Europe helps protect societies worldwide from the threat of cybercrime through the Convention on Cybercrime.[210]
- The purpose of the Messaging Anti-Abuse Working Group (MAAWG) is to bring the messaging industry together to work collaboratively and to successfully address the various forms of messaging abuse, such as spam, viruses, denial-of-service attacks and other messaging exploitations.[211] France Telecom, Facebook, AT&T, Apple, Cisco, Sprint are some of the members of the MAAWG.[212]
- ENISA : The European Network and Information Security Agency (ENISA) is an agency of the European Union with the objective to improve network and information security in the European Union.

Europe

On 14 April 2016, the European Parliament and the Council of the European Union adopted the General Data Protection Regulation (GDPR). The GDPR, which came into force on 25 May 2018, grants individuals within the European Union (EU) and the European Economic Area (EEA) the right to the protection of personal data. The regulation requires that any entity that processes personal data incorporate data protection by design and by default. It also requires that certain organizations appoint a Data Protection Officer (DPO).

National actions

Computer emergency response teams

Most countries have their own computer emergency response team to protect network security.

Canada

Since 2010, Canada has had a cybersecurity strategy.[213][214] This functions as a counterpart document to the National Strategy and Action Plan for Critical Infrastructure.[215] The strategy has three main pillars: securing government systems, securing vital private cyber systems, and helping Canadians to be secure online.[214][215] There is also a Cyber Incident Management Framework to provide a coordinated response in the event of a cyber incident.[216][217]

The Canadian Cyber Incident Response Centre (CCIRC) is responsible for mitigating and responding to threats to Canada's critical infrastructure and cyber systems. It provides support to mitigate cyber threats, technical support to respond & recover from targeted cyber attacks, and provides online tools for members of Canada's critical infrastructure sectors.[218] It posts regular cybersecurity bulletins[219] & operates an online reporting tool where individuals and organizations can report a cyber incident.[220]

To inform the general public on how to protect themselves online, Public Safety Canada has partnered with STOP.THINK.CONNECT, a coalition of non-profit, private sector, and government organizations,[221] and launched the Cyber Security Cooperation Program.[222][223] They also run the GetCyberSafe portal for Canadian citizens, and Cyber Security Awareness Month during October.[224]

Public Safety Canada aims to begin an evaluation of Canada's cybersecurity strategy in early 2015.[215]

China

China's Central Leading Group for Internet Security and Informatization (Chinese: 中央网络安全和信息化领导小组) was established on 27 February 2014. This Leading Small Group (LSG) of the Chinese Communist Party is headed by General Secretary Xi Jinping himself and is staffed with relevant Party and state decision-makers. The LSG was created to overcome the incoherent policies and overlapping responsibilities that characterized China's former cyberspace decision-making mechanisms. The LSG oversees policy-making in the economic, political, cultural, social and military fields as they relate to network security and IT strategy. This LSG also coordinates major policy initiatives in the international arena that promote norms and standards favored by the Chinese government and that emphasizes the principle of national sovereignty in cyberspace.[225]

Germany

Berlin starts National Cyber Defense Initiative: On 16 June 2011, the German Minister for Home Affairs, officially opened the new German NCAZ (National Center for Cyber Defense) Nationales Cyber-Abwehrzentrum located in Bonn. The NCAZ closely cooperates with BSI (Federal Office for Information Security) Bundesamt für Sicherheit in der Informationstechnik, BKA (Federal Police Organisation) Bundeskriminalamt (Deutschland), BND (Federal Intelligence Service) Bundesnachrichtendienst, MAD (Military Intelligence Service) Amt für den Militärischen Abschirmdienst and other national organizations in Germany taking care of national security aspects. According to the Minister, the primary task of the new organization founded on 23 February 2011, is to detect and prevent attacks against the national infrastructure and mentioned incidents like Stuxnet. Germany has also established the largest research institution for IT security in Europe, the Center for Research in Security and Privacy (CRISP) in Darmstadt.

India

Some provisions for cybersecurity have been incorporated into rules framed under the Information Technology Act 2000.[226]

The National Cyber Security Policy 2013 is a policy framework by the Ministry of Electronics and Information Technology (MeitY) which aims to protect the public and private infrastructure from cyberattacks, and safeguard "information, such as personal information (of web users), financial and banking information and sovereign data". CERT- In is the nodal agency which monitors the cyber threats in the country. The post of National Cyber Security Coordinator has also been created in the Prime Minister's Office (PMO).

The Indian Companies Act 2013 has also introduced cyber law and cybersecurity obligations on the part of Indian directors. Some provisions for cybersecurity have been incorporated into rules framed under the Information Technology Act 2000 Update in 2013.[227]

South Korea

Following cyberattacks in the first half of 2013, when the government, news media, television stations, and bank websites were compromised, the national government committed to the training of 5,000 new cybersecurity experts by 2017. The South Korean government blamed its northern counterpart for these attacks, as well as incidents that occurred in 2009, 2011,[228] and 2012, but Pyongyang denies the accusations.[229]

United States

Legislation

The 1986 18 U.S.C. § 1030, the Computer Fraud and Abuse Act is the key legislation. It prohibits unauthorized access or damage of *protected computers* as defined in 18 U.S.C. § 1030€(2). Although various other measures have been proposed[230][231] – none has succeeded.

In 2013, executive order 13636 *Improving Critical Infrastructure Cybersecurity* was signed, which prompted the creation of the NIST Cybersecurity Framework.

In response to the Colonial Pipeline ransomware attack[232] President Joe Biden signed Executive Order 14028[233] on May 12, 2021, to increase software security standards for sales to the government, tighten detection and security on existing systems, improve information sharing and training, establish a Cyber Safety Review Board, and improve incident response.

Standardized government testing services

The General Services Administration (GSA) has[when?] standardized the *penetration test* service as a pre-vetted support service, to rapidly address potential vulnerabilities, and stop adversaries before they impact US federal, state and local governments. These services are commonly referred to as Highly Adaptive Cybersecurity Services (HACS).

Agencies

The Department of Homeland Security has a dedicated division responsible for the response system, risk management program and requirements for cybersecurity in the United States called the National Cyber Security Division.[234][235] The division is home to US-CERT operations and the National Cyber Alert System.[235] The National Cybersecurity and Communications Integration Center brings together government organizations responsible for protecting computer networks and networked infrastructure.[236]

The third priority of the FBI is to: "Protect the United States against cyber-based attacks and high-technology crimes",[237] and they, along with the National White Collar Crime Center (NW3C), and the Bureau of Justice Assistance (BJA) are part of the multi-agency task force, The Internet Crime Complaint Center, also known as IC3.[238]

In addition to its own specific duties, the FBI participates alongside non-profit organizations such as InfraGard.[239][240]

The Computer Crime and Intellectual Property Section (CCIPS) operates in the United States Department of Justice Criminal Division. The CCIPS is in charge of investigating computer crime and intellectual property crime and is specialized in the search and seizure of digital evidence in computers and networks.[241] In 2017, CCIPS published A Framework for a Vulnerability Disclosure Program for Online Systems to help organizations "clearly describe authorized vulnerability disclosure and discovery conduct, thereby substantially reducing the likelihood that such described activities will result in a civil or criminal violation of law under the Computer Fraud and Abuse Act (18 U.S.C. § 1030)."[242]

The United States Cyber Command, also known as USCYBERCOM, "has the mission to direct, synchronize, and coordinate cyberspace planning and operations to defend and advance national interests in collaboration with domestic and international partners."[243] It has no role in the protection of civilian networks.[244][245]

The U.S. Federal Communications Commission's role in cybersecurity is to strengthen the protection of critical communications infrastructure, to assist in maintaining the reliability of networks during disasters, to aid in swift recovery after, and to ensure that first responders have access to effective communications services.[246]

The Food and Drug Administration has issued guidance for medical devices,[247] and the National Highway Traffic Safety Administration[248] is concerned with automotive cybersecurity. After being criticized by the Government Accountability Office,[249] and following successful attacks on airports and claimed attacks on airplanes, the Federal Aviation Administration has devoted funding to securing systems on board the planes of private manufacturers, and the Aircraft Communications Addressing and Reporting System.[250] Concerns have also been raised about the future Next Generation Air Transportation System.[251]

The US Department of Defense (DoD) issued DoD Directive 8570 in 2004, supplemented by DoD Directive 8140, requiring all DoD employees and all DoD contract personnel involved in information assurance roles and activities to earn and maintain various industry Information Technology (IT) certifications in an effort to ensure that all DoD personnel involved in network infrastructure defense have minimum levels of IT industry recognized knowledge, skills and abilities (KSA). Andersson and Reimers (2019) report these certifications range from CompTIA's A+ and Security+ through the ICS2.org's CISSP, etc.. [252]

Computer emergency readiness team

Computer emergency response team is a name given to expert groups that handle computer security incidents. In the US, two distinct organizations exist, although they do work closely together.

- US-CERT: part of the National Cyber Security Division of the United States Department of Homeland Security.[253]
- CERT/CC: created by the Defense Advanced Research Projects Agency (DARPA) and run by the Software Engineering Institute (SEI).

Modern warfare

There is growing concern that cyberspace will become the next theater of warfare. As Mark Clayton from *The Christian Science Monitor* wrote in a 2015 article titled "The New Cyber Arms Race":

In the future, wars will not just be fought by soldiers with guns or with planes that drop bombs. They will also be fought with the click of a mouse a half a world away that unleashes carefully weaponized computer programs that disrupt or destroy critical industries like utilities, transportation, communications, and energy. Such attacks could also disable military networks that control the movement of troops, the path of jet fighters, the command and control of warships.[254]

This has led to new terms such as *cyberwarfare* and *cyberterrorism*. The United States Cyber Command was created in 2009[255] and many other countries have similar forces.

There are a few critical voices that question whether cybersecurity is as significant a threat as it is made out to be.[256][257][258]

Importance of Cyber Security

• Protection of Sensitive Information

Both network security and cybersecurity are important for protecting sensitive information such as personal data, financial information, and trade secrets. A breach of this information can result in significant financial and reputational losses for businesses and individuals alike.

• Protection of Devices and Systems

Network security and cybersecurity are also important for protecting devices and systems from unauthorized access and malicious attacks. This is particularly important for businesses that rely on digital technologies to store and transmit sensitive data.

• Compliance with Regulations

Many industries are subject to regulatory compliance requirements, such as HIPAA, PCI DSS, and GDPR, which mandate the protection of sensitive information. Compliance with these regulations requires implementing robust network security and cybersecurity measures.[23]

Careers

Cybersecurity is a fast-growing field of IT concerned with reducing organizations' risk of hack or data breaches.[259] According to research from the Enterprise Strategy Group, 46% of organizations say that they have a "problematic shortage" of cybersecurity skills in 2016, up from 28% in 2015.[260] Commercial, government and non-governmental organizations all employ cybersecurity professionals. The fastest increases in demand for cybersecurity workers are in industries managing increasing volumes of consumer data such as finance, health care, and retail.[261] However, the use of the term *cybersecurity* is more prevalent in government job descriptions.[262]

Typical cybersecurity job titles and descriptions include:[263]

Security analyst
Analyzes and assesses vulnerabilities in the infrastructure (software, hardware, networks), investigates using available tools and countermeasures to remedy the detected vulnerabilities and recommends solutions and best practices. Analyzes and assesses damage to the data/infrastructure as a result of security incidents, examines available recovery tools and processes, and recommends solutions. Tests for compliance with security policies and procedures. May assist in the creation, implementation, or management of security solutions.

Security engineer
Performs security monitoring, security and data/logs analysis, and forensic analysis, to detect security incidents, and mount the incident response. Investigates and utilizes new technologies and processes to enhance security capabilities and implement improvements. May also review code or perform other security engineering methodologies.

Security architect

Designs a security system or major components of a security system, and may head a security design team building a new security system.[264]

Security administrator
Installs and manages organization-wide security systems. This position may also include taking on some of the tasks of a security analyst in smaller organizations.[265]

Chief Information Security Officer (CISO)
A high-level management position responsible for the entire information security division/staff. The position may include hands-on technical work.[266]

Chief Security Officer (CSO)
A high-level management position responsible for the entire security division/staff. A newer position is now deemed needed as security risks grow.

Data Protection Officer (DPO)
A DPO is tasked with monitoring compliance with the UK GDPR and other data protection laws, our data protection policies, awareness-raising, training, and audits.[267]

Security Consultant/Specialist/Intelligence
Broad titles that encompass any one or all of the other roles or titles tasked with protecting computers, networks, software, data or information systems against viruses, worms, spyware, malware, intrusion detection, unauthorized access, denial-of-service attacks, and an ever-increasing list of attacks by hackers acting as individuals or as part of organized crime or foreign governments.

Student programs are also available for people interested in beginning a career in cybersecurity.[268][269] Meanwhile, a flexible and effective option for information security professionals of all experience levels to keep studying is online security training, including webcasts.[270][271] A wide range of certified courses are also available.[272]

In the United Kingdom, a nationwide set of cybersecurity forums, known as the U.K Cyber Security Forum, were established supported by the Government's cybersecurity strategy[273] in order to encourage start-ups and innovation and to address the skills gap[274] identified by the U.K Government.

In Singapore, the Cyber Security Agency has issued a Singapore Operational Technology (OT) Cybersecurity Competency Framework (OTCCF). The framework defines emerging cybersecurity roles in Operational Technology. The OTCCF was endorsed by the Infocomm Media Development Authority (IMDA). It outlines the different OT cybersecurity job positions as well as the technical skills and core competencies necessary. It also depicts the many career paths available, including vertical and lateral advancement opportunities.[275]

Terminology

The following terms used with regards to computer security are explained below:

- Access authorization restricts access to a computer to a group of users through the use of authentication systems. These systems can protect either the whole computer, such as through an interactive login screen, or individual services, such as a FTP server. There are many methods for identifying and authenticating users, such as passwords, identification cards, smart cards, and biometric systems.

- Anti-virus software consists of computer programs that attempt to identify, thwart, and eliminate computer viruses and other malicious software (malware).
- Applications are executable code, so general corporate practice is to restrict or block users the power to install them; to install them only when there is a demonstrated need (e.g. software needed to perform assignments); to install only those which are known to be reputable (preferably with access to the computer code used to create the application,- and to reduce the attack surface by installing as few as possible. They are typically run with least privilege, with a robust process in place to identify, test and install any released security patches or updates for them.
- For example, programs can be installed into an individual user's account, which limits the program's potential access, as well as being a means control which users have specific exceptions to policy. In Linux], FreeBSD, OpenBSD, and other Unix-like operating systems there is an option to further restrict an application using chroot or other means of restricting the application to its own 'sandbox'. For example. Linux provides namespaces, and Cgroups to further restrict the access of an application to system resources.
- Generalized security frameworks such as SELinux or AppArmor help administrators control access.
- Java and other languages which compile to Java byte code and run in the Java virtual machine can have their access to other applications controlled at the virtual machine level.
- Some software can be run in software containers which can even provide their own set of system libraries, limiting the software's, or anyone controlling it, access to the server's versions of the libraries.
- Authentication techniques can be used to ensure that communication end-points are who they say they are.
- Automated theorem proving and other verification tools can be used to enable critical algorithms and code used in secure systems to be mathematically proven to meet their specifications.
- Backups are one or more copies kept of important computer files. Typically, multiple copies will be kept at different locations so that if a copy is stolen or damaged, other copies will still exist.
- Capability and access control list techniques can be used to ensure privilege separation and mandatory access control. Capabilities vs. ACLs discusses their use.
- Chain of trust techniques can be used to attempt to ensure that all software loaded has been certified as authentic by the system's designers.
- Confidentiality is the nondisclosure of information except to another authorized person.[276]
- Cryptographic techniques can be used to defend data in transit between systems, reducing the probability that the data exchange between systems can be intercepted or modified.
- Cyberwarfare is an Internet-based conflict that involves politically motivated attacks on information and information systems. Such attacks can, for example, disable official websites and networks, disrupt or disable essential services, steal or alter classified data, and cripple financial systems.
- Data integrity is the accuracy and consistency of stored data, indicated by an absence of any alteration in data between two updates of a data record.[277]
- Cryptographic techniques involve transforming information, scrambling it, so it becomes unreadable during transmission. The intended recipient can unscramble the message; ideally, eavesdroppers cannot.

- Encryption is used to protect the confidentiality of a message. Cryptographically secure ciphers are designed to make any practical attempt of breaking them infeasible. Symmetric-key ciphers are suitable for bulk encryption using shared keys, and public-key encryption using digital certificates can provide a practical solution for the problem of securely communicating when no key is shared in advance.
- Endpoint security software aids networks in preventing malware infection and data theft at network entry points made vulnerable by the prevalence of potentially infected devices such as laptops, mobile devices, and USB drives.[278]
- Firewalls serve as a gatekeeper system between networks, allowing only traffic that matches defined rules. They often include detailed logging, and may include intrusion detection and intrusion prevention features. They are near-universal between company local area networks and the Internet, but can also be used internally to impose traffic rules between networks if network segmentation is configured.
- A hacker is someone who seeks to breach defenses and exploit weaknesses in a computer system or network.
- Honey pots are computers that are intentionally left vulnerable to attack by crackers. They can be used to catch crackers and to identify their techniques.
- Intrusion-detection systems are devices or software applications that monitor networks or systems for malicious activity or policy violations.
- A microkernel is an approach to operating system design which has only the near-minimum amount of code running at the most privileged level – and runs other elements of the operating system such as device drivers, protocol stacks and file systems, in the safer, less privileged user space.
- Pinging. The standard ping application can be used to test if an IP address is in use. If it is, attackers may then try a port scan to detect which services are exposed.
- A port scan is used to probe an IP address for open ports to identify accessible network services and applications.
- A key logger is spyware that silently captures and stores each keystroke that a user types on the computer's keyboard.
- Social engineering is the use of deception to manipulate individuals to breach security.
- Logic bombs is a type of malware added to a legitimate program that lies dormant until it is triggered by a specific event.
- Zero trust security means that no one is trusted by default from inside or outside the network, and verification is required from everyone trying to gain access to resources on the network.

Network Security

Network security consists of the policies, processes and practices adopted to prevent, detect and monitor unauthorized access, misuse, modification, or denial of a computer network and network-accessible resources.[1] Network security involves the authorization of access to data in a network, which is controlled by the network administrator. Users choose or are assigned an ID and password or other authenticating information that allows them access to information and programs within their authority. Network security covers a variety of computer networks, both public and private, that are used in everyday jobs: conducting transactions and communications among businesses, government agencies and individuals. Networks can be private, such as within a company, and others which might be open to public access. Network security is involved in organizations, enterprises, and other types of institutions. It does as its title explains: it secures the network, as well as protecting and overseeing operations being done. The most common and simple way of protecting a network resource is by assigning it a unique name and a corresponding password.

Network security concept

Network security starts with authentication, commonly with a username and a password. Since this requires just one detail authenticating the user name—i.e., the password—this is sometimes termed one-factor authentication. With two-factor authentication, something the user 'has' is also used (e.g., a security token or 'dongle', an ATM card, or a mobile phone); and with three-factor authentication, something the user 'is' is also used (e.g., a fingerprint or retinal scan).

Once authenticated, a firewall enforces access policies such as what services are allowed to be accessed by the network users.[2][3] Though effective to prevent unauthorized access, this component may fail to check potentially harmful content such as computer worms or Trojans being transmitted over the network.[4] Anti-virus software or an intrusion prevention system (IPS)[5] help detect and inhibit the action of such malware. An anomaly-based intrusion detection system may also monitor the network like wireshark traffic and may be logged for audit purposes and for later high-level analysis. Newer systems combining unsupervised machine learning with full network traffic analysis can detect active network attackers from malicious insiders or targeted external attackers that have compromised a user machine or account.[6]

Communication between two hosts using a network may be encrypted to maintain security and privacy.

Honeypots, essentially decoy network-accessible resources, may be deployed in a network as surveillance and early-warning tools, as the honeypots are not normally accessed for legitimate purposes. Honeypots are placed at a point in the network where they appear vulnerable and undefended, but they are actually isolated and monitored.[7] Techniques used by the attackers that attempt to compromise these decoy resources are studied during and after an attack to keep an eye on new exploitation techniques. Such analysis may be used to further tighten security of the actual network being protected by the honeypot. A honeypot can also direct an attacker's attention away from legitimate servers. A honeypot encourages attackers to spend their time and energy on the decoy server while distracting their attention from the data on the real server. Similar to a honeypot, a honeynet is a network set up with intentional vulnerabilities.

Its purpose is also to invite attacks so that the attacker's methods can be studied and that information can be used to increase network security. A honeynet typically contains one or more honeypots.[8]

Security management

Security management for networks is different for all kinds of situations. A home or small office may only require basic security while large businesses may require high-maintenance and advanced software and hardware to prevent malicious attacks from hacking and spamming. In order to minimize susceptibility to malicious attacks from external threats to the network, corporations often employ tools which carry out network security verifications].

Types of attack

Networks are subject to attacks from malicious sources. Attacks can be from two categories: "Passive" when a network intruder intercepts data traveling through the network, and "Active" in which an intruder initiates commands to disrupt the network's normal operation or to conduct reconnaissance and lateral movements to find and gain access to assets available via the network.[9]

Honeytoken

In the field of computer security, **honeytokens** are honeypots that are not computer systems. Their value lies not in their use, but in their abuse. As such, they are a generalization of such ideas as the honeypot and the canary values often used in stack protection schemes. Honeytokens do not necessarily prevent any tampering with the data, but instead give the administrator a further measure of confidence in the data integrity.

Honeytokens are fictitious words or records that are added to legitimate databases. They allow administrators to track data in situations they wouldn't normally be able to track, such as cloud-based networks.[1] If data is stolen, honey tokens allow administrators to identify who it was stolen from or how it was leaked. If there are three locations for medical records, different honey tokens in the form of fake medical records could be added to each location. Different honeytokens would be in each set of records.[2]

If they are chosen to be unique and unlikely to ever appear in legitimate traffic, they can also be detected over the network by an intrusion-detection system (IDS), alerting the system administrator to things that would otherwise go unnoticed. This is one case where they go beyond merely ensuring integrity, and with some reactive security mechanisms, may actually prevent the malicious activity, e.g. by dropping all packets containing the honeytoken at the router. However, such mechanisms have pitfalls because it might cause serious problems if the honeytoken was poorly chosen and appeared in otherwise legitimate network traffic, which was then dropped.

The term was first coined by Augusto Paes de Barros in 2003.[3][4]

Physical Security

Physical security describes security measures that are designed to deny unauthorized access to facilities, equipment, and resources and to protect personnel and property from damage or harm (such as espionage, theft, or terrorist attacks).[1] Physical security involves the use of multiple layers of interdependent systems that can include CCTV surveillance, security guards, protective barriers, locks, access control, perimeter intrusion detection, deterrent systems, fire protection, and other systems designed to protect persons and property.

Overview

Physical security systems for protected facilities are generally intended to:[2][3][4]

- deter potential intruders (e.g. warning signs, security lighting and perimeter markings);
- detect intrusions and monitor/record intruders (e.g. intruder alarms and CCTV systems); and
- trigger appropriate incident responses (e.g. by security guards and police).

It is up to security designers, architects and analysts to balance security controls against risks, taking into account the costs of specifying, developing, testing, implementing, using, managing, monitoring and maintaining the controls, along with broader issues such as aesthetics, human rights, health and safety, and societal norms or conventions. Physical access security measures that are appropriate for a high security prison or a military site may be inappropriate in an office, a home or a vehicle, although the principles are similar.

Elements and design

Deterrence methods

The goal of *deterrence* methods is to convince potential attackers that a successful attack is unlikely due to strong defenses.

The initial layer of security for a campus, building, office,, or other physical space uses crime prevention through environmental design to deter threats. Some of the most common examples are also the most basic: warning signs or window stickers, fences, vehicle barriers, vehicle height-restrictors, restricted access points, security lighting and trenches.[5][6][7][8]

Physical barriers

Physical barriers such as fences, walls, and vehicle barriers act as the outermost layer of security. They serve to prevent, or at least delay, attacks, and also act as a psychological deterrent by defining the perimeter of the facility and making intrusions seem more difficult. Tall fencing, topped with barbed wire, razor wire or metal spikes are often emplaced on the perimeter of a property, generally with some type of signage that warns people not to attempt entry. However, in some facilities imposing perimeter walls/fencing will not be possible (e.g. an urban office building that is directly adjacent to public sidewalks) or it may be aesthetically unacceptable (e.g. surrounding a shopping center with tall fences topped with razor wire); in this case, the outer security perimeter will be defined as the walls/windows/doors of the structure itself.[9]

Security lighting

Security lighting is another effective form of deterrence. Intruders are less likely to enter well-lit areas for fear of being seen. Doors, gates, and other entrances, in particular, should be well lit to allow close observation of people entering and exiting. When lighting the grounds of a facility, widely distributed low-intensity lighting is generally superior to small patches of high-intensity lighting, because the latter can have a tendency to create blind spots for security personnel and CCTV cameras. It is important to place lighting in a manner that makes it difficult to tamper with (e.g. suspending lights from tall poles), and to ensure that there is a backup power supply so that security lights will not go out if the electricity is cut off.[10] The introduction of low-voltage LED-based lighting products has enabled new security capabilities, such as instant-on or strobing, while substantially reducing electrical consumption.[11]

Intrusion detection and electronic surveillance

Alarm systems and sensors

Alarm systems can be installed to alert security personnel when unauthorized access is attempted. Alarm systems work in tandem with physical barriers, mechanical systems, and security guards, serving to trigger a response when these other forms of security have been breached. They consist of sensors including perimeter sensors, motion sensors, contact sensors, and glass break detectors.[12]

However, alarms are only useful if there is a prompt response when they are triggered. In the reconnaissance phase prior to an actual attack, some intruders will test the response time of security personnel to a deliberately tripped alarm system. By measuring the length of time it takes for a security team to arrive (if they arrive at all), the attacker can determine if an attack could succeed before authorities arrive to neutralize the threat. Loud audible alarms can also act as a psychological deterrent, by notifying intruders that their presence has been detected.[13] In some jurisdictions, law enforcement will not respond to alarms from intrusion detection systems unless the activation has been verified by an eyewitness or video.[14] Policies like this one have been created to combat the 94–99 percent rate of false alarm activation in the United States.[15]

Video surveillance

Surveillance cameras can be a deterrent[16] when placed in highly visible locations and are useful for incident assessment and historical analysis. For example, if alarms are being generated and there is a camera in place, security personnel assess the situation via the camera feed. In instances when an attack has already occurred and a camera is in place at the point of attack, the recorded video can be reviewed. Although the term closed-circuit television (CCTV) is common, it is quickly becoming outdated as more video systems lose the closed circuit for signal transmission and are instead transmitting on IP camera networks.

Video monitoring does not necessarily guarantee a human response. A human must be monitoring the situation in real time in order to respond in a timely manner; otherwise, video monitoring is simply a means to gather evidence for later analysis. However, technological advances like video analytics are reducing the amount of work required for video monitoring as security personnel can be automatically notified of potential security events.[17][18][19]

Access control

Access control methods are used to monitor and control traffic through specific access points and areas of the secure facility. This is done using a variety of systems including CCTV surveillance, identification cards, security guards, biometric readers, and electronic/mechanical control systems such as locks, doors, turnstiles and gates.[20][21][22]

Mechanical access control systems

Mechanical access control systems include turnstiles, gates, doors, and locks. Key control of the locks becomes a problem with large user populations and any user turnover. Keys quickly become unmanageable, often forcing the adoption of electronic access control.

Electronic access control systems

Electronic access control systems provide secure access to buildings or facilities by controlling who can enter and exit. Some key aspects of these systems include:

- Access credentials – Access cards, fobs, or badges are used to identify and authenticate authorized users. Information encoded on the credentials is read by card readers at entry points.
- Access control panels – These control the system, make access decisions, and are usually located in a secure area. Access control software runs on the panels and interfaces with Card reader.
- Card readers – Installed at access points, these read credentials and send information to the access control panel. Readers can be proximity, magnetic stripe, smart card, Biometrics, etc.
- Door locking hardware – Electrified locks, electric strikes, or maglocks physically secure doors and release when valid credentials are presented. Integration allows doors to unlock when authorized.
- Request to exit devices – These allow free egress through an access point without triggering an alarm. Buttons, motion detectors, and other sensors are commonly used.
- Alarms – Unauthorized access attempts or held/forced doors can trigger audible alarms and alerts. Integration with camera systems also occurs.
- Access levels – Software can limit access to specific users, groups, and times. For example, some employees may have 24/7 access to all areas while others are restricted.
- Event logging – Systems record activity like access attempts, alarms, user tracking, etc. for security auditing and troubleshooting purposes.

Electronic access control uses credential readers, advanced software, and electrified locks to provide programmable, secure access management for facilities. Integration of cameras, alarms and other systems is also common.[23]

An additional sub-layer of mechanical/electronic access control protection is reached by integrating a key management system to manage the possession and usage of mechanical keys to locks or property within a building or campus.

Identification systems and access policies

Another form of access control (*procedural*) includes the use of policies, processes and procedures to manage the ingress into the restricted area. An example of this is the deployment of security personnel conducting checks for authorized entry at predetermined points of entry. This form of access control is usually supplemented by the earlier forms of access control (i.e. mechanical and electronic access control), or simple devices such as physical passes.

Security personnel

Security personnel play a central role in all layers of security. All of the technological systems that are employed to enhance physical security are useless without a security force that is trained in their use and maintenance, and which knows how to properly respond to breaches in security. Security personnel perform many functions: patrolling facilities, administering electronic access control, responding to alarms, and monitoring and analyzing video footage.[24]

Wireless Security

Wireless security is the prevention of unauthorized access or damage to computers or data using wireless networks, which include Wi-Fi networks. The term may also refer to the protection of the wireless network itself from adversaries seeking to damage the confidentiality, integrity, or availability of the network. The most common type is **Wi-Fi security**, which includes Wired Equivalent Privacy (WEP) and Wi-Fi Protected Access (WPA). WEP is an old IEEE 802.11 standard from 1997.[1] It is a notoriously weak security standard: the password it uses can often be cracked in a few minutes with a basic laptop computer and widely available software tools.[2] WEP was superseded in 2003 by WPA, a quick alternative at the time to improve security over WEP. The current standard is WPA2;[3] some hardware cannot support WPA2 without firmware upgrade or replacement. WPA2 uses an encryption device that encrypts the network with a 256-bit key; the longer key length improves security over WEP. Enterprises often enforce security using a certificate-based system to authenticate the connecting device, following the standard 802.11X.

In January 2018, the Wi-Fi Alliance announced WPA3 as a replacement to WPA2. Certification began in June 2018, and WPA3 support has been mandatory for devices which bear the "Wi-Fi CERTIFIED™" logo since July 2020.

Many laptop computers have wireless cards pre-installed. The ability to enter a network while mobile has great benefits. However, wireless networking is prone to some security issues. Hackers have found wireless networks relatively easy to break into, and even use wireless technology to hack into wired networks. As a result, it is very important that enterprises define effective wireless security policies that guard against unauthorized access to important resources.[4] Wireless Intrusion Prevention Systems (WIPS) or Wireless Intrusion Detection Systems (WIDS) are commonly used to enforce wireless security policies.

The risks to users of wireless technology have increased as the service has become more popular. There were relatively few dangers when wireless technology was first introduced. Hackers had not yet had time to latch on to the new technology, and wireless networks were not commonly found in the work place. However, there are many security risks associated with the current wireless protocols and encryption methods, and in the carelessness and ignorance that exists at the user and corporate IT level.[5] Hacking methods have become much more sophisticated and innovative with wireless access. Hacking has also become much easier and more accessible with easy-to-use Windows- or Linux-based tools being made available on the web at no charge.

Some organizations that have no wireless access points installed do not feel that they need to address wireless security concerns. In-Stat MDR and META Group have estimated that 95% of all corporate laptop computers that were planned to be purchased in 2005 were equipped with wireless cards. Issues can arise in a supposedly non-wireless organization when a wireless laptop is plugged into the corporate network. A hacker could sit out in the parking lot and gather information from it through laptops and/or other devices, or even break in through this wireless card–equipped laptop and gain access to the wired network.

Background

Anyone within the geographical network range of an open, unencrypted wireless network can "sniff", or capture and record, the traffic, gain unauthorized access to internal network resources as well as to the internet, and then use the information and resources to perform disruptive or illegal acts. Such security breaches have become important concerns for both enterprise and home networks.

If router security is not activated or if the owner deactivates it for convenience, it creates a free hotspot. Since most 21st-century laptop PCs have wireless networking built in (see Intel "Centrino" technology), they don't need a third-party adapter such as a PCMCIA Card or USB dongle. Built-in wireless networking might be enabled by default, without the owner realizing it, thus broadcasting the laptop's accessibility to any computer nearby.

Modern operating systems such as Linux, macOS, or Microsoft Windows make it fairly easy to set up a PC as a wireless LAN "base station" using Internet Connection Sharing, thus allowing all the PCs in the home to access the Internet through the "base" PC. However, lack of knowledge among users about the security issues inherent in setting up such systems often may allow others nearby access to the connection. Such "piggybacking" is usually achieved without the wireless network operator's knowledge; it may even be without the knowledge of the intruding user if their computer automatically selects a nearby unsecured wireless network to use as an access point.

The threat situation

Wireless security is just an aspect of computer security; however, organizations may be particularly vulnerable to security breaches[6] caused by rogue access points.

If an employee (trusted entity) brings in a wireless router and plugs it into an unsecured switchport, the entire network can be exposed to anyone within range of the signals. Similarly, if an employee adds a wireless interface to a networked computer using an open USB port, they may create a breach in network security that would allow access to confidential materials. However, there are effective countermeasures (like disabling open switchports during switch configuration and VLAN configuration to limit network access) that are available to protect both the network and the information it contains, but such countermeasures must be applied uniformly to all network devices.

Threats and Vulnerabilites in an industrial (M2M) context

Due to its availability and low cost, the use of wireless communication technologies increases in domains beyond the originally intended usage areas, e.g. M2M communication in industrial applications. Such industrial applications often have specific security requirements. Hence, it is important to understand the characteristics of such applications and evaluate the vulnerabilities bearing the highest risk in this context. Evaluation of these vulnerabilities and the resulting vulnerability catalogs in an industrial context when considering WLAN, NFC and ZigBee are available.[7]

The mobility advantage

Wireless networks are very common, both for organizations and individuals. Many laptop computers have wireless cards pre-installed. The ability to enter a network while mobile has great benefits. However, wireless networking is prone to some security issues.[8] Hackers have found wireless networks relatively easy to break into, and even use wireless technology to hack into wired networks.[9] As a result, it is very important that enterprises define effective wireless security policies that guard against unauthorized access to important resources.[4] Wireless Intrusion Prevention Systems (WIPS) or Wireless Intrusion Detection Systems (WIDS) are commonly used to enforce wireless security policies.

The air interface and link corruption risk

There were relatively few dangers when wireless technology was first introduced, as the effort to maintain the communication was high and the effort to intrude is always higher. The variety of risks to users of wireless technology have increased as the service has become more popular and the technology more commonly available. Today there are a great number of security risks associated with the current wireless protocols and encryption methods, as carelessness and ignorance exists at the user and corporate IT level.[5] Hacking methods have become much more sophisticated and innovative with wireless.

Modes of unauthorized access

The modes of unauthorised access to links, to functions and to data is as variable as the respective entities make use of program code. There does not exist a full scope model of such threat. To some extent the prevention relies on known modes and methods of attack and relevant methods for suppression of the applied methods. However, each new mode of operation will create new options of threatening. Hence prevention requires a steady drive for improvement. The described modes of attack are just a snapshot of typical methods and scenarios where to apply.

Accidental association

Violation of the security perimeter of a corporate network can come from a number of different methods and intents. One of these methods is referred to as "accidental association". When a user turns on a computer and it latches on to a wireless access point from a neighboring company's overlapping network, the user may not even know that this has occurred. However, it is a security breach in that proprietary company information is exposed and now there could exist a link from one company to the other. This is especially true if the laptop is also hooked to a wired network.

Accidental association is a case of wireless vulnerability called as "mis-association".[10] Mis-association can be accidental, deliberate (for example, done to bypass corporate firewall) or it can result from deliberate attempts on wireless clients to lure them into connecting to attacker's APs.

Malicious association

"Malicious associations" are when wireless devices can be actively made by attackers to connect to a company network through their laptop instead of a company access point (AP). These types of laptops are known as "soft APs" and are created when a cyber criminal runs some software that makes their wireless network card look like a legitimate access point. Once the thief has gained access, they can steal passwords, launch attacks on the wired network, or plant trojans. Since wireless networks operate at the Layer 2 level, Layer 3 protections such as network authentication and virtual private networks (VPNs) offer no barrier. Wireless 802.1X authentications do help with some protection but are still vulnerable to hacking. The idea behind this type of attack may not be to break into a VPN or other security measures. Most likely the criminal is just trying to take over the client at the Layer 2 level.

Ad hoc networks

Ad hoc networks can pose a security threat. Ad hoc networks are defined as [peer to peer] networks between wireless computers that do not have an access point in between them. While these types of networks usually have little protection, encryption methods can be used to provide security.[11]

The security hole provided by Ad hoc networking is not the Ad hoc network itself but the bridge it provides into other networks, usually in the corporate environment, and the unfortunate default settings in most versions of Microsoft Windows to have this feature turned on unless explicitly disabled. Thus the user may not even know they have an unsecured Ad hoc network in operation on their computer. If they are also using a wired or wireless infrastructure network at the same time, they are providing a bridge to the secured organizational network through the unsecured Ad hoc connection. Bridging is in two forms. A direct bridge, which requires the user actually configure a bridge between the two connections and is thus unlikely to be initiated unless explicitly desired, and an indirect bridge which is the shared resources on the user computer. The indirect bridge may expose private data that is shared from the user's computer to LAN connections, such as shared folders or private Network Attached Storage, making no distinction between authenticated or private connections and unauthenticated Ad-Hoc networks. This presents no threats not already familiar to open/public or unsecured wifi access points, but firewall rules may be circumvented in the case of poorly configured operating systems or local settings.[12]

Non-traditional networks

Non-traditional networks such as personal network Bluetooth devices are not safe from hacking and should be regarded as a security risk.[13] Even barcode readers, handheld PDAs, and wireless printers and copiers should be secured. These non-traditional networks can be easily overlooked by IT personnel who have narrowly focused on laptops and access points.

Identity theft (MAC spoofing)

Identity theft (or MAC spoofing) occurs when a hacker is able to listen in on network traffic and identify the MAC address of a computer with network privileges. Most wireless systems allow some kind of MAC filtering to allow only authorized computers with specific MAC IDs to gain access and utilize the network. However, programs exist that have network "sniffing" capabilities. Combine these programs with other software that allow a computer to pretend it has any MAC address that the hacker desires,[14] and the hacker can easily get around that hurdle.

MAC filtering is effective only for small residential (SOHO) networks, since it provides protection only when the wireless device is "off the air". Any 802.11 device "on the air" freely transmits its unencrypted MAC address in its 802.11 headers, and it requires no special equipment or software to detect it. Anyone with an 802.11 receiver (laptop and wireless adapter) and a freeware wireless packet analyzer can obtain the MAC address of any transmitting 802.11 within range. In an organizational environment, where most wireless devices are "on the air" throughout the active working shift, MAC filtering provides only a false sense of security since it prevents only "casual" or unintended connections to the organizational infrastructure and does nothing to prevent a directed attack.

Man-in-the-middle attacks

A man-in-the-middle attacker entices computers to log into a computer which is set up as a soft AP (Access Point). Once this is done, the hacker connects to a real access point through another wireless card offering a steady flow of traffic through the transparent hacking computer to the real network. The hacker can then sniff the traffic. One type of man-in-the-middle attack relies on security faults in challenge and handshake protocols to execute a "de-authentication attack". This attack forces AP-connected computers to drop their connections and reconnect with the hacker's soft AP (disconnects the user from the modem so they have to connect again using their password which one can extract from the recording of the event). Man-in-the-middle attacks are enhanced by software such as LANjack and AirJack which automate multiple steps of the process, meaning what once required some skill can now be done by script kiddies. Hotspots are particularly vulnerable to any attack since there is little to no security on these networks.

Denial of service

A Denial-of-service attack (DoS) occurs when an attacker continually bombards a targeted AP (Access Point) or network with bogus requests, premature successful connection messages, failure messages, and/or other commands. These cause legitimate users to not be able to get on the network and may even cause the network to crash. These attacks rely on the abuse of protocols such as the Extensible Authentication Protocol (EAP).

The DoS attack in itself does little to expose organizational data to a malicious attacker, since the interruption of the network prevents the flow of data and actually indirectly protects data by preventing it from being transmitted. The usual reason for performing a DoS attack is to observe the recovery of the wireless network, during which all of the initial handshake codes are re-transmitted by all devices, providing an opportunity for the malicious attacker to record these codes and use various cracking tools to analyze security weaknesses and exploit them to gain unauthorized access to the system. This works best on weakly encrypted systems such as WEP, where there are a number of tools available which can launch a dictionary style attack of "possibly accepted" security keys based on the "model" security key captured during the network recovery.

Network injection

In a network injection attack, a hacker can make use of access points that are exposed to non-filtered network traffic, specifically broadcasting network traffic such as "Spanning Tree" (802.1D), OSPF, RIP, and HSRP. The hacker injects bogus networking re-configuration commands that affect routers, switches, and intelligent hubs. A whole network can be brought down in this manner and require rebooting or even reprogramming of all intelligent networking devices.

Caffe Latte attack

The Caffe Latte attack is another way to obtain a WEP key and does not require a nearby access point for the target network.[15] The Caffe Latte attack works by tricking a client with the WEP password stored to connect to a malicious access point with the same SSID as the target network. After the client connects, the client generates ARP requests, which the malicious access point uses to obtain keystream data. The malicious access point then repeatedly sends a deauthentication packet to the client, causing the client to disconnect, reconnect, and send additional ARP requests, which the malicious access point then uses to obtain additional keystream data. Once the malicious access point has collected a sufficient amount of keystream data. the WEP key can be cracked with a tool like [aircrack-ng].

The Caffe Latte attack was demonstrated against the Windows wireless stack, but other operating systems may also be vulnerable.

The attack was named the "Caffe Latte" attack by researcher Vivek Ramachandran because it could be used to obtain the WEP key from a remote traveler in less than the 6 minutes it takes to drink a cup of coffee.[16][17][18]

Wireless intrusion prevention concepts

There are three principal ways to secure a wireless network.

- For closed networks (like home users and organizations) the most common way is to configure access restrictions in the access points. Those restrictions may include encryption and checks on MAC address. Wireless Intrusion Prevention Systems can be used to provide wireless LAN security in this network model.
- For commercial providers, hotspots, and large organizations, the preferred solution is often to have an open and unencrypted, but completely isolated wireless network. The users will at first have no access to the Internet nor to any local network resources. Commercial providers usually forward all web traffic to a captive portal which provides for payment and/or authorization. Another solution is to require the users to connect securely to a privileged network using VPN.
- Wireless networks are less secure than wired ones; in many offices intruders can easily visit and hook up their own computer to the wired network without problems, gaining access to the network, and it is also often possible for remote intruders to gain access to the network through backdoors like Back Orifice. One general solution may be end-to-end encryption, with independent authentication on all resources that shouldn't be available to the public.

There is no ready designed system to prevent from fraudulent usage of wireless communication or to protect data and functions with wirelessly communicating computers and other entities. However, there is a system of qualifying the taken measures as a whole according to a common understanding what shall be seen as state of the art. The system of qualifying is an international consensus as specified in ISO/IEC 15408.

A wireless intrusion prevention system

A Wireless Intrusion Prevention System (WIPS) is a concept for the most robust way to counteract wireless security risks.[19] However such WIPS does not exist as a ready designed solution to implement as a software package. A WIPS is typically implemented as an overlay to an existing Wireless LAN infrastructure, although it may be deployed standalone to enforce no-wireless policies within an organization. WIPS is considered so important to wireless security that in July 2009, the Payment Card Industry Security Standards Council published wireless guidelines[20] for PCI DSS recommending the use of WIPS to automate wireless scanning and protection for large organizations.

Security measures

There are a range of wireless security measures, of varying effectiveness and practicality.

SSID hiding

A simple but ineffective method to attempt to secure a wireless network is to hide the SSID (Service Set Identifier).[21] This provides very little protection against anything but the most casual intrusion efforts.

MAC ID filtering

One of the simplest techniques is to only allow access from known, pre-approved MAC addresses. Most wireless access points contain some type of MAC ID filtering. However, an attacker can simply sniff the MAC address of an authorized client and spoof this address.

Static IP addressing

Typical wireless access points provide IP addresses to clients via DHCP. Requiring clients to set their own addresses makes it more difficult for a casual or unsophisticated intruder to log onto the network, but provides little protection against a sophisticated attacker.[21]

802.11 security

IEEE 802.1X is the IEEE Standard authentication mechanisms to devices wishing to attach to a Wireless LAN.

Regular WEP

The Wired Equivalent Privacy (WEP) encryption standard was the original encryption standard for wireless, but since 2004 with the ratification WPA2 the IEEE has declared it "deprecated",[22] and while often supported, it is seldom or never the default on modern equipment.

Concerns were raised about its security as early as 2001,[23] dramatically demonstrated in 2005 by the FBI,[24] yet in 2007 T.J. Maxx admitted a massive security breach due in part to a reliance on WEP[25] and the Payment Card Industry took until 2008 to prohibit its use – and even then allowed existing use to continue until June 2010.[26]

WPAv1

The Wi-Fi Protected Access (WPA and WPA2) security protocols were later created to address the problems with WEP. If a weak password, such as a dictionary word or short character string is used, WPA and WPA2 can be cracked. Using a long enough random password (e.g. 14 random letters) or passphrase (e.g. 5 randomly chosen words) makes pre-shared key WPA virtually uncrackable. The second generation of the WPA security protocol (WPA2) is based on the final IEEE 802.11i amendment to the 802.11 standard and is eligible for FIPS 140-2 compliance. With all those encryption schemes, any client in the network that knows the keys can read all the traffic.

Wi-Fi Protected Access (WPA) is a software/firmware improvement over WEP. All regular WLAN-equipment that worked with WEP are able to be simply upgraded and no new equipment needs to be bought. WPA is a trimmed-down version of the 802.11i security standard that was developed by the IEEE 802.11 to replace WEP. The TKIP encryption algorithm was developed for WPA to provide improvements to WEP that could be fielded as firmware upgrades to existing 802.11 devices. The WPA profile also provides optional support for the AES-CCMP algorithm that is the preferred algorithm in 802.11i and WPA2.

WPA Enterprise provides RADIUS based authentication using 802.1X. WPA Personal uses a pre-shared Shared Key (PSK) to establish the security using an 8 to 63 character passphrase. The PSK may also be entered as a 64 character hexadecimal string. Weak PSK passphrases can be broken using off-line dictionary attacks by capturing the messages in the four-way exchange when the client reconnects after being deauthenticated. Wireless suites such as aircrack-ng can crack a weak passphrase in less than a minute. Other WEP/WPA crackers are AirSnort and Auditor Security Collection.[27] Still, WPA Personal is secure when used with 'good' passphrases or a full 64-character hexadecimal key.

There was information, however, that Erik Tews (the man who created the fragmentation attack against WEP) was going to reveal a way of breaking the WPA TKIP implementation at Tokyo's PacSec security conference in November 2008, cracking the encryption on a packet in 12 to 15 minutes.[28] Still, the announcement of this 'crack' was somewhat overblown by the media, because as of August, 2009, the best attack on WPA (the Beck-Tews attack) is only partially successful in that it only works on short data packets, it cannot decipher the WPA key, and it requires very specific WPA implementations in order to work.[29]

Additions to WPAv1

In addition to WPAv1, TKIP, WIDS and EAP may be added alongside. Also, VPN-networks (non-continuous secure network connections) may be set up under the 802.11-standard. VPN implementations include PPTP, L2TP, IPsec and SSH. However, this extra layer of security may also be cracked with tools such as Anger, Deceit and Ettercap for PPTP;[30] and ike-scan, IKEProbe, ipsectrace, and IKEcrack for IPsec-connections.

TKIP

This stands for Temporal Key Integrity Protocol and the acronym is pronounced as tee-kip. This is part of the IEEE 802.11i standard. TKIP implements per-packet key mixing with a re-keying system and also provides a message integrity check. These avoid the problems of WEP.

EAP

The WPA-improvement over the IEEE 802.1X standard already improved the authentication and authorization for access of wireless and wired LANs. In addition to this, extra measures such as the Extensible Authentication Protocol (EAP) have initiated an even greater amount of security. This, as EAP uses a central authentication server. Unfortunately, during 2002 a Maryland professor discovered some shortcomings. Over the next few years these shortcomings were addressed with the use of TLS and other enhancements.[31] This new version of EAP is now called Extended EAP and is available in several versions; these include: EAP-MD5, PEAPv0, PEAPv1, EAP-MSCHAPv2, LEAP, EAP-FAST, EAP-TLS, EAP-TTLS, MSCHAPv2, and EAP-SIM.

EAP-versions

EAP-versions include LEAP, PEAP and other EAP's.

LEAP

This stands for the Lightweight Extensible Authentication Protocol. This protocol is based on 802.1X and helps minimize the original security flaws by using WEP and a sophisticated key management system. This EAP-version is safer than EAP-MD5. This also uses MAC address authentication. LEAP is not secure; THC-LeapCracker can be used to break Cisco's version of LEAP and be used against computers connected to an access point in the form of a dictionary attack. Anwrap and asleap finally are other crackers capable of breaking LEAP.[27]

PEAP

This stands for Protected Extensible Authentication Protocol. This protocol allows for a secure transport of data, passwords, and encryption keys without the need of a certificate server. This was developed by Cisco, Microsoft, and RSA Security.

Other EAPs There are other types of Extensible Authentication Protocol implementations that are based on the EAP framework. The framework that was established supports existing EAP types as well as future authentication methods.[32] EAP-TLS offers very good protection because of its mutual authentication. Both the client and the network are authenticated using certificates and per-session WEP keys.[33] EAP-FAST also offers good protection. EAP-TTLS is another alternative made by Certicom and Funk Software. It is more convenient as one does not need to distribute certificates to users, yet offers slightly less protection than EAP-TLS.[34]

Restricted access networks

Solutions include a newer system for authentication, IEEE 802.1X, that promises to enhance security on both wired and wireless networks. Wireless access points that incorporate technologies like these often also have routers built in, thus becoming wireless gateways.

End-to-end encryption

One can argue that both layer 2 and layer 3 encryption methods are not good enough for protecting valuable data like passwords and personal emails. Those technologies add encryption only to parts of the communication path, still allowing people to spy on the traffic if they have gained access to the wired network somehow. The solution may be encryption and authorization in the application layer, using technologies like SSL, SSH, GnuPG, PGP and similar.

The disadvantage with the end-to-end method is, it may fail to cover all traffic. With encryption on the router level or VPN, a single switch encrypts all traffic, even UDP and DNS lookups. With end-to-end encryption on the other hand, each service to be secured must have its encryption "turned on", and often every connection must also be "turned on" separately. For sending emails, every recipient must support the encryption method, and must exchange keys correctly. For Web, not all web sites offer https, and even if they do, the browser sends out IP addresses in clear text.

The most prized resource is often access to the Internet. An office LAN owner seeking to restrict such access will face the nontrivial enforcement task of having each user authenticate themselves for the router.

802.11i security

The newest and most rigorous security to implement into WLAN's today is the 802.11i RSN-standard. This full-fledged 802.11i standard (which uses WPAv2) however does require the newest hardware (unlike WPAv1), thus potentially requiring the purchase of new equipment. This new hardware required may be either AES-WRAP (an early version of 802.11i) or the newer and better AES-CCMP-equipment. One should make sure one needs WRAP or CCMP-equipment, as the 2 hardware standards are not compatible.

WPAv2

WPA2 is a WiFi Alliance branded version of the final 802.11i standard.[35] The primary enhancement over WPA is the inclusion of the AES-CCMP algorithm as a mandatory feature. Both WPA and WPA2 support EAP authentication methods using RADIUS servers and preshared key (PSK).

The number of WPA and WPA2 networks are increasing, while the number of WEP networks are decreasing,[36] because of the security vulnerabilities in WEP.

WPA2 has been found to have at least one security vulnerability, nicknamed Hole196. The vulnerability uses the WPA2 Group Temporal Key (GTK), which is a shared key among all users of the same BSSID, to launch attacks on other users of the same BSSID. It is named after page 196 of the IEEE 802.11i specification, where the vulnerability is discussed. In order for this exploit to be performed, the GTK must be known by the attacker.[37]

Additions to WPAv2

Unlike 802.1X, 802.11i already has most other additional security-services such as TKIP. Just as with WPAv1, WPAv2 may work in cooperation with EAP and a WIDS.

WAPI

This stands for WLAN Authentication and Privacy Infrastructure. This is a wireless security standard defined by the Chinese government.

Smart cards, USB tokens, and software tokens

Security token use is a method of authentication relying upon only authorized users possessing the requisite token. Smart cards are physical tokens in the cards that utilize an embedded integrated circuit chip for authentication, requiring a card reader.[38] USB Tokens are physical tokens that connect via USB port to authenticate the user.[39]

RF shielding

It's practical in some cases to apply specialized wall paint and window film to a room or building to significantly attenuate wireless signals, which keeps the signals from propagating outside a facility. This can significantly improve wireless security because it's difficult for hackers to receive the signals beyond the controlled area of a facility, such as from a parking lot.[40]

Denial of service defense

Most DoS attacks are easy to detect. However, a lot of them are difficult to stop even after detection. Here are three of the most common ways to stop a DoS attack.

Black holing

Black holing is one possible way of stopping a DoS attack. This is a situation where we drop all IP packets from an attacker. This is not a very good long-term strategy because attackers can change their source address very quickly.

This may have negative effects if done automatically. An attacker could knowingly spoof attack packets with the IP address of a corporate partner. Automated defenses could block legitimate traffic from that partner and cause additional problems.

Validating the handshake

Validating the handshake involves creating false opens, and not setting aside resources until the sender acknowledges. Some firewalls address SYN floods by pre-validating the TCP handshake. This is done by creating false opens. Whenever a SYN segment arrives, the firewall sends back a SYN/ACK segment, without passing the SYN segment on to the target server.

Only when the firewall gets back an ACK, which would happen only in a legitimate connection, would the firewall send the original SYN segment on to the server for which it was originally intended. The firewall doesn't set aside resources for a connection when a SYN segment arrives, so handling a large number of false SYN segments is only a small burden.

Rate limiting

Rate limiting can be used to reduce a certain type of traffic down to an amount the can be reasonably dealt with. Broadcasting to the internal network could still be used, but only at a limited rate for example. This is for more subtle DoS attacks. This is good if an attack is aimed at a single server because it keeps transmission lines at least partially open for other communication.

Rate limiting frustrates both the attacker, and the legitimate users. This helps but does not fully solve the problem. Once DoS traffic clogs the access line going to the internet, there is nothing a border firewall can do to help the situation. Most DoS attacks are problems of the community which can only be stopped with the help of ISP's and organizations whose computers are taken over as bots and used to attack other firms.

Mobile devices

With increasing number of mobile devices with 802.1X interfaces, security of such mobile devices becomes a concern. While open standards such as Kismet are targeted towards securing laptops,[41] access points solutions should extend towards covering mobile devices also. Host based solutions for mobile handsets and PDA's with 802.1X interface.

Security within mobile devices fall under three categories:

1. Protecting against ad hoc networks
2. Connecting to rogue access points
3. Mutual authentication schemes such as WPA2 as described above

Wireless IPS solutions now offer wireless security for mobile devices.

Mobile patient monitoring devices are becoming an integral part of healthcare industry and these devices will eventually become the method of choice for accessing and implementing health checks for patients located in remote areas. For these types of patient monitoring systems, security and reliability are critical, because they can influence the condition of patients, and could leave medical professionals in the dark about the condition of the patient if compromised.[42]

Implementing network encryption

In order to implement 802.11i, one must first make sure both that the router/access point(s), as well as all client devices are indeed equipped to support the network encryption. If this is done, a server such as RADIUS, ADS, NDS, or LDAP needs to be integrated. This server can be a computer on the local network, an access point / router with integrated authentication server, or a remote server. AP's/routers with integrated authentication servers are often very expensive and specifically an option for commercial usage like hot spots. Hosted 802.1X servers via the Internet require a monthly fee; running a private server is free yet has the disadvantage that one must set it up and that the server needs to be on continuously.[43]

To set up a server, server and client software must be installed. Server software required is an enterprise authentication server such as RADIUS, ADS, NDS, or LDAP. The required software can be picked from various suppliers as Microsoft, Cisco, Funk Software, Meetinghouse Data, and from some open-source projects. Software includes:

- Aradial RADIUS Server
- Cisco Secure Access Control Software
- freeRADIUS (open-source)
- Funk Software Steel Belted RADIUS (Odyssey)
- Microsoft Internet Authentication Service
- Meetinghouse Data EAGIS
- SkyFriendz (free cloud solution based on freeRADIUS)

Client software comes built-in with Windows XP and may be integrated into other OS's using any of following software:

- AEGIS-client
- Cisco ACU-client
- Intel PROSet/Wireless Software
- Odyssey client
- Xsupplicant (open1X)-project

RADIUS

Remote Authentication Dial In User Service (RADIUS) is an AAA (authentication, authorization and accounting) protocol used for remote network access. RADIUS, developed in 1991, was originally proprietary but then published in 1997 under ISOC documents RFC 2138 and RFC 2139.[44][45] The idea is to have an inside server act as a gatekeeper by verifying identities through a username and password that is already pre-determined by the user. A RADIUS server can also be configured to enforce user policies and restrictions as well as record accounting information such as connection time for purposes such as billing.

Open access points

Today, there is almost full wireless network coverage in many urban areas – the infrastructure for the wireless community network (which some consider to be the future of the internet[who?]) is already in place. One could roam around and always be connected to Internet if the nodes were open to the public, but due to security concerns, most nodes are encrypted and the users don't know how to disable encryption. Many people[who?] consider it proper etiquette to leave access points open to the public, allowing free access to Internet. Others[who?] think the default encryption provides substantial protection at small inconvenience, against dangers of open access that they fear may be substantial even on a home DSL router.

The density of access points can even be a problem – there are a limited number of channels available, and they partly overlap. Each channel can handle multiple networks, but places with many private wireless networks (for example, apartment complexes), the limited number of Wi-Fi radio channels might cause slowness and other problems.

According to the advocates of Open Access Points, it shouldn't involve any significant risks to open up wireless networks for the public:

- The wireless network is after all confined to a small geographical area. A computer connected to the Internet and having improper configurations or other security problems can be exploited by anyone from anywhere in the world, while only clients in a small geographical range can exploit an open wireless access point. Thus the exposure is low with an open wireless access point, and the risks with having an open wireless network are small. However, one should be aware that an open wireless router will give access to the local network, often including access to file shares and printers.
- The only way to keep communication truly secure is to use end-to-end encryption. For example, when accessing an internet bank, one would almost always use strong encryption from the web browser and all the way to the bank – thus it shouldn't be risky to do banking over an unencrypted wireless network. The argument is that anyone can sniff the traffic applies to wired networks too, where system administrators and possible hackers have access to the links and can read the traffic. Also, anyone knowing the keys for an encrypted wireless network can gain access to the data being transferred over the network.
- If services like file shares, access to printers etc. are available on the local net, it is advisable to have authentication (i.e. by password) for accessing it (one should never assume that the private network is not accessible from the outside). Correctly set up, it should be safe to allow access to the local network to outsiders.
- With the most popular encryption algorithms today, a sniffer will usually be able to compute the network key in a few minutes.
- It is very common to pay a fixed monthly fee for the Internet connection, and not for the traffic – thus extra traffic will not be detrimental.
- Where Internet connections are plentiful and cheap, freeloaders will seldom be a prominent nuisance.

On the other hand, in some countries including Germany,[46] persons providing an open access point may be made (partially) liable for any illegal activity conducted via this access point. Also, many contracts with ISPs specify that the connection may not be shared with other persons.

Social Engineering

In the context of information security, **social engineering** is the psychological manipulation of people into performing actions or divulging confidential information. A type of confidence trick for the purpose of information gathering, fraud, or system access, it differs from a traditional "con" in that it is often one of many steps in a more complex fraud scheme.[1] It has also been defined as "any act that influences a person to take an action that may or may not be in their best interests."[2]

Techniques and terms

All social engineering techniques are based on attributes of human decision-making known as cognitive biases.[3][4]

One example of social engineering is an individual who walks into a building and posts an official-looking announcement to the company bulletin that says the number for the help desk has changed. So, when employees call for help the individual asks them for their passwords and IDs thereby gaining the ability to access the company's private information. Another example of social engineering would be that the hacker contacts the target on a social networking site and starts a conversation with the target. Gradually the hacker gains the trust of the target and then uses that trust to get access to sensitive information like password or bank account details.[5]

Other concepts

Pretexting

Pretexting (adj. **pretextual**) is the act of creating and using an invented scenario (the pretext) to engage a targeted victim in a manner that increases the chance the victim will divulge information or perform actions that would be unlikely in ordinary circumstances.[6] An elaborate lie, it most often involves some prior research or setup and the use of this information for impersonation (*e.g.*, date of birth, Social Security number, last bill amount) to establish legitimacy in the mind of the target.[7]

Water holing

Water holing is a targeted social engineering strategy that capitalizes on the trust users have in websites they regularly visit. The victim feels safe to do things they would not do in a different situation. A wary person might, for example, purposefully avoid clicking a link in an unsolicited email, but the same person would not hesitate to follow a link on a website they often visit. So, the attacker prepares a trap for the unwary prey at a favored watering hole. This strategy has been successfully used to gain access to some (supposedly) very secure systems.[8]

Baiting

Baiting is like the real-world Trojan horse that uses physical media and relies on the curiosity or greed of the victim.[9] In this attack, attackers leave malware-infected floppy disks, CD-ROMs, or USB flash drives in locations people will find them (bathrooms, elevators, sidewalks, parking lots, etc.), give them legitimate and curiosity-piquing labels, and wait for victims.

Unless computer controls block infections, insertion compromises PCs "auto-running" media. Hostile devices can also be used.[10] For instance, a "lucky winner" is sent a free digital audio player compromising any computer it is plugged to. A "**road apple**" (the colloquial term for horse manure, suggesting the device's undesirable nature) is any removable media with malicious software left in opportunistic or conspicuous places. It may be a CD, DVD, or USB flash drive, among other media. Curious people take it and plug it into a computer, infecting the host and any attached networks. Again, hackers may give them enticing labels, such as "Employee Salaries" or "Confidential".[11]

One study done in 2016 had researchers drop 297 USB drives around the campus of the University of Illinois. The drives contained files on them that linked to webpages owned by the researchers. The researchers were able to see how many of the drives had files on them opened, but not how many were inserted into a computer without having a file opened. Of the 297 drives that were dropped, 290 (98%) of them were picked up and 135 (45%) of them "called home".[12]

Examples of social engineers

Susan Headley

Susan Headley became involved in phreaking with Kevin Mitnick and Lewis de Payne in Los Angeles, but later framed them for erasing the system files at US Leasing after a falling out, leading to Mitnick's first conviction. She retired to professional poker.[13]

Mike Ridpath

Mike Ridpath Security consultant, published author, and speaker. Previous member of w00w00. Emphasizes techniques and tactics for social engineering cold calling. Became notable after his talks where he would play recorded calls and explain his thought process on what he was doing to get passwords through the phone and his live demonstrations.[14][15][16][17][18] As a child Ridpath was connected with Badir Brothers and was widely known within the phreaking and hacking community for his articles with popular underground ezines, such as, Phrack, B4B0 and 9x on modifying Oki 900s, blueboxing, satellite hacking and RCMAC.[19][20]

Badir Brothers

Brothers Ramy, Muzher, and Shadde Badir—all of whom were blind from birth—managed to set up an extensive phone and computer fraud scheme in Israel in the 1990s using social engineering, voice impersonation, and Braille-display computers.[21][22]

Christopher J. Hadnagy

Christopher J. Hadnagy is an American social engineer and information technology security consultant. He is best known as an author of 4 books on social engineering and cyber security[23][24][25][26] and founder of Innocent Lives Foundation, an organization that helps tracking and identifying child trafficking by seeking the assistance of information security specialists, using data from open-source intelligence (OSINT) and collaborating with law enforcement.[27][28]

Law

In common law, pretexting is an invasion of privacy tort of appropriation.[29]

Pretexting of telephone records

In December 2006, United States Congress approved a Senate sponsored bill making the pretexting of telephone records a federal felony with fines of up to $250,000 and ten years in prison for individuals (or fines of up to $500,000 for companies). It was signed by President George W. Bush on 12 January 2007.[30]

Federal legislation

The 1999 Gramm-Leach-Bliley Act (GLBA) is a U.S. Federal law that specifically addresses pretexting of banking records as an illegal act punishable under federal statutes. When a business entity such as a private investigator, SIU insurance investigator, or an adjuster conducts any type of deception, it falls under the authority of the Federal Trade Commission (FTC). This federal agency has the obligation and authority to ensure that consumers are not subjected to any unfair or deceptive business practices. US Federal Trade Commission Act, Section 5 of the FTCA states, in part: "Whenever the Commission shall have reason to believe that any such person, partnership, or corporation has been or is using any unfair method of competition or unfair or deceptive act or practice in or affecting commerce, and if it shall appear to the Commission that a proceeding by it in respect thereof would be to the interest of the public, it shall issue and serve upon such person, partnership, or corporation a complaint stating its charges in that respect."

The statute states that when someone obtains any personal, non-public information from a financial institution or the consumer, their action is subject to the statute. It relates to the consumer's relationship with the financial institution. For example, a pretexter using false pretenses either to get a consumer's address from the consumer's bank, or to get a consumer to disclose the name of their bank, would be covered. The determining principle is that pretexting only occurs when information is obtained through false pretenses.

While the sale of cell telephone records has gained significant media attention, and telecommunications records are the focus of the two bills currently before the United States Senate, many other types of private records are being bought and sold in the public market. Alongside many advertisements for cell phone records, wireline records and the records associated with calling cards are advertised. As individuals shift to VoIP telephones, it is safe to assume that those records will be offered for sale as well. Currently, it is legal to sell telephone records, but illegal to obtain them.[31]

1st Source Information Specialists

U.S. Rep. Fred Upton (R-Kalamazoo, Michigan), chairman of the Energy and Commerce Subcommittee on Telecommunications and the Internet, expressed concern over the easy access to personal mobile phone records on the Internet during a House Energy & Commerce Committee hearing on "**Phone Records For Sale:** *Why Aren't Phone Records Safe From Pretexting?*" Illinois became the first state to sue an online records broker when Attorney General Lisa Madigan sued 1st Source Information Specialists, Inc. A spokeswoman for Madigan's office said. The Florida-based company operates several Web sites that sell mobile telephone records, according to a copy of the suit. The attorneys general of Florida and Missouri quickly followed Madigan's lead, filing suits respectively, against 1st Source Information Specialists and, in Missouri's case, one other records broker – First Data Solutions, Inc.

Several wireless providers, including T-Mobile, Verizon, and Cingular filed earlier lawsuits against records brokers, with Cingular winning an injunction against First Data Solutions and 1st Source Information Specialists. U.S. Senator Charles Schumer (D-New York) introduced legislation in February 2006 aimed at curbing the practice. The Consumer Telephone Records Protection Act of 2006 would create felony criminal penalties for stealing and selling the records of mobile phone, landline, and Voice over Internet Protocol (VoIP) subscribers.

Hewlett Packard

Patricia Dunn, former chairwoman of Hewlett Packard, reported that the HP board hired a private investigation company to delve into who was responsible for leaks within the board. Dunn acknowledged that the company used the practice of pretexting to solicit the telephone records of board members and journalists. Chairman Dunn later apologized for this act and offered to step down from the board if it was desired by board members.[32] Unlike Federal law, California law specifically forbids such pretexting. The four felony charges brought on Dunn were dismissed.[33]

Malware

Malware (a portmanteau for ***malicious software***)[1] is any software intentionally designed to cause disruption to a computer, server, client, or computer network, leak private information, gain unauthorized access to information or systems, deprive access to information, or which unknowingly interferes with the user's computer security and privacy.[1][2][3][4][5] Researchers tend to classify malware into one or more sub-types (i.e. computer viruses, worms, Trojan horses, ransomware, spyware, adware, rogue software, wiper and keyloggers).[1]

Malware poses serious problems to individuals and businesses on the Internet.[6][7] According to Symantec's 2018 Internet Security Threat Report (ISTR), malware variants number has increased to 669,947,865 in 2017, which is twice as many malware variants as in 2016.[8] Cybercrime, which includes malware attacks as well as other crimes committed by computer, was predicted to cost the world economy $6 trillion USD in 2021, and is increasing at a rate of 15% per year.[9] Since 2021, malware has been designed to target computer systems that run critical infrastructure such as the electricity distribution network.[10]

The defense strategies against malware differ according to the type of malware but most can be thwarted by installing antivirus software, firewalls, applying regular patches, securing networks from intrusion, having regular backups and isolating infected systems. Malware can be designed to evade antivirus software detection algorithms.[8]

History

The notion of a self-reproducing computer program can be traced back to initial theories about the operation of complex automata.[11] John von Neumann showed that in theory a program could reproduce itself. This constituted a plausibility result in computability theory. Fred Cohen experimented with computer viruses and confirmed Neumann's postulate and investigated other properties of malware such as detectability and self-obfuscation using rudimentary encryption. His 1987 doctoral dissertation was on the subject of computer viruses.[12] The combination of cryptographic technology as part of the payload of the virus, exploiting it for attack purposes was initialized and investigated from the mid 1990s, and includes initial ransomware and evasion ideas.[13]

Before Internet access became widespread, viruses spread on personal computers by infecting executable programs or boot sectors of floppy disks. By inserting a copy of itself into the machine code instructions in these programs or boot sectors, a virus causes itself to be run whenever the program is run or the disk is booted. Early computer viruses were written for the Apple II and Macintosh, but they became more widespread with the dominance of the IBM PC and MS-DOS system. The first IBM PC virus in the "wild" was a boot sector virus dubbed (c)Brain,[14] created in 1986 by the Farooq Alvi brothers in Pakistan.[15] Malware distributors would trick the user into booting or running from an infected device or medium. For example, a virus could make an infected computer add autorunnable code to any USB stick plugged into it. Anyone who then attached the stick to another computer set to autorun from USB would in turn become infected, and also pass on the infection in the same way.[16]

Older email software would automatically open HTML email containing potentially malicious JavaScript code. Users may also execute disguised malicious email attachments. The *2018 Data Breach Investigations Report* by Verizon, cited by CSO Online, states that emails are the primary method of malware delivery, accounting for 96% of malware delivery around the world.[17][18]

The first worms, network-borne infectious programs, originated not on personal computers, but on multitasking Unix systems. The first well-known worm was the Internet Worm of 1988, which infected SunOS and VAX BSD systems. Unlike a virus, this worm did not insert itself into other programs. Instead, it exploited security holes (vulnerabilities) in network server programs and started itself running as a separate process.[19] This same behavior is used by today's worms as well.[20]

With the rise of the Microsoft Windows platform in the 1990s, and the flexible macros of its applications, it became possible to write infectious code in the macro language of Microsoft Word and similar programs. These *macro viruses* infect documents and templates rather than applications (executables), but rely on the fact that macros in a Word document are a form of executable code.[21]

Many early infectious programs, including the Morris Worm, the first internet worm, were written as experiments or pranks.[22] Today, malware is used by both black hat hackers and governments to steal personal, financial, or business information.[23][24] Today, any device that plugs into a USB port – even lights, fans, speakers, toys, or peripherals such as a digital microscope – can be used to spread malware. Devices can be infected during manufacturing or supply if quality control is inadequate.[16]

Purposes

Since the rise of widespread broadband Internet access, malicious software has more frequently been designed for profit. Since 2003, the majority of widespread viruses and worms have been designed to take control of users' computers for illicit purposes.[25] Infected "zombie computers" can be used to send email spam, to host contraband data such as child pornography,[26] or to engage in distributed denial-of-service attacks as a form of extortion.[27] Malware is used broadly against government or corporate websites to gather sensitive information,[28] or to disrupt their operation in general. Further, malware can be used against individuals to gain information such as personal identification numbers or details, bank or credit card numbers, and passwords.[29][30]

In addition to criminal money-making, malware can be used for sabotage, often for political motives. Stuxnet, for example, was designed to disrupt very specific industrial equipment. There have been politically motivated attacks which spread over and shut down large computer networks, including massive deletion of files and corruption of master boot records, described as "computer killing." Such attacks were made on Sony Pictures Entertainment (25 November 2014, using malware known as Shamoon or W32.Disttrack) and Saudi Aramco (August 2012).[31][32]

Types

There are many possible ways of categorizing malware and some malicious software may overlap into two or more categories.[1] Broadly, software can categorised into three types:[33] (i) goodware; (ii) greyware and (iii) malware.

Classification of potentially malicious software
Data sourced from: Molina-Coronado et. al. (2023)[33]

Type	Characteristics	Examples	Notes
Goodware	Obtained from trustworthy sources	• Google Play apps • Buggy software	•
Greyware	Insufficient consensus and/or metrics	• Potentially unwanted programs • Spyware • Adware	•
Malware	Broad consensus among antivirus software that program is malicious or obtained from flagged sources.	• Viruses • Worms • Root kits • Backdoors • Ransomware • Trojan horses	•

Malware

Virus

A computer virus is software usually hidden within another seemingly innocuous program that can produce copies of itself and insert them into other programs or files, and that usually performs a harmful action (such as destroying data).[34] They have been likened to biological viruses.[3] An example of this is a portable execution infection, a technique, usually used to spread malware, that inserts extra data or executable code into PE files.[35] A computer virus is software that embeds itself in some other executable software (including the operating system itself) on the target system without the user's knowledge and consent and when it is run, the virus is spread to other executable files.

Worm

A worm is a stand-alone malware software that *actively* transmits itself over a network to infect other computers and can copy itself without infecting files. These definitions lead to the observation that a virus requires the user to run an infected software or operating system for the virus to spread, whereas a worm spreads itself.[36]

Rootkits

Once malicious software is installed on a system, it is essential that it stays concealed, to avoid detection. Software packages known as *rootkits* allow this concealment, by modifying the host's operating system so that the malware is hidden from the user. Rootkits can prevent a harmful process from being visible in the system's list of processes, or keep its files from being read.[37]

Some types of harmful software contain routines to evade identification and/or removal attempts, not merely to hide themselves. An early example of this behavior is recorded in the Jargon File tale of a pair of programs infesting a Xerox CP-V time sharing system:

Each ghost-job would detect the fact that the other had been killed, and would start a new copy of the recently stopped program within a few milliseconds. The only way to kill both ghosts was to kill them simultaneously (very difficult) or to deliberately crash the system.[38]

Backdoors

A backdoor is a broad term for a computer program that allows an attacker persistent unauthorised remote access to a victim's machine often without their knowledge.[39] The attacker typically uses another attack (such as a trojan, worm or virus) to bypass authentication mechanisms usually over an unsecured network such as the Internet to install the backdoor application. A backdoor can also be a side effect of a software bug in legitimate software that is exploited by an attacker to gain access to a victim's computer or network.

The idea has often been suggested that computer manufacturers preinstall backdoors on their systems to provide technical support for customers, but this has never been reliably verified. It was reported in 2014 that US government agencies had been diverting computers purchased by those considered "targets" to secret workshops where software or hardware permitting remote access by the agency was installed, considered to be among the most productive operations to obtain access to networks around the world.[40] Backdoors may be installed by Trojan horses, worms, implants, or other methods.[41][42]

Trojan horse

A Trojan horse misrepresents itself to masquerade as a regular, benign program or utility in order to persuade a victim to install it. A Trojan horse usually carries a hidden destructive function that is activated when the application is started. The term is derived from the Ancient Greek story of the Trojan horse used to invade the city of Troy by stealth.[43][44]

Trojan horses are generally spread by some form of social engineering, for example, where a user is duped into executing an email attachment disguised to be unsuspicious, (e.g., a routine form to be filled in), or by drive-by download. Although their payload can be anything, many modern forms act as a backdoor, contacting a controller (phoning home) which can then have unauthorized access to the affected computer, potentially installing additional software such as a keylogger to steal confidential information, cryptomining software or adware to generate revenue to the operator of the trojan.[45] While Trojan horses and backdoors are not easily detectable by themselves, computers may appear to run slower, emit more heat or fan noise due to heavy processor or network usage, as may occur when cryptomining software is installed. Cryptominers may limit resource usage and/or only run during idle times in an attempt to evade detection.

Unlike computer viruses and worms, Trojan horses generally do not attempt to inject themselves into other files or otherwise propagate themselves.[46]

In spring 2017 Mac users were hit by the new version of Proton Remote Access Trojan (RAT)[47] trained to extract password data from various sources, such as browser auto-fill data, the Mac-OS keychain, and password vaults.[48]

Droppers

Droppers are a sub-type of Trojans that solely aim to deliver malware upon the system that they infect with the desire to subvert detection through stealth and a light payload.[49] It is important not to confuse a dropper with a loader or stager. A loader or stager will merely load an extension of the malware (for example a collection of malicious functions through reflective dynamic link library injection) into memory. The purpose is to keep the initial stage light and undetectable. A dropper merely downloads further malware to the system.

Ransomware

Ransomware prevents a user from accessing their files until a ransom is paid. There are two variations of ransomware, being crypto ransomware and locker ransomware.[50] Locker ransomware just locks down a computer system without encrypting its contents, whereas crypto ransomware locks down a system and encrypts its contents. For example, programs such as CryptoLocker encrypt files securely, and only decrypt them on payment of a substantial sum of money.[51]

Some malware is used to generate money by click fraud, making it appear that the computer user has clicked an advertising link on a site, generating a payment from the advertiser. It was estimated in 2012 that about 60 to 70% of all active malware used some kind of click fraud, and 22% of all ad-clicks were fraudulent.[52]

Lock-screens, or screen lockers is a type of "cyber police" ransomware that blocks screens on Windows or Android devices with a false accusation in harvesting illegal content, trying to scare the victims into paying up a fee.[53] Jisut and SLocker impact Android devices more than other lock-screens, with Jisut making up nearly 60 percent of all Android ransomware detections.[54]

Encryption-based ransomware, like the name suggests, is a type of ransomware that encrypts all files on an infected machine. These types of malware then display a pop-up informing the user that their files have been encrypted and that they must pay (usually in Bitcoin) to recover them. Some examples of encryption-based ransomware are CryptoLocker and WannaCry.[55]

Grayware

Grayware is any unwanted application or file that can worsen the performance of computers and may cause security risks but which there is insufficient consensus or data to classify them as malware.[33] Types of greyware typically includes spyware, adware, fraudulent dialers, joke programs ("jokeware") and remote access tools.[39] For example, at one point, Sony BMG compact discs silently installed a rootkit on purchasers' computers with the intention of preventing illicit copying.[56]

Potentially Unwanted Program (PUP)

Potentially unwanted programs (PUPs) are applications that would be considered unwanted despite often being intentionally downloaded by the user.[57] PUPs include spyware, adware, and fraudulent dialers.

Many security products classify unauthorised key generators as PUPs, although they frequently carry true malware in addition to their ostensible purpose.[58] In fact, Kammerstetter et. al.

(2012)[58] estimated that as much as 55% of key generators could contain malware and that about 36% malicious key generators were not detected by antivirus software.

Adware

Some types of adware (using stolen certificates) turn off anti-malware and virus protection; technical remedies are available.[59]

Spyware

Programs designed to monitor users' web browsing, display unsolicited advertisements, or redirect affiliate marketing revenues are called spyware. Spyware programs do not spread like viruses; instead they are generally installed by exploiting security holes. They can also be hidden and packaged together with unrelated user-installed software.[60] The Sony BMG rootkit was intended to prevent illicit copying; but also reported on users' listening habits, and unintentionally created extra security vulnerabilities.[56]

Detection

Antivirus software typically uses two techniques to detect malware: (i) static analysis and (ii) dynamic/heuristic analysis.[61] Static analysis involves studying the software code of a potentially malicious program and producing a signature of that program. This information is then used to compare scanned files by an antivirus program. Because this approach is not useful for malware that has not yet been studied, antivirus software can use dynamic analysis to monitor how the program runs on a computer and block it if it performs unexpected activity.

The aim of any malware is to conceal itself from detection by users or antivirus software.[1] Detecting potential malware is difficult for two reasons. The first is that it is difficult to determine if software is malicious.[33] The second is that malware uses technical measures to make it more difficult to detect it.[61] An estimated 33% of malware is not detected by antivirus software.[58]

The most commonly employed anti-detection technique involves encrypting the malware payload in order to prevent antivirus software from recognizing the signature.[33] Tools such as crypters come with an encrypted blob of malicious code and a decryption stub. The stub decrypts the blob and loads it into memory. Because anntivirus does not typically scan memory and only scans files on the drive, this allows the malware to evade detection. Advanced malware has the ability to transform itself into different variations, making it less likely to be detected due to the differences in its signatures. This is known as polymorphic malware. Other common techniques used to evade detection include, from common to uncommon:[62] (1) evasion of analysis and detection by fingerprinting the environment when executed;[63] (2) confusing automated tools' detection methods. This allows malware to avoid detection by technologies such as signature-based antivirus software by changing the server used by the malware;[62] (3) timing-based evasion. This is when malware runs at certain times or following certain actions taken by the user, so it executes during certain vulnerable periods, such as during the boot process, while remaining dormant the rest of the time; (4) obfuscating internal data so that automated tools do not detect the malware;[64] (v) information hiding techniques, namely stegomalware;[65] and (5) fileless malware which runs within memory instead of using files and utilizes existing system tools to carry out malicious acts. The use of existing binaries to carry out malicious activities is a technique known as LotL, or Living off the Land.[66] This reduces the amount of forensic artifacts available to analyze. Recently these types of attacks have become more frequent with a 432%

increase in 2017 and makeup 35% of the attacks in 2018. Such attacks are not easy to perform but are becoming more prevalent with the help of exploit-kits.[67][68]

Risks

Vulnerable software

A vulnerability is a weakness, flaw or software bug in an application, a complete computer, an operating system, or a computer network that is exploited by malware to bypass defenses or gain privileges it requires to run. For example, TestDisk 6.4 or earlier contained a vulnerability that allowed attackers to inject code into Windows.[69] Malware can exploit security defects (security bugs or vulnerabilities) in the operating system, applications (such as browsers, e.g. older versions of Microsoft Internet Explorer supported by Windows XP[70]), or in vulnerable versions of browser plugins such as Adobe Flash Player, Adobe Acrobat or Reader, or Java SE.[71][72] For example, a common method is exploitation of a buffer overrun vulnerability, where software designed to store data in a specified region of memory does not prevent more data than the buffer can accommodate being supplied. Malware may provide data that overflows the buffer, with malicious executable code or data after the end; when this payload is accessed it does what the attacker, not the legitimate software, determines.

Malware can exploit recently discovered vulnerabilities before developers have had time to release a suitable patch.[6] Even when new patches addressing the vulnerability have been released, they may not necessarily be installed immediately, allowing malware to take advantage of systems lacking patches. Sometimes even applying patches or installing new versions does not automatically uninstall the old versions. Security advisories from plug-in providers announce security-related updates.[73] Common vulnerabilities are assigned CVE IDs and listed in the US National Vulnerability Database. Secunia PSI[74] is an example of software, free for personal use, that will check a PC for vulnerable out-of-date software, and attempt to update it. Other approaches involve using firewalls and intrusion prevention systems to monitor unusual traffic patterns on the local computer network.[75]

Excessive privileges

Users and programs can be assigned more privileges than they require, and malware can take advantage of this. For example, of 940 Android apps sampled, one third of them asked for more privileges than they required.[76] Apps targeting the Android platform can be a major source of malware infection but one solution is to use third party software to detect apps that have been assigned excessive privileges.[77]

Some systems allow all users to modify their internal structures, and such users today would be considered over-privileged users. This was the standard operating procedure for early microcomputer and home computer systems, where there was no distinction between an *administrator* or *root*, and a regular user of the system. In some systems, non-administrator users are over-privileged by design, in the sense that they are allowed to modify internal structures of the system. In some environments, users are over-privileged because they have been inappropriately granted administrator or equivalent status.[78] This can be because users tend to demand more privileges than they need, so often end up being assigned unnecessary privileges.[79]

Some systems allow code executed by a user to access all rights of that user, which is known as over-privileged code. This was also standard operating procedure for early microcomputer and home computer systems. Malware, running as over-privileged code, can use this privilege to subvert the system. Almost all currently popular operating systems, and also many scripting applications allow code too many privileges, usually in the sense that when a user executes code, the system allows that code all rights of that user.

Weak passwords

A credential attack occurs when a user account with administrative privileges is cracked and that account is used to provide malware with appropriate privileges.[80] Typically, the attack succeeds because the weakest form of account security is used, which is typically a short password that can be cracked using a dictionary or brute force attack. Using strong passwords and enabling two-factor authentication can reduce this risk. With the latter enabled, even if an attacker can crack the password, they cannot use the account without also having the token possessed by the legitimate user of that account.

Use of the same operating system

Homogeneity can be a vulnerability. For example, when all computers in a network run the same operating system, upon exploiting one, one worm can exploit them all:[81] In particular, Microsoft Windows or Mac OS X have such a large share of the market that an exploited vulnerability concentrating on either operating system could subvert a large number of systems. It is estimated that approximately 83% of malware infections between January and March 2020 were spread via systems running Windows 10.[82] This risk is mitigated by segmenting the networks into different subnetworks and setting up firewalls to block traffic between them.[83][84]

Mitigation

Antivirus / Anti-malware software

Anti-malware (sometimes also called antivirus) programs block and remove some or all types of malware. For example, Microsoft Security Essentials (for Windows XP, Vista, and Windows 7) and Windows Defender (for Windows 8, 10 and 11) provides real-time protection. The Windows Malicious Software Removal Tool removes malicious software from the system.[85] Additionally, several capable antivirus software programs are available for free download from the Internet (usually restricted to non-commercial use).[86] Tests found some free programs to be competitive with commercial ones.[86][87][88]

Typically, antivirus software can combat malware in the following ways:

1. **Real-time protection:** They can provide real time protection against the installation of malware software on a computer. This type of malware protection works the same way as that of antivirus protection in that the anti-malware software scans all incoming network data for malware and blocks any threats it comes across.
2. **Removal:** Anti-malware software programs can be used solely for detection and removal of malware software that has already been installed onto a computer. This type of anti-malware software scans the contents of the Windows registry, operating system files, and installed programs on a computer and will provide a list of any threats found, allowing the user to choose which files to delete or keep, or to compare this list to a list of known malware components, removing files that match.[89]

3. **Sandboxing:** Provide sandboxing of apps considered dangerous (such as web browsers where most vulnerabilities are likely to be installed from).[90]

Real-time protection

A specific component of anti-malware software, commonly referred to as an on-access or real-time scanner, hooks deep into the operating system's core or kernel and functions in a manner similar to how certain malware itself would attempt to operate, though with the user's informed permission for protecting the system. Any time the operating system accesses a file, the on-access scanner checks if the file is infected or not. Typically, when an infected file is found, execution is stopped and the file is quarantined to prevent further damage with the intention to prevent irreversible system damage. Most AVs allow users to override this behaviour. This can have a considerable performance impact on the operating system, though the degree of impact is dependent on how many pages it creates in virtual memory.[91]

Sandboxing

Because many malware components are installed as a result of browser exploits or user error, using security software (some of which are anti-malware, though many are not) to "sandbox" browsers (essentially isolate the browser from the computer and hence any malware induced change) can also be effective in helping to restrict any damage done.[90]

Website security scans

Website vulnerability scans check the website, detect malware, may note outdated software, and may report known security issues, in order to reduce the risk of the site being compromised.

Network Segregation

Structuring a network as a set of smaller networks, and limiting the flow of traffic between them to that known to be legitimate, can hinder the ability of infectious malware to replicate itself across the wider network. Software Defined Networking provides techniques to implement such controls.

"Air gap" isolation or "parallel network"

As a last resort, computers can be protected from malware, and the risk of infected computers disseminating trusted information can be greatly reduced by imposing an "air gap" (i.e. completely disconnecting them from all other networks) and applying enhanced controls over the entry and exit of software and data from the outside world. However, malware can still cross the air gap in some situations, not least due to the need to introduce software into the air-gapped network and can damage the availability or integrity of assets thereon. Stuxnet is an example of malware that is introduced to the target environment via a USB drive, causing damage to processes supported on the environment without the need to exfiltrate data.

AirHopper,[92] BitWhisper,[93] GSMem [94] and Fansmitter[95] are four techniques introduced by researchers that can leak data from air-gapped computers using electromagnetic, thermal and acoustic emissions.

Security Testing

Security testing is a process intended to detect flaws in the security mechanisms of an information system and as such help enable it to protect data and maintain functionality as intended.[1] Due to the logical limitations of security testing, passing the security testing process is not an indication that no flaws exist or that the system adequately satisfies the security requirements.

Typical security requirements may include specific elements of confidentiality, integrity, authentication, availability, authorization and non-repudiation.[2] Actual security requirements tested depend on the security requirements implemented by the system. Security testing as a term has a number of different meanings and can be completed in a number of different ways. As such, a Security Taxonomy helps us to understand these different approaches and meanings by providing a base level to work from.

Confidentiality

- A security measure which protects against the disclosure of information to parties other than the intended recipient is by no means the only way of ensuring the security. [3]

Integrity

Integrity of information refers to protecting information from being modified by unauthorized parties

- A measure intended to allow the receiver to determine that the information provided by a system is correct.
- Integrity schemes often use some of the same underlying technologies as confidentiality schemes, but they usually involve adding information to a communication, to form the basis of an algorithmic check, rather than the encoding all of the communication.
- To check if the correct information is transferred from one application to other. [3]

Authentication

This might involve confirming the identity of a person, tracing the origins of an artifact, ensuring that a product is what its packaging and labelling claims to be, or assuring that a computer program is a trusted one. [3]

Authorization

- The process of determining that a requester is allowed to receive a service or perform an operation.
- Access control is an example of authorization.

Availability

- Assuring information and communications services will be ready for use when expected.
- Information must be kept available to authorized persons when they need it.

Non-repudiation

- In reference to digital security, non-repudiation means to ensure that a transferred message has been sent and received by the parties claiming to have sent and received the message. Non-repudiation is a way to guarantee that the sender of a message cannot later deny having sent the message and that the recipient cannot deny having received the message.
- A sender-id is usually a header transmitted along with message which recognises the message source.

Taxonomy

Common terms used for the delivery of security testing:

- **Discovery** - The purpose of this stage is to identify systems within scope and the services in use. It is not intended to discover vulnerabilities, but version detection may highlight deprecated versions of software / firmware and thus indicate potential vulnerabilities.
- **Vulnerability Scan** - Following the discovery stage this looks for known security issues by using automated tools to match conditions with known vulnerabilities. The reported risk level is set automatically by the tool with no manual verification or interpretation by the test vendor. This can be supplemented with credential based scanning that looks to remove some common false positives by using supplied credentials to authenticate with a service (such as local windows accounts).
- **Vulnerability Assessment** - This uses discovery and vulnerability scanning to identify security vulnerabilities and places the findings into the context of the environment under test. An example would be removing common false positives from the report and deciding risk levels that should be applied to each report finding to improve business understanding and context.
- **Security Assessment** - Builds upon Vulnerability Assessment by adding manual verification to confirm exposure, but does not include the exploitation of vulnerabilities to gain further access. Verification could be in the form of authorized access to a system to confirm system settings and involve examining logs, system responses, error messages, codes, etc. A Security Assessment is looking to gain a broad coverage of the systems under test but not the depth of exposure that a specific vulnerability could lead to.
- **Penetration Test** - Penetration test simulates an attack by a malicious party. Building on the previous stages and involves exploitation of found vulnerabilities to gain further access. Using this approach will result in an understanding of the ability of an attacker to gain access to confidential information, affect data integrity or availability of a service and the respective impact. Each test is approached using a consistent and complete methodology in a way that allows the tester to use their problem solving abilities, the output from a range of tools and their own knowledge of networking and systems to

find vulnerabilities that would/ could not be identified by automated tools. This approach looks at the depth of attack as compared to the Security Assessment approach that looks at the broader coverage.
- **Security Audit** - Driven by an Audit / Risk function to look at a specific control or compliance issue. Characterized by a narrow scope, this type of engagement could make use of any of the earlier approaches discussed (vulnerability assessment, security assessment, penetration test).
- **Security Review** - Verification that industry or internal security standards have been applied to system components or product. This is typically completed through gap analysis and utilizes build / code reviews or by reviewing design documents and architecture diagrams. This activity does not utilize any of the earlier approaches (Vulnerability Assessment, Security Assessment, Penetration Test, Security Audit)

Cryptography

Cryptography, or **cryptology** (from Ancient Greek: κρυπτός, romanized: *kryptós* "hidden, secret"; and γράφειν *graphein*, "to write", or -λογία *-logia*, "study", respectively[1]), is the practice and study of techniques for secure communication in the presence of adversarial behavior.[2] More generally, cryptography is about constructing and analyzing protocols that prevent third parties or the public from reading private messages.[3] Modern cryptography exists at the intersection of the disciplines of mathematics, computer science, information security, electrical engineering, digital signal processing, physics, and others.[4] Core concepts related to information security (data confidentiality, data integrity, authentication, and non-repudiation) are also central to cryptography.[5] Practical applications of cryptography include electronic commerce, chip-based payment cards, digital currencies, computer passwords, and military communications.

Cryptography prior to the modern age was effectively synonymous with encryption, converting readable information (plaintext) to unintelligible nonsense text (ciphertext), which can only be read by reversing the process (decryption). The sender of an encrypted (coded) message shares the decryption (decoding) technique only with the intended recipients to preclude access from adversaries. The cryptography literature often uses the names "Alice" (or "A") for the sender, "Bob" (or "B") for the intended recipient, and "Eve" (or "E") for the eavesdropping adversary.[6] Since the development of rotor cipher machines in World War I and the advent of computers in World War II, cryptography methods have become increasingly complex and their applications more varied.

Modern cryptography is heavily based on mathematical theory and computer science practice; cryptographic algorithms are designed around computational hardness assumptions, making such algorithms hard to break in actual practice by any adversary. While it is theoretically possible to break into a well-designed system, it is infeasible in actual practice to do so. Such schemes, if well designed, are therefore termed "computationally secure". Theoretical advances (e.g., improvements in integer factorization algorithms) and faster computing technology require these designs to be continually reevaluated and, if necessary, adapted. Information-theoretically secure schemes that provably cannot be broken even with unlimited computing power, such as the one-time pad, are much more difficult to use in practice than the best theoretically breakable but computationally secure schemes.

The growth of cryptographic technology has raised a number of legal issues in the Information Age. Cryptography's potential for use as a tool for espionage and sedition has led many governments to classify it as a weapon and to limit or even prohibit its use and export.[7] In some jurisdictions where the use of cryptography is legal, laws permit investigators to compel the disclosure of encryption keys for documents relevant to an investigation.[8][9] Cryptography also plays a major role in digital rights management and copyright infringement disputes with regard to digital media.[10]

Terminology

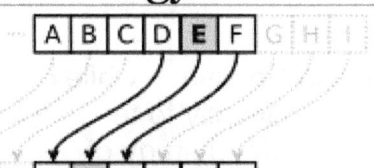

Alphabet shift ciphers are believed to have been used by Julius Caesar over 2,000 years ago.[6] This is an example with $k = 3$. In other words, the letters in the alphabet are shifted three in one direction to encrypt and three in the other direction to decrypt.

The first use of the term "cryptograph" (as opposed to "cryptogram") dates back to the 19th century—originating from "The Gold-Bug," a story by Edgar Allan Poe.[11][12]

Until modern times, cryptography referred almost exclusively to "encryption", which is the process of converting ordinary information (called plaintext) into an unintelligible form (called ciphertext).[13] Decryption is the reverse, in other words, moving from the unintelligible ciphertext back to plaintext. A cipher (or cypher) is a pair of algorithms that carry out the encryption and the reversing decryption. The detailed operation of a cipher is controlled both by the algorithm and, in each instance, by a "key". The key is a secret (ideally known only to the communicants), usually a string of characters (ideally short so it can be remembered by the user), which is needed to decrypt the ciphertext. In formal mathematical terms, a "cryptosystem" is the ordered list of elements of finite possible plaintexts, finite possible cyphertexts, finite possible keys, and the encryption and decryption algorithms that correspond to each key. Keys are important both formally and in actual practice, as ciphers without variable keys can be trivially broken with only the knowledge of the cipher used and are therefore useless (or even counter-productive) for most purposes. Historically, ciphers were often used directly for encryption or decryption without additional procedures such as authentication or integrity checks.

There are two main types of cryptosystems: symmetric and asymmetric. In symmetric systems, the only ones known until the 1970s, the same secret key encrypts and decrypts a message. Data manipulation in symmetric systems is significantly faster than in asymmetric systems. Asymmetric systems use a "public key" to encrypt a message and a related "private key" to decrypt it. The advantage of asymmetric systems is that the public key can be freely published, allowing parties to establish secure communication without having a shared secret key. In practice, asymmetric systems are used to first exchange a secret key, and then secure communication proceeds via a more efficient symmetric system using that key.[14] Examples of asymmetric systems include Diffie–Hellman key exchange, RSA (Rivest–Shamir–Adleman), ECC (Elliptic Curve Cryptography), and Post-quantum cryptography. Secure symmetric algorithms include the commonly used AES (Advanced Encryption Standard) which replaced the older DES

(Data Encryption Standard).[15] Insecure symmetric algorithms include children's language tangling schemes such as Pig Latin or other cant, and all historical cryptographic schemes, however seriously intended, prior to the invention of the one-time pad early in the 20th century.

In colloquial use, the term "code" is often used to mean any method of encryption or concealment of meaning. However, in cryptography, code has a more specific meaning: the replacement of a unit of plaintext (i.e., a meaningful word or phrase) with a code word (for example, "wallaby" replaces "attack at dawn"). A cypher, in contrast, is a scheme for changing or substituting an element below such a level (a letter, a syllable, or a pair of letters, etc.) in order to produce a cyphertext.

Cryptanalysis is the term used for the study of methods for obtaining the meaning of encrypted information without access to the key normally required to do so; i.e., it is the study of how to "crack" encryption algorithms or their implementations.

Some use the terms "cryptography" and "cryptology" interchangeably in English,[16] while others (including US military practice generally) use "cryptography" to refer specifically to the use and practice of cryptographic techniques and "cryptology" to refer to the combined study of cryptography and cryptanalysis.[17][18] English is more flexible than several other languages in which "cryptology" (done by cryptologists) is always used in the second sense above. RFC 2828 advises that steganography is sometimes included in cryptology.[19]

The study of characteristics of languages that have some application in cryptography or cryptology (e.g. frequency data, letter combinations, universal patterns, etc.) is called cryptolinguistics. Cryptolingusitics is especially used in military intelligence applications for deciphering foreign communications.[20][21]

History

Before the modern era, cryptography focused on message confidentiality (i.e., encryption)—conversion of messages from a comprehensible form into an incomprehensible one and back again at the other end, rendering it unreadable by interceptors or eavesdroppers without secret knowledge (namely the key needed for decryption of that message). Encryption attempted to ensure secrecy in communications, such as those of spies, military leaders, and diplomats. In recent decades, the field has expanded beyond confidentiality concerns to include techniques for message integrity checking, sender/receiver identity authentication, digital signatures, interactive proofs and secure computation, among others.

Classic cryptography

The main classical cipher types are transposition ciphers, which rearrange the order of letters in a message (e.g., 'hello world' becomes 'ehlol owrdl' in a trivially simple rearrangement scheme), and substitution ciphers, which systematically replace letters or groups of letters with other letters or groups of letters (e.g., 'fly at once' becomes 'gmz bu podf' by replacing each letter with the one following it in the Latin alphabet).[22] Simple versions of either have never offered much confidentiality from enterprising opponents. An early substitution cipher was the Caesar cipher, in which each letter in the plaintext was replaced by a letter some fixed number of positions further down the alphabet. Suetonius reports that Julius Caesar used it with a shift of three to communicate with his generals. Atbash is an example of an early Hebrew cipher. The earliest known use of cryptography is some carved ciphertext on stone in Egypt (c. 1900 BCE), but this may have been done for the amusement of literate observers rather than as a way of concealing information.

The Greeks of Classical times are said to have known of ciphers (e.g., the scytale transposition cipher claimed to have been used by the Spartan military).[23] Steganography (i.e., hiding even the existence of a message so as to keep it confidential) was also first developed in ancient times. An early example, from Herodotus, was a message tattooed on a slave's shaved head and concealed under the regrown hair.[13] More modern examples of steganography include the use of invisible ink, microdots, and digital watermarks to conceal information.

In India, the 2000-year-old Kamasutra of Vātsyāyana speaks of two different kinds of ciphers called Kautiliyam and Mulavediya. In the Kautiliyam, the cipher letter substitutions are based on phonetic relations, such as vowels becoming consonants. In the Mulavediya, the cipher alphabet consists of pairing letters and using the reciprocal ones.[13]

In Sassanid Persia, there were two secret scripts, according to the Muslim author Ibn al-Nadim: the *šāh-dabīrīya* (literally "King's script") which was used for official correspondence, and the *rāz-saharīya* which was used to communicate secret messages with other countries.[24]

David Kahn notes in *The Codebreakers* that modern cryptology originated among the Arabs, the first people to systematically document cryptanalytic methods.[25] Al-Khalil (717–786) wrote the *Book of Cryptographic Messages*, which contains the first use of permutations and combinations to list all possible Arabic words with and without vowels.[26]

Ciphertexts produced by a classical cipher (and some modern ciphers) will reveal statistical information about the plaintext, and that information can often be used to break the cipher. After the discovery of frequency analysis, perhaps by the Arab mathematician and polymath Al-Kindi (also known as *Alkindus*) in the 9th century,[27] nearly all such ciphers could be broken by an informed attacker. Such classical ciphers still enjoy popularity today, though mostly as puzzles (see cryptogram). Al-Kindi wrote a book on cryptography entitled *Risalah fi Istikhraj al-Mu'amma* (*Manuscript for the Deciphering Cryptographic Messages*), which described the first known use of frequency analysis cryptanalysis techniques.[27][28]

Language letter frequencies may offer little help for some extended historical encryption techniques such as homophonic cipher that tend to flatten the frequency distribution. For those ciphers, language letter group (or n-gram) frequencies may provide an attack.

Essentially all ciphers remained vulnerable to cryptanalysis using the frequency analysis technique until the development of the polyalphabetic cipher, most clearly by Leon Battista Alberti around the year 1467, though there is some indication that it was already known to Al-Kindi.[28] Alberti's innovation was to use different ciphers (i.e., substitution alphabets) for various parts of a message (perhaps for each successive plaintext letter at the limit). He also invented what was probably the first automatic cipher device, a wheel that implemented a partial realization of his invention. In the Vigenère cipher, a polyalphabetic cipher, encryption uses a *key word*, which controls letter substitution depending on which letter of the key word is used. In the mid-19th century Charles Babbage showed that the Vigenère cipher was vulnerable to Kasiski examination, but this was first published about ten years later by Friedrich Kasiski.[29]

Although frequency analysis can be a powerful and general technique against many ciphers, encryption has still often been effective in practice, as many a would-be cryptanalyst was unaware of the technique. Breaking a message without using frequency analysis essentially required knowledge of the cipher used and perhaps of the key involved, thus making espionage, bribery, burglary, defection, etc., more attractive approaches to the cryptanalytically uninformed. It was finally explicitly recognized in the 19th century that secrecy of a cipher's algorithm is not a sensible nor practical safeguard of message security; in fact, it was further realized that any adequate cryptographic scheme (including ciphers) should remain secure even if the adversary fully understands the cipher algorithm itself. Security of the key used should alone be sufficient for a good cipher to maintain confidentiality under an attack. This fundamental principle was first explicitly stated in 1883 by Auguste Kerckhoffs and is generally called Kerckhoffs's Principle; alternatively and more bluntly, it was restated by Claude Shannon, the inventor of information theory and the fundamentals of theoretical cryptography, as *Shannon's Maxim*—'the enemy knows the system'.

Different physical devices and aids have been used to assist with ciphers. One of the earliest may have been the scytale of ancient Greece, a rod supposedly used by the Spartans as an aid for a transposition cipher. In medieval times, other aids were invented such as the cipher grille, which was also used for a kind of steganography. With the invention of polyalphabetic ciphers came more sophisticated aids such as Alberti's own cipher disk, Johannes Trithemius' tabula recta scheme, and Thomas Jefferson's wheel cypher (not publicly known, and reinvented independently by Bazeries around 1900). Many mechanical encryption/decryption devices were invented early in the 20th century, and several patented, among them rotor machines—famously including the Enigma machine used by the German government and military from the late 1920s and during World War II.[30] The ciphers implemented by better quality examples of these machine designs brought about a substantial increase in cryptanalytic difficulty after WWI.[31]

Early computer-era cryptography

Cryptanalysis of the new mechanical ciphering devices proved to be both difficult and laborious. In the United Kingdom, cryptanalytic efforts at Bletchley Park during WWII spurred the development of more efficient means for carrying out repetitive tasks, such as military code breaking (decryption). This culminated in the development of the Colossus, the world's first fully electronic, digital, programmable computer, which assisted in the decryption of ciphers generated by the German Army's Lorenz SZ40/42 machine.

Extensive open academic research into cryptography is relatively recent, beginning in the mid-1970s. In the early 1970s IBM personnel designed the Data Encryption Standard (DES) algorithm that became the first federal government cryptography standard in the United States.[32] In 1976 Whitfield Diffie and Martin Hellman published the Diffie–Hellman key exchange algorithm.[33] In 1977 the RSA algorithm was published in Martin Gardner's *Scientific American* column.[34] Since then, cryptography has become a widely used tool in communications, computer networks, and computer security generally.

Some modern cryptographic techniques can only keep their keys secret if certain mathematical problems are intractable, such as the integer factorization or the discrete logarithm problems, so there are deep connections with abstract mathematics. There are very few cryptosystems that are proven to be unconditionally secure. The one-time pad is one, and was proven to be so by Claude Shannon. There are a few important algorithms that have been proven secure under certain assumptions. For example, the infeasibility of factoring extremely large integers is the basis for believing that RSA is secure, and some other systems, but even so, proof of unbreakability is unavailable since the underlying mathematical problem remains open. In practice, these are widely used, and are believed unbreakable in practice by most competent observers. There are systems similar to RSA, such as one by Michael O. Rabin that are provably secure provided factoring $n = pq$ is impossible; it is quite unusable in practice. The discrete logarithm problem is the basis for believing some other cryptosystems are secure, and again, there are related, less practical systems that are provably secure relative to the solvability or insolvability discrete log problem.[35]

As well as being aware of cryptographic history, cryptographic algorithm and system designers must also sensibly consider probable future developments while working on their designs. For instance, continuous improvements in computer processing power have increased the scope of brute-force attacks, so when specifying key lengths, the required key lengths are similarly advancing.[36] The potential impact of quantum computing are already being considered by some cryptographic system designers developing post-quantum cryptography.[when?] The announced imminence of small implementations of these machines may be making the need for preemptive caution rather more than merely speculative.[5]

Modern cryptography

Prior to the early 20th century, cryptography was mainly concerned with linguistic and lexicographic patterns. Since then cryptography has broadened in scope, and now makes extensive use of mathematical subdisciplines, including information theory, computational complexity, statistics, combinatorics, abstract algebra, number theory, and finite mathematics.[37] Cryptography is also a branch of engineering, but an unusual one since it deals with active, intelligent, and malevolent opposition; other kinds of engineering (e.g., civil or chemical engineering) need deal only with neutral natural forces. There is also active research examining the relationship between cryptographic problems and quantum physics.

Just as the development of digital computers and electronics helped in cryptanalysis, it made possible much more complex ciphers. Furthermore, computers allowed for the encryption of any kind of data representable in any binary format, unlike classical ciphers which only encrypted written language texts; this was new and significant. Computer use has thus supplanted linguistic cryptography, both for cipher design and cryptanalysis. Many computer ciphers can be characterized by their operation on binary bit sequences (sometimes in groups or blocks), unlike classical and mechanical schemes, which generally manipulate traditional characters (i.e., letters and digits) directly. However, computers have also assisted cryptanalysis, which has compensated to some extent for increased cipher complexity. Nonetheless, good modern ciphers have stayed ahead of cryptanalysis; it is typically the case that use of a quality cipher is very efficient (i.e., fast and requiring few resources, such as memory or CPU capability), while breaking it requires an effort many orders of magnitude larger, and vastly larger than that required for any classical cipher, making cryptanalysis so inefficient and impractical as to be effectively impossible.

Modern cryptography

Symmetric-key cryptography

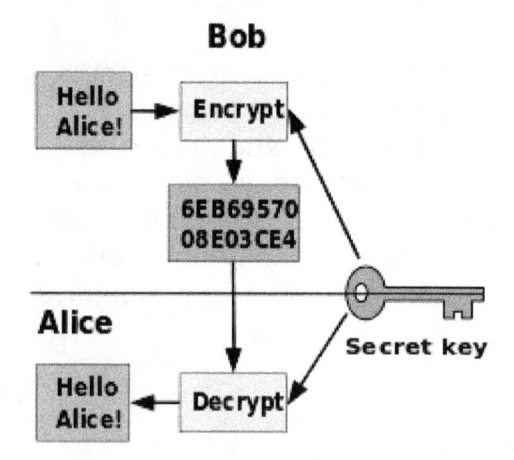

Symmetric-key cryptography, where a single key is used for encryption and decryption

Symmetric-key cryptography refers to encryption methods in which both the sender and receiver share the same key (or, less commonly, in which their keys are different, but related in an easily computable way). This was the only kind of encryption publicly known until June 1976.[33]

Symmetric key ciphers are implemented as either block ciphers or stream ciphers. A block cipher enciphers input in blocks of plaintext as opposed to individual characters, the input form used by a stream cipher.

The Data Encryption Standard (DES) and the Advanced Encryption Standard (AES) are block cipher designs that have been designated cryptography standards by the US government (though DES's designation was finally withdrawn after the AES was adopted).[38] Despite its deprecation as an official standard, DES (especially its still-approved and much more secure triple-DES variant) remains quite popular; it is used across a wide range of applications, from ATM encryption[39] to e-mail privacy[40] and secure remote access.[41] Many other block ciphers have been designed and released, with considerable variation in quality. Many, even some designed by capable practitioners, have been thoroughly broken, such as FEAL.[5][42]

Stream ciphers, in contrast to the 'block' type, create an arbitrarily long stream of key material, which is combined with the plaintext bit-by-bit or character-by-character, somewhat like the one-time pad. In a stream cipher, the output stream is created based on a hidden internal state that changes as the cipher operates. That internal state is initially set up using the secret key material. RC4 is a widely used stream cipher.[5] Block ciphers can be used as stream ciphers by generating blocks of a keystream (in place of a Pseudorandom number generator) and applying an XOR operation to each bit of the plaintext with each bit of the keystream.[43]

Message authentication codes (MACs) are much like cryptographic hash functions, except that a secret key can be used to authenticate the hash value upon receipt;[5][44] this additional complication blocks an attack scheme against bare digest algorithms, and so has been thought worth the effort. Cryptographic hash functions are a third type of cryptographic algorithm. They take a message of any length as input, and output a short, fixed-length hash, which can be used in (for example) a digital signature. For good hash functions, an attacker cannot find two messages that produce the same hash. MD4 is a long-used hash function that is now broken; MD5, a strengthened variant of MD4, is also widely used but broken in practice. The US National Security Agency developed the Secure Hash Algorithm series of MD5-like hash functions: SHA-0 was a flawed algorithm that the agency withdrew; SHA-1 is widely deployed and more secure than MD5, but cryptanalysts have identified attacks against it; the SHA-2 family improves on SHA-1, but is vulnerable to clashes as of 2011; and the US standards authority thought it "prudent" from a security perspective to develop a new standard to "significantly improve the robustness of NIST's overall hash algorithm toolkit."[45] Thus, a hash function design competition was meant to select a new U.S. national standard, to be called SHA-3, by 2012. The competition ended on October 2, 2012, when the NIST announced that Keccak would be the new SHA-3 hash algorithm.[46] Unlike block and stream ciphers that are invertible, cryptographic hash functions produce a hashed output that cannot be used to retrieve the original input data. Cryptographic hash functions are used to verify the authenticity of data retrieved from an untrusted source or to add a layer of security.

Public-key cryptography

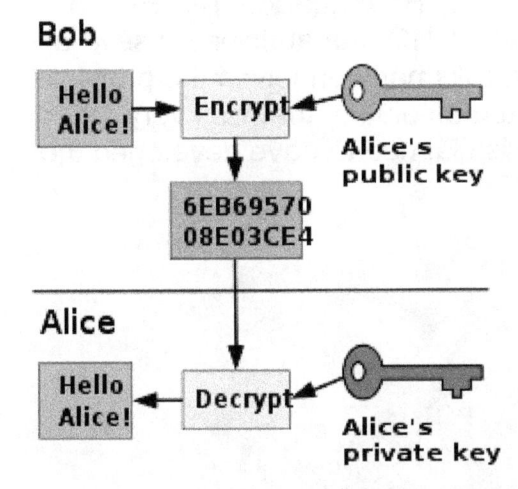

Public-key cryptography, where different keys are used for encryption and decryption.

Symmetric-key cryptosystems use the same key for encryption and decryption of a message, although a message or group of messages can have a different key than others. A significant disadvantage of symmetric ciphers is the key management necessary to use them securely. Each distinct pair of communicating parties must, ideally, share a different key, and perhaps for each ciphertext exchanged as well. The number of keys required increases as the square of the number of network members, which very quickly requires complex key management schemes to keep them all consistent and secret.

In a groundbreaking 1976 paper, Whitfield Diffie and Martin Hellman proposed the notion of *public-key* (also, more generally, called *asymmetric key*) cryptography in which two different but mathematically related keys are used—a *public* key and a *private* key.[47] A public key system is so constructed that calculation of one key (the 'private key') is computationally infeasible from the other (the 'public key'), even though they are necessarily related. Instead, both keys are generated secretly, as an interrelated pair.[48] The historian David Kahn described public-key cryptography as "the most revolutionary new concept in the field since polyalphabetic substitution emerged in the Renaissance".[49]

In public-key cryptosystems, the public key may be freely distributed, while its paired private key must remain secret. In a public-key encryption system, the *public key* is used for encryption, while the *private* or *secret key* is used for decryption. While Diffie and Hellman could not find such a system, they showed that public-key cryptography was indeed possible by presenting the Diffie–Hellman key exchange protocol, a solution that is now widely used in secure communications to allow two parties to secretly agree on a shared encryption key.[33] The X.509 standard defines the most commonly used format for public key certificates.[50]

Diffie and Hellman's publication sparked widespread academic efforts in finding a practical public-key encryption system. This race was finally won in 1978 by Ronald Rivest, Adi Shamir, and Len Adleman, whose solution has since become known as the RSA algorithm.[51]

The Diffie–Hellman and RSA algorithms, in addition to being the first publicly known examples of high-quality public-key algorithms, have been among the most widely used. Other asymmetric-key algorithms include the Cramer–Shoup cryptosystem, ElGamal encryption, and various elliptic curve techniques.

A document published in 1997 by the Government Communications Headquarters (GCHQ), a British intelligence organization, revealed that cryptographers at GCHQ had anticipated several academic developments.[52] Reportedly, around 1970, James H. Ellis had conceived the principles of asymmetric key cryptography. In 1973, Clifford Cocks invented a solution that was very similar in design rationale to RSA.[52][53] In 1974, Malcolm J. Williamson is claimed to have developed the Diffie–Hellman key exchange.[54]

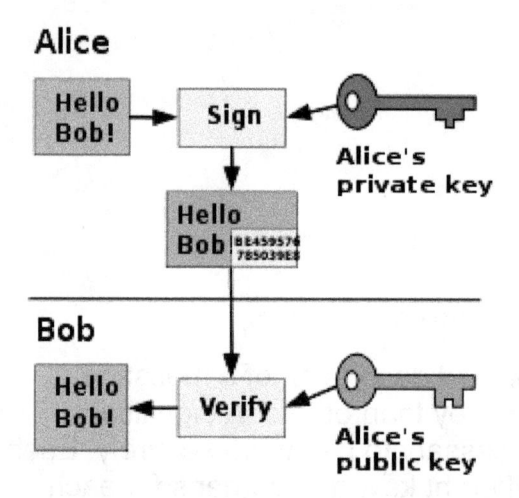

In this example the message is only signed and not encrypted. 1) Alice signs a message with her private key. 2) Bob can verify that Alice sent the message and that the message has not been modified.

Public-key cryptography is also used for implementing digital signature schemes. A digital signature is reminiscent of an ordinary signature; they both have the characteristic of being easy for a user to produce, but difficult for anyone else to forge. Digital signatures can also be permanently tied to the content of the message being signed; they cannot then be 'moved' from one document to another, for any attempt will be detectable. In digital signature schemes, there are two algorithms: one for *signing*, in which a secret key is used to process the message (or a hash of the message, or both), and one for *verification*, in which the matching public key is used with the message to check the validity of the signature. RSA and DSA are two of the most popular digital signature schemes. Digital signatures are central to the operation of public key infrastructures and many network security schemes (e.g., SSL/TLS, many VPNs, etc.).[42]

Public-key algorithms are most often based on the computational complexity of "hard" problems, often from number theory. For example, the hardness of RSA is related to the integer factorization problem, while Diffie–Hellman and DSA are related to the discrete logarithm problem. The security of elliptic curve cryptography is based on number theoretic problems involving elliptic curves. Because of the difficulty of the underlying problems, most public-key algorithms involve operations such as modular multiplication and exponentiation, which are much more computationally expensive than the techniques used in most block ciphers, especially with typical key sizes. As a result, public-key cryptosystems are commonly hybrid cryptosystems, in which a fast high-quality symmetric-key encryption algorithm is used for the message itself, while the relevant symmetric key is sent with the message, but encrypted using a public-key algorithm. Similarly, hybrid signature schemes are often used, in which a cryptographic hash function is computed, and only the resulting hash is digitally signed.[5]

Cryptographic hash functions

Cryptographic hash functions are cryptographic algorithms that generate and use keys to encrypt data, and such functions may be viewed as keys themselves. They take a message of any length as input, and output a short, fixed-length hash, which can be used in (for example) a digital signature. For good hash functions, an attacker cannot find two messages that produce the same hash. MD4 is a long-used hash function that is now broken; MD5, a strengthened variant of MD4, is also widely used but broken in practice. The US National Security Agency developed the Secure Hash Algorithm series of MD5-like hash functions: SHA-0 was a flawed algorithm that the agency withdrew; SHA-1 is widely deployed and more secure than MD5, but cryptanalysts have identified attacks against it; the SHA-2 family improves on SHA-1, but is vulnerable to clashes as of 2011; and the US standards authority thought it "prudent" from a security perspective to develop a new standard to "significantly improve the robustness of NIST's overall hash algorithm toolkit."[45] Thus, a hash function design competition was meant to select a new U.S. national standard, to be called SHA-3, by 2012. The competition ended on October 2, 2012, when the NIST announced that Keccak would be the new SHA-3 hash algorithm.[46] Unlike block and stream ciphers that are invertible, cryptographic hash functions produce a hashed output that cannot be used to retrieve the original input data. Cryptographic hash functions are used to verify the authenticity of data retrieved from an untrusted source or to add a layer of security.

Cryptanalysis

The goal of cryptanalysis is to find some weakness or insecurity in a cryptographic scheme, thus permitting its subversion or evasion.

It is a common misconception that every encryption method can be broken. In connection with his WWII work at Bell Labs, Claude Shannon proved that the one-time pad cipher is unbreakable, provided the key material is truly random, never reused, kept secret from all possible attackers, and of equal or greater length than the message.[55] Most ciphers, apart from the one-time pad, can be broken with enough computational effort by brute force attack, but the amount of effort needed may be exponentially dependent on the key size, as compared to the effort needed to make use of the cipher. In such cases, effective security could be achieved if it is proven that the effort required (i.e., "work factor", in Shannon's terms) is beyond the ability of any adversary. This means it must be shown that no efficient method (as opposed to the time-consuming brute force method) can be found to break the cipher. Since no such proof has been found to date, the one-time-pad remains the only theoretically unbreakable cipher. Although well-implemented one-time-pad encryption cannot be broken, traffic analysis is still possible.

There are a wide variety of cryptanalytic attacks, and they can be classified in any of several ways. A common distinction turns on what Eve (an attacker) knows and what capabilities are available. In a ciphertext-only attack, Eve has access only to the ciphertext (good modern cryptosystems are usually effectively immune to ciphertext-only attacks). In a known-plaintext attack, Eve has access to a ciphertext and its corresponding plaintext (or to many such pairs). In a chosen-plaintext attack, Eve may choose a plaintext and learn its corresponding ciphertext (perhaps many times); an example is gardening, used by the British during WWII. In a chosen-ciphertext attack, Eve may be able to *choose* ciphertexts and learn their corresponding plaintexts.[5] Finally in a man-in-the-middle attack Eve gets in between Alice (the sender) and Bob (the recipient), accesses and modifies the traffic and then forwards it to the recipient.[56] Also important, often overwhelmingly so, are mistakes (generally in the design or use of one of the protocols involved).

Cryptanalysis of symmetric-key ciphers typically involves looking for attacks against the block ciphers or stream ciphers that are more efficient than any attack that could be against a perfect cipher. For example, a simple brute force attack against DES requires one known plaintext and 2^{55} decryptions, trying approximately half of the possible keys, to reach a point at which chances are better than even that the key sought will have been found. But this may not be enough assurance; a linear cryptanalysis attack against DES requires 2^{43} known plaintexts (with their corresponding ciphertexts) and approximately 2^{43} DES operations.[57] This is a considerable improvement over brute force attacks.

Public-key algorithms are based on the computational difficulty of various problems. The most famous of these are the difficulty of integer factorization of semiprimes and the difficulty of calculating discrete logarithms, both of which are not yet proven to be solvable in polynomial time (**P**) using only a classical Turing-complete computer. Much public-key cryptanalysis concerns designing algorithms in **P** that can solve these problems, or using other technologies, such as quantum computers. For instance, the best-known algorithms for solving the elliptic curve-based version of discrete logarithm are much more time-consuming than the best-known algorithms for factoring, at least for problems of more or less equivalent size. Thus, to achieve an equivalent strength of encryption, techniques that depend upon the difficulty of factoring large composite numbers, such as the RSA cryptosystem, require larger keys than elliptic curve techniques. For this reason, public-key cryptosystems based on elliptic curves have become popular since their invention in the mid-1990s.

While pure cryptanalysis uses weaknesses in the algorithms themselves, other attacks on cryptosystems are based on actual use of the algorithms in real devices, and are called *side-channel attacks*. If a cryptanalyst has access to, for example, the amount of time the device took to encrypt a number of plaintexts or report an error in a password or PIN character, he may be able to use a timing attack to break a cipher that is otherwise resistant to analysis. An attacker might also study the pattern and length of messages to derive valuable information; this is known as traffic analysis[58] and can be quite useful to an alert adversary. Poor administration of a cryptosystem, such as permitting too short keys, will make any system vulnerable, regardless of other virtues. Social engineering and other attacks against humans
(e.g., bribery, extortion, blackmail, espionage, rubber-hose cryptanalysis or torture) are usually

employed due to being more cost-effective and feasible to perform in a reasonable amount of time compared to pure cryptanalysis by a high margin.

Cryptographic primitives

Much of the theoretical work in cryptography concerns cryptographic *primitives*—algorithms with basic cryptographic properties—and their relationship to other cryptographic problems. More complicated cryptographic tools are then built from these basic primitives. These primitives provide fundamental properties, which are used to develop more complex tools called *cryptosystems* or *cryptographic protocols*, which guarantee one or more high-level security properties. Note, however, that the distinction between cryptographic *primitives* and cryptosystems, is quite arbitrary; for example, the RSA algorithm is sometimes considered a cryptosystem, and sometimes a primitive. Typical examples of cryptographic primitives include pseudorandom functions, one-way functions, etc.

Cryptosystems

One or more cryptographic primitives are often used to develop a more complex algorithm, called a cryptographic system, or *cryptosystem*. Cryptosystems (e.g., El-Gamal encryption) are designed to provide particular functionality (e.g., public key encryption) while guaranteeing certain security properties (e.g., chosen-plaintext attack (CPA) security in the random oracle model). Cryptosystems use the properties of the underlying cryptographic primitives to support the system's security properties. As the distinction between primitives and cryptosystems is somewhat arbitrary, a sophisticated cryptosystem can be derived from a combination of several more primitive cryptosystems. In many cases, the cryptosystem's structure involves back and forth communication among two or more parties in space (e.g., between the sender of a secure message and its receiver) or across time (e.g., cryptographically protected backup data). Such cryptosystems are sometimes called *cryptographic protocols*.

Some widely known cryptosystems include RSA, Schnorr signature, ElGamal encryption, and Pretty Good Privacy (PGP). More complex cryptosystems include electronic cash[59] systems, signcryption systems, etc. Some more 'theoretical' cryptosystems include interactive proof systems,[60] (like zero-knowledge proofs),[61] systems for secret sharing,[62][63] etc.

Lightweight cryptography

Lightweight cryptography (LWC) concerns cryptographic algorithms developed for a strictly constrained environment. The growth of Internet of Things (IoT) has spiked research into the development of lightweight algorithms that are better suited for the environment. An IoT environment requires strict constraints on power consumption, processing power, and security.[64] Algorithms such as PRESENT, AES, and SPECK are examples of the many LWC algorithms that have been developed to achieve the standard set by the National Institute of Standards and Technology.[65]

Applications

General

Cryptography is widely used on the internet to help protect user-data and prevent eavesdropping. To ensure secrecy during transmission, many systems use private key cryptography to protect

transmitted information. With public-key systems, one can maintain secrecy without a master key or a large number of keys.[66] But, some algorithms like Bitlocker and Veracrypt are generally not private-public key cryptography. For example, Veracrypt uses a password hash to generate the single private key. However, it can be configured to run in public-private key systems.
The C++ opensource encryption library OpenSSL provides free and opensource encryption software and tools. The most commonly used encryption cipher suit is AES,[67] as it has hardware acceleration for all x86 based processors that has AES-NI. A close contender is ChaCha20-Poly1305, which is a stream cipher, however it is commonly used for mobile devices as they are ARM based which does not feature AES-NI instruction set extension.

Cybersecurity

Cryptography can be used to secure communications by encrypting them. Websites use encryption via HTTPS.[68] "End-to-end" encryption, where only sender and receiver can read messages, is implemented for email in Pretty Good Privacy and for secure messaging in general in WhatsApp, Signal and Telegram.[68]

Operating systems use encryption to keep passwords secret, conceal parts of the system, and ensure that software updates are truly from the system maker.[68] Instead of storing plaintext passwords, computer systems store hashes thereof; then, when a user logs in, the system passes the given password through a cryptographic hash function and compares it to the hashed value on file. In this manner, neither the system nor an attacker has at any point access to the password in plaintext.[68]

Encryption is sometimes used to encrypt one's entire drive. For example, University College London has implemented BitLocker (a program by Microsoft) to render drive data opaque without users logging in.[68]

Cryptocurrencies and cryptoeconomics

Cryptographic techniques enable cryptocurrency technologies, such as distributed ledger technologies (e.g., blockchains), which finance cryptoeconomics applications such as decentralized finance (DeFi). Key cryptographic techniques that enable cryptocurrencies and cryptoeconomics include, but are not limited to: cryptographic keys, cryptographic hash functions, asymmetric (public key) encryption, Multi-Factor Authentication (MFA), End-to-End Encryption (E2EE), and Zero Knowledge Proofs (ZKP).

Legal issues

Prohibitions

Cryptography has long been of interest to intelligence gathering and law enforcement agencies.[9] Secret communications may be criminal or even treasonous. Because of its facilitation of privacy, and the diminution of privacy attendant on its prohibition, cryptography is also of considerable interest to civil rights supporters. Accordingly, there has been a history of controversial legal issues surrounding cryptography, especially since the advent of inexpensive computers has made widespread access to high-quality cryptography possible.

In some countries, even the domestic use of cryptography is, or has been, restricted. Until 1999, France significantly restricted the use of cryptography domestically, though it has since relaxed many of these rules. In China and Iran, a license is still required to use cryptography.[7] Many countries have tight restrictions on the use of cryptography. Among the more restrictive are laws in Belarus, Kazakhstan, Mongolia, Pakistan, Singapore, Tunisia, and Vietnam.[69]

In the United States, cryptography is legal for domestic use, but there has been much conflict over legal issues related to cryptography.[9] One particularly important issue has been the export of cryptography and cryptographic software and hardware. Probably because of the importance of cryptanalysis in World War II and an expectation that cryptography would continue to be important for national security, many Western governments have, at some point, strictly regulated export of cryptography. After World War II, it was illegal in the US to sell or distribute encryption technology overseas; in fact, encryption was designated as auxiliary military equipment and put on the United States Munitions List.[70] Until the development of the personal computer, asymmetric key algorithms (i.e., public key techniques), and the Internet, this was not especially problematic. However, as the Internet grew and computers became more widely available, high-quality encryption techniques became well known around the globe.

Export controls

In the 1990s, there were several challenges to US export regulation of cryptography. After the source code for Philip Zimmermann's Pretty Good Privacy (PGP) encryption program found its way onto the Internet in June 1991, a complaint by RSA Security (then called RSA Data Security, Inc.) resulted in a lengthy criminal investigation of Zimmermann by the US Customs Service and the FBI, though no charges were ever filed.[71][72] Daniel J. Bernstein, then a graduate student at UC Berkeley, brought a lawsuit against the US government challenging some aspects of the restrictions based on free speech grounds. The 1995 case *Bernstein v. United States* ultimately resulted in a 1999 decision that printed source code for cryptographic algorithms and systems was protected as free speech by the United States Constitution.[73]

In 1996, thirty-nine countries signed the Wassenaar Arrangement, an arms control treaty that deals with the export of arms and "dual-use" technologies such as cryptography. The treaty stipulated that the use of cryptography with short key-lengths (56-bit for symmetric encryption, 512-bit for RSA) would no longer be export-controlled.[74] Cryptography exports from the US became less strictly regulated as a consequence of a major relaxation in 2000;[75] there are no longer very many restrictions on key sizes in US-exported mass-market software. Since this relaxation in US export restrictions, and because most personal computers connected to the Internet include US-sourced web browsers such as Firefox or Internet Explorer, almost every Internet user worldwide has potential access to quality cryptography via their browsers (e.g., via Transport Layer Security). The Mozilla Thunderbird and Microsoft Outlook E-mail client programs similarly can transmit and receive emails via TLS, and can send and receive email encrypted with S/MIME. Many Internet users do not realize that their basic application software contains such extensive cryptosystems. These browsers and email programs are so ubiquitous that even governments whose intent is to regulate civilian use of cryptography generally do not find it practical to do much to control distribution or use of cryptography of this quality, so even when such laws are in force, actual enforcement is often effectively impossible.

NSA involvement

Another contentious issue connected to cryptography in the United States is the influence of the National Security Agency on cipher development and policy.[9] The NSA was involved with the design of DES during its development at IBM and its consideration by the National Bureau of

Standards as a possible Federal Standard for cryptography.[76] DES was designed to be resistant to differential cryptanalysis,[77] a powerful and general cryptanalytic technique known to the NSA and IBM, that became publicly known only when it was rediscovered in the late 1980s.[78] According to Steven Levy, IBM discovered differential cryptanalysis,[72] but kept the technique secret at the NSA's request. The technique became publicly known only when Biham and Shamir re-discovered and announced it some years later. The entire affair illustrates the difficulty of determining what resources and knowledge an attacker might actually have.

Another instance of the NSA's involvement was the 1993 Clipper chip affair, an encryption microchip intended to be part of the Capstone cryptography-control initiative. Clipper was widely criticized by cryptographers for two reasons. The cipher algorithm (called Skipjack) was then classified (declassified in 1998, long after the Clipper initiative lapsed). The classified cipher caused concerns that the NSA had deliberately made the cipher weak in order to assist its intelligence efforts. The whole initiative was also criticized based on its violation of Kerckhoffs's Principle, as the scheme included a special escrow key held by the government for use by law enforcement (i.e. wiretapping).[72]

Digital rights management

Cryptography is central to digital rights management (DRM), a group of techniques for technologically controlling use of copyrighted material, being widely implemented and deployed at the behest of some copyright holders. In 1998, U.S. President Bill Clinton signed the Digital Millennium Copyright Act (DMCA), which criminalized all production, dissemination, and use of certain cryptanalytic techniques and technology (now known or later discovered); specifically, those that could be used to circumvent DRM technological schemes.[79] This had a noticeable impact on the cryptography research community since an argument can be made that any cryptanalytic research violated the DMCA. Similar statutes have since been enacted in several countries and regions, including the implementation in the EU Copyright Directive. Similar restrictions are called for by treaties signed by World Intellectual Property Organization member-states.

The United States Department of Justice and FBI have not enforced the DMCA as rigorously as had been feared by some, but the law, nonetheless, remains a controversial one. Niels Ferguson, a well-respected cryptography researcher, has publicly stated that he will not release some of his research into an Intel security design for fear of prosecution under the DMCA.[80] Cryptologist Bruce Schneier has argued that the DMCA encourages vendor lock-in, while inhibiting actual measures toward cyber-security.[81] Both Alan Cox (longtime Linux kernel developer) and Edward Felten (and some of his students at Princeton) have encountered problems related to the Act. Dmitry Sklyarov was arrested during a visit to the US from Russia, and jailed for five months pending trial for alleged violations of the DMCA arising from work he had done in Russia, where the work was legal. In 2007, the cryptographic keys responsible for Blu-ray and HD DVD content scrambling were discovered and released onto the Internet. In both cases, the Motion Picture Association of America sent out numerous DMCA takedown notices, and there was a massive Internet backlash[10] triggered by the perceived impact of such notices on fair use and free speech.

Forced disclosure of encryption keys

In the United Kingdom, the Regulation of Investigatory Powers Act gives UK police the powers to force suspects to decrypt files or hand over passwords that protect encryption keys. Failure to comply is an offense in its own right, punishable on conviction by a two-year jail sentence or up to five years in cases involving national security.[8] Successful prosecutions have occurred under the Act; the first, in 2009,[82] resulted in a term of 13 months' imprisonment.[83] Similar forced disclosure laws in Australia, Finland, France, and India compel individual suspects under investigation to hand over encryption keys or passwords during a criminal investigation.

In the United States, the federal criminal case of *United States v. Fricosu* addressed whether a search warrant can compel a person to reveal an encryption passphrase or password.[84] The Electronic Frontier Foundation (EFF) argued that this is a violation of the protection from self-incrimination given by the Fifth Amendment.[85] In 2012, the court ruled that under the All Writs Act, the defendant was required to produce an unencrypted hard drive for the court.[86]

In many jurisdictions, the legal status of forced disclosure remains unclear.

The 2016 FBI–Apple encryption dispute concerns the ability of courts in the United States to compel manufacturers' assistance in unlocking cell phones whose contents are cryptographically protected.

As a potential counter-measure to forced disclosure some cryptographic software supports plausible deniability, where the encrypted data is indistinguishable from unused random data (for example such as that of a drive which has been securely wiped).

Electronic Authentication

Electronic authentication is the process of establishing confidence in user identities electronically presented to an information system.[1] **Digital authentication, or e-authentication,** may be used synonymously when referring to the authentication process that confirms or certifies a person's identity and works. When used in conjunction with an electronic signature, it can provide evidence of whether data received has been tampered with after being signed by its original sender. Electronic authentication can reduce the risk of fraud and identity theft by verifying that a person is who they say they are when performing transactions online.[2]

Various e-authentication methods can be used to authenticate a user's identify ranging from a password to higher levels of security that utilize multifactor authentication (MFA).[3] Depending on the level of security used, the user might need to prove his or her identity through the use of security tokens, challenge questions, or being in possession of a certificate from a third-party certificate authority that attests to their identity.[4]

Overview

The American National Institute of Standards and Technology (NIST) has developed a generic electronic authentication model[5] that provides a basic framework on how the authentication process is accomplished regardless of jurisdiction or geographic region. According to this model, the enrollment process begins with an individual applying to a Credential Service Provider (CSP). The CSP will need to prove the applicant's identity before proceeding with the transaction. Once the applicant's identity has been confirmed by the CSP, he or she receives the status of "subscriber", is given an authenticator, such as a token and a credential, which may be in the form of a username.

The CSP is responsible for managing the credential along with the subscriber's enrollment data for the life of the credential. The subscriber will be tasked with maintaining the authenticators. An example of this is when a user normally uses a specific computer to do their online banking. If he or she attempts to access their bank account from another computer, the authenticator will not be present. In order to gain access, the subscriber would need to verify their identity to the CSP, which might be in the form of answering a challenge question successfully before being given access.[4]

Use of electronic authorization in medical field

New invention on medicines, and novel development on medical technologies had been widely deployed and adopted in modern societies. In consequence, the average lifetime of human being is much longer than it was before. Therefore, to safely establish and manage personal health records for each individual during his/her lifetime within the electronic form has gradually become an interesting topic for individual citizens and social welfare departments; the reason is that a well-maintained health records document of an individual can help doctors and hospitals know important and necessary medical and body conditions of the targeted patient in time before conducting any therapy.

History

The need for authentication has been prevalent throughout history. In ancient times, people would identify each other through eye contact and physical appearance. The Sumerians in ancient Mesopotamia attested to the authenticity of their writings by using seals embellished with identifying symbols. As time moved on, the most common way to provide authentication would be the handwritten signature.[2]

Authentication factors

There are three generally accepted factors that are used to establish a digital identity for electronic authentication, including:

- Knowledge factor, which is something that the user knows, such as a password, answers to challenge questions, ID numbers or a PIN.
- Possession factor, which is something that the user has, such as mobile phone, PC or token
- Biometric factor, which is something that the user is, such as his or her fingerprints, eye scan or voice pattern

Out of the three factors, the biometric factor is the most convenient and convincing to prove an individual's identity, but it is the most expensive to implement. Each factor has its weaknesses; hence, reliable and strong authentication depends on combining two or more factors. This is known as multi-factor authentication,[2] of which two-factor authentication and two-step verification are subtypes.

Multi-factor authentication can still be vulnerable to attacks, including man-in-the-middle attacks and Trojan attacks.[6]

Methods

Token

A sample of token

Tokens generically are something the claimant possesses and controls that may be used to authenticate the claimant's identity. In e-authentication, the claimant authenticates to a system or application over a network. Therefore, a token used for e-authentication is a secret and the token must be protected. The token may, for example, be a cryptographic key, that is protected by encrypting it under a password. An impostor must steal the encrypted key and learn the password to use the token.

Passwords and PIN-based authentication

Passwords and PINs are categorized as "something you know" method. A combination of numbers, symbols, and mixed cases are considered to be stronger than all-letter password. Also, the adoption of Transport Layer Security (TLS) or Secure Socket Layer (SSL) features during the information transmission process will as well create an encrypted channel for data exchange and to further protect information delivered. Currently, most security attacks target on password-based authentication systems.[7]

Public-key authentication

This type of authentication has two parts. One is a public key, the other is a private key. A public key is issued by a Certification Authority and is available to any user or server. A private key is known by the user only.[8]

Symmetric-key authentication

The user shares a unique key with an authentication server. When the user sends a randomly generated message (the challenge) encrypted by the secret key to the authentication server, if the message can be matched by the server using its shared secret key, the user is authenticated. When implemented together with the password authentication, this method also provides a possible solution for two-factor authentication systems.[9]

SMS-based authentication

The user receives password by reading the message in the cell phone, and types back the password to complete the authentication. Short Message Service (SMS) is very effective when cell phones are commonly adopted. SMS is also suitable against man-in-the-middle (MITM) attacks, since the use of SMS does not involve the Internet.[10]

Biometric authentication

Biometric authentication is the use of unique physical attributes and body measurements as the intermediate for better identification and access control. Physical characteristics that are often used for authentication include fingerprints, voice recognition, face recognition, and iris scans because all of these are unique to every individual. Traditionally, biometric authentication based on token-based identification systems, such as passport, and nowadays becomes one of the most secure identification systems to user protections. A new technological innovation which provides a wide variety of either behavioral or physical characteristics which are defining the proper concept of biometric authentication.[11]

Digital identity authentication

Digital identity authentication refers to the combined use of device, behavior, location and other data, including email address, account and credit card information, to authenticate online users in real time. For example, recent work have explored how to exploit browser fingerprinting as part of a multi-factor authentication scheme.[12]

Electronic credentials

Paper credentials are documents that attest to the identity or other attributes of an individual or entity called the subject of the credentials. Some common paper credentials include passports, birth certificates, driver's licenses, and employee identity cards. The credentials themselves are authenticated in a variety of ways: traditionally perhaps by a signature or a seal, special papers and inks, high quality engraving, and today by more complex mechanisms, such as holograms, that make the credentials recognizable and difficult to copy or forge. In some cases, simple possession of the credentials is sufficient to establish that the physical holder of the credentials is indeed the subject of the credentials. More commonly, the credentials contain biometric information such as the subject's description, a picture of the subject or the handwritten signature of the subject that can be used to authenticate that the holder of the credentials is indeed the subject of the credentials. When these paper credentials are presented in-person, authentication biometrics contained in those credentials can be checked to confirm that the physical holder of the credential is the subject.

Electronic identity credentials bind a name and perhaps other attributes to a token. There are a variety of electronic credential types in use today, and new types of credentials are constantly being created (eID, electronic voter ID card, biometric passports, bank cards, etc.) At a minimum, credentials include identifying information that permits recovery of the records of the registration associated with the credentials and a name that is associated with the subscriber.

Verifiers

In any authenticated on-line transaction, the verifier is the party that verifies that the claimant has possession and control of the token that verifies his or her identity. A claimant authenticates his or her identity to a verifier by the use of a token and an authentication protocol. This is called Proof of Possession (PoP). Many PoP protocols are designed so that a verifier, with no knowledge of the token before the authentication protocol run, learns nothing about the token from the run. The verifier and CSP may be the same entity, the verifier and relying party may be the same entity or they may all three be separate entities. It is undesirable for verifiers to learn shared secrets unless they are a part of the same entity as the CSP that registered the tokens. Where the verifier and the relying party are separate entities, the verifier must convey the result of the authentication protocol to the relying party. The object created by the verifier to convey this result is called an assertion.[13]

Authentication schemes

There are four types of authentication schemes: local authentication, centralized authentication, global centralized authentication, global authentication and web application (portal).

When using a local authentication scheme, the application retains the data that pertains to the user's credentials. This information is not usually shared with other applications. The onus is on the user to maintain and remember the types and number of credentials that are associated with the service in which they need to access. This is a high risk scheme because of the possibility that the storage area for passwords might become compromised.

Using the central authentication scheme allows for each user to use the same credentials to access various services. Each application is different and must be designed with interfaces and the ability to interact with a central system to successfully provide authentication for the user. This allows the user to access important information and be able to access private keys that will allow him or her to electronically sign documents.

Using a third party through a global centralized authentication scheme allows the user direct access to authentication services. This then allows the user to access the particular services they need.

The most secure scheme is the global centralized authentication and web application (portal). It is ideal for E-Government use because it allows a wide range of services. It uses a single authentication mechanism involving a minimum of two factors to allow access to required services and the ability to sign documents.[2]

Authentication and digital signing working together

Often, authentication and digital signing are applied in conjunction. In advanced electronic signatures, the signatory has authenticated and uniquely linked to a signature. In the case of a qualified electronic signature as defined in the eIDAS-regulation, the signer's identity is even certified by a qualified trust service provider. This linking of signature and authentication firstly supports the probative value of the signature – commonly referred to as non-repudiation of origin. The protection of the message on the network-level is called non-repudiation of emission. The authenticated sender and the message content are linked to each other. If a 3rd party tries to change the message content, the signature loses validity.[14]

Risk assessment

When developing electronic systems, there are some industry standards requiring United States agencies to ensure the transactions provide an appropriate level of assurance. Generally, servers adopt the US' Office of Management and Budget's (OMB's) E-Authentication Guidance for Federal Agencies (M-04-04) as a guideline, which is published to help federal agencies provide secure electronic services that protect individual privacy. It asks agencies to check whether their transactions require e-authentication, and determine a proper level of assurance.[15]

It established four levels of assurance:[16]

Assurance Level 1: Little or no confidence in the asserted identity's validity.
Assurance Level 2: Some confidence in the asserted identity's validity.
Assurance Level 3: High confidence in the asserted identity's validity.
Assurance Level 4: Very high confidence in the asserted identity's validity.

Determining assurance levels

The OMB proposes a five-step process to determine the appropriate assurance level for their applications:

- Conduct a risk assessment, which measures possible negative impacts.
- Compare with the five assurance levels and decide which one suits this case.
- Select technology according to the technical guidance issued by NIST.
- Confirm the selected authentication process satisfies requirements.
- Reassess the system regularly and adjust it with changes.[17]

The required level of authentication assurance are assessed through the factors below:

- Inconvenience, distress, or damage to standing or reputation;
- Financial loss or agency liability;
- Harm to agency programs or public interests;
- Unauthorized release of sensitive information;
- Personal safety; and/or civil or criminal violations.[17]

Determining technical requirements

National Institute of Standards and Technology (NIST) guidance defines technical requirements for each of the four levels of assurance in the following areas:[18]

- Tokens are used for proving identity. Passwords and symmetric cryptographic keys are private information that the verifier needs to protect. Asymmetric cryptographic keys have a private key (which only the subscriber knows) and a related public key.
- Identity proofing, registration, and the delivery of credentials that bind an identity to a token. This process can involve a far distance operation.
- Credentials, tokens, and authentication protocols can also be combined to identify that a claimant is in fact the claimed subscriber.
- An assertion mechanism that involves either a digital signature of the claimant or is acquired directly by a trusted third party through a secure authentication protocol.

Guidelines and regulations

Triggered by the growth of new cloud solutions and online transactions, person-to-machine and machine-to-machine identities play a significant role in identifying individuals and accessing information. According to the Office of Management and Budget in the U.S., more than $70 million was spent on identity management solutions in both 2013 and 2014.[19]

Governments use e-authentication systems to offer services and reduce time people traveling to a government office. Services ranging from applying for visas to renewing driver's licenses can all be achieved in a more efficient and flexible way. Infrastructure to support e-authentication is regarded as an important component in successful e-government.[20] Poor coordination and poor technical design might be major barriers to electronic authentication.[21]

In several countries there has been established nationwide common e-authentication schemes to ease the reuse of digital identities in different electronic services.[22] Other policy initiatives have included the creation of frameworks for electronic authentication, in order to establish common levels of trust and possibly interoperability between different authentication schemes.[23]

United States

E-authentication is a centerpiece of the United States government's effort to expand electronic government, or e-government, as a way of making government more effective and efficient and easier to access. The e-authentication service enables users to access government services online using log-in IDs (identity credentials) from other web sites that both the user and the government trust.

E-authentication is a government-wide partnership that is supported by the agencies that comprise the Federal CIO Council. The United States General Services Administration (GSA) is the lead agency partner. E-authentication works through an association with a trusted credential issuer, making it necessary for the user to log into the issuer's site to obtain the authentication credentials. Those credentials or e-authentication ID are then transferred the supporting government web site causing authentication. The system was created in response a December 16, 2003 memorandum was issued through the Office of Management and Budget. Memorandum M04-04 Whitehouse.[17] That memorandum updates the guidance issued in the *Paperwork Elimination Act* of 1998, 44 U.S.C. § 3504 and implements section 203 of the E-Government Act, 44 U.S.C. ch. 36.

NIST provides guidelines for digital authentication standards and does away with most knowledge-based authentication methods. A stricter standard has been drafted on more complicated passwords that at least 8 characters long or passphrases that are at least 64 characters long.[24]

Europe

In Europe, eIDAS provides guidelines to be used for electronic authentication in regards to electronic signatures and certificate services for website authentication. Once confirmed by the issuing Member State, other participating States are required to accept the user's electronic signature as valid for cross border transactions.

Under eIDAS, electronic identification refers to a material/immaterial unit that contains personal identification data to be used for authentication for an online service. Authentication is referred to as an electronic process that allows for the electronic identification of a natural or legal person. A trust service is an electronic service that is used to create, verify and validate electronic signatures, in addition to creating, verifying and validating certificates for website authentication.

Article 8 of eIDAS allows for the authentication mechanism that is used by a natural or legal person to use electronic identification methods in confirming their identity to a relying party. Annex IV provides requirements for qualified certificates for website authentication.[25] [26]

Russia

E-authentication is a centerpiece of the Russia government's effort to expand e-government, as a way of making government more effective and efficient and easier for the Russian people to access. The e-authentication service[27] enables users to access government services online using log-in IDs (identity credentials) they already have from web sites that they and the government trust.

Other applications

Apart from government services, e-authentication is also widely used in other technology and industries. These new applications combine the features of authorizing identities in traditional database and new technology to provide a more secure and diverse use of e-authentication. Some examples are described below.

Mobile authentication

Mobile authentication is the verification of a user's identity through the use a mobile device. It can be treated as an independent field or it can also be applied with other multifactor authentication schemes in the e-authentication field.[28]

For mobile authentication, there are five levels of application sensitivity from Level 0 to Level 4. Level 0 is for public use over a mobile device and requires no identity authentications, while level 4 has the most multi-procedures to identify users.[29] For either level, mobile authentication is relatively easy to process. Firstly, users send a one-time password (OTP) through offline channels. Then, a server identifies the information and makes adjustment in the database. Since only the user has the access to a PIN code and can send information through their mobile devices, there is a low risk of attacks.[30]

E-commerce authentication

In the early 1980s, electronic data interchange (EDI) systems was implemented, which was considered as an early representative of E-commerce. But ensuring its security is not a significant issue since the systems are all constructed around closed networks. However, more recently, business-to-consumer transactions have transformed. Remote transacting parties have forced the implementation of E-commerce authentication systems.[31]

Generally speaking, the approaches adopted in E-commerce authentication are basically the same as e-authentication. The difference is E-commerce authentication is a more narrow field that focuses on the transactions between customers and suppliers. A simple example of E-commerce authentication includes a client communicating with a merchant server via the Internet. The merchant server usually utilizes a web server to accept client requests, a database management system to manage data and a payment gateway to provide online payment services.[32]

Self-sovereign identity

With self-sovereign identity (SSI) the individual identity holders fully create and control their credentials. Whereas the verifiers can authenticate the provided identities on a decentralized network.

Perspectives

To keep up with the evolution of services in the digital world, there is continued need for security mechanisms. While passwords will continue to be used, it is important to rely on authentication mechanisms, most importantly multifactor authentication. As the usage of e-signatures continues to significantly expand throughout the United States, the EU and throughout the world, there is expectation that regulations such as eIDAS will eventually be amended to reflect changing conditions along with regulations in the United States.[33]

Public Key Infrastructure

A **public key infrastructure** (**PKI**) is a set of roles, policies, hardware, software and procedures needed to create, manage, distribute, use, store and revoke digital certificates and manage public-key encryption. The purpose of a PKI is to facilitate the secure electronic transfer of information for a range of network activities such as e-commerce, internet banking and confidential email. It is required for activities where simple passwords are an inadequate authentication method and more rigorous proof is required to confirm the identity of the parties involved in the communication and to validate the information being transferred.

In cryptography, a PKI is an arrangement that *binds* public keys with respective identities of entities (like people and organizations).[1] The binding is established through a process of registration and issuance of certificates at and by a certificate authority (CA). Depending on the assurance level of the binding, this may be carried out by an automated process or under human supervision. When done over a network, this requires using a secure certificate enrollment or certificate management protocol such as CMP.

The PKI role that may be delegated by a CA to assure valid and correct registration is called a *registration authority* (RA). Basically, an RA is responsible for accepting requests for digital certificates and authenticating the entity making the request.[2] The Internet Engineering Task Force's RFC 3647 defines an RA as "An entity that is responsible for one or more of the following functions: the identification and authentication of certificate applicants, the approval or rejection of certificate applications, initiating certificate revocations or suspensions under certain circumstances, processing subscriber requests to revoke or suspend their certificates, and approving or rejecting requests by subscribers to renew or re-key their certificates. RAs, however, do not sign or issue certificates (i.e., an RA is delegated certain tasks on behalf of a CA)."[3] While Microsoft may have referred to a subordinate CA as an RA,[4] this is incorrect according to the X.509 PKI standards. RAs do not have the signing authority of a CA and only manage the vetting and provisioning of certificates. So in the Microsoft PKI case, the RA functionality is provided either by the Microsoft Certificate Services web site or through Active Directory Certificate Services which enforces Microsoft Enterprise CA and certificate policy through certificate templates and manages certificate enrollment (manual or auto-enrollment). In the case of Microsoft Standalone CAs, the function of RA does not exist since all of the procedures controlling the CA are based on the administration and access procedure associated with the system hosting the CA and the CA itself rather than Active Directory. Most non-Microsoft commercial PKI solutions offer a stand-alone RA component.

An entity must be uniquely identifiable within each CA domain on the basis of information about that entity. A third-party validation authority (VA) can provide this entity information on behalf of the CA.

The X.509 standard defines the most commonly used format for public key certificates.[5]

Capabilities

PKI provides "trust services" - in plain terms trusting the actions or outputs of entities, be they people or computers. Trust service objectives respect one or more of the following capabilities: Confidentiality, Integrity and Authenticity (CIA).

Confidentiality: Assurance that no entity can maliciously or unwittingly view a payload in clear text. Data is encrypted to make it secret, such that even if it was read, it appears as gibberish. Perhaps the most common use of PKI for confidentiality purposes is in the context of Transport Layer Security (TLS). TLS is a capability underpinning the security of data in transit, i.e. during transmission. A classic example of TLS for confidentiality is when using an internet browser to log on to a service hosted on an internet based web site by entering a password.

Integrity: Assurance that if an entity changed (tampered) with transmitted data in the slightest way, it would be obvious it happened as its integrity would have been compromised. Often it is not of utmost importance to prevent the integrity being compromised (tamper proof), however, it is of utmost importance that if integrity is compromised there is clear evidence of it having done so (tamper evident).

Authenticity: Assurance that every entity has certainty of what it is connecting to, or can evidence its legitimacy when connecting to a protected service. The former is termed server-side authentication - typically used when authenticating to a web server using a password. The latter is termed client-side authentication - sometimes used when authenticating using a smart card (hosting a digital certificate and private key).

Design

Public-key cryptography is a cryptographic technique that enables entities to securely communicate on an insecure public network, and reliably verify the identity of an entity via digital signatures.[6]

A public key infrastructure (PKI) is a system for the creation, storage, and distribution of digital certificates which are used to verify that a particular public key belongs to a certain entity. The PKI creates digital certificates which map public keys to entities, securely stores these certificates in a central repository and revokes them if needed.[7][8][9]

A PKI consists of:[8][10][11]

- A *certificate authority* (CA) that stores, issues and signs the digital certificates;
- A *registration authority* (RA) which verifies the identity of entities requesting their digital certificates to be stored at the CA;
- A *central directory*—i.e., a secure location in which keys are stored and indexed;
- A *certificate management system* managing things like the access to stored certificates or the delivery of the certificates to be issued;
- A *certificate policy* stating the PKI's requirements concerning its procedures. Its purpose is to allow outsiders to analyze the PKI's trustworthiness.

Methods of certification

Broadly speaking, there have traditionally been three approaches to getting this trust: certificate authorities (Cas), web of trust (WoT), and simple public-key infrastructure (SPKI).

Certificate authorities

The primary role of the CA is to digitally sign and publish the public key bound to a given user. This is done using the CA's own private key, so that trust in the user key relies on one's trust in the validity of the CA's key. When the CA is a third party separate from the user and the system, then it is called the Registration Authority (RA), which may or may not be separate from the CA.[12] The key-to-user binding is established, depending on the level of assurance the binding has, by software or under human supervision.

The term trusted third party (TTP) may also be used for certificate authority (CA). Moreover, PKI is itself often used as a synonym for a CA implementation.[13]

Certificate revocation

A certificate may be revoked before it expires, which signals that it is no longer valid. Without revocation, an attacker would be able to exploit such a compromised or misissued certificate until expiry.[14] Hence, revocation is an important part of a public key infrastructure.[15] Revocation is performed by the issuing certificate authority, which produces a cryptographically authenticated statement of revocation.[16]

For distributing revocation information to clients, timeliness of the discovery of revocation (and hence the window for an attacker to exploit a compromised certificate) trades off against resource usage in querying revocation statuses and privacy concerns.[17] If revocation information is unavailable (either due to accident or an attack), clients must decide whether to *fail-hard* and treat a certificate as if it is revoked (and so degrade availability) or to *fail-soft* and treat it as unrevoked (and allow attackers to sidestep revocation).[18]

Due to the cost of revocation checks and the availability impact from potentially-unreliable remote services, Web browsers limit the revocation checks they will perform, and will fail-soft where they do.[19] Certificate revocation lists are too bandwidth-costly for routine use, and the Online Certificate Status Protocol presents connection latency and privacy issues. Other schemes have been proposed but have not yet been successfully deployed to enable fail-hard checking.[15]

Issuer market share

In this model of trust relationships, a CA is a trusted third party – trusted both by the subject (owner) of the certificate and by the party relying upon the certificate.

According to NetCraft report from 2015,[20] the industry standard for monitoring active Transport Layer Security (TLS) certificates, states that "Although the global [TLS] ecosystem is competitive, it is dominated by a handful of major Cas — three certificate authorities (Symantec, Sectigo, GoDaddy) account for three-quarters of all issued [TLS] certificates on public-facing web servers. The top spot has been held by Symantec (or VeriSign before it was purchased by Symantec) ever since [our] survey began, with it currently accounting for just under a third of all certificates. To illustrate the effect of differing methodologies, amongst the million busiest sites Symantec issued 44% of the valid, trusted certificates in use — significantly more than its overall market share."

Following major issues in how certificate issuing were managed, all major players gradually distrusted Symantec issued certificates starting from 2017.[21][22][23]

Temporary certificates and single sign-on

This approach involves a server that acts as an offline certificate authority within a single sign-on system. A single sign-on server will issue digital certificates into the client system, but never stores them. Users can execute programs, etc. with the temporary certificate. It is common to find this solution variety with X.509-based certificates.[24]

Starting Sep 2020, TLS Certificate Validity reduced to 13 Months.

Web of trust

An alternative approach to the problem of public authentication of public key information is the web-of-trust scheme, which uses self-signed certificates and third-party attestations of those certificates. The singular term "web of trust" does not imply the existence of a single web of trust, or common point of trust, but rather one of any number of potentially disjoint "webs of trust". Examples of implementations of this approach are PGP (Pretty Good Privacy) and GnuPG (an implementation of OpenPGP, the standardized specification of PGP). Because PGP and implementations allow the use of e-mail digital signatures for self-publication of public key information, it is relatively easy to implement one's own web of trust.

One of the benefits of the web of trust, such as in PGP, is that it can interoperate with a PKI CA fully trusted by all parties in a domain (such as an internal CA in a company) that is willing to guarantee certificates, as a trusted introducer. If the "web of trust" is completely trusted then, because of the nature of a web of trust, trusting one certificate is granting trust to all the certificates in that web. A PKI is only as valuable as the standards and practices that control the issuance of certificates and including PGP or a personally instituted web of trust could significantly degrade the trustworthiness of that enterprise's or domain's implementation of PKI.[25]

The web of trust concept was first put forth by PGP creator Phil Zimmermann in 1992 in the manual for PGP version 2.0:

As time goes on, you will accumulate keys from other people that you may want to designate as trusted introducers. Everyone else will each choose their own trusted introducers. And everyone will gradually accumulate and distribute with their key a collection of certifying signatures from other people, with the expectation that anyone receiving it will trust at least one or two of the signatures. This will cause the emergence of a decentralized fault-tolerant web of confidence for all public keys.

Simple public key infrastructure

Another alternative, which does not deal with public authentication of public key information, is the simple public key infrastructure (SPKI) that grew out of three independent efforts to overcome the complexities of X.509 and PGP's web of trust. SPKI does not associate users with persons, since the *key* is what is trusted, rather than the person. SPKI does not use any notion of trust, as the verifier is also the issuer. This is called an "authorization loop" in SPKI terminology, where authorization is integral to its design.[26] This type of PKI is specially useful for making integrations of PKI that do not rely on third parties for certificate authorization, certificate information, etc.; a good example of this is an air-gapped network in an office.

Decentralized PKI

Decentralized identifiers (DIDs) eliminates dependence on centralized registries for identifiers as well as centralized certificate authorities for key management, which is the standard in hierarchical PKI. In cases where the DID registry is a distributed ledger, each entity can serve as its own root authority. This architecture is referred to as decentralized PKI (DPKI).[27][28]

History

Developments in PKI occurred in the early 1970s at the British intelligence agency GCHQ, where James Ellis, Clifford Cocks and others made important discoveries related to encryption algorithms and key distribution.[29] Because developments at GCHQ are highly classified, the results of this work were kept secret and not publicly acknowledged until the mid-1990s.

The public disclosure of both secure key exchange and asymmetric key algorithms in 1976 by Diffie, Hellman, Rivest, Shamir, and Adleman changed secure communications entirely. With the further development of high-speed digital electronic communications (the Internet and its predecessors), a need became evident for ways in which users could securely communicate with each other, and as a further consequence of that, for ways in which users could be sure with whom they were actually interacting.

Assorted cryptographic protocols were invented and analyzed within which the new cryptographic primitives could be effectively used. With the invention of the World Wide Web and its rapid spread, the need for authentication and secure communication became still more acute. Commercial reasons alone (e.g., e-commerce, online access to proprietary databases from web browsers) were sufficient. Taher Elgamal and others at Netscape developed the SSL protocol ('https' in Web URLs); it included key establishment, server authentication (prior to v3, one-way only), and so on. A PKI structure was thus created for Web users/sites wishing secure communications.

Vendors and entrepreneurs saw the possibility of a large market, started companies (or new projects at existing companies), and began to agitate for legal recognition and protection from liability. An American Bar Association technology project published an extensive analysis of some of the foreseeable legal aspects of PKI operations (see ABA digital signature guidelines), and shortly thereafter, several U.S. states (Utah being the first in 1995) and other jurisdictions throughout the world began to enact laws and adopt regulations. Consumer groups raised questions about privacy, access, and liability considerations, which were more taken into consideration in some jurisdictions than in others.

The enacted laws and regulations differed, there were technical and operational problems in converting PKI schemes into successful commercial operation, and progress has been much slower than pioneers had imagined it would be.

By the first few years of the 21st century, the underlying cryptographic engineering was clearly not easy to deploy correctly. Operating procedures (manual or automatic) were not easy to correctly design (nor even if so designed, to execute perfectly, which the engineering required). The standards that existed were insufficient.

PKI vendors have found a market, but it is not quite the market envisioned in the mid-1990s, and it has grown both more slowly and in somewhat different ways than were anticipated.[30] PKIs have not solved some of the problems they were expected to, and several major vendors have gone out of business or been acquired by others. PKI has had the most success in government implementations; the largest PKI implementation to date is the Defense Information Systems Agency (DISA) PKI infrastructure for the Common Access Cards program.

Uses

PKIs of one type or another, and from any of several vendors, have many uses, including providing public keys and bindings to user identities which are used for:

- Encryption and/or sender authentication of e-mail messages (e.g., using OpenPGP or S/MIME);
- Encryption and/or authentication of documents (e.g., the XML Signature or XML Encryption standards if documents are encoded as XML);
- Authentication of users to applications (e.g., smart card logon, client authentication with SSL/TLS). There's experimental usage for digitally signed HTTP authentication in the Enigform and mod_openpgp projects;
- Bootstrapping secure communication protocols, such as Internet key exchange (IKE) and SSL/TLS. In both of these, initial set-up of a secure channel (a "security association") uses asymmetric key—i.e., public key—methods, whereas actual communication uses faster symmetric key—i.e., secret key—methods;
- Mobile signatures are electronic signatures that are created using a mobile device and rely on signature or certification services in a location independent telecommunication environment;[31]
- Internet of things requires secure communication between mutually trusted devices. A public key infrastructure enables devices to obtain and renew X.509 certificates which are used to establish trust between devices and encrypt communications using TLS.

Open source implementations

- OpenSSL is the simplest form of CA and tool for PKI. It is a toolkit, developed in C, that is included in all major Linux distributions, and can be used both to build your own (simple) CA and to PKI-enable applications. (Apache licensed)
- EJBCA is a full-featured, enterprise-grade, CA implementation developed in Java. It can be used to set up a CA both for internal use and as a service. (LGPL licensed)
- XiPKI,[32] CA and OCSP responder. With SHA-3 support, implemented in Java. (Apache licensed)
- XCA is a graphical interface, and database. XCA uses OpenSSL for the underlying PKI operations.
- DogTag is a full featured CA developed and maintained as part of the Fedora Project.
- CFSSL[33][34] open source toolkit developed by CloudFlare for signing, verifying, and bundling TLS certificates. (BSD 2-clause licensed)
- Vault[35] tool for securely managing secrets (TLS certificates included) developed by HashiCorp. (Mozilla Public License 2.0 licensed)
- Boulder, an ACME-based CA written in Go. Boulder is the software that runs Let's Encrypt.

Criticism

Some argue that purchasing certificates for securing websites by SSL/TLS and securing software by code signing is a costly venture for small businesses.[36] However, the emergence of free alternatives, such as Let's Encrypt, has changed this. HTTP/2, the latest version of HTTP protocol, allows unsecured connections in theory; in practice, major browser companies have made it clear that they would support this protocol only over a PKI secured TLS connection.[37] Web browser implementation of HTTP/2 including Chrome, Firefox, Opera, and Edge supports HTTP/2 only over TLS by using the ALPN extension of the TLS protocol. This would mean that, to get the speed benefits of HTTP/2, website owners would be forced to purchase SSL/TLS certificates controlled by corporations.

Currently the majority of web browsers are shipped with pre-installed intermediate certificates issued and signed by a certificate authority, by public keys certified by so-called root certificates. This means browsers need to carry a large number of different certificate providers, increasing the risk of a key compromise.[38]

When a key is known to be compromised, it could be fixed by revoking the certificate, but such a compromise is not easily detectable and can be a huge security breach. Browsers have to issue a security patch to revoke intermediary certificates issued by a compromised root certificate authority.[39]

Certificate Authority

In cryptography, a **certificate authority** or **certification authority** (**CA**) is an entity that stores, signs, and issues digital certificates. A digital certificate certifies the ownership of a public key by the named subject of the certificate. This allows others (relying parties) to rely upon signatures or on assertions made about the private key that corresponds to the certified public key. A CA acts as a trusted third party—trusted both by the subject (owner) of the certificate and by the party relying upon the certificate.[1] The format of these certificates is specified by the X.509 or EMV standard.

One particularly common use for certificate authorities is to sign certificates used in HTTPS, the secure browsing protocol for the World Wide Web. Another common use is in issuing identity cards by national governments for use in electronically signing documents.[2]

Overview

Trusted certificates can be used to create secure connections to a server via the Internet. A certificate is essential in order to circumvent a malicious party which happens to be on the route to a target server which acts as if it were the target. Such a scenario is commonly referred to as a man-in-the-middle attack. The client uses the CA certificate to authenticate the CA signature on the server certificate, as part of the authorizations before launching a secure connection.[3] Usually, client software—for example, browsers—include a set of trusted CA certificates. This makes sense, as many users need to trust their client software. A malicious or compromised client can skip any security check and still fool its users into believing otherwise.

The clients of a CA are server supervisors who call for a certificate that their servers will bestow to users. Commercial CAs charge money to issue certificates, and their customers anticipate the CA's certificate to be contained within the majority of web browsers, so that safe connections to the certified servers work efficiently out-of-the-box. The quantity of internet browsers, other devices and applications which trust a particular certificate authority is referred to as ubiquity. Mozilla, which is a non-profit business, issues several commercial CA certificates with its products.[4] While Mozilla developed their own policy, the CA/Browser Forum developed similar guidelines for CA trust. A single CA certificate may be shared among multiple CAs or their resellers. A *root* CA certificate may be the base to issue multiple *intermediate* CA certificates with varying validation requirements.

In addition to commercial CAs, some non-profits issue publicly-trusted digital certificates without charge, for example Let's Encrypt. Some large cloud computing and web hosting companies are also publicly-trusted CAs and issue certificates to services hosted on their infrastructure, for example IBM Cloud, Amazon Web Services, Cloudflare, and Google Cloud Platform.

Large organizations or government bodies may have their own PKIs (public key infrastructure), each containing their own CAs. Any site using self-signed certificates acts as its own CA.

Commercial banks that issue EMV payment cards are governed by the EMV Certificate Authority,[5] payment schemes that route payment transactions initiated at Point of Sale Terminals (POS) to a Card Issuing Bank to transfer the funds from the card holder's bank account to the payment recipient's bank account. Each payment card presents along with its card data also the Card Issuer Certificate to the POS. The Issuer Certificate is signed by EMV CA Certificate. The POS retrieves the public key of EMV CA from its storage, validates the Issuer Certificate and authenticity of the payment card before sending the payment request to the payment scheme.

Browsers and other clients of sorts characteristically allow users to add or do away with CA certificates at will. While server certificates regularly last for a relatively short period, CA certificates are further extended,[6] so, for repeatedly visited servers, it is less error-prone importing and trusting the CA issued, rather than confirm a security exemption each time the server's certificate is renewed.

Less often, trustworthy certificates are used for encrypting or signing messages. CAs dispense end-user certificates too, which can be used with S/MIME. However, encryption entails the receiver's public key and, since authors and receivers of encrypted messages, apparently, know one another, the usefulness of a trusted third party remains confined to the signature verification of messages sent to public mailing lists.

Providers

Worldwide, the certificate authority business is fragmented, with national or regional providers dominating their home market. This is because many uses of digital certificates, such as for legally binding digital signatures, are linked to local law, regulations, and accreditation schemes for certificate authorities.

However, the market for globally trusted TLS/SSL server certificates is largely held by a small number of multinational companies. This market has significant barriers to entry due to the technical requirements.[7] While not legally required, new providers may choose to undergo annual security audits (such as WebTrust[8] for certificate authorities in North America and ETSI in Europe[9]) to be included as a trusted root by a web browser or operating system.

As of 24 August 2020, 147 root certificates, representing 52 organizations, are trusted in the Mozilla Firefox web browser,[10] 168 root certificates, representing 60 organizations, are trusted by macOS,[11] and 255 root certificates, representing 101 organizations, are trusted by Microsoft

Windows.[12] As of Android 4.2 (Jelly Bean), Android currently contains over 100 CAs that are updated with each release.[13]

On November 18, 2014, a group of companies and nonprofit organizations, including the Electronic Frontier Foundation, Mozilla, Cisco, and Akamai, announced Let's Encrypt, a nonprofit certificate authority that provides free domain validated X.509 certificates as well as software to enable installation and maintenance of certificates.[14] Let's Encrypt is operated by the newly formed Internet Security Research Group, a California nonprofit recognized as federally tax-exempt.[15]

According to Netcraft in May 2015, the industry standard for monitoring active TLS certificates, "Although the global [TLS] ecosystem is competitive, it is dominated by a handful of major CAs — three certificate authorities (Symantec, Comodo, GoDaddy) account for three-quarters of all issued [TLS] certificates on public-facing web servers. The top spot has been held by Symantec (or VeriSign before it was purchased by Symantec) ever since [our] survey began, with it currently accounting for just under a third of all certificates. To illustrate the effect of differing methodologies, amongst the million busiest sites Symantec issued 44% of the valid, trusted certificates in use — significantly more than its overall market share."[16]

In 2020, according to independent survey company Netcraft, "DigiCert is the world's largest high-assurance certificate authority, commanding 60% of the Extended Validation Certificate market, and 96% of organization-validated certificates globally.[17]

As of April 2023 the survey company W3Techs, which collects statistics on certificate authority usage among the Alexa top 10 million and the Tranco top 1 million websites, lists the six largest authorities by absolute usage share as below. [18]

Rank	Issuer	Usage	Market Share
1	IdenTrust	38.5%	43.6%
2	DigiCert Group	13.1%	14.5%
3	Sectigo (Comodo Cybersecurity)	12.1%	13.4%
4	GlobalSign	16.1%	16.7%
5	Let's Encrypt	5.8%	6.4%
6	GoDaddy Group	4.8%	5.3%

Validation standards

The commercial CAs that issue the bulk of certificates for HTTPS servers typically use a technique called "domain validation" to authenticate the recipient of the certificate. The techniques used for domain validation vary between CAs, but in general domain validation techniques are meant to prove that the certificate applicant controls a given domain name, not any information about the applicant's identity.

Many Certificate Authorities also offer Extended Validation (EV) certificates as a more rigorous alternative to domain validated certificates. Extended validation is intended to verify not only control of a domain name, but additional identity information to be included in the certificate. Some browsers display this additional identity information in a green box in the URL bar. One limitation of EV as a solution to the weaknesses of domain validation is that attackers could still obtain a domain validated certificate for the victim domain, and deploy it during an attack; if that occurred, the difference observable to the victim user would be the absence of a green bar with the company name. There is some question as to whether users would be likely to recognise this absence as indicative of an attack being in progress: a test using Internet Explorer 7 in 2009 showed that the absence of IE7's EV warnings were not noticed by users, however Microsoft's current browser, Edge, shows a significantly greater difference between EV and domain validated certificates, with domain validated certificates having a hollow, grey lock.

Validation weaknesses

Domain validation suffers from certain structural security limitations. In particular, it is always vulnerable to attacks that allow an adversary to observe the domain validation probes that CAs send. These can include attacks against the DNS, TCP, or BGP protocols (which lack the cryptographic protections of TLS/SSL), or the compromise of routers. Such attacks are possible either on the network near a CA, or near the victim domain itself.

One of the most common domain validation techniques involves sending an email containing an authentication token or link to an email address that is likely to be administratively responsible for the domain. This could be the technical contact email address listed in the domain's WHOIS entry, or an administrative email like `admin@`, `administrator@`, `webmaster@`, `hostmaster@` or `postmaster@` the domain.[19][20] Some Certificate Authorities may accept confirmation using `root@`, `info@`, or `support@` in the domain.[21] The theory behind domain validation is that only the legitimate owner of a domain would be able to read emails sent to these administrative addresses.

Domain validation implementations have sometimes been a source of security vulnerabilities. In one instance, security researchers showed that attackers could obtain certificates for webmail sites because a CA was willing to use an email address like `ssladmin@domain.com` for domain.com, but not all webmail systems had reserved the "ssladmin" username to prevent attackers from registering it.[22]

Prior to 2011, there was no standard list of email addresses that could be used for domain validation, so it was not clear to email administrators which addresses needed to be reserved. The first version of the CA/Browser Forum Baseline Requirements, adopted November 2011, specified a list of such addresses. This allowed mail hosts to reserve those addresses for administrative use, though such precautions are still not universal. In January 2015, a Finnish man registered the username "hostmaster" at the Finnish version of Microsoft Live and was able to obtain a domain-validated certificate for live.fi, despite not being the owner of the domain name.[23]

Issuing a certificate

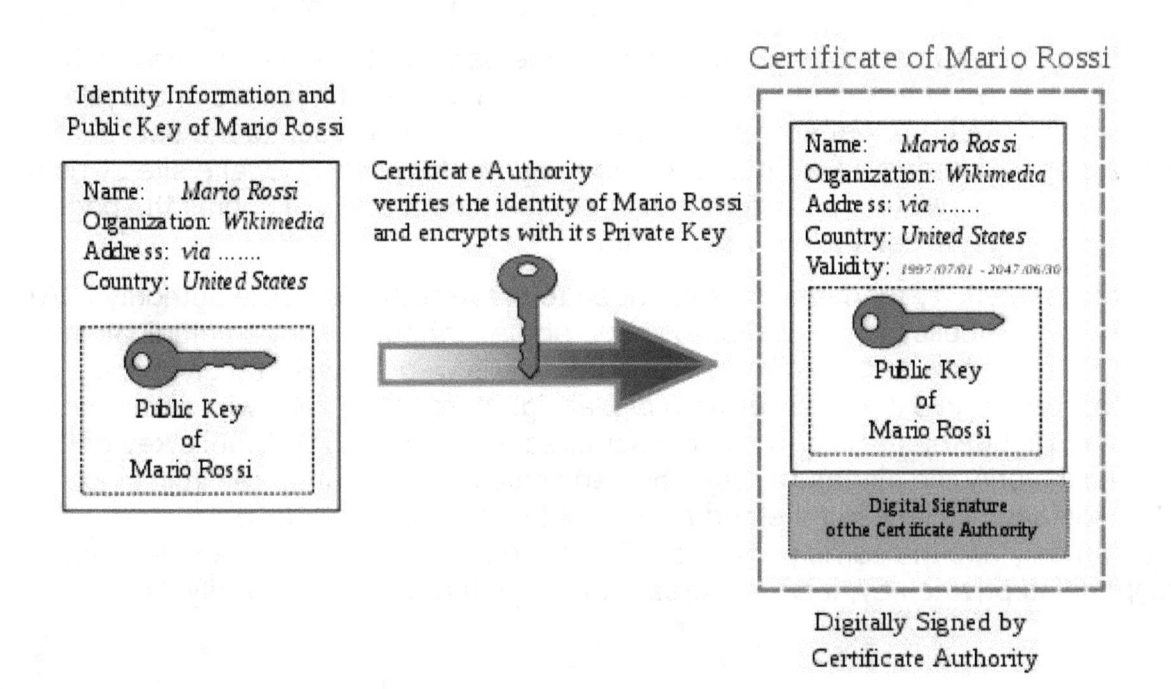

The procedure of obtaining a Public key certificate

A CA issues digital certificates that contain a public key and the identity of the owner. The matching private key is not made available publicly, but kept secret by the end user who generated the key pair. The certificate is also a confirmation or validation by the CA that the public key contained in the certificate belongs to the person, organization, server or other entity noted in the certificate. A CA's obligation in such schemes is to verify an applicant's credentials, so that users and relying parties can trust the information in the issued certificate. CAs use a variety of standards and tests to do so. In essence, the certificate authority is responsible for saying "yes, this person is who they say they are, and we, the CA, certify that".[24]

If the user trusts the CA and can verify the CA's signature, then they can also assume that a certain public key does indeed belong to whoever is identified in the certificate.[25]

Example

Public-key cryptography can be used to encrypt data communicated between two parties. This can typically happen when a user logs on to any site that implements the HTTP Secure protocol. In this example let us suppose that the user logs on to their bank's homepage www.bank.example to do online banking. When the user opens www.bank.example homepage, they receive a public key along with all the data that their web-browser displays. The public key could be used to encrypt data from the client to the server but the safe procedure is to use it in a protocol that determines a temporary shared symmetric encryption key; messages in such a key exchange protocol can be enciphered with the bank's public key in such a way that only the bank server has the private key to read them.[26]

The rest of the communication then proceeds using the new (disposable) symmetric key, so when the user enters some information to the bank's page and submits the page (sends the information back to the bank) then the data the user has entered to the page will be encrypted by their web browser. Therefore, even if someone can access the (encrypted) data that was communicated from the user to www.bank.example, such eavesdropper cannot read or decipher it.

This mechanism is only safe if the user can be sure that it is the bank that they see in their web browser. If the user types in www.bank.example, but their communication is hijacked and a fake website (that pretends to be the bank website) sends the page information back to the user's browser, the fake web-page can send a fake public key to the user (for which the fake site owns a matching private key). The user will fill the form with their personal data and will submit the page. The fake web-page will then get access to the user's data.

This is what the certificate authority mechanism is intended to prevent. A certificate authority (CA) is an organization that stores public keys and their owners, and every party in a communication trusts this organization (and knows its public key). When the user's web browser receives the public key from www.bank.example it also receives a digital signature of the key (with some more information, in a so-called X.509 certificate). The browser already possesses the public key of the CA and consequently can verify the signature, trust the certificate and the public key in it: since www.bank.example uses a public key that the certification authority certifies, a fake www.bank.example can only use the same public key. Since the fake www.bank.example does not know the corresponding private key, it cannot create the signature needed to verify its authenticity.[27]

Security

It is difficult to assure correctness of match between data and entity when the data are presented to the CA (perhaps over an electronic network), and when the credentials of the person/company/program asking for a certificate are likewise presented. This is why commercial CAs often use a combination of authentication techniques including leveraging government bureaus, the payment infrastructure, third parties' databases and services, and custom heuristics. In some enterprise systems, local forms of authentication such as Kerberos can be used to obtain a certificate which can in turn be used by external relying parties. Notaries are required in some cases to personally know the party whose signature is being notarized; this is a higher standard than is reached by many CAs. According to the American Bar Association outline on Online Transaction Management the primary points of US Federal and State statutes enacted regarding digital signatures has been to "prevent conflicting and overly burdensome local regulation and to establish that electronic writings satisfy the traditional requirements associated with paper documents." Further the US E-Sign statute and the suggested UETA code[28] help ensure that:

1. a signature, contract or other record relating to such transaction may not be denied legal effect, validity, or enforceability solely because it is in electronic form; and
2. a contract relating to such transaction may not be denied legal effect, validity or enforceability solely because an electronic signature or electronic record was used in its formation.

Despite the security measures undertaken to correctly verify the identities of people and companies, there is a risk of a single CA issuing a bogus certificate to an imposter. It is also possible to register individuals and companies with the same or very similar names, which may lead to confusion. To minimize this hazard, the *certificate transparency* initiative proposes auditing all certificates in a public unforgeable log, which could help in the prevention of phishing.[29][30]

In large-scale deployments, Alice may not be familiar with Bob's certificate authority (perhaps they each have a different CA server), so Bob's certificate may also include his CA's public key signed by a different CA_2, which is presumably recognizable by Alice. This process typically leads to a hierarchy or mesh of CAs and CA certificates.

Certificate revocation

A certificate may be revoked before it expires, which signals that it is no longer valid. Without revocation, an attacker would be able to exploit such a compromised or misissued certificate until expiry.[31] Hence, revocation is an important part of a public key infrastructure.[32] Revocation is performed by the issuing CA, which produces a cryptographically authenticated statement of revocation.[33]

For distributing revocation information to clients, timeliness of the discovery of revocation (and hence the window for an attacker to exploit a compromised certificate) trades off against resource usage in querying revocation statuses and privacy concerns.[34] If revocation information is unavailable (either due to accident or an attack), clients must decide whether to *fail-hard* and treat a certificate as if it is revoked (and so degrade availability) or to *fail-soft* and treat it as unrevoked (and allow attackers to sidestep revocation).[35]

Due to the cost of revocation checks and the availability impact from potentially-unreliable remote services, Web browsers limit the revocation checks they will perform, and will fail-soft where they do.[36] Certificate revocation lists are too bandwidth-costly for routine use, and the Online Certificate Status Protocol presents connection latency and privacy issues. Other schemes have been proposed but have not yet been successfully deployed to enable fail-hard checking.[32]

Industry organizations

- Certificate Authority Security Council (CASC) – In February 2013, the CASC was founded as an industry advocacy organization dedicated to addressing industry issues and educating the public on internet security. The founding members are the seven largest Certificate Authorities.[37][38]
- Common Computing Security Standards Forum (CCSF) – In 2009 the CCSF was founded to promote industry standards that protect end users. Comodo Group CEO Melih Abdulhayoğlu is considered the founder of the CCSF.[39]
- CA/Browser Forum – In 2005, a new consortium of Certificate Authorities and web browser vendors was formed to promote industry standards and baseline requirements for internet security. Comodo Group CEO Melih Abdulhayoğlu organized the first meeting and is considered the founder of the CA/Browser Forum.[40][41]

Baseline requirements

The CA/Browser Forum publishes the Baseline Requirements,[42] a list of policies and technical requirements for CAs to follow. These are a requirement for inclusion in the certificate stores of Firefox[43] and Safari.[44]

CA compromise

If the CA can be subverted, then the security of the entire system is lost, potentially subverting all the entities that trust the compromised CA.

For example, suppose an attacker, Eve, manages to get a CA to issue to her a certificate that claims to represent Alice. That is, the certificate would publicly state that it represents Alice, and might include other information about Alice. Some of the information about Alice, such as her employer name, might be true, increasing the certificate's credibility. Eve, however, would have the all-important private key associated with the certificate. Eve could then use the certificate to send a digitally signed email to Bob, tricking Bob into believing that the email was from Alice. Bob might even respond with encrypted email, believing that it could only be read by Alice, when Eve is actually able to decrypt it using the private key.

A notable case of CA subversion like this occurred in 2001, when the certificate authority VeriSign issued two certificates to a person claiming to represent Microsoft. The certificates have the name "Microsoft Corporation", so they could be used to spoof someone into believing that updates to Microsoft software came from Microsoft when they actually did not. The fraud was detected in early 2001. Microsoft and VeriSign took steps to limit the impact of the problem.[45][46]

In 2008, Comodo reseller Certstar sold a certificate for mozilla.com to Eddy Nigg, who had no authority to represent Mozilla.[47]

In 2011 fraudulent certificates were obtained from Comodo and DigiNotar,[48][49] allegedly by Iranian hackers. There is evidence that the fraudulent DigiNotar certificates were used in a man-in-the-middle attack in Iran.[50]

In 2012, it became known that Trustwave issued a subordinate root certificate that was used for transparent traffic management (man-in-the-middle) which effectively permitted an enterprise to sniff SSL internal network traffic using the subordinate certificate.[51]

Key storage

An attacker who steals a certificate authority's private keys is able to forge certificates as if they were CA, without needed ongoing access to the CA's systems. Key theft is therefore one of the main risks certificate authorities defend against. Publicly trusted CAs almost always store their keys on a hardware security module (HSM), which allows them to sign certificates with a key, but generally prevent extraction of that key with both physical and software controls. CAs typically take the further precaution of keeping the key for their long-term root certificates in an HSM that is kept offline, except when it is needed to sign shorter-lived intermediate certificates. The intermediate certificates, stored in an online HSM, can do the day-to-day work of signing end-entity certificates and keeping revocation information up to date.

CAs sometimes use a key ceremony when generating signing keys, in order to ensure that the keys are not tampered with or copied.

Implementation weakness of the trusted third party scheme

The critical weakness in the way that the current X.509 scheme is implemented is that any CA trusted by a particular party can then issue certificates for any domain they choose. Such certificates will be accepted as valid by the trusting party whether they are legitimate and authorized or not.[52] This is a serious shortcoming given that the most commonly encountered technology employing X.509 and trusted third parties is the HTTPS protocol. As all major web browsers are distributed to their end-users pre-configured with a list of trusted CAs that numbers in the dozens this means that any one of these pre-approved trusted CAs can issue a valid certificate for any domain whatsoever.[53] The industry response to this has been muted.[54] Given that the contents of a browser's pre-configured trusted CA list is determined independently by the party that is distributing or causing to be installed the browser application there is really nothing that the CAs themselves can do.

This issue is the driving impetus behind the development of the DNS-based Authentication of Named Entities (DANE) protocol. If adopted in conjunction with Domain Name System Security Extensions (DNSSEC) DANE will greatly reduce if not eliminate the role of trusted third parties in a domain's PKI.

Vulnerability

Vulnerabilities are flaws in a computer system that weaken the overall security of the device/system. Vulnerabilities can be weaknesses in either the hardware itself, or the software that runs on the hardware. Vulnerabilities can be exploited by a threat actor, such as an attacker, to cross privilege boundaries (i.e. perform unauthorized actions) within a computer system. To exploit a vulnerability, an attacker must have at least one applicable tool or technique that can connect to a system weakness. In this frame, vulnerabilities are also known as the attack surface.

Vulnerability management is a cyclical practice that varies in theory but contains common processes which include: discover all assets, prioritize assets, assess or perform a complete vulnerability scan, report on results, remediate vulnerabilities, verify remediation - repeat. This practice generally refers to software vulnerabilities in computing systems.[1] Agile vulnerability management refers to preventing attacks by identifying all vulnerabilities as quickly as possible.[2]

A security risk is often incorrectly classified as a vulnerability. The use of vulnerability with the same meaning of risk can lead to confusion. The risk is the potential of a significant impact resulting from the exploit of a vulnerability. Then there are vulnerabilities without risk: for example when the affected asset has no value. A vulnerability with one or more known instances of working and fully implemented attacks is classified as an exploitable vulnerability—a vulnerability for which an exploit exists. The window of vulnerability is the time from when the security hole was introduced or manifested in deployed software, to when access was removed, a security fix was available/deployed, or the attacker was disabled—see zero-day attack.

Security bug (security defect) is a narrower concept. There are vulnerabilities that are not related to software: hardware, site, personnel vulnerabilities are examples of vulnerabilities that are not software security bugs.

Constructs in programming languages that are difficult to use properly can manifest large numbers of vulnerabilities.

Definitions

ISO 27005 defines **vulnerability** as:[3]

> *A weakness of an asset or group of assets that can be exploited by one or more threats, where an asset is anything that has value to the organization, its business operations, and their continuity, including information resources that support the organization's mission*[4]

IETF RFC 4949 **vulnerability** as:[5]

> *A flaw or weakness in a system's design, implementation, or operation and management that could be exploited to violate the system's security policy*

The Committee on National Security Systems of United States of America defined **vulnerability** in CNSS Instruction No. 4009 dated 26 April 2010 National Information Assurance Glossary:[6]

> *Vulnerability—Weakness in an information system, system security procedures, internal controls, or implementation that could be exploited by a threat source.*

Many NIST publications define **vulnerability** in IT context in different publications: FISMApedia[7] term[8] provide a list. Between them SP 800-30,[9] give a broader one:

> *A flaw or weakness in system security procedures, design, implementation, or internal controls that could be exercised (accidentally triggered or intentionally exploited) and result in a security breach or a violation of the system's security policy.*

ENISA defines **vulnerability** in[10] as:

> *The existence of a weakness, design, or implementation error that can lead to an unexpected, undesirable event [G.11] compromising the security of the computer system, network, application, or protocol involved.(ITSEC)*

The Open Group defines **vulnerability** in[11] as

> *The probability that threat capability exceeds the ability to resist the threat.*

Factor Analysis of Information Risk (FAIR) defines **vulnerability** as:[12]

> *The probability that an asset will be unable to resist the actions of a threat agent*

According to FAIR vulnerability is related to Control Strength, i.e. the strength of control as compared to a standard measure of force and the threat Capabilities, i.e. the probable level of force that a threat agent is capable of applying against an asset.

ISACA defines **vulnerability** in Risk It framework as:

> *A weakness in design, implementation, operation or internal control*

Data and Computer Security: Dictionary of standards concepts and terms, authors Dennis Longley and Michael Shain, Stockton Press, ISBN 0-935859-17-9, defines **vulnerability** as:

1) In computer security, a weakness in automated systems security procedures, administrative controls, Internet controls, etc., that could be exploited by a threat to gain unauthorized access to information or to disrupt critical processing. 2) In computer security, a weakness in the physical layout, organization, procedures, personnel, management, administration, hardware or software that may be exploited to cause harm to the ADP system or activity. 3) In computer security, any weakness or flaw existing in a system. The attack or harmful event, or the opportunity available to a threat agent to mount that attack.

Matt Bishop and Dave Bailey[13] give the following definition of computer **vulnerability**:

A computer system is composed of states describing the current configuration of the entities that make up the computer system. The system computes through the application of state transitions that change the state of the system. All states reachable from a given initial state using a set of state transitions fall into the class of authorized or unauthorized, as defined by a security policy. In this paper, the definitions of these classes and transitions is considered axiomatic. A vulnerable state is an authorized state from which an unauthorized state can be reached using authorized state transitions. A compromised state is the state so reached. An attack is a sequence of authorized state transitions which end in a compromised state. By definition, an attack begins in a vulnerable state. A vulnerability is a characterization of a vulnerable state which distinguishes it from all non-vulnerable states. If generic, the vulnerability may characterize many vulnerable states; if specific, it may characterize only one...

National Information Assurance Training and Education Center defines **vulnerability**:[14][15]

A weakness in automated system security procedures, administrative controls, internal controls, and so forth, that could be exploited by a threat to gain unauthorized access to information or disrupt critical processing. 2. A weakness in system security procedures, hardware design, internal controls, etc., which could be exploited to gain unauthorized access to classified or sensitive information. 3. A weakness in the physical layout, organization, procedures, personnel, management, administration, hardware, or software that may be exploited to cause harm to the ADP system or activity. The presence of a vulnerability does not in itself cause harm; a vulnerability is merely a condition or set of conditions that may allow the ADP system or activity to be harmed by an attack. 4. An assertion primarily concerning entities of the internal environment (assets); we say that an asset (or class of assets) is vulnerable (in some way, possibly involving an agent or collection of agents); we write: $V(i,e)$ where: e may be an empty set. 5. Susceptibility to various threats. 6. A set of properties of a specific internal entity that, in union with a set of properties of a specific external entity, implies a risk. 7. The characteristics of a system which cause it to suffer a definite degradation (incapability to perform the designated mission) as a result of having been subjected to a certain level of effects in an unnatural (manmade) hostile environment.

Vulnerability and risk factor models

A resource (either physical or logical) may have one or more vulnerabilities that can be exploited by a threat actor. The result can potentially compromise the confidentiality, integrity or availability of resources (not necessarily the vulnerable one) belonging to an organization and/or other parties involved (customers, suppliers). The so-called CIA triad is a cornerstone of Information Security.

An attack can be *active* when it attempts to alter system resources or affect their operation, compromising integrity or availability. A "*passive attack*" attempts to learn or make use of information from the system but does not affect system resources, compromising confidentiality.[5]

OWASP (see figure) depicts the same phenomenon in slightly different terms: a threat agent through an attack vector exploits a weakness (vulnerability) of the system and the related security controls, causing a technical impact on an IT resource (asset) connected to a business impact.

The overall picture represents the risk factors of the risk scenario.[16]

Information security management system

A set of policies concerned with the information security management system (ISMS), has been developed to manage, according to Risk management principles, the countermeasures to ensure a security strategy is set up following the rules and regulations applicable to a given organization. These countermeasures are also called Security controls, but when applied to the transmission of information, they are called security services.[17]

Classification

Vulnerabilities are classified according to the asset class they are related to:[3]

- hardware
    - susceptibility to humidity or dust
    - susceptibility to unprotected storage
    - age-based wear that causes failure
    - over-heating
- software
    - insufficient testing
    - insecure coding
    - lack of audit trail
    - design flaw
- network
    - unprotected communication lines (e.g. lack of cryptography)
    - insecure network architecture
- personnel
    - inadequate recruiting process
    - inadequate security awareness
    - insider threat
- physical site
    - area subject to natural disasters (e.g. flood, earthquake)
    - interruption of power source

- organizational
    - lack of regular audits
    - lack of continuity plans
    - lack of security

Causes

- Complexity: Large, complex systems increase the probability of flaws and unintended access points.[18]
- Familiarity: Using common, well-known code, software, operating systems, and/or hardware increases the probability an attacker has or can find the knowledge and tools to exploit the flaw.[19]
- Connectivity: More physical connections, privileges, ports, protocols, and services and time each of those are accessible increase vulnerability.[12]
- Password management flaws: The computer user uses weak passwords that could be discovered by brute force.[20] The computer user stores the password on the computer where a program can access it. Users re-use passwords between many programs and websites.[18]
- Fundamental operating system design flaws: The operating system designer chooses to enforce suboptimal policies on user/program management. For example, operating systems with policies such as default permit grant every program and every user full access to the entire computer.[18] This operating system flaw allows viruses and malware to execute commands on behalf of the administrator.[21]
- Internet Website Browsing: Some internet websites may contain harmful Spyware or Adware that can be installed automatically on the computer systems. After visiting those websites, the computer systems become infected and personal information will be collected and passed on to third party individuals.[22]
- Software bugs: The programmer leaves an exploitable bug in a software program. The software bug may allow an attacker to misuse an application.[18]
- Unchecked user input: The program assumes that all user input is safe. Programs that do not check user input can allow unintended direct execution of commands or SQL statements (known as Buffer overflows, SQL injection or other non-validated inputs).[18]
- Not learning from past mistakes:[23][24] for example most vulnerabilities discovered in IPv4 protocol software were discovered in the new IPv6 implementations.[25]

The research has shown that the most vulnerable point in most information systems is the human user, operator, designer, or other human:[26] so humans should be considered in their different roles as asset, threat, information resources. Social engineering is an increasing security concern.

Consequences

The impact of a security breach can be very high.[27] Most legislation sees the failure of IT managers to address IT systems and applications vulnerabilities if they are known to them as misconduct; IT managers have a responsibility to manage IT risk.[28] Privacy law forces managers to act to reduce the impact or likelihood of that security risk. Information technology security audit is a way to let other independent people certify that the IT environment is managed properly and lessen the responsibilities, at least having demonstrated the good faith. Penetration test is a form of verification of the weakness and countermeasures adopted by an organization: a White hat hacker tries to attack an organization's information technology assets, to find out how easy or difficult it is to compromise the IT security.[29] The proper way to professionally manage the IT risk is to adopt an Information Security Management System, such as ISO/IEC 27002 or Risk IT and follow them, according to the security strategy set forth by the upper management.[17]

One of the key concept of information security is the principle of defence in depth, i.e. to set up a multilayer defense system that can:[27]

- prevent the exploit
- detect and intercept the attack
- find out the threat agents and prosecute them

Intrusion detection system is an example of a class of systems used to detect attacks.

Physical security is a set of measures to physically protect an information asset: if somebody can get physical access to the information asset, it is widely accepted that an attacker can access any information on it or make the resource unavailable to its legitimate users.

Some sets of criteria to be satisfied by a computer, its operating system and applications in order to meet a good security level have been developed: ITSEC and Common criteria are two examples.

Vulnerability disclosure

Coordinated disclosure (some refer to it as 'responsible disclosure' but that is considered a biased term by others) of vulnerabilities is a topic of great debate. As reported by The Tech Herald in August 2010, "Google, Microsoft, TippingPoint, and Rapid7 have issued guidelines and statements addressing how they will deal with disclosure going forward."[30] The other method is typically full disclosure, when all the details of a vulnerability is publicized, sometimes with the intent to put pressure on the software author to publish a fix more quickly. In January 2014 when Google revealed a Microsoft vulnerability before Microsoft released a patch to fix it, a Microsoft representative called for coordinated practices among software companies in revealing disclosures.[31]

Vulnerability inventory

Mitre Corporation maintains an incomplete list of publicly disclosed vulnerabilities in a system called Common Vulnerabilities and Exposures. This information is immediately shared with the National Institute of Standards and Technology (NIST), where each vulnerability is given a risk score using Common Vulnerability Scoring System (CVSS), Common Platform Enumeration (CPE) scheme, and Common Weakness Enumeration.

Cloud service providers often do not list security issues in their services using the CVE system.[32] There is currently no universal standard for cloud computing vulnerability enumeration, severity assessment, and no unified tracking mechanism.[33] The Open CVDB initiative is a community-driven centralized cloud vulnerability database that catalogs CSP vulnerabilities, and lists the steps users can take to detect or prevent these issues in their own environments.[34]

OWASP maintains a list of vulnerability classes with the aim of educating system designers and programmers, therefore reducing the likelihood of vulnerabilities being written unintentionally into the software.[35]

Vulnerability disclosure date

The time of disclosure of a vulnerability is defined differently in the security community and industry. It is most commonly referred to as "a kind of public disclosure of security information by a certain party". Usually, vulnerability information is discussed on a mailing list or published on a security web site and results in a security advisory afterward.

The **time of disclosure** is the first date a security vulnerability is described on a channel where the disclosed information on the vulnerability has to fulfill the following requirement:

- The information is freely available to the public
- The vulnerability information is published by a trusted and independent channel/source
- The vulnerability has undergone analysis by experts such that risk rating information is included upon disclosure

Identifying and removing vulnerabilities

Many software tools exist that can aid in the discovery (and sometimes removal) of vulnerabilities in a computer system. Though these tools can provide an auditor with a good overview of possible vulnerabilities present, they can not replace human judgment. Relying solely on scanners will yield false positives and a limited-scope view of the problems present in the system.

Vulnerabilities have been found in every major operating system [36] including Windows, macOS, various forms of Unix and Linux, OpenVMS, and others. The only way to reduce the chance of a vulnerability being used against a system is through constant vigilance, including careful system maintenance (e.g. applying software patches), best practices in deployment (e.g. the use of firewalls and access controls) and auditing (both during development and throughout the deployment lifecycle).

Locations in which vulnerabilities manifest

Vulnerabilities are related to and can manifest in:

- physical environment of the system
- the personnel (i.e. employees, management)
- administration procedures and security policy
- business operation and service delivery
- hardware including peripheral devices [37] [38]
- software (i.e. on premises or in cloud)
- connectivity (i.e. communication equipment and facilities)

It is evident that a pure technical approach cannot always protect physical assets: one should have administrative procedure to let maintenance personnel to enter the facilities and people with adequate knowledge of the procedures, motivated to follow it with proper care. However, technical protections do not necessarily stop Social engineering (security) attacks.

Examples of vulnerabilities:

- an attacker finds and uses a buffer overflow weakness to install malware to then exfiltrate sensitive data;
- an attacker convinces a user to open an email message with attached malware;
- a flood damages one's computer systems installed at ground floor.

Software vulnerabilities

Common types of software flaws that lead to vulnerabilities include:
- Memory safety violations, such as:
    - Buffer overflows and over-reads
    - Dangling pointers
- Input validation errors, such as:
    - Code injection
    - Cross-site scripting in web applications
    - Directory traversal
    - Email injection
    - Format string attacks
    - HTTP header injection
    - HTTP response splitting
    - SQL injection
- Privilege-confusion bugs, such as:
    - Clickjacking
    - Cross-site request forgery in web applications
    - FTP bounce attack
- Privilege escalation
- Race conditions, such as:
    - Symlink races
    - Time-of-check-to-time-of-use bugs
- Side-channel attack
    - Timing attack
- User interface failures, such as:
    - Blaming the Victim prompting a user to make a security decision without giving the user enough information to answer it[39]
    - Race conditions[40][41]
    - Warning fatigue[42] or user conditioning.

Some set of coding guidelines have been developed and a large number of static code analyzers has been used to verify that the code follows the guidelines.

Computer Network

A **computer network** is a set of computers sharing resources located on or provided by network nodes. Computers use common communication protocols over digital interconnections to communicate with each other. These interconnections are made up of telecommunication network technologies based on physically wired, optical, and wireless radio-frequency methods that may be arranged in a variety of network topologies.

The nodes of a computer network can include personal computers, servers, networking hardware, or other specialized or general-purpose hosts. They are identified by network addresses and may have hostnames. Hostnames serve as memorable labels for the nodes and are rarely changed after initial assignment. Network addresses serve for locating and identifying the nodes by communication protocols such as the Internet Protocol.

Computer networks may be classified by many criteria, including the transmission medium used to carry signals, bandwidth, communications protocols to organize network traffic, the network size, the topology, traffic control mechanisms, and organizational intent.

Computer networks support many applications and services, such as access to the World Wide Web, digital video and audio, shared use of application and storage servers, printers and fax machines, and use of email and instant messaging applications.

History

Computer networking may be considered a branch of computer science, computer engineering, and telecommunications, since it relies on the theoretical and practical application of the related disciplines. Computer networking was influenced by a wide array of technology developments and historical milestones.

- In the late 1950s, a network of computers was built for the U.S. military Semi-Automatic Ground Environment (SAGE) radar system[1][2][3] using the Bell 101 modem. It was the first commercial modem for computers, released by AT&T Corporation in 1958. The modem allowed digital data to be transmitted over regular unconditioned telephone lines at a speed of 110 bits per second (bit/s).
- In 1959, Christopher Strachey filed a patent application for time-sharing and John McCarthy initiated the first project to implement time-sharing of user programs at MIT.[4][5][6][7] Stratchey passed the concept on to J. C. R. Licklider at the inaugural UNESCO Information Processing Conference in Paris that year.[8] McCarthy was instrumental in the creation of three of the earliest time-sharing systems (the Compatible Time-Sharing System in 1961, the BBN Time-Sharing System in 1962, and the Dartmouth Time Sharing System in 1963).
- In 1959, Anatoly Kitov proposed to the Central Committee of the Communist Party of the Soviet Union a detailed plan for the re-organisation of the control of the Soviet armed forces and of the Soviet economy on the basis of a network of computing centres.[9] Kitov's proposal was rejected, as later was the 1962 OGAS economy management network project.[10]
- In 1960, the commercial airline reservation system semi-automatic business research environment (SABRE) went online with two connected mainframes.
- In 1963, J. C. R. Licklider sent a memorandum to office colleagues discussing the concept of the "Intergalactic Computer Network", a computer network intended to allow general communications among computer users.
- Throughout the 1960s, Paul Baran and Donald Davies independently developed the concept of packet switching to transfer information between computers over a network.[11][12][13] Davies pioneered the implementation of the concept. The NPL network,

a local area network at the National Physical Laboratory (United Kingdom) used a line speed of 768 kbit/s and later high-speed T1 links (1.544 Mbit/s line rate).[14][15][16]

- In 1965, Western Electric introduced the first widely used telephone switch that implemented computer control in the switching fabric.
- In 1969, the first four nodes of the ARPANET were connected using 50 kbit/s circuits between the University of California at Los Angeles, the Stanford Research Institute, the University of California at Santa Barbara, and the University of Utah.[17] In the early 1970s, Leonard Kleinrock carried out mathematical work to model the performance of packet-switched networks, which underpinned the development of the ARPANET.[18][19] His theoretical work on hierarchical routing in the late 1970s with student Farouk Kamoun remains critical to the operation of the Internet today.
- In 1972, commercial services were first deployed on public data networks in Europe,[20][21][22] which began using X.25 in the late 1970s and spread across the globe.[14] The underlying infrastructure was used for expanding TCP/IP networks in the 1980s.[23]
- In 1973, the French CYCLADES network, directed by Louis Pouzin was the first to make the hosts responsible for the reliable delivery of data, rather than this being a centralized service of the network itself.[24]
- In 1973, Peter Kirstein put internetworking into practice at University College London (UCL), connecting the ARPANET to British academic networks, the first international heterogeneous computer network.[25][26]
- In 1973, Robert Metcalfe wrote a formal memo at Xerox PARC describing Ethernet, a networking system that was based on the Aloha network, developed in the 1960s by Norman Abramson and colleagues at the University of Hawaii. In July 1976, Robert Metcalfe and David Boggs published their paper "Ethernet: Distributed Packet Switching for Local Computer Networks"[27] and collaborated on several patents received in 1977 and 1978.
- In 1974, Vint Cerf, Yogen Dalal, and Carl Sunshine published the Transmission Control Protocol (TCP) specification, RFC 675, coining the term *Internet* as a shorthand for internetworking.[28]
- In 1976, John Murphy of Datapoint Corporation created ARCNET, a token-passing network first used to share storage devices.
- In 1977, the first long-distance fiber network was deployed by GTE in Long Beach, California.
- In 1977, Xerox Network Systems (XNS) was developed by Robert Metcalfe and Yogen Dalal at Xerox.[29]
- In 1979, Robert Metcalfe pursued making Ethernet an open standard.[30]
- In 1980, Ethernet was upgraded from the original 2.94 Mbit/s protocol to the 10 Mbit/s protocol, which was developed by Ron Crane, Bob Garner, Roy Ogus,[31] and Yogen Dalal.[32]
- In 1995, the transmission speed capacity for Ethernet increased from 10 Mbit/s to 100 Mbit/s. By 1998, Ethernet supported transmission speeds of 1 Gbit/s. Subsequently, higher speeds of up to 400 Gbit/s were added (as of 2018). The scaling of Ethernet has been a contributing factor to its continued use.[30]

Use

Computer networks extend interpersonal communications by electronic means with various technologies, such as email, instant messaging, online chat, voice and video telephone calls, and video conferencing. A network allows sharing of network and computing resources. Users may access and use resources provided by devices on the network, such as printing a document on a shared network printer or use of a shared storage device. A network allows sharing of files, data, and other types of information giving authorized users the ability to access information stored on other computers on the network. Distributed computing uses computing resources across a network to accomplish tasks.

Network packet

Most modern computer networks use protocols based on packet-mode transmission. A network packet is a formatted unit of data carried by a packet-switched network.

Packets consist of two types of data: control information and user data (payload). The control information provides data the network needs to deliver the user data, for example, source and destination network addresses, error detection codes, and sequencing information. Typically, control information is found in packet headers and trailers, with payload data in between.

With packets, the bandwidth of the transmission medium can be better shared among users than if the network were circuit switched. When one user is not sending packets, the link can be filled with packets from other users, and so the cost can be shared, with relatively little interference, provided the link is not overused. Often the route a packet needs to take through a network is not immediately available. In that case, the packet is queued and waits until a link is free.

The physical link technologies of packet networks typically limit the size of packets to a certain maximum transmission unit (MTU). A longer message may be fragmented before it is transferred and once the packets arrive, they are reassembled to construct the original message.

Network topology

The physical or geographic locations of network nodes and links generally have relatively little effect on a network, but the topology of interconnections of a network can significantly affect its throughput and reliability. With many technologies, such as bus or star networks, a single failure can cause the network to fail entirely. In general, the more interconnections there are, the more robust the network is; but the more expensive it is to install. Therefore, most network diagrams are arranged by their network topology which is the map of logical interconnections of network hosts.

Common topologies are:

- Bus network: all nodes are connected to a common medium along this medium. This was the layout used in the original Ethernet, called 10BASE5 and 10BASE2. This is still a common topology on the data link layer, although modern physical layer variants use point-to-point links instead, forming a star or a tree.
- Star network: all nodes are connected to a special central node. This is the typical layout found in a small switched Ethernet LAN, where each client connects to a central

network switch, and logically in a wireless LAN, where each wireless client associates with the central wireless access point.
- Ring network: each node is connected to its left and right neighbor node, such that all nodes are connected and that each node can reach each other node by traversing nodes left- or rightwards. Token ring networks, and the Fiber Distributed Data Interface (FDDI), made use of such a topology.
- Mesh network: each node is connected to an arbitrary number of neighbors in such a way that there is at least one traversal from any node to any other.
- Fully connected network: each node is connected to every other node in the network.
- Tree network: nodes are arranged hierarchically. This is the natural topology for a larger Ethernet network with multiple switches and without redundant meshing.

The physical layout of the nodes in a network may not necessarily reflect the network topology. As an example, with FDDI, the network topology is a ring, but the physical topology is often a star, because all neighboring connections can be routed via a central physical location. Physical layout is not completely irrelevant, however, as common ducting and equipment locations can represent single points of failure due to issues like fires, power failures and flooding.

Overlay network

An overlay network is a virtual network that is built on top of another network. Nodes in the overlay network are connected by virtual or logical links. Each link corresponds to a path, perhaps through many physical links, in the underlying network. The topology of the overlay network may (and often does) differ from that of the underlying one. For example, many peer-to-peer networks are overlay networks. They are organized as nodes of a virtual system of links that run on top of the Internet.[33]

Overlay networks have been around since the invention of networking when computer systems were connected over telephone lines using modems before any data network existed.

The most striking example of an overlay network is the Internet itself. The Internet itself was initially built as an overlay on the telephone network.[33] Even today, each Internet node can communicate with virtually any other through an underlying mesh of sub-networks of wildly different topologies and technologies. Address resolution and routing are the means that allow mapping of a fully connected IP overlay network to its underlying network.

Another example of an overlay network is a distributed hash table, which maps keys to nodes in the network. In this case, the underlying network is an IP network, and the overlay network is a table (actually a map) indexed by keys.

Overlay networks have also been proposed as a way to improve Internet routing, such as through quality of service guarantees achieve higher-quality streaming media. Previous proposals such as IntServ, DiffServ, and IP multicast have not seen wide acceptance largely because they require modification of all routers in the network. On the other hand, an overlay network can be incrementally deployed on end-hosts running the overlay protocol software, without cooperation from Internet service providers. The overlay network has no control over how packets are routed in the underlying network between two overlay nodes, but it can control, for example, the sequence of overlay nodes that a message traverses before it reaches its destination.

For example, Akamai Technologies manages an overlay network that provides reliable, efficient content delivery (a kind of multicast). Academic research includes end system multicast,[34] resilient routing and quality of service studies, among others.

Network links

The transmission media (often referred to in the literature as the *physical medium*) used to link devices to form a computer network include electrical cable, optical fiber, and free space. In the OSI model, the software to handle the media is defined at layers 1 and 2 — the physical layer and the data link layer.

A widely adopted *family* that uses copper and fiber media in local area network (LAN) technology are collectively known as Ethernet. The media and protocol standards that enable communication between networked devices over Ethernet are defined by IEEE 802.3. Wireless LAN standards use radio waves, others use infrared signals as a transmission medium. Power line communication uses a building's power cabling to transmit data.

Wired

The following classes of wired technologies are used in computer networking.

- *Coaxial cable* is widely used for cable television systems, office buildings, and other work-sites for local area networks. Transmission speed ranges from 200 million bits per second to more than 500 million bits per second.
- ITU-T G.hn technology uses existing home wiring (coaxial cable, phone lines and power lines) to create a high-speed local area network.
- *Twisted pair* cabling is used for wired Ethernet and other standards. It typically consists of 4 pairs of copper cabling that can be utilized for both voice and data transmission. The use of two wires twisted together helps to reduce crosstalk and electromagnetic induction. The transmission speed ranges from 2 Mbit/s to 10 Gbit/s. Twisted pair cabling comes in two forms: unshielded twisted pair (UTP) and shielded twisted-pair (STP). Each form comes in several category ratings, designed for use in various scenarios.

- An *optical fiber* is a glass fiber. It carries pulses of light that represent data via lasers and optical amplifiers. Some advantages of optical fibers over metal wires are very low transmission loss and immunity to electrical interference. Using dense wave division multiplexing, optical fibers can simultaneously carry multiple streams of data on different wavelengths of light, which greatly increases the rate that data can be sent to up to trillions of bits per second. Optic fibers can be used for long runs of cable carrying very high data rates, and are used for undersea communications cables to interconnect continents. There are two basic types of fiber optics, single-mode optical fiber (SMF) and multi-mode optical fiber (MMF). Single-mode fiber has the advantage of being able to sustain a coherent signal for dozens or even a hundred kilometers. Multimode fiber is cheaper to terminate but is limited to a few hundred or even only a few dozens of meters, depending on the data rate and cable grade.[35]

Wireless

Network connections can be established wirelessly using radio or other electromagnetic means of communication.

- *Terrestrial microwave* – Terrestrial microwave communication uses Earth-based transmitters and receivers resembling satellite dishes. Terrestrial microwaves are in the low gigahertz range, which limits all communications to line-of-sight. Relay stations are spaced approximately 40 miles (64 km) apart.
- *Communications satellites* – Satellites also communicate via microwave. The satellites are stationed in space, typically in geosynchronous orbit 35,400 km (22,000 mi) above the equator. These Earth-orbiting systems are capable of receiving and relaying voice, data, and TV signals.
- *Cellular networks* use several radio communications technologies. The systems divide the region covered into multiple geographic areas. Each area is served by a low-power transceiver.
- *Radio and spread spectrum technologies* – Wireless LANs use a high-frequency radio technology similar to digital cellular. Wireless LANs use spread spectrum technology to enable communication between multiple devices in a limited area. IEEE 802.11 defines a common flavor of open-standards wireless radio-wave technology known as Wi-Fi.
- *Free-space optical communication* uses visible or invisible light for communications. In most cases, line-of-sight propagation is used, which limits the physical positioning of communicating devices.
- Extending the Internet to interplanetary dimensions via radio waves and optical means, the Interplanetary Internet.[36]
- IP over Avian Carriers was a humorous April fool's Request for Comments, issued as RFC 1149. It was implemented in real life in 2001.[37]

The last two cases have a large round-trip delay time, which gives slow two-way communication but does not prevent sending large amounts of information (they can have high throughput).

Network nodes

Apart from any physical transmission media, networks are built from additional basic system building blocks, such as network interface controllers, repeaters, hubs, bridges, switches, routers, modems, and firewalls. Any particular piece of equipment will frequently contain multiple building blocks and so may perform multiple functions.

Network interfaces

An ATM network interface in the form of an accessory card. A lot of network interfaces are built-in.

A network interface controller (NIC) is computer hardware that connects the computer to the network media and has the ability to process low-level network information. For example, the NIC may have a connector for accepting a cable, or an aerial for wireless transmission and reception, and the associated circuitry.

In Ethernet networks, each NIC has a unique Media Access Control (MAC) address—usually stored in the controller's permanent memory. To avoid address conflicts between network devices, the Institute of Electrical and Electronics Engineers (IEEE) maintains and administers MAC address uniqueness. The size of an Ethernet MAC address is six octets. The three most significant octets are reserved to identify NIC manufacturers. These manufacturers, using only their assigned prefixes, uniquely assign the three least-significant octets of every Ethernet interface they produce.

Repeaters and hubs

A repeater is an electronic device that receives a network signal, cleans it of unnecessary noise and regenerates it. The signal is retransmitted at a higher power level, or to the other side of obstruction so that the signal can cover longer distances without degradation. In most twisted-pair Ethernet configurations, repeaters are required for cable that runs longer than 100 meters. With fiber optics, repeaters can be tens or even hundreds of kilometers apart.

Repeaters work on the physical layer of the OSI model but still require a small amount of time to regenerate the signal. This can cause a propagation delay that affects network performance and may affect proper function. As a result, many network architectures limit the number of repeaters used in a network, e.g., the Ethernet 5-4-3 rule.

An Ethernet repeater with multiple ports is known as an Ethernet hub. In addition to reconditioning and distributing network signals, a repeater hub assists with collision detection and fault isolation for the network. Hubs and repeaters in LANs have been largely obsoleted by modern network switches.

Bridges and switches

Network bridges and network switches are distinct from a hub in that they only forward frames to the ports involved in the communication whereas a hub forwards to all ports.[38] Bridges only have two ports but a switch can be thought of as a multi-port bridge. Switches normally have numerous ports, facilitating a star topology for devices, and for cascading additional switches.

Bridges and switches operate at the data link layer (layer 2) of the OSI model and bridge traffic between two or more network segments to form a single local network. Both are devices that forward frames of data between ports based on the destination MAC address in each frame.[39] They learn the association of physical ports to MAC addresses by examining the source addresses of received frames and only forward the frame when necessary. If an unknown destination MAC is targeted, the device broadcasts the request to all ports except the source, and discovers the location from the reply.

Bridges and switches divide the network's collision domain but maintain a single broadcast domain. Network segmentation through bridging and switching helps break down a large, congested network into an aggregation of smaller, more efficient networks.

Routers

A router is an internetworking device that forwards packets between networks by processing the addressing or routing information included in the packet. The routing information is often processed in conjunction with the routing table. A router uses its routing table to determine where to forward packets and does not require broadcasting packets which is inefficient for very big networks.

Modems

Modems (modulator-demodulator) are used to connect network nodes via wire not originally designed for digital network traffic, or for wireless. To do this one or more carrier signals are modulated by the digital signal to produce an analog signal that can be tailored to give the required properties for transmission. Early modems modulated audio signals sent over a standard voice telephone line. Modems are still commonly used for telephone lines, using a digital subscriber line technology and cable television systems using DOCSIS technology.

Firewalls

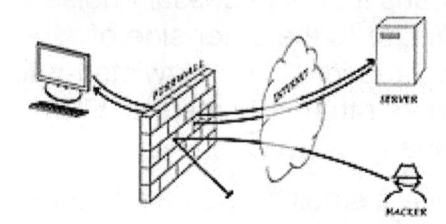

Firewall

A firewall is a network device or software for controlling network security and access rules. Firewalls are inserted in connections between secure internal networks and potentially insecure external networks such as the Internet. Firewalls are typically configured to reject access requests from unrecognized sources while allowing actions from recognized ones. The vital role firewalls play in network security grows in parallel with the constant increase in cyber attacks.

Communication protocols

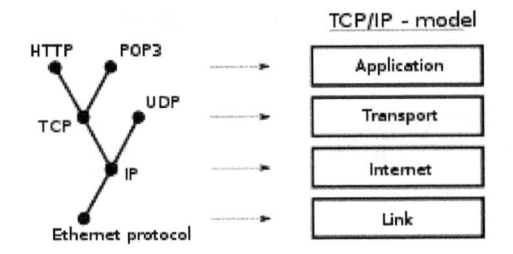

The TCP/IP model and its relation to common protocols used at different layers of the model.

A communication protocol is a set of rules for exchanging information over a network. Communication protocols have various characteristics. They may be connection-oriented or connectionless, they may use circuit mode or packet switching, and they may use hierarchical addressing or flat addressing.

In a protocol stack, often constructed per the OSI model, communications functions are divided up into protocol layers, where each layer leverages the services of the layer below it until the lowest layer controls the hardware that sends information across the media. The use of protocol layering is ubiquitous across the field of computer networking. An important example of a protocol stack is HTTP (the World Wide Web protocol) running over TCP over IP (the Internet protocols) over IEEE 802.11 (the Wi-Fi protocol). This stack is used between the wireless router and the home user's personal computer when the user is surfing the web.

There are many communication protocols, a few of which are described below.

Common protocols

Internet protocol suite

The Internet protocol suite, also called TCP/IP, is the foundation of all modern networking. It offers connection-less and connection-oriented services over an inherently unreliable network traversed by datagram transmission using Internet protocol (IP). At its core, the protocol suite defines the addressing, identification, and routing specifications for Internet Protocol Version 4 (IPv4) and for IPv6, the next generation of the protocol with a much enlarged addressing capability. The Internet protocol suite is the defining set of protocols for the Internet.[40]

IEEE 802

IEEE 802 is a family of IEEE standards dealing with local area networks and metropolitan area networks. The complete IEEE 802 protocol suite provides a diverse set of networking capabilities. The protocols have a flat addressing scheme. They operate mostly at layers 1 and 2 of the OSI model.

For example, MAC bridging (IEEE 802.1D) deals with the routing of Ethernet packets using a Spanning Tree Protocol. IEEE 802.1Q describes VLANs, and IEEE 802.1X defines a port-based Network Access Control protocol, which forms the basis for the authentication mechanisms used in VLANs[41] (but it is also found in WLANs[42]) – it is what the home user sees when the user has to enter a "wireless access key".

Ethernet

Ethernet is a family of technologies used in wired LANs. It is described by a set of standards together called IEEE 802.3 published by the Institute of Electrical and Electronics Engineers.

Wireless LAN

Wireless LAN based on the IEEE 802.11 standards, also widely known as WLAN or WiFi, is probably the most well-known member of the IEEE 802 protocol family for home users today. IEEE 802.11 shares many properties with wired Ethernet.

SONET/SDH

Synchronous optical networking (SONET) and Synchronous Digital Hierarchy (SDH) are standardized multiplexing protocols that transfer multiple digital bit streams over optical fiber using lasers. They were originally designed to transport circuit mode communications from a variety of different sources, primarily to support circuit-switched digital telephony. However, due to its protocol neutrality and transport-oriented features, SONET/SDH also was the obvious choice for transporting Asynchronous Transfer Mode (ATM) frames.

Asynchronous Transfer Mode

Asynchronous Transfer Mode (ATM) is a switching technique for telecommunication networks. It uses asynchronous time-division multiplexing and encodes data into small, fixed-sized cells. This differs from other protocols such as the Internet protocol suite or Ethernet that use variable-sized packets or frames. ATM has similarities with both circuit and packet switched networking. This makes it a good choice for a network that must handle both traditional high-throughput data traffic, and real-time, low-latency content such as voice and video. ATM uses a connection-oriented model in which a virtual circuit must be established between two endpoints before the actual data exchange begins.

ATM still plays a role in the last mile, which is the connection between an Internet service provider and the home user.[43][needs update]

Cellular standards

There are a number of different digital cellular standards, including: Global System for Mobile Communications (GSM), General Packet Radio Service (GPRS), cdmaOne, CDMA2000, Evolution-Data Optimized (EV-DO), Enhanced Data Rates for GSM Evolution (EDGE), Universal Mobile Telecommunications System (UMTS), Digital Enhanced Cordless Telecommunications (DECT), Digital AMPS (IS-136/TDMA), and Integrated Digital Enhanced Network (iDEN).[44]

Routing

Routing is the process of selecting network paths to carry network traffic. Routing is performed for many kinds of networks, including circuit switching networks and packet switched networks.

In packet-switched networks, routing protocols direct packet forwarding through intermediate nodes. Intermediate nodes are typically network hardware devices such as routers, bridges, gateways, firewalls, or switches. General-purpose computers can also forward packets and perform routing, though because they lack specialized hardware, may offer limited performance. The routing process directs forwarding on the basis of routing tables, which maintain a record of the routes to various network destinations. Most routing algorithms use only one network path at a time. Multipath routing techniques enable the use of multiple alternative paths.

Routing can be contrasted with bridging in its assumption that network addresses are structured and that similar addresses imply proximity within the network. Structured addresses allow a single routing table entry to represent the route to a group of devices. In large networks, the structured addressing used by routers outperforms unstructured addressing used by bridging. Structured IP addresses are used on the Internet. Unstructured MAC addresses are used for bridging on Ethernet and similar local area networks.

Geographic scale

Networks may be characterized by many properties or features, such as physical capacity, organizational purpose, user authorization, access rights, and others. Another distinct classification method is that of the physical extent or geographic scale.

Nanoscale network

A nanoscale network has key components implemented at the nanoscale, including message carriers, and leverages physical principles that differ from macroscale communication mechanisms. Nanoscale communication extends communication to very small sensors and actuators such as those found in biological systems and also tends to operate in environments that would be too harsh for other communication techniques.[45]

Personal area network

A personal area network (PAN) is a computer network used for communication among computers and different information technological devices close to one person. Some examples of devices that are used in a PAN are personal computers, printers, fax machines, telephones, PDAs, scanners, and video game consoles. A PAN may include wired and wireless devices. The reach of a PAN typically extends to 10 meters.[46] A wired PAN is usually constructed with USB and FireWire connections while technologies such as Bluetooth and infrared communication typically form a wireless PAN.

Local area network

A local area network (LAN) is a network that connects computers and devices in a limited geographical area such as a home, school, office building, or closely positioned group of buildings. Wired LANs are most commonly based on Ethernet technology. Other networking technologies such as ITU-T G.hn also provide a way to create a wired LAN using existing wiring, such as coaxial cables, telephone lines, and power lines.[47]

A LAN can be connected to a wide area network (WAN) using a router. The defining characteristics of a LAN, in contrast to a WAN, include higher data transfer rates, limited geographic range, and lack of reliance on leased lines to provide connectivity. Current Ethernet or other IEEE 802.3 LAN technologies operate at data transfer rates up to and in excess of 100 Gbit/s,[48] standardized by IEEE in 2010.

Home area network

A home area network (HAN) is a residential LAN used for communication between digital devices typically deployed in the home, usually a small number of personal computers and accessories, such as printers and mobile computing devices. An important function is the sharing of Internet access, often a broadband service through a cable Internet access or digital subscriber line (DSL) provider.

Storage area network

A storage area network (SAN) is a dedicated network that provides access to consolidated, block-level data storage. SANs are primarily used to make storage devices, such as disk arrays, tape libraries, and optical jukeboxes, accessible to servers so that the storage appears as locally attached devices to the operating system. A SAN typically has its own network of storage devices that are generally not accessible through the local area network by other devices. The cost and complexity of SANs dropped in the early 2000s to levels allowing wider adoption across both enterprise and small to medium-sized business environments.

Campus area network

A campus area network (CAN) is made up of an interconnection of LANs within a limited geographical area. The networking equipment (switches, routers) and transmission media (optical fiber, Cat5 cabling, etc.) are almost entirely owned by the campus tenant or owner (an enterprise, university, government, etc.).

For example, a university campus network is likely to link a variety of campus buildings to connect academic colleges or departments, the library, and student residence halls.

Backbone network

A backbone network is part of a computer network infrastructure that provides a path for the exchange of information between different LANs or subnetworks. A backbone can tie together diverse networks within the same building, across different buildings, or over a wide area. When designing a network backbone, network performance and network congestion are critical factors to take into account. Normally, the backbone network's capacity is greater than that of the individual networks connected to it.

For example, a large company might implement a backbone network to connect departments that are located around the world. The equipment that ties together the departmental networks constitutes the network backbone. Another example of a backbone network is the Internet backbone, which is a massive, global system of fiber-optic cable and optical networking that carry the bulk of data between wide area networks (WANs), metro, regional, national and transoceanic networks.

Metropolitan area network

A metropolitan area network (MAN) is a large computer network that interconnects users with computer resources in a geographic region of the size of a metropolitan area.

Wide area network

A wide area network (WAN) is a computer network that covers a large geographic area such as a city, country, or spans even intercontinental distances. A WAN uses a communications channel that combines many types of media such as telephone lines, cables, and airwaves. A WAN often makes use of transmission facilities provided by common carriers, such as telephone companies. WAN technologies generally function at the lower three layers of the OSI model: the physical layer, the data link layer, and the network layer.

Enterprise private network

An enterprise private network is a network that a single organization builds to interconnect its office locations (e.g., production sites, head offices, remote offices, shops) so they can share computer resources.

Virtual private network

A virtual private network (VPN) is an overlay network in which some of the links between nodes are carried by open connections or virtual circuits in some larger network (e.g., the Internet) instead of by physical wires. The data link layer protocols of the virtual network are said to be tunneled through the larger network. One common application is secure communications through the public Internet, but a VPN need not have explicit security features, such as authentication or content encryption. VPNs, for example, can be used to separate the traffic of different user communities over an underlying network with strong security features.

VPN may have best-effort performance or may have a defined service level agreement (SLA) between the VPN customer and the VPN service provider.

Global area network

A global area network (GAN) is a network used for supporting mobile users across an arbitrary number of wireless LANs, satellite coverage areas, etc. The key challenge in mobile communications is handing off communications from one local coverage area to the next. In IEEE Project 802, this involves a succession of terrestrial wireless LANs.[49]

Organizational scope

Networks are typically managed by the organizations that own them. Private enterprise networks may use a combination of intranets and extranets. They may also provide network access to the Internet, which has no single owner and permits virtually unlimited global connectivity.

Intranet

An intranet is a set of networks that are under the control of a single administrative entity. An intranet typically uses the Internet Protocol and IP-based tools such as web browsers and file transfer applications. The administrative entity limits the use of the intranet to its authorized users. Most commonly, an intranet is the internal LAN of an organization. A large intranet typically has at least one web server to provide users with organizational information.

Extranet

An extranet is a network that is under the administrative control of a single organization but supports a limited connection to a specific external network. For example, an organization may provide access to some aspects of its intranet to share data with its business partners or customers. These other entities are not necessarily trusted from a security standpoint. The network connection to an extranet is often, but not always, implemented via WAN technology.

Internet

An internetwork is the connection of multiple different types of computer networks to form a single computer network using higher-layer network protocols and connecting them together using routers.

The Internet is the largest example of internetwork. It is a global system of interconnected governmental, academic, corporate, public, and private computer networks. It is based on the networking technologies of the Internet protocol suite. It is the successor of the Advanced Research Projects Agency Network (ARPANET) developed by DARPA of the United States Department of Defense. The Internet utilizes copper communications and an optical networking backbone to enable the World Wide Web (WWW), the Internet of things, video transfer, and a broad range of information services.

Participants on the Internet use a diverse array of methods of several hundred documented, and often standardized, protocols compatible with the Internet protocol suite and the IP addressing system administered by the Internet Assigned Numbers Authority and address registries. Service providers and large enterprises exchange information about the reachability of their address spaces through the Border Gateway Protocol (BGP), forming a redundant worldwide mesh of transmission paths.

Darknet

A darknet is an overlay network, typically running on the Internet, that is only accessible through specialized software. It is an anonymizing network where connections are made only between trusted peers — sometimes called *friends* (F2F)[51] — using non-standard protocols and ports.

Darknets are distinct from other distributed peer-to-peer networks as sharing is anonymous (that is, IP addresses are not publicly shared), and therefore users can communicate with little fear of governmental or corporate interference.[52]

Network service

Network services are applications hosted by servers on a computer network, to provide some functionality for members or users of the network, or to help the network itself to operate.

The World Wide Web, E-mail,[53] printing and network file sharing are examples of well-known network services. Network services such as Domain Name System (DNS) give names for IP and MAC addresses (people remember names like *nm.lan* better than numbers like *210.121.67.18*),[54] and Dynamic Host Configuration Protocol (DHCP) to ensure that the equipment on the network has a valid IP address.[55]

Services are usually based on a service protocol that defines the format and sequencing of messages between clients and servers of that network service.

Network performance

Bandwidth

Bandwidth in bit/s may refer to consumed bandwidth, corresponding to achieved throughput or goodput, i.e., the average rate of successful data transfer through a communication path. The throughput is affected by processes such as bandwidth shaping, bandwidth management, bandwidth throttling, bandwidth cap and bandwidth allocation (using, for example, bandwidth allocation protocol and dynamic bandwidth allocation).

Network delay

Network delay is a design and performance characteristic of a telecommunications network. It specifies the latency for a bit of data to travel across the network from one communication endpoint to another. It is typically measured in multiples or fractions of a second. Delay may differ slightly, depending on the location of the specific pair of communicating endpoints. Engineers usually report both the maximum and average delay, and they divide the delay into several parts:

- Processing delay – time it takes a router to process the packet header
- Queuing delay – time the packet spends in routing queues
- Transmission delay – time it takes to push the packet's bits onto the link
- Propagation delay – time for a signal to propagate through the media

A certain minimum level of delay is experienced by signals due to the time it takes to transmit a packet serially through a link. This delay is extended by more variable levels of delay due to network congestion. IP network delays can range from a few milliseconds to several hundred milliseconds.

Quality of service

Depending on the installation requirements, network performance is usually measured by the quality of service of a telecommunications product. The parameters that affect this typically can include throughput, jitter, bit error rate and latency.

The following list gives examples of network performance measures for a circuit-switched network and one type of packet-switched network, viz. ATM:

- Circuit-switched networks: In circuit switched networks, network performance is synonymous with the grade of service. The number of rejected calls is a measure of how well the network is performing under heavy traffic loads.[56] Other types of performance measures can include the level of noise and echo.
- ATM: In an Asynchronous Transfer Mode (ATM) network, performance can be measured by line rate, quality of service (QoS), data throughput, connect time, stability, technology, modulation technique, and modem enhancements.[57][verification needed][full citation needed]

There are many ways to measure the performance of a network, as each network is different in nature and design. Performance can also be modeled instead of measured. For example, state transition diagrams are often used to model queuing performance in a circuit-switched network. The network planner uses these diagrams to analyze how the network performs in each state, ensuring that the network is optimally designed.[58]

Network congestion

Network congestion occurs when a link or node is subjected to a greater data load than it is rated for, resulting in a deterioration of its quality of service. When networks are congested and queues become too full, packets have to be discarded, and so networks rely on re-transmission. Typical effects of congestion include queueing delay, packet loss or the blocking of new connections. A consequence of these latter two is that incremental increases in offered load lead either to only a small increase in the network throughput or to a reduction in network throughput.

Network protocols that use aggressive retransmissions to compensate for packet loss tend to keep systems in a state of network congestion—even after the initial load is reduced to a level that would not normally induce network congestion. Thus, networks using these protocols can exhibit two stable states under the same level of load. The stable state with low throughput is known as *congestive collapse*.

Modern networks use congestion control, congestion avoidance and traffic control techniques to try to avoid congestion collapse (i.e. endpoints typically slow down or sometimes even stop transmission entirely when the network is congested). These techniques include: exponential backoff in protocols such as 802.11's CSMA/CA and the original Ethernet, window reduction in TCP, and fair queueing in devices such as routers. Another method to avoid the negative effects of network congestion is implementing priority schemes so that some packets are transmitted with higher priority than others. Priority schemes do not solve network congestion by themselves, but they help to alleviate the effects of congestion for some services. An example of this is 802.1p. A third method to avoid network congestion is the explicit allocation of network resources to specific flows. One example of this is the use of Contention-Free Transmission Opportunities (CFTXOPs) in the ITU-T G.hn standard, which provides high-speed (up to 1 Gbit/s) Local area networking over existing home wires (power lines, phone lines and coaxial cables).

For the Internet, RFC 2914 addresses the subject of congestion control in detail.

Network resilience

Network resilience is "the ability to provide and maintain an acceptable level of service in the face of faults and challenges to normal operation."[59]

Security

Computer networks are also used by security hackers to deploy computer viruses or computer worms on devices connected to the network, or to prevent these devices from accessing the network via a denial-of-service attack.

Network security

Network Security consists of provisions and policies adopted by the network administrator to prevent and monitor unauthorized access, misuse, modification, or denial of the computer network and its network-accessible resources.[60] Network security is the authorization of access to data in a network, which is controlled by the network administrator. Users are assigned an ID and password that allows them access to information and programs within their authority. Network security is used on a variety of computer networks, both public and private, to secure daily transactions and communications among businesses, government agencies, and individuals.

Network surveillance

Network surveillance is the monitoring of data being transferred over computer networks such as the Internet. The monitoring is often done surreptitiously and may be done by or at the behest of governments, by corporations, criminal organizations, or individuals. It may or may not be legal and may or may not require authorization from a court or other independent agency.

Computer and network surveillance programs are widespread today, and almost all Internet traffic is or could potentially be monitored for clues to illegal activity.

Surveillance is very useful to governments and law enforcement to maintain social control, recognize and monitor threats, and prevent/investigate criminal activity. With the advent of programs such as the Total Information Awareness program, technologies such as high-speed surveillance computers and biometrics software, and laws such as the Communications Assistance For Law Enforcement Act, governments now possess an unprecedented ability to monitor the activities of citizens.[61]

However, many civil rights and privacy groups—such as Reporters Without Borders, the Electronic Frontier Foundation, and the American Civil Liberties Union—have expressed concern that increasing surveillance of citizens may lead to a mass surveillance society, with limited political and personal freedoms. Fears such as this have led to numerous lawsuits such as *Hepting v. AT&T*.[61][62] The hacktivist group Anonymous has hacked into government websites in protest of what it considers "draconian surveillance".[63][64]

End to end encryption

End-to-end encryption (E2EE) is a digital communications paradigm of uninterrupted protection of data traveling between two communicating parties. It involves the originating party encrypting data so only the intended recipient can decrypt it, with no dependency on third parties. End-to-end encryption prevents intermediaries, such as Internet service providers or application service providers, from discovering or tampering with communications. End-to-end encryption generally protects both confidentiality and integrity.

Examples of end-to-end encryption include HTTPS for web traffic, PGP for email, OTR for instant messaging, ZRTP for telephony, and TETRA for radio.

Typical server-based communications systems do not include end-to-end encryption. These systems can only guarantee the protection of communications between clients and servers, not between the communicating parties themselves. Examples of non-E2EE systems are Google Talk, Yahoo Messenger, Facebook, and Dropbox. Some such systems, for example, LavaBit and SecretInk, have even described themselves as offering "end-to-end" encryption when they do not. Some systems that normally offer end-to-end encryption have turned out to contain a back door that subverts negotiation of the encryption key between the communicating parties, for example Skype or Hushmail.

The end-to-end encryption paradigm does not directly address risks at the endpoints of the communication themselves, such as the technical exploitation of clients, poor quality random number generators, or key escrow. E2EE also does not address traffic analysis, which relates to things such as the identities of the endpoints and the times and quantities of messages that are sent.

SSL/TLS

The introduction and rapid growth of e-commerce on the World Wide Web in the mid-1990s made it obvious that some form of authentication and encryption was needed. Netscape took the first shot at a new standard. At the time, the dominant web browser was Netscape Navigator. Netscape created a standard called secure socket layer (SSL). SSL requires a server with a certificate. When a client requests access to an SSL-secured server, the server sends a copy of the certificate to the client. The SSL client checks this certificate (all web browsers come with an exhaustive list of CA root certificates preloaded), and if the certificate checks out, the server is authenticated and the client negotiates a symmetric-key cipher for use in the session. The session is now in a very secure encrypted tunnel between the SSL server and the SSL client.[35]

Views of networks

Users and network administrators typically have different views of their networks. Users can share printers and some servers from a workgroup, which usually means they are in the same geographic location and are on the same LAN, whereas a Network Administrator is responsible to keep that network up and running. A community of interest has less of a connection of being in a local area and should be thought of as a set of arbitrarily located users who share a set of servers, and possibly also communicate via peer-to-peer technologies.

Network administrators can see networks from both physical and logical perspectives. The physical perspective involves geographic locations, physical cabling, and the network elements (e.g., routers, bridges and application layer gateways) that interconnect via the transmission media. Logical networks, called, in the TCP/IP architecture, subnets, map onto one or more transmission media. For example, a common practice in a campus of buildings is to make a set of LAN cables in each building appear to be a common subnet, using VLAN technology.

Both users and administrators are aware, to varying extents, of the trust and scope characteristics of a network. Again using TCP/IP architectural terminology, an intranet is a community of interest under private administration usually by an enterprise, and is only accessible by authorized users (e.g. employees).[65] Intranets do not have to be connected to the Internet, but generally have a limited connection. An extranet is an extension of an intranet that allows secure communications to users outside of the intranet (e.g. business partners, customers).[65]

Unofficially, the Internet is the set of users, enterprises, and content providers that are interconnected by Internet Service Providers (ISP). From an engineering viewpoint, the Internet is the set of subnets, and aggregates of subnets, that share the registered IP address space and exchange information about the reachability of those IP addresses using the Border Gateway Protocol. Typically, the human-readable names of servers are translated to IP addresses, transparently to users, via the directory function of the Domain Name System (DNS).

Over the Internet, there can be business-to-business (B2B), business-to-consumer (B2C) and consumer-to-consumer (C2C) communications. When money or sensitive information is exchanged, the communications are apt to be protected by some form of communications security mechanism. Intranets and extranets can be securely superimposed onto the Internet, without any access by general Internet users and administrators, using secure Virtual Private Network (VPN) technology.

Cloud Computing

Cloud computing[1] is the on-demand availability of computer system resources, especially data storage (cloud storage) and computing power, without direct active management by the user.[2] Large clouds often have functions distributed over multiple locations, each of which is a data center. Cloud computing relies on sharing of resources to achieve coherence and typically uses a pay-as-you-go model, which can help in reducing capital expenses but may also lead to unexpected operating expenses for users.[3]

Definition

The United States National Institute of Standards and Technology's definition of cloud computing identifies "five essential characteristics":

- **On-demand self-service.** A consumer can unilaterally provision computing capabilities, such as server time and network storage, as needed automatically without requiring human interaction with each service provider.
- **Broad network access.** Capabilities are available over the network and accessed through standard mechanisms that promote use by heterogeneous thin or thick client platforms (e.g., mobile phones, tablets, laptops, and workstations).
- **Resource pooling.** The provider's computing resources are pooled to serve multiple consumers using a multi-tenant model, with different physical and virtual resources dynamically assigned and reassigned according to consumer demand.
- **Rapid elasticity.** Capabilities can be elastically provisioned and released, in some cases automatically, to scale rapidly outward and inward commensurate with demand. To the consumer, the capabilities available for provisioning often appear unlimited and can be appropriated in any quantity at any time.
- **Measured service.** Cloud systems automatically control and optimize resource use by leveraging a metering capability at some level of abstraction appropriate to the type of service (e.g., storage, processing, bandwidth, and active user accounts). Resource usage can be monitored, controlled, and reported, providing transparency for both the provider and consumer of the utilized service.[4]

History

Cloud computing has a rich history that extends back to the 1960s, with the initial concepts of time-sharing becoming popularized via Remote Job Entry (RJE). The "data center" model, where users submitted jobs to operators to run on mainframes, was predominantly used during this era. This was a time of exploration and experimentation with ways to make large-scale computing power available to more users through time-sharing, optimizing the infrastructure, platform, and applications, and increasing efficiency for end users.[5]

The use of the "cloud" metaphor to denote virtualized services traces back to 1994, when it was used by General Magic to describe the universe of "places" that mobile agents in the Telescript environment could go. This metaphor is credited to David Hoffman, a General Magic communications employee, based on its long-standing use in networking and telecom.[6] The expression *cloud computing* became more widely known in 1996 when the Compaq Computer Corporation drew up a business plan for future computing and the Internet. The company's ambition was to supercharge sales with "cloud computing-enabled applications". The business plan foresaw that online consumer file storage would most likely be commercially successful. As a result, Compaq decided to sell server hardware to internet service providers.[7]

In the 2000s, the application of cloud computing began to take shape with the establishment of Amazon Web Services in 2002, which allowed developers to build applications independently. In 2006 the beta version of Google Docs was released, Amazon Simple Storage Service, known as Amazon S3, and the Amazon Elastic Compute Cloud (EC2), in 2008 NASA's development of the first open-source software for deploying private and hybrid clouds.[8][9]

The following decade saw the launch of various cloud services. In 2010, Microsoft launched Microsoft Azure, and Rackspace Hosting and NASA initiated an open-source cloud-software project, OpenStack. IBM introduced the IBM SmartCloud framework in 2011, and Oracle announced the Oracle Cloud in 2012. In December 2019, Amazon launched AWS Outposts, a service that extends AWS infrastructure, services, APIs, and tools to customer data centers, co-location spaces, or on-premises facilities.[10][11]

Since the global pandemic of 2020, cloud technology has surged in popularity due to the level of data security it offers and the flexibility of working options it provides for all employees, notably remote workers.[12]

Value proposition

Advocates of public and hybrid clouds claim that cloud computing allows companies to avoid or minimize up-front IT infrastructure costs. Proponents also claim that cloud computing allows enterprises to get their applications up and running faster, with improved manageability and less maintenance, and that it enables IT teams to more rapidly adjust resources to meet fluctuating and unpredictable demand,[13][14][15] providing **burst computing** capability: high computing power at certain periods of peak demand.[16]

Additional value propositions of cloud computing include:

Topic	Description
Cost reductions	A public-cloud delivery model converts capital expenditures (e.g., buying servers) to operational expenditure.[17] This purportedly lowers barriers to entry, as infrastructure is typically provided by a third party and need not be purchased for one-time or infrequent intensive computing tasks. Pricing on a utility computing basis is "fine-grained", with usage-based billing options. As well, less in-house IT skills are required for implementation of projects that use cloud computing.[18] The e-FISCAL project's state-of-the-art repository[19] contains several articles looking into cost aspects in more detail, most of them concluding that costs savings depend on the type of activities supported and the type of infrastructure available in-house.
Device independence	Device and location independence[20] enable users to access systems using a web browser regardless of their location or what device they use (e.g., PC, mobile phone). As infrastructure is off-site (typically provided by a third-party) and accessed via the Internet, users can connect to it from anywhere.[18]
Maintenance	Maintenance of cloud environment is easier because the data is hosted on an outside server maintained by a provider without the need to invest in data center hardware. IT maintenance of

	cloud computing is managed and updated by the cloud provider's IT maintenance team which reduces cloud computing costs compared with on-premises data centers.
Multitenancy	Multitenancy enables sharing of resources and costs across a large pool of users thus allowing for: - centralization of infrastructure in locations with lower costs (such as real estate, electricity, etc.) - peak-load capacity increases (users need not engineer and pay for the resources and equipment to meet their highest possible load-levels) - utilization and efficiency improvements for systems that are often only 10–20% utilized.[21][22]
Performance	Performance is monitored by IT experts from the service provider, and consistent and loosely coupled architectures are constructed using web services as the system interface.[18][23]
Productivity	Productivity may be increased when multiple users can work on the same data simultaneously, rather than waiting for it to be saved and emailed. Time may be saved as information does not need to be re-entered when fields are matched, nor do users need to install application software upgrades to their computer.
Availability	Availability improves with the use of multiple redundant sites, which makes well-designed cloud computing suitable for business continuity and disaster recovery.[24]
Scalability and Elasticity	Scalability and elasticity via dynamic ("on-demand") provisioning of resources on a fine-grained, self-service basis in near real-time[25][26] (Note, the VM startup time varies by VM type, location, OS and cloud providers[25]), without users having to engineer for peak loads.[27][28][29] This gives the ability to scale up when the usage need increases or down if resources are not being used.[30] The time-efficient benefit of cloud scalability also means faster time to market, more business flexibility, and adaptability, as adding new resources does not take as much time as it used to.[31] Emerging approaches for managing elasticity include the use of machine learning techniques to propose efficient elasticity models.[32]
Security	Security can improve due to centralization of data, increased security-focused resources, etc., but concerns can persist about loss of control over certain sensitive data, and the lack of security for stored kernels. Security is often as good as or better than other traditional systems, in part because service providers are able to devote resources to solving security issues that many customers cannot afford to tackle or which they lack the technical skills to address.[33] However, the complexity of security is greatly increased when data is distributed over a wider area or over a greater number of devices, as well as in multi-tenant systems shared by unrelated users. In addition, user access to security audit logs may be difficult or impossible. Private cloud installations are in part motivated by users' desire to retain control over the infrastructure and avoid losing control of information security.

Challenges and limitations

One of the main challenges of cloud computing, in comparison to more traditional on-premises computing, is data security and privacy. Cloud users entrust their sensitive data to third-party providers, who may not have adequate measures to protect it from unauthorized access, breaches, or leaks. Cloud users also face compliance risks if they have to adhere to certain regulations or standards regarding data protection, such as GDPR or HIPAA.[34]

Another challenge of cloud computing is reduced visibility and control. Cloud users may not have full insight into how their cloud resources are managed, configured, or optimized by their providers. They may also have limited ability to customize or modify their cloud services according to their specific needs or preferences.[34] Complete understanding of all technology may be impossible, especially given the scale, complexity, and deliberate opacity of contemporary systems; however, there is a need for understanding complex technologies and their interconnections to have power and agency within them.[35] The metaphor of the cloud can be seen as problematic as cloud computing retains the aura of something noumenal and numinous; it is something experienced without precisely understanding what it is or how it works.[36]

In addition, cloud migration is a significant issue. Cloud migration is the process of moving data, applications, or workloads from one cloud environment to another or from on-premises to the cloud. Cloud migration can be complex, time-consuming, and costly, especially if there are incompatibility issues between different cloud platforms or architectures. Cloud migration can also cause downtime, performance degradation, or data loss if not planned and executed properly.[37]

Service models

Cloud clients
Web browser, mobile app, thin client, IoT devices, machines, ...

Cloud application (SaaS)
CRM, ERP, web conferencing, group chat, email, analytics, virtual desktop, games, ...

Cloud platform (PaaS)
Application runtime, database, web server, developer services, data lake, ...

Resources more abstracted (e.g. serverless)

Cloud infrastructure (IaaS)
Virtual machines, bare metal servers, storage, load balancers, networking, ...

Resources less abstracted

Deployment model
Public cloud, hybrid cloud, multicloud, private cloud

Cloud computing service models arranged as layers in a stack

The service-oriented architecture (SOA) promotes the idea of "Everything as a Service" (EaaS or XaaS, or simply aAsS).[38] This concept is operationalized in cloud computing through several service models as defined by the National Institute of Standards and Technology (NIST). The three standard service models are Infrastructure as a Service (IaaS), Platform as a Service (PaaS), and Software as a Service (SaaS).[4] They are commonly depicted as layers in a stack, providing different levels of abstraction. However, these layers are not necessarily interdependent. For instance, SaaS can be delivered on bare metal, bypassing PaaS and IaaS, and a program can run directly on IaaS without being packaged as SaaS.

Infrastructure as a service (IaaS)

"Infrastructure as a service" (IaaS) refers to online services that provide high-level APIs used to abstract various low-level details of underlying network infrastructure like physical computing resources, location, data partitioning, scaling, security, backup, etc. A hypervisor runs the virtual machines as guests. Pools of hypervisors within the cloud operational system can support large numbers of virtual machines and the ability to scale services up and down according to customers' varying requirements. Linux containers run in isolated partitions of a single Linux kernel running directly on the physical hardware. Linux cgroups and namespaces are the underlying Linux kernel technologies used to isolate, secure and manage the containers. The use of containers offers higher performance than virtualization because there is no hypervisor overhead. IaaS clouds often offer additional resources such as a virtual-machine disk-image library, raw block storage, file or object storage, firewalls, load balancers, IP addresses, virtual local area networks (VLANs), and software bundles.[39]

The NIST's definition of cloud computing describes IaaS as "where the consumer is able to deploy and run arbitrary software, which can include operating systems and applications. The consumer does not manage or control the underlying cloud infrastructure but has control over operating systems, storage, and deployed applications; and possibly limited control of select networking components (e.g., host firewalls)."[4]

IaaS-cloud providers supply these resources on-demand from their large pools of equipment installed in data centers. For wide-area connectivity, customers can use either the Internet or carrier clouds (dedicated virtual private networks). To deploy their applications, cloud users install operating-system images and their application software on the cloud infrastructure. In this model, the cloud user patches and maintains the operating systems and the application software. Cloud providers typically bill IaaS services on a utility computing basis: cost reflects the number of resources allocated and consumed.[40]

Platform as a service (PaaS)

The NIST's definition of cloud computing defines Platform as a Service as:[4]

The capability provided to the consumer is to deploy onto the cloud infrastructure consumer-created or acquired applications created using programming languages, libraries, services, and tools supported by the provider. The consumer does not manage or control the underlying cloud infrastructure including network, servers, operating systems, or storage, but has control over the deployed applications and possibly configuration settings for the application-hosting environment.

PaaS vendors offer a development environment to application developers. The provider typically develops toolkit and standards for development and channels for distribution and payment. In the PaaS models, cloud providers deliver a computing platform, typically including an operating system, programming-language execution environment, database, and the web server. Application developers develop and run their software on a cloud platform instead of directly buying and managing the underlying hardware and software layers. With some PaaS, the underlying computer and storage resources scale automatically to match application demand so that the cloud user does not have to allocate resources manually.[41][need quotation to verify]

Some integration and data management providers also use specialized applications of PaaS as delivery models for data. Examples include **iPaaS (Integration Platform as a Service)** and **dPaaS (Data Platform as a Service)**. iPaaS enables customers to develop, execute and govern integration flows.[42] Under the iPaaS integration model, customers drive the development and deployment of integrations without installing or managing any hardware or middleware.[43] dPaaS delivers integration—and data-management—products as a fully managed service.[44] Under the dPaaS model, the PaaS provider, not the customer, manages the development and execution of programs by building data applications for the customer. dPaaS users access data through data-visualization tools.[45]

Software as a service (SaaS)

The NIST's definition of cloud computing defines Software as a Service as:[4]

The capability provided to the consumer is to use the provider's applications running on a cloud infrastructure. The applications are accessible from various client devices through either a thin client interface, such as a web browser (e.g., web-based email), or a program interface. The consumer does not manage or control the underlying cloud infrastructure including network, servers, operating systems, storage, or even individual application capabilities, with the possible exception of limited user-specific application configuration settings.

In the software as a service (SaaS) model, users gain access to application software and databases. Cloud providers manage the infrastructure and platforms that run the applications. SaaS is sometimes referred to as "on-demand software" and is usually priced on a pay-per-use basis or using a subscription fee.[46] In the SaaS model, cloud providers install and operate application software in the cloud and cloud users access the software from cloud clients. Cloud users do not manage the cloud infrastructure and platform where the application runs. This eliminates the need to install and run the application on the cloud user's own computers, which simplifies maintenance and support. Cloud applications differ from other applications in their scalability—which can be achieved by cloning tasks onto multiple virtual machines at run-time to meet changing work demand.[47] Load balancers distribute the work over the set of virtual machines. This process is transparent to the cloud user, who sees only a single access-point. To accommodate a large number of cloud users, cloud applications can be *multitenant*, meaning that any machine may serve more than one cloud-user organization.

The pricing model for SaaS applications is typically a monthly or yearly flat fee per user,[48] so prices become scalable and adjustable if users are added or removed at any point. It may also be free.[49] Proponents claim that SaaS gives a business the potential to reduce IT operational costs by outsourcing hardware and software maintenance and support to the cloud provider. This enables the business to reallocate IT operations costs away from hardware/software spending and from personnel expenses, towards meeting other goals. In addition, with applications hosted centrally, updates can be released without the need for users to install new software. One drawback of SaaS comes with storing the users' data on the cloud provider's server. As a result, there could be unauthorized access to the data.[50] Examples of applications offered as SaaS are games and productivity software like Google Docs and Office Online. SaaS applications may be integrated with cloud storage or File hosting services, which is the case with Google Docs being integrated with Google Drive, and Office Online being integrated with OneDrive.[51]

Mobile "backend" as a service (MBaaS)

In the mobile "backend" as a service (m) model, also known as "backend as a service" (BaaS), web app and mobile app developers are provided with a way to link their applications to cloud storage and cloud computing services with application programming interfaces (APIs) exposed to their applications and custom software development kits (SDKs). Services include user management, push notifications, integration with social networking services[52] and more. This is a relatively recent model in cloud computing,[53] with most BaaS startups dating from 2011 or later[54][55][56] but trends indicate that these services are gaining significant mainstream traction with enterprise consumers.[57]

Serverless computing or Function-as-a-Service (FaaS)

Serverless computing is a cloud computing code execution model in which the cloud provider fully manages starting and stopping virtual machines as necessary to serve requests. Requests are billed by an abstract measure of the resources required to satisfy the request, rather than per virtual machine per hour.[58] Despite the name, serverless computing does not actually involve running code without servers.[58] The business or person using the system does not have to purchase, rent or provide servers or virtual machines for the back-end code to run on.

Function as a service (FaaS) is a service-hosted remote procedure call that utilizes serverless computing to enable deploying individual functions in the cloud to run in response to events.[59] Some consider FaaS to fall under the umbrella of serverless computing, while others use the terms interchangeably.[60]

Deployment models

Private

Private cloud is cloud infrastructure operated solely for a single organization, whether managed internally or by a third party, and hosted either internally or externally.[4] Undertaking a private cloud project requires significant engagement to virtualize the business environment, and requires the organization to reevaluate decisions about existing resources. It can improve business, but every step in the project raises security issues that must be addressed to prevent serious vulnerabilities. Self-run data centers[61] are generally capital intensive. They have a significant physical footprint, requiring allocations of space, hardware, and environmental controls. These assets have to be refreshed periodically, resulting in additional capital expenditures. They have attracted criticism because users "still have to buy, build, and manage them" and thus do not benefit from less hands-on management,[62] essentially "[lacking] the economic model that makes cloud computing such an intriguing concept".[63][64]

Public

Cloud services are considered "public" when they are delivered over the public Internet, and they may be offered as a paid subscription, or free of charge.[65] Architecturally, there are few differences between public- and private-cloud services, but security concerns increase substantially when services (applications, storage, and other resources) are shared by multiple customers. Most public-cloud providers offer direct-connection services that allow customers to securely link their legacy data centers to their cloud-resident applications.[18][66]

Several factors like the functionality of the solutions, cost, integrational and organizational aspects as well as safety & security are influencing the decision of enterprises and organizations to choose a public cloud or on-premises solution.[67]

Hybrid

Hybrid cloud is a composition of a public cloud and a private environment, such as a private cloud or on-premises resources,[68][69] that remain distinct entities but are bound together, offering the benefits of multiple deployment models. Hybrid cloud can also mean the ability to connect collocation, managed and/or dedicated services with cloud resources.[4] Gartner defines a hybrid cloud service as a cloud computing service that is composed of some combination of private, public and community cloud services, from different service providers.[70] A hybrid cloud service crosses isolation and provider boundaries so that it cannot be simply put in one category of private, public, or community cloud service. It allows one to extend either the capacity or the capability of a cloud service, by aggregation, integration or customization with another cloud service.

Varied use cases for hybrid cloud composition exist. For example, an organization may store sensitive client data in house on a private cloud application, but interconnect that application to a business intelligence application provided on a public cloud as a software service.[71] This example of hybrid cloud extends the capabilities of the enterprise to deliver a specific business service through the addition of externally available public cloud services. Hybrid cloud adoption depends on a number of factors such as data security and compliance requirements, level of control needed over data, and the applications an organization uses.[72]

Another example of hybrid cloud is one where IT organizations use public cloud computing resources to meet temporary capacity needs that can not be met by the private cloud.[73] This capability enables hybrid clouds to employ cloud bursting for scaling across clouds.[4] Cloud bursting is an application deployment model in which an application runs in a private cloud or data center and "bursts" to a public cloud when the demand for computing capacity increases. A primary advantage of cloud bursting and a hybrid cloud model is that an organization pays for extra compute resources only when they are needed.[74] Cloud bursting enables data centers to create an in-house IT infrastructure that supports average workloads, and use cloud resources from public or private clouds, during spikes in processing demands.[75]

Others

Community

Community cloud shares infrastructure between several organizations from a specific community with common concerns (security, compliance, jurisdiction, etc.), whether managed internally or by a third-party, and either hosted internally or externally. The costs are spread over fewer users than a public cloud (but more than a private cloud), so only some of the cost savings potential of cloud computing are realized.[4]

Distributed

A cloud computing platform can be assembled from a distributed set of machines in different locations, connected to a single network or hub service. It is possible to distinguish between two types of distributed clouds: public-resource computing and volunteer cloud.

- **Public-resource computing** – This type of distributed cloud results from an expansive definition of cloud computing, because they are more akin to distributed computing than cloud computing. Nonetheless, it is considered a sub-class of cloud computing.
- **Volunteer cloud** – Volunteer cloud computing is characterized as the intersection of public-resource computing and cloud computing, where a cloud computing infrastructure is built using volunteered resources. Many challenges arise from this type of infrastructure, because of the volatility of the resources used to build it and the dynamic environment it operates in. It can also be called peer-to-peer clouds, or ad-hoc clouds. An interesting effort in such direction is Cloud@Home, it aims to implement a cloud computing infrastructure using volunteered resources providing a business-model to incentivize contributions through financial restitution.[76]

Multi

Multicloud is the use of multiple cloud computing services in a single heterogeneous architecture to reduce reliance on single vendors, increase flexibility through choice, mitigate against disasters, etc. It differs from hybrid cloud in that it refers to multiple cloud services, rather than multiple deployment modes (public, private, legacy).[77][78][79]

Poly

Poly cloud refers to the use of multiple public clouds for the purpose of leveraging specific services that each provider offers. It differs from Multi cloud in that it is not designed to increase flexibility or mitigate against failures but is rather used to allow an organization to achieve more that could be done with a single provider.[80]

Big data

The issues of transferring large amounts of data to the cloud as well as data security once the data is in the cloud initially hampered adoption of cloud for big data, but now that much data originates in the cloud and with the advent of bare-metal servers, the cloud has become[81] a solution for use cases including business analytics and geospatial analysis.[82]

HPC

HPC cloud refers to the use of cloud computing services and infrastructure to execute high-performance computing (HPC) applications.[83] These applications consume a considerable amount of computing power and memory and are traditionally executed on clusters of computers. In 2016 a handful of companies, including R-HPC, Amazon Web Services, Univa, Silicon Graphics International, Sabalcore, Gomput, and Penguin Computing offered a high-performance computing cloud. The Penguin On Demand (POD) cloud was one of the first non-virtualized remote HPC services offered on a pay-as-you-go basis.[84][85] Penguin Computing launched its HPC cloud in 2016 as an alternative to Amazon's EC2 Elastic Compute Cloud, which uses virtualized computing nodes.[86][87]

Architecture

Cloud architecture,[88] the systems architecture of the software systems involved in the delivery of cloud computing, typically involves multiple *cloud components* communicating with each other over a loose coupling mechanism such as a messaging queue. Elastic provision implies intelligence in the use of tight or loose coupling as applied to mechanisms such as these and others.

Cloud engineering

Cloud engineering is the application of engineering disciplines of cloud computing. It brings a systematic approach to the high-level concerns of commercialization, standardization and governance in conceiving, developing, operating and maintaining cloud computing systems. It is a multidisciplinary method encompassing contributions from diverse areas such as systems, software, web, performance, information technology engineering, security, platform, risk, and quality engineering.

Security and privacy

Cloud computing poses privacy concerns because the service provider can access the data that is in the cloud at any time. It could accidentally or deliberately alter or delete information.[89] Many cloud providers can share information with third parties if necessary for purposes of law and order without a warrant. That is permitted in their privacy policies, which users must agree to before they start using cloud services. Solutions to privacy include policy and legislation as well as end-users' choices for how data is stored.[89] Users can encrypt data that is processed or stored within the cloud to prevent unauthorized access.[89] Identity management systems can also provide practical solutions to privacy concerns in cloud computing. These systems distinguish between authorized and unauthorized users and determine the amount of data that is accessible to each entity.[90] The systems work by creating and describing identities, recording activities, and getting rid of unused identities.

According to the Cloud Security Alliance, the top three threats in the cloud are *Insecure Interfaces and APIs*, *Data Loss & Leakage*, and *Hardware Failure*—which accounted for 29%, 25% and 10% of all cloud security outages respectively. Together, these form shared technology vulnerabilities. In a cloud provider platform being shared by different users, there may be a possibility that information belonging to different customers resides on the same data server. Additionally, Eugene Schultz, chief technology officer at Emagined Security, said that hackers are spending substantial time and effort looking for ways to penetrate the cloud. "There are some real Achilles' heels in the cloud infrastructure that are making big holes for the bad guys to get into". Because data from hundreds or thousands of companies can be stored on large cloud servers, hackers can theoretically gain control of huge stores of information through a single attack—a process he called "hyperjacking". Some examples of this include the Dropbox security breach, and iCloud 2014 leak.[91] Dropbox had been breached in October 2014, having over 7 million of its users passwords stolen by hackers in an effort to get monetary value from it by Bitcoins (BTC). By having these passwords, they are able to read private data as well as have this data be indexed by search engines (making the information public).[91]

There is the problem of legal ownership of the data (If a user stores some data in the cloud, can the cloud provider profit from it?). Many Terms of Service agreements are silent on the question of ownership.[92] Physical control of the computer equipment (private cloud) is more secure than having the equipment off-site and under someone else's control (public cloud). This delivers great incentive to public cloud computing service providers to prioritize building and maintaining strong management of secure services.[93] Some small businesses that do not have expertise in IT security could find that it is more secure for them to use a public cloud. There is the risk that end users do not understand the issues involved when signing on to a cloud service (persons sometimes do not read the many pages of the terms of service agreement, and just click "Accept" without reading). This is important now that cloud computing is common and required for some services to work, for example for an intelligent personal assistant (Apple's Siri or Google Assistant). Fundamentally, private cloud is seen as more secure with higher levels of control for the owner, however public cloud is seen to be more flexible and requires less time and money investment from the user.[94]

Market

According to International Data Corporation (IDC), global spending on cloud computing services has reached $706 billion and expected to reach $1.3 trillion by 2025.[95] While Gartner estimated that global public cloud services end-user spending would reach $600 billion by 2023.[96] As per a McKinsey & Company report, cloud cost-optimization levers and value-oriented business use cases foresee more than $1 trillion in run-rate EBITDA across Fortune 500 companies as up for grabs in 2030.[97] In 2022, more than $1.3 trillion in enterprise IT spending was at stake from the shift to the cloud, growing to almost $1.8 trillion in 2025, according to Gartner.[98]

Similar concepts

The goal of cloud computing is to allow users to take benefit from all of these technologies, without the need for deep knowledge about or expertise with each one of them. The cloud aims to cut costs and helps the users focus on their core business instead of being impeded by IT obstacles.[99] The main enabling technology for cloud computing is virtualization. Virtualization software separates a physical computing device into one or more "virtual" devices, each of which can be easily used and managed to perform computing tasks. With operating system–level virtualization essentially creating a scalable system of multiple independent computing devices, idle computing resources can be allocated and used more efficiently. Virtualization provides the agility required to speed up IT operations and reduces cost by increasing infrastructure utilization. Autonomic computing automates the process through which the user can provision resources on-demand. By minimizing user involvement, automation speeds up the process, reduces labor costs and reduces the possibility of human errors.[99]

Cloud computing uses concepts from utility computing to provide metrics for the services used. Cloud computing attempts to address QoS (quality of service) and reliability problems of other grid computing models.[99]

Cloud computing shares characteristics with:

- Client–server model – *Client–server computing* refers broadly to any distributed application that distinguishes between service providers (servers) and service requestors (clients).[100]
- Computer bureau – A service bureau providing computer services, particularly from the 1960s to 1980s.
- Grid computing – A form of distributed and parallel computing, whereby a 'super and virtual computer' is composed of a cluster of networked, loosely coupled computers acting in concert to perform very large tasks.
- Fog computing – Distributed computing paradigm that provides data, compute, storage and application services closer to the client or near-user edge devices, such as network routers. Furthermore, fog computing handles data at the network level, on smart devices and on the end-user client-side (e.g. mobile devices), instead of sending data to a remote location for processing.
- Utility computing – The "packaging of computing resources, such as computation and storage, as a metered service similar to a traditional public utility, such as electricity."[101][102]

- Peer-to-peer – A distributed architecture without the need for central coordination. Participants are both suppliers and consumers of resources (in contrast to the traditional client-server model).
- Cloud sandbox – A live, isolated computer environment in which a program, code or file can run without affecting the application in which it runs.

Cloud Computing Security

Cloud computing security or, more simply, **cloud security**, refers to a broad set of policies, technologies, applications, and controls utilized to protect virtualized IP, data, applications, services, and the associated infrastructure of cloud computing. It is a sub-domain of computer security, network security, and, more broadly, information security.

Security issues associated with the cloud

Cloud computing and storage provide users with the capabilities to store and process their data in third-party data centers.[1] Organizations use the cloud in a variety of different service models (with acronyms such as SaaS, PaaS, and IaaS) and deployment models (private, public, hybrid, and community).[2]

Security concerns associated with cloud computing are typically categorized in two ways: as security issues faced by cloud providers (organizations providing software-, platform-, or infrastructure-as-a-service via the cloud) and security issues faced by their customers (companies or organizations who host applications or store data on the cloud).[3] The responsibility is shared, however, and is often detailed in a cloud provider's "shared security responsibility model" or "shared responsibility model."[4][5][6] The provider must ensure that their infrastructure is secure and that their clients' data and applications are protected, while the user must take measures to fortify their application and use strong passwords and authentication measures.[5][6]

When an organization elects to store data or host applications on the public cloud, it loses its ability to have physical access to the servers hosting its information. As a result, potentially sensitive data is at risk from insider attacks. According to a 2010 Cloud Security Alliance report, insider attacks are one of the top seven biggest threats in cloud computing.[7] Therefore, cloud service providers must ensure that thorough background checks are conducted for employees who have physical access to the servers in the data center. Additionally, data centers are recommended to be frequently monitored for suspicious activity.

In order to conserve resources, cut costs, and maintain efficiency, cloud service providers often store more than one customer's data on the same server. As a result, there is a chance that one user's private data can be viewed by other users (possibly even competitors). To handle such sensitive situations, cloud service providers should ensure proper data isolation and logical storage segregation.[2]

The extensive use of virtualization in implementing cloud infrastructure brings unique security concerns for customers or tenants of a public cloud service.[8] Virtualization alters the relationship between the OS and underlying hardware – be it computing, storage or even networking. This introduces an additional layer – virtualization – that itself must be properly configured, managed and secured.[9] Specific concerns include the potential to compromise the virtualization software, or "hypervisor". While these concerns are largely theoretical, they do exist.[10] For example, a breach in the administrator workstation with the management software of the virtualization software can cause the whole data center to go down or be reconfigured to an attacker's liking.

Cloud security controls

Cloud security architecture is effective only if the correct defensive implementations are in place. An efficient cloud security architecture should recognize the issues that will arise with security management and follow all of the best practices, procedures, and guidelines to ensure a secure cloud environment. Security management addresses these issues with security controls. These controls protect cloud environments and are put in place to safeguard any weaknesses in the system and reduce the effect of an attack. While there are many types of controls behind a cloud security architecture, they can usually be found in one of the following categories:

Deterrent controls

These controls are administrative mechanisms intended to reduce attacks on a cloud system and are utilized to ensure compliance with external controls. Much like a warning sign on a fence or a property, deterrent controls typically reduce the threat level by informing potential attackers that there will be adverse consequences for them if they proceed.[11] (Some consider them a subset of preventive controls.) Examples of such controls could be considered as policies, procedures, standards, guidelines, laws, and regulations that guide an organization towards security. Although most malicious actors ignore such deterrent controls, such controls are intended to ward off those who are inexperienced or curious about compromising the IT infrastructure of an organization.

Preventive controls

The main objective of preventive controls is to strengthen the system against incidents, generally by reducing if not actually eliminating vulnerabilities, as well as preventing unauthorized intruders from accessing or entering the system.[12] This could be achieved by either *adding* software or feature implementations (such as firewall protection, endpoint protection, and multi-factor authentication), or *removing* unneeded functionalities so that the attack surface is minimized (as in unikernel applications). Additionally, educating individuals through security awareness training and exercises is included in such controls due to human error being the weakest point of security. Strong authentication of cloud users, for instance, makes it less likely that unauthorized users can access cloud systems, and more likely that cloud users are positively identified. All in all, preventative controls affect the likelihood of a loss event occurring and are intended to prevent or eliminate the systems' exposure to malicious action.

Detective controls

Detective controls are intended to detect and react appropriately to any incidents that occur. In the event of an attack, a detective control will signal the preventative or corrective controls to address the issue. Detective security controls function not only when such an activity is in progress and after it has occurred. System and network security monitoring, including intrusion detection and prevention arrangements, are typically employed to detect attacks on cloud systems and the supporting communications infrastructure. Most organizations acquire or create a dedicated security operations center (SOC), where dedicated members continuously monitor the organization's IT infrastructure through logs and Security Information and Event Management (SIEM) software. SIEMs are security solutions that help organizations and security teams analyze "log data in real-time for swift detection of security incidents."[13] SIEMS are not the only examples of detective controls. There are also Physical security controls, Intrusion detection systems, and anti-virus/anti-malware tools, which all have different functions centered around the exact purpose of detecting security compromises within an IT infrastructure.

Corrective controls

Corrective controls reduce the consequences of an incident, generally by limiting the damage. Such controls include technical, physical, and administrative measures that occur during or after an incident to restore the systems or resources to their previous state after a security incident.[14] There are plenty of examples of corrective controls, both physical and technical. For instance, re-issuing an access card or repairing physical damage can be considered corrective controls. However, technical controls such as terminating a process and administrative controls such as implementing an incident response plan could also be considered corrective controls. Corrective controls are focused on recovering and repairing any damage caused by a security incident or unauthorized activity. The value is needed to change the function of security.

Dimensions of cloud security

Cloud security engineering is characterized by the security layers, plan, design, programming, and best practices that exist inside a cloud security arrangement. Cloud security engineering requires the composed and visual model (design and UI) to be characterized by the tasks inside the Cloud. This cloud security engineering process includes such things as access to the executives, techniques, and controls to ensure applications and information. It also includes ways to deal with and keep up with permeability, consistency, danger stance, and by and large security. Processes for imparting security standards into cloud administrations and activities assume an approach that fulfills consistent guidelines and essential framework security parts.[15]

For interest in Cloud advancements to be viable, companies should recognize the various parts of the Cloud and how they remain to impact and help them. These interests may include investments in cloud computing and security, for example. This of course leads to leads to driving push for the Cloud advancements to succeed.

Though the idea of cloud computing isn't new, associations are increasingly enforcing it because of its flexible scalability, relative trustability, and cost frugality of services. However, despite its rapid-fire relinquishment in some sectors and disciplines, it's apparent from exploration and statistics that security-related pitfalls are the most conspicuous hedge to its wide relinquishment.

It is generally recommended that information security controls be selected and implemented according to and in proportion to the risks, typically by assessing the threats, vulnerabilities and impacts. Cloud security concerns can be grouped in various ways; Gartner named seven[16] while the Cloud Security Alliance identified twelve areas of concern.[17] Cloud access security brokers (CASBs) are software that sits between cloud users and cloud applications to provide visibility into cloud application usage, data protection and governance to monitor all activity and enforce security policies.[18]

Security and privacy

Any service without a "hardened" environment is considered a "soft" target. Virtual servers should be protected just like a physical server against data leakage, malware, and exploited vulnerabilities. "Data loss or leakage represents 24.6% and cloud related malware 3.4% of threats causing cloud outages"[19]

Identity management

Every enterprise will have its own identity management system to control access to information and computing resources. Cloud providers either integrate the customer's identity management system into their own infrastructure, using federation or SSO technology or a biometric-based identification system,[1] or provide an identity management system of their own.[20] CloudID,[1] for instance, provides privacy-preserving cloud-based and cross-enterprise biometric identification. It links the confidential information of the users to their biometrics and stores it in an encrypted fashion. Making use of a searchable encryption technique, biometric identification is performed in the encrypted domain to make sure that the cloud provider or potential attackers do not gain access to any sensitive data or even the contents of the individual queries.[1]

Physical security

Cloud service providers physically secure the IT hardware (servers, routers, cables etc.) against unauthorized access, interference, theft, fires, floods etc. and ensure that essential supplies (such as electricity) are sufficiently robust to minimize the possibility of disruption. This is normally achieved by serving cloud applications from professionally specified, designed, constructed, managed, monitored and maintained data centers.

Personnel security

Various information security concerns relating to the IT and other professionals associated with cloud services are typically handled through pre-, para- and post-employment activities such as security screening potential recruits, security awareness and training programs, and proactive.

Privacy

Providers ensure that all critical data (credit card numbers, for example) are masked or encrypted and that only authorized users have access to data in its entirety. Moreover, digital identities and credentials must be protected as should any data that the provider collects or produces about customer activity in the cloud.

Penetration testing

Penetration testing is the process of performing offensive security tests on a system, service, or computer network to find security weaknesses in it. Since the cloud is a shared environment with other customers or tenants, following penetration testing rules of engagement step-by-step is a mandatory requirement. Scanning and penetration testing from inside or outside the cloud should be authorized by the cloud provider. Violation of acceptable use policies can lead to termination of the service.[21]

Cloud vulnerability and penetration testing

Scanning the cloud from outside and inside using free or commercial products is crucial because without a hardened environment your service is considered a soft target. Virtual servers should be hardened just like a physical server against data leakage, malware, and exploited vulnerabilities. "Data loss or leakage represents 24.6% and cloud-related malware 3.4% of threats causing cloud outages"

Scanning and penetration testing from inside or outside the cloud must be authorized by the cloud provider. Since the cloud is a shared environment with other customers or tenants, following penetration testing rules of engagement step-by-step is a mandatory requirement. Violation of acceptable use policies can lead to the termination of the service. Some key terminology to grasp when discussing penetration testing is the difference between application and network layer testing. Understanding what is asked of you as the tester is sometimes the most important step in the process. The network-layer testing refers to testing that includes internal/external connections as well as the interconnected systems throughout the local network. Oftentimes, social engineering attacks are carried out, as the most vulnerable link in security is often the employee.

White-box testing

Testing under the condition that the "attacker" has full knowledge of the internal network, its design, and implementation.

Grey-box testing

Testing under the condition that the "attacker" has partial knowledge of the internal network, its design, and implementation.

Black-box testing

Testing under the condition that the "attacker" has no prior knowledge of the internal network, its design, and implementation.

Data security

There are numerous security threats associated with cloud data services. This includes traditional threats and non-traditional threats. Traditional threats include: network eavesdropping, illegal invasion, and denial of service attacks, but also specific cloud computing threats, such as side channel attacks, virtualization vulnerabilities, and abuse of cloud services. In order to mitigate these threats security controls often rely on monitoring the three areas of the CIA triad. The CIA Triad refers to confidentiality (including access controllability which can be further understood from the following.[22]), integrity and availability.

It is important to note that many effective security measures cover several or all of the three categories. Encryption for example can be used to prevent unauthorized access, and also ensure integrity of the data). Backups on the other hand generally cover integrity and availability and firewalls only cover confidentiality and access controllability.[23]

Confidentiality

Data confidentiality is the property in that data contents are not made available or disclosed to illegal users. Outsourced data is stored in a cloud and out of the owners' direct control. Only authorized users can access the sensitive data while others, including CSPs, should not gain any information about the data. Meanwhile, data owners expect to fully utilize cloud data services, e.g., data search, data computation, and data sharing, without the leakage of the data contents to CSPs or other adversaries. Confidentiality refers to how data must be kept strictly confidential to the owner of said data

An example of security control that covers confidentiality is encryption so that only authorized users can access the data. Symmetric or asymmetric key paradigm can be used for encryption.[24]

Access controllability

Access controllability means that a data owner can perform the selective restriction of access to their data outsourced to the cloud. Legal users can be authorized by the owner to access the data, while others can not access it without permission. Further, it is desirable to enforce fine-grained access control to the outsourced data, i.e., different users should be granted different access privileges with regard to different data pieces. The access authorization must be controlled only by the owner in untrusted cloud environments.

Access control can also be referred to as availability. While unauthorized access should be strictly prohibited, access for administrative or even consumer uses should be allowed but monitored as well. Availability and Access control ensure that the proper amount of permissions is granted to the correct persons.

Integrity

Data integrity demands maintaining and assuring the accuracy and completeness of data. A data owner always expects that her or his data in a cloud can be stored correctly and trustworthy. It means that the data should not be illegally tampered with, improperly modified, deliberately deleted, or maliciously fabricated. If any undesirable operations corrupt or delete the data, the owner should be able to detect the corruption or loss. Further, when a portion of the outsourced data is corrupted or lost, it can still be retrieved by the data users. Effective integrity security controls go beyond protection from malicious actors and protect data from unintentional alterations as well.

An example of security control that covers integrity is automated backups of information.

Risks and vulnerabilities of Cloud Computing

While cloud computing is on the cutting edge of information technology there are risks and vulnerabilities to consider before investing fully in it. Security controls and services do exist for the cloud but as with any security system they are not guaranteed to succeed. Furthermore, some risks extend beyond asset security and may involve issues in productivity and even privacy as well.[25]

Privacy Concerns

Cloud computing is still an emerging technology and thus is developing in relatively new technological structures. As a result, all cloud services must undertake Privacy Impact Assessments or PIAs before releasing their platform. Consumers as well that intend to use clouds to store their customer's data must also be aware of the vulnerabilities of having non-physical storage for private information.[26]

Unauthorized Access to Management interface

Due to the autonomous nature of the cloud, consumers are often given management interfaces to monitor their databases. By having controls in such a congregated location and by having the interface be easily accessible for convenience for users, there is a possibility that a single actor could gain access to the cloud's management interface; giving them a great deal of control and power over the database.[27]

Data Recovery Vulnerabilities

The cloud's capabilities with allocating resources as needed often result in resources in memory and otherwise being recycled to another user at a later event. For these memory or storage resources, it could be possible for current users to access information left by previous ones.[27]

Internet Vulnerabilities

The cloud requires an internet connection and therefore internet protocols to access. Therefore, it is open to many internet protocol vulnerabilities such as man-in-the-middle attacks. Furthermore, by having a heavy reliance on internet connectivity, if the connection fails consumers will be completely cut off from any cloud resources.[27]

Encryption Vulnerabilities

Cryptography is an ever-growing field and technology. What was secure 10 years ago may be considered a significant security risk by today's standards. As technology continues to advance and older technologies grow old, new methods of breaking encryptions will emerge as well as fatal flaws in older encryption methods. Cloud providers must keep up to date with their encryption as the data they typically contain is especially valuable.[28]

Legal issues

Privacy legislation often varies from country to country. By having information stored via the cloud it is difficult to determine under which jurisdictions the data falls under. Transborder clouds are especially popular given that the largest companies transcend several countries. Other legal dilemmas from the ambiguity of the cloud refer to how there is a difference in privacy regulation between information shared between and information shared inside of organizations.[26]

Attacks

There are several different types of attacks on cloud computing, one that is still very much untapped is infrastructure compromise. Though not completely known it is listed as the attack with the highest amount of payoff.[29] What makes this so dangerous is that the person carrying out the attack is able to gain a level of privilege of having essentially root access to the machine. It is very hard to defend against attacks like these because they are so unpredictable and unknown, attacks of this type are also called zero day exploits because they are difficult to defend against since the vulnerabilities were previously unknown and unchecked until the attack has already occurred.

DoS attacks aim to have systems be unavailable to their users. Since cloud computing software is used by large numbers of people, resolving these attacks is increasingly difficult. Now with cloud computing on the rise, this has left new opportunities for attacks because of the virtualization of data centers and cloud services being utilized more.[30]

With the global pandemic that started early in 2020 taking effect, there was a massive shift to remote work, because of this companies became more reliant on the cloud. This massive shift has not gone unnoticed, especially by cybercriminals and bad actors, many of which saw the opportunity to attack the cloud because of this new remote work environment. Companies have to constantly remind their employees to keep constant vigilance especially remotely. Constantly keeping up to date with the latest security measures and policies, mishaps in communication are some of the things that these cybercriminals are looking for and will prey upon.

Moving work to the household was critical for workers to be able to continue, but as the move to remote work happened, several security issues arose quickly. The need for data privacy, using applications, personal devices, and the internet all came to the forefront. The pandemic has had large amounts of data being generated especially in the healthcare sector. Big data is accrued for the healthcare sector now more than ever due to the growing coronavirus pandemic. The cloud has to be able to organize and share the data with its users securely. Quality of data looks for four things: accuracy, redundancy, completeness and consistency.[31]

Users had to think about the fact that massive amounts of data are being shared globally. Different countries have certain laws and regulations that have to be adhered to. Differences in policy and jurisdiction give rise to the risk involved with the cloud. Workers are using their personal devices more now that they are working from home. Criminals see this increase as an opportunity to exploit people, software is developed to infect people's devices and gain access to their cloud. The current pandemic has put people in a situation where they are incredibly vulnerable and susceptible to attacks. The change to remote work was so sudden that many companies simply were unprepared to deal with the tasks and subsequent workload they have found themselves deeply entrenched in. Tighter security measures have to be put in place to ease that newfound tension within organizations.

Encryption

Some advanced encryption algorithms which have been applied to cloud computing increase the protection of privacy. In a practice called crypto-shredding, the keys can simply be deleted when there is no more use of the data.

Attribute-based encryption (ABE)

Attribute-based encryption is a type of public-key encryption in which the secret key of a user and the ciphertext are dependent upon attributes (e.g. the country in which he lives, or the kind of subscription he has). In such a system, the decryption of a ciphertext is possible only if the set of attributes of the user key matches the attributes of the ciphertext.

Some of the strengths of Attribute-based encryption are that it attempts to solve issues that exist in current public-key infrastructure(PKI) and identity-based encryption(IBE) implementations. By relying on attributes ABE circumvents needing to share keys directly, as with PKI, as well as having to know the identity of the receiver, as with IBE.

These benefits come at a cost as ABE suffers from the decryption key re-distribution problem. Since decryption keys in ABE only contain information regarding access structure or the attributes of the user it is hard to verify the user's actual identity. Thus malicious users can intentionally leak their attribute information so that unauthorized users can imitate and gain access.[32]

Ciphertext-policy ABE (CP-ABE)

Ciphertext-policy ABE (CP-ABE) is a type of public-key encryption. In the CP-ABE, the encryptor controls the access strategy. The main research work of CP-ABE is focused on the design of the access structure. A Ciphertext-policy attribute-based encryption scheme consists of four algorithms: Setup, Encrypt, KeyGen, and Decrypt.[33] The Setup algorithm takes security parameters and an attribute universe description as input and outputs public parameters and a master key. The encryption algorithm takes data as input. It then encrypts it to produce ciphertext that only a user that possesses a set of attributes that satisfies the access structure will decrypt the message. The KeyGen algorithm then takes the master key and the user's attributes to develop a private key. Finally, the Decrypt algorithm takes the public parameters, the ciphertext, the private key, and user attributes as input. With this information, the algorithm first checks if the users' attributes satisfy the access structure and then decrypts the ciphertext to return the data.

Key-policy ABE (KP-ABE)

Key-policy Attribute-Based Encryption, or KP-ABE, is an important type of Attribute-Based Encryption. KP-ABE allows senders to encrypt their messages under a set of attributes, much like any Attribute Based Encryption system. For each encryption, private user keys are then generated which contain decryption algorithms for deciphering the message and these private user keys grant users access to specific messages that they correspond to. In a KP-ABE system, ciphertexts, or the encrypted messages, are tagged by the creators with a set of attributes, while the user's private keys are issued that specify which type of ciphertexts the key can decrypt.[34] The private keys control which ciphertexts a user is able to decrypt.[35] In KP-ABE, the attribute sets are used to describe the encrypted texts and the private keys are associated to the specified policy that users will have for the decryption of the ciphertexts. A drawback to KP-ABE is that in KP-ABE the encryptor does not control who has access to the encrypted data, except through descriptive attributes, which creates a reliance on the key-issuer granting and denying access to users. Hence, the creation of other ABE systems such as Ciphertext-Policy Attribute-Based Encryption.[36]

Fully homomorphic encryption (FHE)

Fully Homomorphic Encryption is a cryptosystem that supports arbitrary computation on ciphertext and also allows computing sum and product for the encrypted data without decryption. Another interesting feature of Fully Homomorphic Encryption or FHE for short is that it allows operations to be executed without the need for a secret key.[37] FHE has been linked not only to cloud computing but to electronic voting as well. Fully Homomorphic Encryption has been especially helpful with the development of cloud computing and computing technologies. However, as these systems are developing the need for cloud security has also increased. FHE aims to secure data transmission as well as cloud computing storage with its encryption algorithms.[38] Its goal is to be a much more secure and efficient method of encryption on a larger scale to handle the massive capabilities of the cloud.

Searchable encryption (SE)

Searchable encryption is a cryptographic system that offers secure search functions over encrypted data.[39][40] SE schemes can be classified into two categories: SE based on secret-key (or symmetric-key) cryptography, and SE based on public-key cryptography. In order to improve search efficiency, symmetric-key SE generally builds keyword indexes to answer user queries. This has the obvious disadvantage of providing multimodal access routes for unauthorized data retrieval, bypassing the encryption algorithm by subjecting the framework to alternative parameters within the shared cloud environment.[41]

Compliance

Numerous laws and regulations pertaining to the storage and use of data. In the US these include privacy or data protection laws, Payment Card Industry Data Security Standard (PCI DSS), the Health Insurance Portability and Accountability Act (HIPAA), the Sarbanes-Oxley Act, the Federal Information Security Management Act of 2002 (FISMA), and Children's Online

Privacy Protection Act of 1998, among others. Similar standards exist in other jurisdictions, e.g. Singapore's Multi-Tier Cloud Security Standard.

Similar laws may apply in different legal jurisdictions and may differ quite markedly from those enforced in the US. Cloud service users may often need to be aware of the legal and regulatory differences between the jurisdictions. For example, data stored by a cloud service provider may be located in, say, Singapore and mirrored in the US.[42]

Many of these regulations mandate particular controls (such as strong access controls and audit trails) and require regular reporting. Cloud customers must ensure that their cloud providers adequately fulfill such requirements as appropriate, enabling them to comply with their obligations since, to a large extent, they remain accountable.

Business continuity and data recovery

Cloud providers have business continuity and data recovery plans in place to ensure that service can be maintained in case of a disaster or an emergency and that any data loss will be recovered.[43] These plans may be shared with and reviewed by their customers, ideally dovetailing with the customers' own continuity arrangements. Joint continuity exercises may be appropriate, simulating a major Internet or electricity supply failure for instance.

Log and audit trail

In addition to producing logs and audit trails, cloud providers work with their customers to ensure that these logs and audit trails are properly secured, maintained for as long as the customer requires, and are accessible for the purposes of forensic investigation (e.g., eDiscovery).

Unique compliance requirements

In addition to the requirements to which customers are subject, the data centers used by cloud providers may also be subject to compliance requirements. Using a cloud service provider (CSP) can lead to additional security concerns around data jurisdiction since customer or tenant data may not remain on the same system, in the same data center, or even within the same provider's cloud.[44]

The European Union's GDPR has introduced new compliance requirements for customer data.

Legal and contractual issues

Aside from the security and compliance issues enumerated above, cloud providers and their customers will negotiate terms around liability (stipulating how incidents involving data loss or compromise will be resolved, for example), intellectual property, and end-of-service (when data and applications are ultimately returned to the customer). In addition, there are considerations for acquiring data from the cloud that may be involved in litigation.[45] These issues are discussed in service-level agreements (SLA).

Public records

Legal issues may also include records-keeping requirements in the public sector, where many agencies are required by law to retain and make available electronic records in a specific fashion. This may be determined by legislation, or law may require agencies to conform to the rules and practices set by a records-keeping agency. Public agencies using cloud computing and storage must take these concerns into account.

Computer Access Control

In computer security, general access control includes identification, authorization, authentication, access approval, and audit. A more narrow definition of access control would cover only access approval, whereby the system makes a decision to grant or reject an access request from an already authenticated subject, based on what the subject is authorized to access. Authentication and access control are often combined into a single operation, so that access is approved based on successful authentication, or based on an anonymous access token. Authentication methods and tokens include passwords, biometric scans, physical keys, electronic keys and devices, hidden paths, social barriers, and monitoring by humans and automated systems.

Software entities

In any access-control model, the entities that can perform actions on the system are called *subjects*, and the entities representing resources to which access may need to be controlled are called *objects*. Subjects and objects should both be considered as software entities, rather than as human users: any human users can only have an effect on the system via the software entities that they control.

Although some systems equate subjects with *user IDs*, so that all processes started by a user by default have the same authority, this level of control is not fine-grained enough to satisfy the principle of least privilege, and arguably is responsible for the prevalence of malware in such systems (see computer insecurity).

In some models, for example the object-capability model, any software entity can potentially act as both subject and object.

As of 2014, access-control models tend to fall into one of two classes: those based on capabilities and those based on access control lists (ACLs).

- In a capability-based model, holding an unforged-able reference or *capability* to an object, that provides access to the object (roughly analogous to how possession of one's house key grants one access to one's house); access is conveyed to another party by transmitting such a capability over a secure channel.
- In an ACL-based model, a subject's access to an object depends on whether its identity appears on a list associated with the object (roughly analogous to how a bouncer at a private party would check an ID to see if a name appears on the guest list); access is conveyed by editing the list. (Different ACL systems have a variety of different conventions regarding who or what is responsible for editing the list and how it is edited.)

Both capability-based and ACL-based models have mechanisms to allow access rights to be granted to all members of a *group* of subjects (often the group is itself modeled as a subject).

Services

Access control systems provide the essential services of *authorization*, *identification and authentication (I&A)*, *access approval*, and *accountability* where:

- authorization specifies what a subject can do
- identification and authentication ensure that only legitimate subjects can log on to a system

- access approval grants access during operations, by association of users with the resources that they are allowed to access, based on the authorization policy
- accountability identifies what a subject (or all subjects associated with a user) did

Authorization

Authorization involves the act of defining access-rights for subjects. An authorization policy specifies the operations that subjects are allowed to execute within a system.

Most modern operating systems implement authorization policies as formal sets of permissions that are variations or extensions of three basic types of access:

- Read (R): The subject can:
    - Read file contents
    - List directory contents
- Write (W): The subject can change the contents of a file or directory with the following tasks:
    - Add
    - Update
    - Delete
    - Rename
- Execute (X): If the file is a program, the subject can cause the program to be run. (In Unix-style systems, the "execute" permission doubles as a "traverse directory" permission when granted for a directory.)

These rights and permissions are implemented differently in systems based on *discretionary access control* (*DAC*) and *mandatory access control* (*MAC*).

Identification and authentication

Identification and authentication (I&A) is the process of verifying that an identity is bound to the entity that makes an assertion or claim of identity. The I&A process assumes that there was an initial validation of the identity, commonly called identity proofing. Various methods of identity proofing are available, ranging from in-person validation using government issued identification, to anonymous methods that allow the claimant to remain anonymous, but known to the system if they return. The method used for identity proofing and validation should provide an assurance level commensurate with the intended use of the identity within the system. Subsequently, the entity asserts an identity together with an authenticator as a means for validation. The only requirements for the identifier is that it must be unique within its security domain.

Authenticators are commonly based on at least one of the following four factors:

- *Something you know*, such as a password or a personal identification number (PIN). This assumes that only the owner of the account knows the password or PIN needed to access the account.
- *Something you have*, such as a smart card or security token. This assumes that only the owner of the account has the necessary smart card or token needed to unlock the account.
- *Something you are*, such as fingerprint, voice, retina, or iris characteristics.
- *Where you are*, for example inside or outside a company firewall, or proximity of login location to a personal GPS device.

Access approval

Access approval is the function that actually grants or rejects access during operations.[1]

During access approval, the system compares the formal representation of the authorization policy with the access request, to determine whether the request shall be granted or rejected. Moreover, the access evaluation can be done online/ongoing.[2]

Accountability

Accountability uses such system components as *audit trails* (records) and *logs*, to associate a subject with its actions. The information recorded should be sufficient to map the subject to a controlling user. Audit trails and logs are important for

- Detecting security violations
- Re-creating security incidents

If no one is regularly reviewing your logs and they are not maintained in a secure and consistent manner, they may not be admissible as evidence.

Many systems can generate automated reports, based on certain predefined criteria or thresholds, known as *clipping levels*. For example, a clipping level may be set to generate a report for the following:

- More than three failed logon attempts in a given period
- Any attempt to use a disabled user account

These reports help a system administrator or security administrator to more easily identify possible break-in attempts. – Definition of clipping level:[3] a disk's ability to maintain its magnetic properties and hold its content. A high-quality level range is 65–70%; low quality is below 55%.

Access controls

Access control models are sometimes categorized as either discretionary or non-discretionary. The three most widely recognized models are Discretionary Access Control (DAC), Mandatory Access Control (MAC), and Role Based Access Control (RBAC). MAC is non-discretionary.

Discretionary access control

Discretionary access control (DAC) is a policy determined by the owner of an object. The owner decides who is allowed to access the object, and what privileges they have.

Two important concepts in DAC are

- File and data ownership: Every object in the system has an *owner*. In most DAC systems, each object's initial owner is the subject that caused it to be created. The access policy for an object is determined by its owner.
- Access rights and permissions: These are the controls that an owner can assign to other subjects for specific resources.

Access controls may be discretionary in ACL-based or capability-based access control systems. (In capability-based systems, there is usually no explicit concept of 'owner', but the creator of an object has a similar degree of control over its access policy.)

Mandatory access control

Mandatory access control refers to allowing access to a resource if and only if rules exist that allow a given user to access the resource. It is difficult to manage, but its use is usually justified when used to protect highly sensitive information. Examples include certain government and military information. Management is often simplified (over what is required) if the information can be protected using hierarchical access control, or by implementing sensitivity labels. What makes the method "mandatory" is the use of either rules or sensitivity labels.

- Sensitivity labels: In such a system subjects and objects must have labels assigned to them. A subject's sensitivity label specifies its level of trust. An object's sensitivity label specifies the level of trust required for access. In order to access a given object, the subject must have a sensitivity level equal to or higher than the requested object.
- Data import and export: Controlling the import of information from other systems and export to other systems (including printers) is a critical function of these systems, which must ensure that sensitivity labels are properly maintained and implemented so that sensitive information is appropriately protected at all times.

Two methods are commonly used for applying mandatory access control:

- Rule-based (or label-based) access control: This type of control further defines specific conditions for access to a requested object. A Mandatory Access Control system implements a simple form of rule-based access control to determine whether access should be granted or denied by matching:
    - An object's sensitivity label
    - A subject's sensitivity label
- Lattice-based access control: These can be used for complex access control decisions involving multiple objects and/or subjects. A lattice model is a mathematical structure that defines greatest lower-bound and least upper-bound values for a pair of elements, such as a subject and an object.

Few systems implement MAC; XTS-400 and SELinux are examples of systems that do.

Role-based access control

Role-based access control (RBAC) is an access policy determined by the system, not by the owner. RBAC is used in commercial applications and also in military systems, where multi-level security requirements may also exist. RBAC differs from DAC in that DAC allows users to control access to their resources, while in RBAC, access is controlled at the system level, outside of the user's control. Although RBAC is non-discretionary, it can be distinguished from MAC primarily in the way permissions are handled. MAC controls read and write permissions based on a user's clearance level and additional labels. RBAC controls collections of permissions that may include complex operations such as an e-commerce transaction, or may be as simple as read or write. A role in RBAC can be viewed as a set of permissions.

Three primary rules are defined for RBAC:

1. Role assignment: A subject can execute a transaction only if the subject has selected or been assigned a suitable role.
2. Role authorization: A subject's active role must be authorized for the subject. With rule 1 above, this rule ensures that users can take on only roles for which they are authorized.

3. Transaction authorization: A subject can execute a transaction only if the transaction is authorized for the subject's active role. With rules 1 and 2, this rule ensures that users can execute only transactions for which they are authorized.

Additional constraints may be applied as well, and roles can be combined in a hierarchy where higher-level roles subsume permissions owned by lower-level sub-roles.

Most IT vendors offer RBAC in one or more products.

Attribute-based access control

In attribute-based access control (ABAC),[4][5] access is granted not based on the rights of the subject associated with a user after authentication, but based on the attributes of the user. The user has to prove so-called claims about his or her attributes to the access control engine. An attribute-based access control policy specifies which claims need to be satisfied in order to grant access to an object. For instance the claim could be "older than 18". Any user that can prove this claim is granted access. Users can be anonymous when authentication and identification are not strictly required. One does, however, require means for proving claims anonymously. This can for instance be achieved using anonymous credentials. XACML (extensible access control markup language) is a standard for attribute-based access control. XACML 3.0 was standardized in January 2013.[6]

Break-Glass Access Control Models

Traditionally, access has the purpose of restricting access, thus most access control models follow the "default deny principle", i.e. if a specific access request is not explicitly allowed, it will be denied. This behavior might conflict with the regular operations of a system. In certain situations, humans are willing to take the risk that might be involved in violating an access control policy, if the potential benefit that can be achieved outweighs this risk. This need is especially visible in the health-care domain, where a denied access to patient records can cause the death of a patient. Break-Glass (also called break-the-glass) try to mitigate this by allowing users to override access control decision. Break-Glass can either be implemented in an access control specific manner (e.g. into RBAC),[7] or generic (i.e., independent from the underlying access control model).[8]

Host-based access control (HBAC)

The initialism HBAC stands for "host-based access control".[9]

Data Backup

In information technology, a **backup**, or **data backup** is a copy of computer data taken and stored elsewhere so that it may be used to restore the original after a data loss event. The verb form, referring to the process of doing so, is "back up", whereas the noun and adjective form is "backup".[1] Backups can be used to recover data after its loss from data deletion or corruption, or to recover data from an earlier time.[2] Backups provide a simple form of disaster recovery;

however not all backup systems are able to reconstitute a computer system or other complex configuration such as a computer cluster, active directory server, or database server.[3]

A backup system contains at least one copy of all data considered worth saving. The data storage requirements can be large. An information repository model may be used to provide structure to this storage. There are different types of data storage devices used for copying backups of data that is already in secondary storage onto archive files.[note 1][4] There are also different ways these devices can be arranged to provide geographic dispersion, data security, and portability.

Data is selected, extracted, and manipulated for storage. The process can include methods for dealing with live data, including open files, as well as compression, encryption, and de-duplication. Additional techniques apply to enterprise client-server backup. Backup schemes may include dry runs that validate the reliability of the data being backed up. There are limitations[5] and human factors involved in any backup scheme.

Storage

A backup strategy requires an information repository, "a secondary storage space for data"[6] that aggregates backups of data "sources". The repository could be as simple as a list of all backup media (DVDs, etc.) and the dates produced, or could include a computerized index, catalog, or relational database.

The backup data needs to be stored, requiring a backup rotation scheme,[4] which is a system of backing up data to computer media that limits the number of backups of different dates retained separately, by appropriate re-use of the data storage media by overwriting of backups no longer needed. The scheme determines how and when each piece of removable storage is used for a backup operation and how long it is retained once it has backup data stored on it. The 3-2-1 rule can aid in the backup process. It states that there should be at least 3 copies of the data, stored on 2 different types of storage media, and one copy should be kept offsite, in a remote location (this can include cloud storage). 2 or more different media should be used to eliminate data loss due to similar reasons (for example, optical discs may tolerate being underwater while LTO tapes may not, and SSDs cannot fail due to head crashes or damaged spindle motors since they don't have any moving parts, unlike hard drives). An offsite copy protects against fire, theft of physical media (such as tapes or discs) and natural disasters like floods and earthquakes. Physically protected hard drives are an alternative to an offsite copy, but they have limitations like only being able to resist fire for a limited period of time, so an offsite copy still remains as the ideal choice.

Backup methods

Unstructured

An unstructured repository may simply be a stack of tapes, DVD-Rs or external HDDs with minimal information about what was backed up and when. This method is the easiest to implement, but unlikely to achieve a high level of recoverability as it lacks automation.

Full only/System imaging

A repository using this backup method contains complete source data copies taken at one or more specific points in time. Copying system images, this method is frequently used by computer technicians to record known good configurations. However, imaging[7] is generally more useful as a way of deploying a standard configuration to many systems rather than as a tool for making ongoing backups of diverse systems.

Incremental

An incremental backup stores data changed since a reference point in time. Duplicate copies of unchanged data are not copied. Typically a full backup of all files is made once or at infrequent intervals, serving as the reference point for an incremental repository. Subsequently, a number of incremental backups are made after successive time periods. Restores begin with the last full backup and then apply the incrementals.[8] Some backup systems[9] can create a synthetic full backup from a series of incrementals, thus providing the equivalent of frequently doing a full backup. When done to modify a single archive file, this speeds restores of recent versions of files.

Near-CDP

Continuous Data Protection (CDP) refers to a backup that instantly saves a copy of every change made to the data. This allows restoration of data to any point in time and is the most comprehensive and advanced data protection.[10] Near-CDP backup applications— often marketed as "CDP"—automatically take incremental backups at a specific interval, for example every 15 minutes, one hour, or 24 hours. They can therefore only allow restores to an interval boundary.[10] Near-CDP backup applications use journaling and are typically based on periodic "snapshots",[11] read-only copies of the data frozen at a particular point in time.

Near-CDP (except for Apple Time Machine)[12] intent-logs every change on the host system,[13] often by saving byte or block-level differences rather than file-level differences. This backup method differs from simple disk mirroring in that it enables a roll-back of the log and thus a restoration of old images of data. Intent-logging allows precautions for the consistency of live data, protecting *self-consistent* files but requiring *applications* "be quiesced and made ready for backup."

Near-CDP is more practicable for ordinary personal backup applications, as opposed to *true* CDP, which must be run in conjunction with a virtual machine[14][15] or equivalent[16] and is therefore generally used in enterprise client-server backups.

Software may create copies of individual files such as written documents, multimedia projects, or user preferences, to prevent failed write events caused by power outages, operating system crashes, or exhausted disk space, from causing data loss. A common implementation is an appended ".bak" extension to the file name.

Reverse incremental

A Reverse incremental backup method stores a recent archive file "mirror" of the source data and a series of differences between the "mirror" in its current state and its previous states. A reverse incremental backup method starts with a non-image full backup. After the full backup is performed, the system periodically synchronizes the full backup with the live copy, while storing the data necessary to reconstruct older versions. This can either be done using hard links—as Apple Time Machine does, or using binary diffs.

Differential

A differential backup saves only the data that has changed since the last full backup. This means a maximum of two backups from the repository are used to restore the data. However, as time from the last full backup (and thus the accumulated changes in data) increases, so does the time to perform the differential backup. Restoring an entire system requires starting from the most recent full backup and then applying just the last differential backup.

A differential backup copies files that have been created or changed since the last full backup, regardless of whether any other differential backups have been made since, whereas an incremental backup copies files that have been created or changed since the most recent backup of any type (full or incremental). Changes in files may be detected through a more recent date/time of last modification file attribute, and/or changes in file size. Other variations of incremental backup include multi-level incrementals and block-level incrementals that compare parts of files instead of just entire files.

Storage media

Regardless of the repository model that is used, the data has to be copied onto an archive file data storage medium. The medium used is also referred to as the type of backup destination.

Magnetic tape

Magnetic tape was for a long time the most commonly used medium for bulk data storage, backup, archiving, and interchange. It was previously a less expensive option, but this is no longer the case for smaller amounts of data.[17] Tape is a sequential access medium, so the rate of continuously writing or reading data can be very fast. While tape media itself has a low cost per space, tape drives are typically dozens of times as expensive as hard disk drives and optical drives.

Many tape formats have been proprietary or specific to certain markets like mainframes or a particular brand of personal computer. By 2014 LTO had become the primary tape technology.[18] The other remaining viable "super" format is the IBM 3592 (also referred to as the TS11xx series). The Oracle StorageTek T10000 was discontinued in 2016.[19]

Hard disk

The use of hard disk storage has increased over time as it has become progressively cheaper. Hard disks are usually easy to use, widely available, and can be accessed quickly.[18] However, hard disk backups are close-tolerance mechanical devices and may be more easily damaged than tapes, especially while being transported.[20] In the mid-2000s, several drive manufacturers began to produce portable drives employing ramp loading and accelerometer technology (sometimes termed a "shock sensor"),[21][22] and by 2010 the industry average in drop tests for drives with that technology showed drives remaining intact and working after a 36-inch non-operating drop onto industrial carpeting.[23] Some manufacturers also offer 'ruggedized' portable hard drives, which include a shock-absorbing case around the hard disk, and claim a range of higher drop specifications.[23][24][25] Over a period of years the stability of hard disk backups is shorter than that of tape backups.[19][26][20]

External hard disks can be connected via local interfaces like SCSI, USB, FireWire, or eSATA, or via longer-distance technologies like Ethernet, iSCSI, or Fibre Channel. Some disk-based backup systems, via Virtual Tape Libraries or otherwise, support data deduplication, which can reduce the amount of disk storage capacity consumed by daily and weekly backup data.[27][28][29]

Optical storage

Optical storage uses lasers to store and retrieve data. Recordable CDs, DVDs, and Blu-ray Discs are commonly used with personal computers and are generally cheap. In the past, the capacities and speeds of these discs have been lower than hard disks or tapes, although advances in optical media are slowly shrinking that gap.[30][31]

Potential future data losses caused by gradual media degradation can be predicted by measuring the rate of correctable minor data errors, of which consecutively too many increase the risk of uncorrectable sectors. Support for error scanning varies among optical drive vendors.[32]

Many optical disc formats are WORM type, which makes them useful for archival purposes since the data cannot be changed. Moreover, optical discs are not vulnerable to head crashes, magnetism, imminent water ingress or power surges; and, a fault of the drive typically just halts the spinning.

Optical media is modular; the storage controller is not tied to media itself like with hard drives or flash storage (→flash memory controller), allowing it to be removed and accessed through a different drive. However, recordable media may degrade earlier under long-term exposure to light.[33]

Some optical storage systems allow for cataloged data backups without human contact with the discs, allowing for longer data integrity. A French study in 2008 indicated that the lifespan of typically-sold CD-Rs was 2–10 years,[34] but one manufacturer later estimated the longevity of its CD-Rs with a gold-sputtered layer to be as high as 100 years.[35] Sony's proprietary Optical Disc Archive[18] can in 2016 reach a read rate of 250MB/s.[36]

Solid-state drive

Solid-state drives (SSDs) use integrated circuit assemblies to store data. Flash memory, thumb drives, USB flash drives, CompactFlash, SmartMedia, Memory Sticks, and Secure Digital card devices are relatively expensive for their low capacity, but convenient for backing up relatively low data volumes. A solid-state drive does not contain any movable parts, making it less susceptible to physical damage, and can have huge throughput of around 500 Mbit/s up to 6 Gbit/s. Available SSDs have become more capacious and cheaper.[37][24] Flash memory backups are stable for fewer years than hard disk backups.[19]

Remote backup service

Remote backup services or cloud backups involve service providers storing data offsite. This has been used to protect against events such as fires, floods, or earthquakes which could destroy locally stored backups.[38] Cloud-based backup (through services like or similar to Google Drive, and Microsoft OneDrive) provides a layer of data protection.[20] However, the users must trust the provider to maintain the privacy and integrity of their data, with confidentiality enhanced by the use of encryption. Because speed and availability are limited by a user's online connection,[20] users with large amounts of data may need to use cloud seeding and large-scale recovery.

Management

Various methods can be used to manage backup media, striking a balance between accessibility, security and cost. These media management methods are not mutually exclusive and are frequently combined to meet the user's needs. Using on-line disks for staging data before it is sent to a near-line tape library is a common example.[39][40]

Online

Online backup storage is typically the most accessible type of data storage, and can begin a restore in milliseconds. An internal hard disk or a disk array (maybe connected to SAN) is an example of an online backup. This type of storage is convenient and speedy, but is vulnerable to being deleted or overwritten, either by accident, by malevolent action, or in the wake of a data-deleting virus payload.

Near-line

Nearline storage is typically less accessible and less expensive than online storage, but still useful for backup data storage. A mechanical device is usually used to move media units from storage into a drive where the data can be read or written. Generally it has safety properties similar to on-line storage. An example is a tape library with restore times ranging from seconds to a few minutes.

Off-line

Off-line storage requires some direct action to provide access to the storage media: for example, inserting a tape into a tape drive or plugging in a cable. Because the data is not accessible via any computer except during limited periods in which they are written or read back, they are largely immune to on-line backup failure modes. Access time varies depending on whether the media are on-site or off-site.

Off-site data protection

Backup media may be sent to an off-site vault to protect against a disaster or other site-specific problem. The vault can be as simple as a system administrator's home office or as sophisticated as a disaster-hardened, temperature-controlled, high-security bunker with facilities for backup media storage. A data replica can be off-site but also on-line (e.g., an off-site RAID mirror). Such a replica has fairly limited value as a backup.

Backup site

A backup site or disaster recovery center is used to store data that can enable computer systems and networks to be restored and properly configured in the event of a disaster. Some organisations have their own data recovery centres, while others contract this out to a third-party. Due to high costs, backing up is rarely considered the preferred method of moving data to a DR site. A more typical way would be remote disk mirroring, which keeps the DR data as up to date as possible.

Selection and extraction of data

A backup operation starts with selecting and extracting coherent units of data. Most data on modern computer systems is stored in discrete units, known as files. These files are organized into filesystems. Deciding what to back up at any given time involves tradeoffs. By backing up too much redundant data, the information repository will fill up too quickly. Backing up an insufficient amount of data can eventually lead to the loss of critical information.[41]

Files

- Copying files: Making copies of files is the simplest and most common way to perform a backup. A means to perform this basic function is included in all backup software and all operating systems.

- Partial file copying: A backup may include only the blocks or bytes within a file that have changed in a given period of time. This can substantially reduce needed storage space, but requires higher sophistication to reconstruct files in a restore situation. Some implementations require integration with the source file system.
- Deleted files: To prevent the unintentional restoration of files that have been intentionally deleted, a record of the deletion must be kept.
- Versioning of files: Most backup applications, other than those that do only full only/System imaging, also back up files that have been modified since the last backup. "That way, you can retrieve many different versions of a given file, and if you delete it on your hard disk, you can still find it in your [information repository] archive."[4]

Filesystems

- Filesystem dump: A copy of the whole filesystem in block-level can be made. This is also known as a "raw partition backup" and is related to disk imaging. The process usually involves unmounting the filesystem and running a program like dd (Unix).[42] Because the disk is read sequentially and with large buffers, this type of backup can be faster than reading every file normally, especially when the filesystem contains many small files, is highly fragmented, or is nearly full. But because this method also reads the free disk blocks that contain no useful data, this method can also be slower than conventional reading, especially when the filesystem is nearly empty. Some filesystems, such as XFS, provide a "dump" utility that reads the disk sequentially for high performance while skipping unused sections. The corresponding restore utility can selectively restore individual files or the entire volume at the operator's choice.[43]
- Identification of changes: Some filesystems have an archive bit for each file that says it was recently changed. Some backup software looks at the date of the file and compares it with the last backup to determine whether the file was changed.
- Versioning file system: A versioning filesystem tracks all changes to a file. The NILFS versioning filesystem for Linux is an example.[44]

Live data

Files that are actively being updated present a challenge to back up. One way to back up live data is to temporarily quiesce them (e.g., close all files), take a "snapshot", and then resume live operations. At this point the snapshot can be backed up through normal methods.[45] A snapshot is an instantaneous function of some filesystems that presents a copy of the filesystem as if it were frozen at a specific point in time, often by a copy-on-write mechanism. Snapshotting a file while it is being changed results in a corrupted file that is unusable. This is also the case across interrelated files, as may be found in a conventional database or in applications such as Microsoft Exchange Server.[11] The term fuzzy backup can be used to describe a backup of live data that looks like it ran correctly, but does not represent the state of the data at a single point in time.[46]

Backup options for data files that cannot be or are not quiesced include:[47]

- Open file backup: Many backup software applications undertake to back up open files in an internally consistent state.[48] Some applications simply check whether open files are in use and try again later.[45] Other applications exclude open files that are updated very frequently.[49] Some low-availability interactive applications can be backed up via natural/induced pausing.
- Interrelated database files backup: Some interrelated database file systems offer a means to generate a "hot backup"[50] of the database while it is online and usable. This may include a snapshot of the data files plus a snapshotted log of changes made while the backup is running. Upon a restore, the changes in the log files are applied to bring the copy of the database up to

the point in time at which the initial backup ended.[51] Other low-availability interactive applications can be backed up via coordinated snapshots. However, genuinely-high-availability interactive applications can be only be backed up via Continuous Data Protection.

Metadata

Not all information stored on the computer is stored in files. Accurately recovering a complete system from scratch requires keeping track of this non-file data too.[52]

- System description: System specifications are needed to procure an exact replacement after a disaster.
- Boot sector: The boot sector can sometimes be recreated more easily than saving it. It usually isn't a normal file and the system won't boot without it.
- Partition layout: The layout of the original disk, as well as partition tables and filesystem settings, is needed to properly recreate the original system.
- File metadata: Each file's permissions, owner, group, ACLs, and any other metadata need to be backed up for a restore to properly recreate the original environment.
- System metadata: Different operating systems have different ways of storing configuration information. Microsoft Windows keeps a registry of system information that is more difficult to restore than a typical file.

Manipulation of data and dataset optimization

It is frequently useful or required to manipulate the data being backed up to optimize the backup process. These manipulations can improve backup speed, restore speed, data security, media usage and/or reduced bandwidth requirements.

Automated data grooming

Out-of-date data can be automatically deleted, but for personal backup applications—as opposed to enterprise client-server backup applications where automated data "grooming" can be customized—the deletion[note 2][53][54] can at most[55] be globally delayed or be disabled.[56]

Compression

Various schemes can be employed to shrink the size of the source data to be stored so that it uses less storage space. Compression is frequently a built-in feature of tape drive hardware.[57]

Deduplication

Redundancy due to backing up similarly configured workstations can be reduced, thus storing just one copy. This technique can be applied at the file or raw block level. This potentially large reduction[57] is called deduplication. It can occur on a server before any data moves to backup media, sometimes referred to as source/client side deduplication. This approach also reduces bandwidth required to send backup data to its target media. The process can also occur at the target storage device, sometimes referred to as inline or back-end deduplication.

Duplication

Sometimes backups are duplicated to a second set of storage media. This can be done to rearrange the archive files to optimize restore speed, or to have a second copy at a different location or on a different storage medium—as in the disk-to-disk-to-tape capability of Enterprise client-server backup.

Encryption

High-capacity removable storage media such as backup tapes present a data security risk if they are lost or stolen.[58] Encrypting the data on these media can mitigate this problem, however encryption is a CPU intensive process that can slow down backup speeds, and the security of the encrypted backups is only as effective as the security of the key management policy.[57]

Multiplexing

When there are many more computers to be backed up than there are destination storage devices, the ability to use a single storage device with several simultaneous backups can be useful.[59] However cramming the scheduled backup window via "multiplexed backup" is only used for tape destinations.[59]

Refactoring

The process of rearranging the sets of backups in an archive file is known as refactoring. For example, if a backup system uses a single tape each day to store the incremental backups for all the protected computers, restoring one of the computers could require many tapes. Refactoring could be used to consolidate all the backups for a single computer onto a single tape, creating a "synthetic full backup". This is especially useful for backup systems that do incrementals forever style backups.

Staging

Sometimes backups are copied to a staging disk before being copied to tape.[59] This process is sometimes referred to as D2D2T, an acronym for Disk-to-disk-to-tape. It can be useful if there is a problem matching the speed of the final destination device with the source device, as is frequently faced in network-based backup systems. It can also serve as a centralized location for applying other data manipulation techniques.

Objectives

- Recovery point objective (RPO): The point in time that the restarted infrastructure will reflect, expressed as "the maximum targeted period in which data (transactions) might be lost from an IT service due to a major incident". Essentially, this is the roll-back that will be experienced as a result of the recovery. The most desirable RPO would be the point just prior to the data loss event. Making a more recent recovery point achievable requires increasing the frequency of synchronization between the source data and the backup repository.[60]
- Recovery time objective (RTO): The amount of time elapsed between disaster and restoration of business functions.[61]
- Data security: In addition to preserving access to data for its owners, data must be restricted from unauthorized access. Backups must be performed in a manner that does not compromise the original owner's undertaking. This can be achieved with data encryption and proper media handling policies.[62]
- Data retention period: Regulations and policy can lead to situations where backups are expected to be retained for a particular period, but not any further. Retaining backups after this period can lead to unwanted liability and sub-optimal use of storage media.[62]
- Checksum or hash function validation: Applications that back up to tape archive files need this option to verify that the data was accurately copied.[63]
- Backup process monitoring: Enterprise client-server backup applications need a user interface that allows administrators to monitor the backup process, and proves compliance to regulatory

bodies outside the organization; for example, an insurance company in the USA might be required under HIPAA to demonstrate that its client data meet records retention requirements.[64]
- User-initiated backups and restores: To avoid or recover from *minor* disasters, such as inadvertently deleting or overwriting the "good" versions of one or more files, the computer user—rather than an administrator—may initiate backups and restores (from not necessarily the most-recent backup) of files or folders.

IT Risk Management

IT risk management is the application of risk management methods to information technology in order to manage IT risk, i.e.:

> The business risk associated with the use, ownership, operation, involvement, influence and adoption of IT within an enterprise or organization

IT risk management can be considered a component of a wider enterprise risk management system.[1]

The establishment, maintenance and continuous update of an information security management system (ISMS) provide a strong indication that a company is using a systematic approach for the identification, assessment and management of information security risks.[2]

Different methodologies have been proposed to manage IT risks, each of them divided into processes and steps.[3]

According to the Risk IT framework,[1] this encompasses not only the negative impact of operations and service delivery which can bring destruction or reduction of the value of the organization, but also the benefit enabling risk associated to missing opportunities to use technology to enable or enhance business or the IT project management for aspects like overspending or late delivery with adverse business impact.

Because risk is strictly tied to uncertainty, decision theory should be applied to manage risk as a science, i.e. rationally making choices under uncertainty.

Generally speaking, risk is the product of likelihood times impact (Risk = Likelihood * Impact).[4]

The measure of an IT risk can determined as a product of threat, vulnerability and asset values:[5]

A more current risk management framework for IT Risk would be the TIK framework:

> The *process* of risk management is an ongoing iterative process. It must be repeated indefinitely. The business environment is constantly changing and new threats and vulnerabilities emerge every day. The choice of countermeasures (controls) used to manage risks must strike a balance between productivity, cost, effectiveness of the countermeasure, and the value of the informational asset being protected.

Definitions

The Certified Information Systems Auditor Review Manual 2006 produced by ISACA, an international professional association focused on IT Governance, provides the following definition of risk management: *"Risk management is the process of identifying vulnerabilities and threats to the information resources used by an organization in achieving business objectives, and deciding what countermeasures, if any, to take in reducing risk to an acceptable level, based on the value of the information resource to the organization."*[6]

Risk management is the process that allows IT managers to balance the operational and economic costs of protective measures and achieve gains in mission capability by protecting the IT systems and data that support their organizations' missions. This process is not unique to the IT environment; indeed it pervades decision-making in all areas of our daily lives.[7]

The head of an organizational unit must ensure that the organization has the capabilities needed to accomplish its mission. These mission owners must determine the security capabilities that their IT systems must have to provide the desired level of mission support in the face of real world threats. Most organizations have tight budgets for IT security; therefore, IT security spending must be reviewed as thoroughly as other management decisions. A well-structured risk management methodology, when used effectively, can help management identify appropriate controls for providing the mission-essential security capabilities.[7]

Risk management in the IT world is quite a complex, multi faced activity, with a lot of relations with other complex activities. The picture to the right shows the relationships between different related terms.

The American National Information Assurance Training and Education Center defines risk management in the IT field as:[8]

1. The total process to identify, control, and minimize the impact of uncertain events. The objective of the risk management program is to reduce risk and obtain and maintain DAA approval. The process facilitates the management of security risks by each level of management throughout the system life cycle. The approval process consists of three elements: risk analysis, certification, and approval.
2. An element of managerial science concerned with the identification, measurement, control, and minimization of uncertain events. An effective risk management program encompasses the following four phases:
    a. a Risk assessment, as derived from an evaluation of threats and vulnerabilities.
    b. Management decision.
    c. Control implementation.
    d. Effectiveness review.
3. The total process of identifying, measuring, and minimizing uncertain events affecting AIS resources. It includes risk analysis, cost benefit analysis, safeguard selection, security test and evaluation, safeguard implementation, and systems review.
4. The total process of identifying, controlling, and eliminating or minimizing uncertain events that may affect system resources. It includes risk analysis, cost benefit analysis, selection, implementation and test, security evaluation of safeguards, and overall security review.

Risk management as part of enterprise risk management

Some organizations have and many others should have a comprehensive Enterprise risk management (ERM) in place. The four objective categories addressed, according to Committee of Sponsoring Organizations of the Treadway Commission (COSO) are:

- Strategy - high-level goals, aligned with and supporting the organization's mission
- Operations - effective and efficient use of resources
- Financial Reporting - reliability of operational and financial reporting
- Compliance - compliance with applicable laws and regulations

According to the Risk IT framework by ISACA,[9] IT risk is transversal to all four categories. The IT risk should be managed in the framework of Enterprise risk management: Risk appetite and Risk sensitivity of the whole enterprise should guide the IT risk management process. ERM should provide the context and business objectives to IT risk management

Risk management methodology

Whilst a methodology does not describe specific methods ; nevertheless it does specify several processes (constitute a generic framework) that need to be followed. These processes may be broken down in sub-processes, they may be combined, or their sequence may change. A risk management exercise must carry out these processes in one form or another, The following table compares the processes foreseen by three leading standards.[3] The ISACA Risk IT framework is more recent. The Risk IT Practitioner-Guide[10] compares Risk IT and ISO 27005.

The term methodology means an organized set of principles and rules that drive action in a particular field of knowledge.[3]

The overall comparison is illustrated in the following table.

Risk management constituent processes

ISO/IEC 27005:2008	BS 7799-3:2006	NIST SP 800-39	Risk IT
Context establishment	Organizational context	Frame	RG and RE Domains more precisely - RG1.2 Propose IT risk tolerance, - RG2.1 Establish and maintain accountability for IT risk management - RG2.3 Adapt IT risk practices to enterprise risk practices, - RG2.4 Provide adequate resources for IT risk management, - RE2.1 Define IT risk analysis scope.

Risk assessment	Risk assessment	Assess	RE2 process includes: - RE2.1 Define IT risk analysis scope. - RE2.2 Estimate IT risk. - RE2.3 Identify risk response options. - RE2.4 Perform a peer review of IT risk analysis. In general, the elements as described in the ISO 27005 process are all included in Risk IT; however, some are structured and named differently.
Risk treatment	Risk treatment and management decision making	Respond	- RE 2.3 Identify risk response options - RR2.3 Respond to discovered risk exposure and opportunity
Risk acceptance			RG3.4 Accept IT risk
Risk communication	Ongoing risk management activities		- RG1.5 Promote IT risk-aware culture - RG1.6 Encourage effective communication of IT risk - RE3.6 Develop IT risk indicators.
Risk monitoring and review		Monitor	- RG2 Integrate with ERM. - RE2.4 Perform a peer review of IT risk analysis. - RG2.5 Provide independent assurance over IT risk management

Due to the probabilistic nature and the need of cost benefit analysis, IT risks are managed following a process that according to NIST SP 800-30 can be divided in the following steps:[7]

1. risk assessment,
2. risk mitigation, and
3. evaluation and assessment.

Effective risk management must be totally integrated into the Systems Development Life Cycle.[7]

Information risk analysis conducted on applications, computer installations, networks and systems under development should be undertaken using structured methodologies.[11]

Context establishment

This step is the first step in ISO ISO/IEC 27005 framework. Most of the elementary activities are foreseen as the first sub process of Risk assessment according to NIST SP 800–30. This step implies the acquisition of all relevant information about the organization and the determination of the basic criteria, purpose, scope and boundaries of risk management activities and the organization in charge of risk management activities. The purpose is usually the compliance with legal requirements and provide evidence of due diligence supporting an ISMS that can be certified. The scope can be an incident reporting plan, a business continuity plan.

Another area of application can be the certification of a product.

Criteria include the risk evaluation, risk acceptance and impact evaluation criteria. These are conditioned by:[12]

- legal and regulatory requirements
- the strategic value for the business of information processes
- stakeholder expectations
- negative consequences for the reputation of the organization

Establishing the scope and boundaries, the organization should be studied: its mission, its values, its structure; its strategy, its locations and cultural environment. The constraints (budgetary, cultural, political, technical) of the organization are to be collected and documented as guide for next steps.

Organization for security management

The set up of the organization in charge of risk management is foreseen as partially fulfilling the requirement to provide the resources needed to establish, implement, operate, monitor, review, maintain and improve an ISMS.[13] The main roles inside this organization are:[7]

- Senior Management
- Chief information officer (CIO)
- System and Information owners, such as the Chief Data Officer (CDO) or Chief Privacy Officer (CPO)
- the business and functional managers
- the [https://www.elits.ae/services/ Information System Security Officer] (ISSO) or Chief information security officer (CISO)
- IT Security Practitioners
- Security Awareness Trainers

Risk assessment

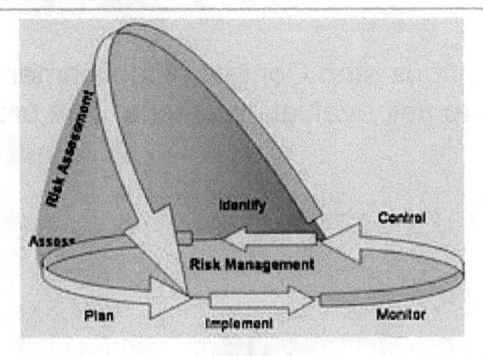

ENISA: Risk assessment inside risk management

Risk Management is a recurrent activity that deals with the analysis, planning, implementation, control, and monitoring of implemented measurements and the enforced security policy. On the contrary, Risk Assessment is executed at discrete time points (e.g. once a year, on demand, etc.) and – until the performance of the next assessment – provides a temporary view of assessed risks and while parameterizing the entire Risk Management process. This view of the relationship of Risk Management to Risk Assessment is depicted in figure as adopted from OCTAVE.[2]

Risk assessment is often conducted in more than one iteration, the first being a high-level assessment to identify high risks, while the other iterations detailed the analysis of the major risks and other risks.

According to National Information Assurance Training and Education Center risk assessment in the IT field is:[8]

1. A study of the vulnerabilities, threats, likelihood, loss or impact, and theoretical effectiveness of security measures. Managers use the results of a risk assessment to develop security requirements and specifications.
2. The process of evaluating threats and vulnerabilities, known and postulated, to determine expected loss and establish the degree of acceptability to system operations.
3. An identification of a specific ADP facility's assets, the threats to these assets, and the ADP facility's vulnerability to those threats.
4. An analysis of system assets and vulnerabilities to establish an expected loss from certain events based on estimated probabilities of the occurrence of those events. The purpose of a risk assessment is to determine if countermeasures are adequate to reduce the probability of loss or the impact of loss to an acceptable level.
5. A management tool which provides a systematic approach for determining the relative value and sensitivity of computer installation assets, assessing vulnerabilities, assessing loss expectancy or perceived risk exposure levels, assessing existing protection features and additional protection alternatives or acceptance of risks and documenting management decisions. Decisions for implementing additional protection features are normally based on the existence of a reasonable ratio between cost/benefit of the safeguard and sensitivity/value of the assets to be protected. Risk assessments may vary from an informal review of a small scale microcomputer installation to a more formal and fully documented analysis (i. e., risk analysis) of a large scale computer installation. Risk assessment methodologies may vary from qualitative or quantitative approaches to any combination of these two approaches.

ISO 27005 framework

Risk assessment receives as input the output of the previous step Context establishment; the output is the list of assessed risks prioritized according to risk evaluation criteria. The process can be divided into the following steps:[12]

- Risk analysis, further divided in:
    - Risk identification
    - Risk estimation
    - Risk evaluation

The following table compares these ISO 27005 processes with Risk IT framework processes:[10]

Risk assessment constituent processes	
ISO 27005	Risk IT
Risk analysis	• RE2 Analyse risk comprises more than what is described by the ISO 27005 process step. RE2 has as its objective developing useful information to support risk decisions that take into account the business relevance of risk factors. • RE1 Collect data serves as input to the analysis of risk (e.g., identifying risk factors, collecting data on the external environment).
Risk identification	This process is included in RE2.2 Estimate IT risk. The identification of risk comprises the following elements: • Risk scenarios • Risk factors
Risk estimation	RE2.2 Estimate IT risk
Risk evaluation	RE2.2 Estimate IT risk

The ISO/IEC 27002:2005 Code of practice for information security management recommends the following be examined during a risk assessment:

- security policy,
- organization of information security,
- asset management,
- human resources security,
- physical and environmental security,
- communications and operations management,
- access control,
- information systems acquisition, development and maintenance, (see Systems Development Life Cycle)
- information security incident management,
- business continuity management, and
- regulatory compliance.

Risk identification

Risk identification states what could cause a potential loss; the following are to be identified:[12]

- assets, primary (i.e. Business processes and related information) and supporting (i.e. hardware, software, personnel, site, organization structure)
- threats
- existing and planned security measures

- vulnerabilities
- consequence
- related business processes

The output of sub process is made up of:

- list of asset and related business processes to be risk managed with associated list of threats, existing and planned security measures
- list of vulnerabilities unrelated to any identified threats
- list of incident scenarios with their consequences.

Risk estimation

There are two methods of risk assessment in information security field, quantitative and qualitative.[14]

Purely quantitative risk assessment is a mathematical calculation based on security metrics on the asset (system or application). For each risk scenario, taking into consideration the different risk factors a Single loss expectancy (SLE) is determined. Then, considering the probability of occurrence on a given period basis, for example the annual rate of occurrence (ARO), the Annualized Loss Expectancy is determined as the product of ARO and SLE.[5] It is important to point out that the values of assets to be considered are those of all involved assets, not only the value of the directly affected resource.

For example, if you consider the risk scenario of a Laptop theft threat, you should consider the value of the data (a related asset) contained in the computer and the reputation and liability of the company (other assets) deriving from the loss of availability and confidentiality of the data that could be involved. It is easy to understand that intangible assets (data, reputation, liability) can be worth much more than physical resources at risk (the laptop hardware in the example).[15] Intangible asset value can be huge, but is not easy to evaluate: this can be a consideration against a pure quantitative approach.[16]

Qualitative risk assessment (three to five steps evaluation, from Very High to Low) is performed when the organization requires a risk assessment be performed in a relatively short time or to meet a small budget, a significant quantity of relevant data is not available, or the persons performing the assessment don't have the sophisticated mathematical, financial, and risk assessment expertise required.[14] Qualitative risk assessment can be performed in a shorter period of time and with less data. Qualitative risk assessments are typically performed through interviews of a sample of personnel from all relevant groups within an organization charged with the security of the asset being assessed. Qualitative risk assessments are descriptive versus measurable. Usually a qualitative classification is done followed by a quantitative evaluation of the highest risks to be compared to the costs of security measures.

Risk estimation has as input the output of risk analysis and can be split in the following steps:

- assessment of the consequences through the valuation of assets
- assessment of the likelihood of the incident (through threat and vulnerability valuation)
- assign values to the likelihood and consequence of the risks

The output is the list of risks with value levels assigned. It can be documented in a risk register.

Risks arising from security threats and adversary attacks may be particularly difficult to estimate. This difficulty is made worse because, at least for any IT system connected to the Internet, any adversary with intent and capability may attack because physical closeness or access is not necessary. Some initial models have been proposed for this problem.[17]

During risk estimation there are generally three values of a given asset, one for the loss of one of the CIA properties: Confidentiality, Integrity, Availability.[18]

Risk evaluation

The risk evaluation process receives as input the output of risk analysis process. It compares each risk level against the risk acceptance criteria and prioritise the risk list with risk treatment indications.

NIST SP 800 30 framework

To determine the likelihood of a future adverse event, threats to an IT system must be in conjunction with the potential vulnerabilities and the controls in place for the IT system. Impact refers to the magnitude of harm that could be caused by a threat's exercise of vulnerability. The level of impact is governed by the potential mission impacts and produces a relative value for the IT assets and resources affected (e.g., the criticality sensitivity of the IT system components and data). The risk assessment methodology encompasses nine primary steps:[7]

- Step 1 System Characterization
- Step 2 Threat Identification
- Step 3 Vulnerability Identification
- Step 4 Control Analysis
- Step 5 Likelihood Determination
- Step 6 Impact Analysis
- Step 7 Risk Determination
- Step 8 Control Recommendations
- Step 9 Results Documentation

Risk mitigation

Risk mitigation, the second process according to SP 800–30, the third according to ISO 27005 of risk management, involves prioritizing, evaluating, and implementing the appropriate risk-reducing controls recommended from the risk assessment process. Because the elimination of all risk is usually impractical or close to impossible, it is the responsibility of senior management and functional and business managers to use the least-cost approach and implement the most appropriate controls to decrease mission risk to an acceptable level, with minimal adverse impact on the organization's resources and mission.

ISO 27005 framework

The risk treatment process aim at selecting security measures to:

- reduce
- retain

- avoid
- transfer

risk and produce a risk treatment plan, that is the output of the process with the residual risks subject to the acceptance of management.

There are some list to select appropriate security measures,[13] but is up to the single organization to choose the most appropriate one according to its business strategy, constraints of the environment and circumstances. The choice should be rational and documented. The importance of accepting a risk that is too costly to reduce is very high and led to the fact that risk acceptance is considered a separate process.[12]

Risk transfer apply were the risk has a very high impact but is not easy to reduce significantly the likelihood by means of security controls: the insurance premium should be compared against the mitigation costs, eventually evaluating some mixed strategy to partially treat the risk. Another option is to outsource the risk to somebody more efficient to manage the risk.[19]

Risk avoidance describe any action where ways of conducting business are changed to avoid any risk occurrence. For example, the choice of not storing sensitive information about customers can be an avoidance for the risk that customer data can be stolen.

The *residual risks*, i.e. the risk remaining after risk treatment decision have been taken, should be estimated to ensure that sufficient protection is achieved. If the residual risk is unacceptable, the risk treatment process should be iterated.

NIST SP 800 30 framework

Risk mitigation is a systematic methodology used by senior management to reduce mission risk.[7] Risk mitigation can be achieved through any of the following risk mitigation options:

- **Risk Assumption**. To accept the potential risk and continue operating the IT system or to implement controls to lower the risk to an acceptable level
- **Risk Avoidance**. To avoid the risk by eliminating the risk cause and/or consequence (e.g., forgo certain functions of the system or shut down the system when risks are identified)
- **Risk Limitation**. To limit the risk by implementing controls that minimize the adverse impact of a threat's exercising a vulnerability (e.g., use of supporting, preventive, detective controls)
- **Risk Planning**. To manage risk by developing a risk mitigation plan that prioritizes, implements, and maintains controls
- **Research and Acknowledgement**. To lower the risk of loss by acknowledging the vulnerability or flaw and researching controls to correct the vulnerability
- **Risk Transference**. To transfer the risk by using other options to compensate for the loss, such as purchasing insurance.

Address the greatest risks and strive for sufficient risk mitigation at the lowest cost, with minimal impact on other mission capabilities: this is the suggestion contained in[7]

Risk communication

Risk communication is a horizontal process that interacts bidirectionally with all other processes of risk management. Its purpose is to establish a common understanding of all aspect of risk among all the organization's stakeholder. Establishing a common understanding is important, since it influences decisions to be taken. The Risk Reduction Overview method [20] is specifically designed for this process. It presents a comprehensible overview of the coherence of risks, measures and residual risks to achieve this common understanding.

Risk monitoring and review

Risk management is an ongoing, never ending process. Within this process implemented security measures are regularly monitored and reviewed to ensure that they work as planned and that changes in the environment rendered them ineffective. Business requirements, vulnerabilities and threats can change over the time.

Regular audits should be scheduled and should be conducted by an independent party, i.e. somebody not under the control of whom is responsible for the implementations or daily management of ISMS.

IT evaluation and assessment

Security controls should be validated. Technical controls are possible complex systems that are to tested and verified. The hardest part to validate is people knowledge of procedural controls and the effectiveness of the real application in daily business of the security procedures.[7]

Vulnerability assessment, both internal and external, and Penetration test are instruments for verifying the status of security controls.

Information technology security audit is an organizational and procedural control with the aim of evaluating security. The IT systems of most organization are evolving quite rapidly. Risk management should cope with these changes through change authorization after risk re evaluation of the affected systems and processes and periodically review the risks and mitigation actions.[5]

Monitoring system events according to a security monitoring strategy, an incident response plan and security validation and metrics are fundamental activities to assure that an optimal level of security is obtained.
It is important to monitor the new vulnerabilities, apply procedural and technical security controls like regularly updating software, and evaluate other kinds of controls to deal with zero-day attacks.

The attitude of involved people to benchmark against best practice and follow the seminars of professional associations in the sector are factors to assure the state of art of an organization IT risk management practice.

Integrating risk management into system development life cycle

Effective risk management must be totally integrated into the SDLC. An IT system's SDLC has five phases: initiation, development or acquisition, implementation, operation or maintenance, and disposal. The risk management methodology is the same regardless of the SDLC phase for which the assessment is being conducted. Risk management is an iterative process that can be performed during each major phase of the SDLC.[7]

Table 2-1 Integration of Risk Management into the SDLC[7]

SDLC Phases	Phase Characteristics	Support from Risk Management Activities
Phase 1: Initiation	The need for an IT system is expressed and the purpose and scope of the IT system is documented	Identified risks are used to support the development of the system requirements, including security requirements, and a security concept of operations (strategy)
Phase 2: Development or Acquisition	The IT system is designed, purchased, programmed, developed, or otherwise constructed	The risks identified during this phase can be used to support the security analyses of the IT system that may lead to architecture and design tradeoffs during system development
Phase 3: Implementation	The system security features should be configured, enabled, tested, and verified	The risk management process supports the assessment of the system implementation against its requirements and within its modeled operational environment. Decisions regarding risks identified must be made prior to system operation
Phase 4: Operation or Maintenance	The system performs its functions. Typically the system is being modified on an ongoing basis through the addition of hardware and software and by changes to organizational processes, policies, and procedures	Risk management activities are performed for periodic system reauthorization (or reaccreditation) or whenever major changes are made to an IT system in its operational, production environment (e.g., new system interfaces)

Phase 5: Disposal	This phase may involve the disposition of information, hardware, and software. Activities may include moving, archiving, discarding, or destroying information and sanitizing the hardware and software	Risk management activities are performed for system components that will be disposed of or replaced to ensure that the hardware and software are properly disposed of, that residual data is appropriately handled, and that system migration is conducted in a secure and systematic manner

NIST SP 800-64[21] is devoted to this topic.

Early integration of security in the SDLC enables agencies to maximize return on investment in their security programs, through:[21]

- Early identification and mitigation of security vulnerabilities and misconfigurations, resulting in lower cost of security control implementation and vulnerability mitigation;
- Awareness of potential engineering challenges caused by mandatory security controls;
- Identification of shared security services and reuse of security strategies and tools to reduce development cost and schedule while improving security posture through proven methods and techniques; and
- Facilitation of informed executive decision making through comprehensive risk management in a timely manner.

This guide[21] focuses on the information security components of the SDLC. First, descriptions of the key security roles and responsibilities that are needed in most information system developments are provided. Second, sufficient information about the SDLC is provided to allow a person who is unfamiliar with the SDLC process to understand the relationship between information security and the SDLC. The document integrates the security steps into the linear, sequential (a.k.a. waterfall) SDLC. The five-step SDLC cited in the document is an example of one method of development and is not intended to mandate this methodology. Lastly, SP 800-64 provides insight into IT projects and initiatives that are not as clearly defined as SDLC-based developments, such as service-oriented architectures, cross-organization projects, and IT facility developments.

Security can be incorporated into information systems acquisition, development and maintenance by implementing effective security practices in the following areas.[22]

- Security requirements for information systems
- Correct processing in applications
- Cryptographic controls
- Security of system files
- Security in development and support processes
- Technical vulnerability management

Information systems security begins with incorporating security into the requirements process for any new application or system enhancement. Security should be designed into the system from the beginning. Security requirements are presented to the vendor during the requirements phase of a product purchase. Formal testing should be done to determine whether the product meets the required security specifications prior to purchasing the product.

Correct processing in applications is essential in order to prevent errors and to mitigate loss, unauthorized modification or misuse of information. Effective coding techniques include validating input and output data, protecting message integrity using encryption, checking for processing errors, and creating activity logs.

Applied properly, cryptographic controls provide effective mechanisms for protecting the confidentiality, authenticity and integrity of information. An institution should develop policies on the use of encryption, including proper key management. Disk Encryption is one way to protect data at rest. Data in transit can be protected from alteration and unauthorized viewing using SSL certificates issued through a Certificate Authority that has implemented a Public Key Infrastructure.

System files used by applications must be protected in order to ensure the integrity and stability of the application. Using source code repositories with version control, extensive testing, production back-off plans, and appropriate access to program code are some effective measures that can be used to protect an application's files.

Security in development and support processes is an essential part of a comprehensive quality assurance and production control process, and would usually involve training and continuous oversight by the most experienced staff.

Applications need to be monitored and patched for technical vulnerabilities. Procedures for applying patches should include evaluating the patches to determine their appropriateness, and whether or not they can be successfully removed in case of a negative impact.

Critique of risk management as a methodology

Risk management as a scientific methodology has been criticized as being shallow.[3] Major IT risk management programmes for large organizations, such as mandated by the US Federal Information Security Management Act, have been criticized.

By avoiding the complexity that accompanies the formal probabilistic model of risks and uncertainty, risk management looks more like a process that attempts to guess rather than formally predict the future on the basis of statistical evidence. It is highly subjective in assessing the value of assets, the likelihood of threats occurrence and the significance of the impact.

However, a better way to deal with the subject has not emerged.[3]

Risk managements methods

It is quite hard to list most of the methods that at least partially support the IT risk management process. Efforts in this direction were done by:

- NIST Description of Automated Risk Management Packages That NIST/NCSC Risk Management Research Laboratory Has Examined, updated 1991
- ENISA[23] in 2006; a list of methods and tools is available on line with a comparison engine.[24] Among them the most widely used are:[3]

- CRAMM Developed by British government is compliant to ISO/IEC 17799, Gramm–Leach–Bliley Act (GLBA) and Health Insurance Portability and Accountability Act (HIPAA)
- EBIOS developed by the French government it is compliant with major security standards: ISO/IEC 27001, ISO/IEC 13335, ISO/IEC 15408, ISO/IEC 17799 and ISO/IEC 21287
- Standard of Good Practice developed by Information Security Forum (ISF)
- Mehari developed by Clusif Club de la Sécurité de l'Information Français[25]
- TIK IT Risk Framework developed by IT Risk Institute[26]
- Octave developed by Carnegie Mellon University, SEI (Software Engineering Institute) The Operationally Critical Threat, Asset, and Vulnerability Evaluation (OCTAVE^{SM}) approach defines a risk-based strategic assessment and planning technique for security.
- IT-Grundschutz (IT Baseline Protection Manual) developed by Federal Office for Information Security (BSI) (Germany); IT-Grundschutz provides a method for an organization to establish an Information Security Management System (ISMS). It comprises both generic IT security recommendations for establishing an applicable IT security process and detailed technical recommendations to achieve the necessary IT security level for a specific domain

Enisa report[2] classified the different methods regarding completeness, free availability, tool support; the result is that:

- EBIOS, ISF methods, IT-Grundschutz cover deeply all the aspects (Risk Identification, Risk analysis, Risk evaluation, Risk assessment, Risk treatment, Risk acceptance, Risk communication),
- EBIOS and IT-Grundschutz are the only ones freely available and
- only EBIOS has an open source tool to support it.

The Factor Analysis of Information Risk (FAIR) main document, "An Introduction to Factor Analysis of Information Risk (FAIR)", Risk Management Insight LLC, November 2006;[16] outline that most of the methods above lack of rigorous definition of risk and its factors. FAIR is not another methodology to deal with risk management, but it complements existing methodologies.[27]

FAIR has had a good acceptance, mainly by The Open Group and ISACA.

ISACA developed a methodology, called Risk IT, to address various kind of IT related risks, chiefly security related risks. It is integrated with COBIT, a general framework to manage IT. Risk IT has a broader concept of IT risk than other methodologies, it encompasses not just only the negative impact of operations and service delivery which can bring destruction or reduction of the value of the organization, but also the benefit\value enabling risk associated to missing opportunities to use technology to enable or enhance business or the IT project management for aspects like overspending or late delivery with adverse business impact.[1]

The "*Build Security In*" initiative of Homeland Security Department of United States, cites FAIR.[28] The initiative Build Security In is a collaborative effort that provides practices, tools, guidelines, rules, principles, and other resources that software developers, architects, and security practitioners can use to build security into software in every phase of its development. So it chiefly address Secure coding.

In 2016, Threat Sketch launched an abbreviated cyber security risk assessment specifically for small organizations.[29][30] The methodology uses real options to forecast and prioritize a fixed list of high-level threats.

In the US, data and privacy legislation continue to evolve to focus on **'reasonable security'** for sensitive information risk management. The goal is to ensure organizations establish their duty of care when it comes to managing data. Businesses are responsible to understand their risk posture to prevent foreseeable harm reasonable safeguards based on their specific working environment.

1. ^ *Curry, Michael; Marshall, Byron; Crossler, Robert E.; Correia, John (2018-04-25). "InfoSec Process Action Model (IPAM): Systematically Addressing Individual Security Behavior". ACM SIGMIS Database: The DATABASE for Advances in Information Systems. **49** (SI): 49–66. doi:10.1145/3210530.3210535. ISSN 0095-0033. S2CID 14003960.*
2. ^ *Joshi, Chanchala; Singh, Umesh Kumar (August 2017). "Information security risks management framework – A step towards mitigating security risks in university network". Journal of Information Security and Applications. **35**: 128–137. doi:10.1016/j.jisa.2017.06.006. ISSN 2214-2126.*
3. ^ *Fletcher, Martin (14 December 2016). "An introduction to information risk". The National Archives. Retrieved 23 February 2022.*
4. ^ *"SANS Institute: Information Security Resources". www.sans.org. Retrieved 2020-10-31.*[circular reference]
5. ^ *Daniel, Kent; Titman, Sheridan (August 2006). "Market Reactions to Tangible and Intangible Information". The Journal of Finance. **61** (4): 1605–1643. doi:10.1111/j.1540-6261.2006.00884.x. SSRN 414701.*
6. ^ *Fink, Kerstin (2004). Knowledge Potential Measurement and Uncertainty. Deutscher Universitätsverlag. ISBN 978-3-322-81240-7. OCLC 851734708.*
7. ^ *Keyser, Tobias (2018-04-19), "Security policy", The Information Governance Toolkit, CRC Press, pp. 57–62, doi:10.1201/9781315385488-13, ISBN 978-1-315-38548-8, retrieved 2021-05-28*
8. ^ *Danzig, Richard (1995). "The big three: Our greatest security risks and how to address them" (Document). DTIC ADA421883.* {{cite document}}: Cite document requires |publisher= (help)
9. ^ *Lyu, M.R.; Lau, L.K.Y. (2000). "Firewall security: Policies, testing and performance evaluation". Proceedings 24th Annual International Computer Software and Applications Conference. COMPSAC2000. IEEE Comput. Soc. pp. 116–121. doi:10.1109/cmpsac.2000.884700. ISBN 0-7695-0792-1. S2CID 11202223.*
10. ^ *"How the Lack of Data Standardization Impedes Data-Driven Healthcare", Data-Driven Healthcare, Hoboken, NJ, US: John Wiley & Sons, Inc., p. 29, 2015-10-17, doi:10.1002/9781119205012.ch3, ISBN 978-1-119-20501-2, retrieved 2021-05-28*
11. ^ *Lent, Tom; Walsh, Bill (2009), "Rethinking Green Building Standards for Comprehensive Continuous Improvement", Common Ground, Consensus Building and Continual Improvement: International Standards and Sustainable Building, West Conshohocken, PA: ASTM International, pp. 1–1–10, doi:10.1520/stp47516s, ISBN 978-0-8031-4507-8, retrieved 2021-05-28*
12. ^ *a b* Cherdantseva Y. and Hilton J.: "Information Security and Information Assurance. The Discussion about the Meaning, Scope and Goals". In: *Organizational, Legal, and Technological Dimensions of Information System Administrator*. Almeida F., Portela, I. (eds.). IGI Global Publishing. (2013)
13. ^ ISO/IEC 27000:2018 (E). (2018). Information technology – Security techniques – Information security management systems – Overview and vocabulary. ISO/IEC.
14. ^ Committee on National Security Systems: National Information Assurance (IA) Glossary, CNSS Instruction No. 4009, 26 April 2010.
15. ^ ISACA. (2008). Glossary of terms, 2008. Retrieved from http://www.isaca.org/Knowledge-Center/Documents/Glossary/glossary.pdf
16. ^ Pipkin, D. (2000). *Information security: Protecting the global enterprise*. New York: Hewlett-Packard Company.
17. ^ B., McDermott, E., & Geer, D. (2001). Information security is information risk management. In Proceedings of the 2001 Workshop on New Security Paradigms NSPW '01, (pp. 97 – 104). ACM. doi:10.1145/508171.508187
18. ^ *Anderson, J. M. (2003). "Why we need a new definition of information security". Computers & Security. **22** (4): 308–313. doi:10.1016/S0167-4048(03)00407-3.*
19. ^ *Venter, H. S.; Eloff, J. H. P. (2003). "A taxonomy for information security technologies". Computers & Security. **22** (4): 299–307. doi:10.1016/S0167-4048(03)00406-1.*
20. ^ *Gold, S (December 2004). "Threats looming beyond the perimeter". Information Security Technical Report. **9** (4): 12–14. doi:10.1016/s1363-4127(04)00047-0. ISSN 1363-4127.*
21. ^ *Parker, Donn B. (January 1993). "A Comprehensive List of Threats To Information". Information Systems Security. **2** (2): 10–14. doi:10.1080/19393559308551348. ISSN 1065-898X.*
22. ^ *Sullivant, John (2016), "The Evolving Threat Environment", Building a Corporate Culture of Security, Elsevier, pp. 33–50, doi:10.1016/b978-0-12-802019-7.00004-3, ISBN 978-0-12-802019-7, retrieved 2021-05-28*
23. ^ *Бучик, С. С.; Юдін, О. К.; Нетребко, Р. В. (2016-12-21). "The analysis of methods of determination of functional types of security of the information-telecommunication system from an unauthorized access". Problems of Informatization and Management. **4** (56). doi:10.18372/2073-4751.4.13135. ISSN 2073-4751.*
24. ^ *a b Samonas, S.; Coss, D. (2014). "The CIA Strikes Back: Redefining Confidentiality, Integrity and Availability in Security". Journal of Information System Security. **10** (3): 21–45. Archived from the original on 2018-09-22. Retrieved 2018-01-25.*
25. ^ *"Gartner Says Digital Disruptors Are Impacting All Industries; Digital KPIs Are Crucial to Measuring Success". Gartner. 2 October 2017. Retrieved 25 January 2018.*
26. ^ *"Gartner Survey Shows 42 Percent of CEOs Have Begun Digital Business Transformation". Gartner. 24 April 2017. Retrieved 25 January 2018.*
27. ^ *Forte, Dario; Power, Richard (December 2007). "Baseline controls in some vital but often-overlooked areas of your information protection programme". Computer Fraud & Security. **2007** (12): 17–20. doi:10.1016/s1361-3723(07)70170-7. ISSN 1361-3723.*
28. ^ *Low-voltage switchgear and controlgear. Device profiles for networked industrial devices, BSI British Standards, doi:10.3403/bsen61915, retrieved 2021-05-28*
29. ^ *Fetzer, James; Highfill, Tina; Hossiso, Kassu; Howells, Thomas; Strassner, Erich; Young, Jeffrey (November 2018). "Accounting for Firm Heterogeneity within U.S. Industries: Extended Supply-Use Tables and Trade in Value Added using Enterprise and Establishment Level Data". Cambridge, MA. doi:10.3386/w25249. S2CID 169324096.*
30. ^ *"Secure estimation subject to cyber stochastic attacks", Cloud Control Systems, Emerging Methodologies and Applications in Modelling, Elsevier: 373–404, 2020, doi:10.1016/b978-0-12-818701-2.00021-4, ISBN 978-0-12-818701-2, S2CID 240746156, retrieved 2021-05-28*
31. ^ *Nijmeijer, H. (2003). Synchronization of mechanical systems. World Scientific. ISBN 978-981-279-497-0. OCLC 262846185.*
32. ^ *"Chapter 1. How students' use of computers has evolved in recent years". dx.doi.org. doi:10.1787/888933277851. Retrieved 2021-05-28.*
33. ^ *Information technology. Security techniques. Competence requirements for information security management systems professionals, BSI British Standards, doi:10.3403/30342674, retrieved 2021-05-29*
34. ^ *"Information Security Qualifications Fact Sheet" (PDF). IT Governance. Archived from the original (PDF) on 16 March 2018. Retrieved 16 March 2018.*
35. ^ *Ma, Ruiqing Ray (March 2016). "Flexible Displays Come in Many Forms". Information Display. **32** (2): 4–49. doi:10.1002/j.2637-496x.2016.tb00883.x. ISSN 0362-0972.*
36. ^ *Rahim, Noor H. (March 2006). Human Rights and Internal Security in Malaysia: Rhetoric and Reality. Defense Technical Information Center. OCLC 74288358.*
37. ^ *Kramer, David (2018-09-14). "Nuclear theft and sabotage threats remain high, report warns". Physics Today. doi:10.1063/pt.6.2.20180914a. ISSN 1945-0699. S2CID 240223415.*
38. ^ *Wilding, Edward (2 March 2017). Information risk and security : preventing and investigating workplace computer crime. Routledge. ISBN 978-1-351-92755-0. OCLC 1052118207.*
39. ^ *Stewart, James (2012). CISSP Study Guide. Canada: John Wiley & Sons. pp. 255–257. ISBN 978-1-118-31417-3.*
40. ^ *"2.2. Productivity growth has been trending down in many sectors". dx.doi.org. doi:10.1787/734700048756. Retrieved 2021-05-28.*
41. ^ *"Identity Theft: The Newest Digital Attackking Industry Must Take Seriously". Issues in Information Systems. 2007. doi:10.48009/2_iis_2007_297-302. ISSN 1529-7314.*
42. ^ *Wendel-Persson, Anna; Ronnhed, Fredrik (2017). IT-säkerhet och människan : De har världens starkaste mur men porten står alltid på glänt. Umeå universitet, Institutionen för informatik. OCLC 1233659973.*
43. ^ *Enge, Eric (5 April 2017). "Stone Temple". Archived from the original on 27 April 2018. Retrieved 17 November 2017.* Cell phones
44. ^ *Shao, Ruodan; Skarlicki, Daniel P. (2014). "Sabotage toward the Customers who Mistreated Employees Scale". PsycTESTS Dataset. doi:10.1037/t31653-000. Retrieved 2021-05-28.*
45. ^ *Kitchen, Julie (June 2008). "7side – Company Information, Company Formations and Property Searches". Legal Information Management. **8** (2): 146. doi:10.1017/s1472669608000364. ISSN 1472-6696. S2CID 144325193.*
46. ^ *Young, Courtenay (2018-05-08), "Working with panic attacks", Help Yourself Towards Mental Health, Routledge, pp. 209–214, doi:10.4324/9780429475474-32, ISBN 978-0-429-47547-4, retrieved 2021-05-28*
47. ^ *"Introduction: Inside the Insider Threat", Insider Threats, Cornell University Press, pp. 1–9, 2017-12-31, doi:10.7591/9781501705946-003, ISBN 978-1-5017-0594-6, retrieved 2021-05-28*
48. ^ *"Table 7.7 France: Comparison of the profit shares of non-financial corporations and non-financial corporations plus unincorporated enterprises". dx.doi.org. doi:10.1787/888933144055. Retrieved 2021-05-28.*
49. ^ *"How Did it All Come About?", The Compliance Business and Its Customers, Basingstoke: Palgrave Macmillan, 2012, doi:10.1057/9781137271150.0007, ISBN 978-1-137-27115-0, retrieved 2021-05-28*
50. ^ *Gordon, Lawrence A.; Loeb, Martin P. (November 2002). "The Economics of Information Security Investment". ACM Transactions on Information and System Security. **5** (4): 438–457. doi:10.1145/581271.581274. S2CID 1500788.*
51. ^ *Cho Kim, Byung; Khansa, Lara; James, Tabitha (July 2011). "Individual Trust and Consumer Risk Perception". Journal of Information Privacy and Security. **7** (3): 3–22. doi:10.1080/15536548.2011.10855915. ISSN 1553-6548. S2CID 144643691.*
52. ^ *Stewart, James (2012). CISSP Certified Information Systems Security Professional Study Guide Sixth Edition. Canada: John Wiley & Sons, Inc. pp. 255–257. ISBN 978-1-118-31417-3.*
53. ^ *Gillett, John (March 1994). "The cost-benefit of outsourcing: assessing the true cost of your outsourcing strategy". European Journal of Purchasing & Supply Management. **1** (1): 45–47. doi:10.1016/0969-7012(94)90042-6. ISSN 0969-7012.*
54. ^ *"2.1. Despite strong growth, Austria has lost some ground since the early 1990s". dx.doi.org. doi:10.1787/645173688502. Retrieved 2021-05-29.*
55. ^ *"Introduction : Caesar Is Dead. Long Live Caesar!", Julius Caesar's Self-Created Image and Its Dramatic Afterlife, Bloomsbury Academic, 2018, doi:10.5040/9781474245784.0005, ISBN 978-1-4742-4578-4, retrieved 2021-05-29*
56. ^ *Suetonius Tranquillus, Gaius (2008). Lives of the Caesars (Oxford World's Classics). New York: Oxford University Press. p. 28. ISBN 978-0-19-953756-3.*
57. ^ *Singh, Simon (2000). The Code Book. Anchor. pp. 289–290. ISBN 978-0-385-49532-5.*
58. ^ *Tan, Heng Chuan (2017). Towards trusted and secure communications in a vehicular environment (Thesis). Nanyang Technological University. doi:10.32657/10356/72758.*
59. ^ *Johnson, John (1997). The Evolution of British Sigint: 1653–1939. Her Majesty's Stationery Office. ASIN B00GYX1GX2.*
60. ^ *Willison, Matthew (14 September 2018). "Were Banks Special? Contrasting Viewpoints in Mid-Nineteenth Century Britain". doi:10.2139/ssrn.3249510. S2CID 169606130.*
61. ^ *Ruppert, K. (2011). "Official Secrets Act (1889; New 1911; Amended 1920, 1939, 1989)". In Hastedt, G.P. (ed.). Spies, Wiretaps, and Secret Operations: An Encyclopedia of American Espionage. Vol. 2. ABC-CLIO. pp. 589–590. ISBN 9781851098088.*
62. ^ *"2. The Clayton Act: A consideration of section 2, defining unlawful price discrimination.", The Federal Anti-Trust Law, Columbia University Press, pp. 18–28, 1930-12-31, doi:10.7312/dunn93452-003, ISBN 978-0-231-89377-0, retrieved 2021-05-29*
63. ^ *Maer, Lucinda; Gay (30 December 2008). "Official Secrecy" (PDF). Federation of American Scientists.*

64. ^ "The Official Secrets Act 1989 which replaced section 2 of the 1911 Act", *Espionage and Secrecy (Routledge Revivals)*, Routledge, pp. 267–282, 2016-06-10, doi:10.4324/9781315542515-21, ISBN 978-1-315-54251-5, retrieved 2021-05-29
65. ^ "Official Secrets Act: what it covers; when it has been used, questioned". *The Indian Express*. 2019-03-08. Retrieved 2020-08-07.
66. ^ Singh, Gajendra (November 2015). ""Breaking the Chains with Which We were Bound": The Interrogation Chamber, the Indian National Army and the Negation of Military Identities, 1941–1947". *Brill's Digital Library of World War I*. doi:10.1163/2352-3786_dlws1_b9789004211452_019. Retrieved 2021-05-28.
67. ^ Duncanson, Dennis (June 1982). "The scramble to unscramble French Indochina". *Asian Affairs*. **13** (2): 161–170. doi:10.1080/03068378208730070. ISSN 0306-8374.
68. ^ Whitman et al. 2017, pp. 3.
69. ^ "Allied Power. Mobilizing Hydro-Electricity During Canada'S Second World War", *Allied Power*, University of Toronto Press, pp. 1–2, 2015-12-31, doi:10.3138/9781442617117-003, ISBN 978-1-4426-1711-7, retrieved 2021-05-29
70. ^ Glatthaar, Joseph T. (2011-06-15), "Officers and Enlisted Men", *Soldiering in the Army of Northern Virginia*, University of North Carolina Press, pp. 83–96, doi:10.5149/9780807877869_glatthaar.11, ISBN 978-0-8078-3492-3, retrieved 2021-05-28
71. ^ [a][b] Sebag–Montefiore, H. (2011). *Enigma: The Battle for the Code*. Orion. p. 576. ISBN 9781780221236.
72. ^ Whitman et al. 2017, pp. 4–5.
73. ^ [a][b] Whitman et al. 2017, p. 5.
74. ^ "Twentieth-Century Wisdom for Twenty-First-Century Communities", *Thomas Merton*, The Lutterworth Press, pp. 160–184, 2012-04-26, doi:10.2307/j.ctt1cg4k28.13, ISBN 978-0-7188-4069-3, retrieved 2021-05-29
75. ^ Murphy, Richard C. (2009-09-01). "Building more powerful less expensive supercomputers using Processing-In-Memory (PIM) LDRD final report". doi:10.2172/993898.
76. ^ "A Brief History of the Internet". www.usg.edu. Retrieved 2020-08-07.
77. ^ "Walking through the view of Delft - on Internet". *Computers & Graphics*. **25** (5): 927. October 2001. doi:10.1016/s0097-8493(01)00149-2. ISSN 0097-8493.
78. ^ DeNardis, L. (2007). "Chapter 24: A History of Internet Security". In de Leeuw, K.M.M.; Bergstra, J. (eds.). *The History of Information Security: A Comprehensive Handbook*. Elsevier. pp. 681–704. ISBN 9780080550589.
79. ^ Perrin, Chad (30 June 2008). "The CIA Triad". Retrieved 31 May 2012.
80. ^ Sandhu, Ravi; Jajodia, Sushil (2000-10-20), "Relational Database Security", *Information Security Management Handbook, Four Volume Set*, Auerbach Publications, doi:10.1201/9780203325438.ch120, ISBN 978-0-8493-1068-3, retrieved 2021-05-29
81. ^ [a][b] Stoneburner, G.; Hayden, C.; Feringa, A. (2004). "Engineering Principles for Information Technology Security" (PDF). csrc.nist.gov. doi:10.6028/NIST.SP.800-27rA. Archived from the original (PDF) on 2011-08-15. Retrieved 2011-08-28.
82. ^ A. J. Neumann, N. Statland and R. D. Webb (1977). "Post-processing audit tools and techniques" (PDF). US Department of Commerce, National Bureau of Standards. pp. 11-3–-11-4.
83. ^ "oecd.org" (PDF). Archived from the original (PDF) on May 16, 2011. Retrieved 2014-01-17.
84. ^ "GSSP (Generally-Accepted system Security Principles): A trip to abilene". *Computers & Security*. **15** (5): 417. January 1996. doi:10.1016/0167-4048(96)82630-7. ISSN 0167-4048.
85. ^ Slade, Rob. "(ICS)2 Blog".
86. ^ Aceituno, Vicente. "Open Information Security Maturity Model". Retrieved 12 February 2017.
87. ^ "George Cybenko – George Cybenko's Personal Home Page" (PDF). Archived from the original (PDF) on 2018-03-29. Retrieved 2018-01-05.
88. ^ Hughes, Jeff; Cybenko, George (21 June 2018). "Quantitative Metrics and Risk Assessment: The Three Tenets Model of Cybersecurity". *Technology Innovation Management Review*. **3** (8).
89. ^ Teplow, Lily. "Are Your Clients Falling for These IT Security Myths? [CHART]". continuum.net.
90. ^ Beckers, K. (2015). *Pattern and Security Requirements: Engineering-Based Establishment of Security Standards*. Springer. p. 100. ISBN 9783319166643.
91. ^ Fienberg, Stephen E.; Slavković, Aleksandra B. (2011), "Data Privacy and Confidentiality", *International Encyclopedia of Statistical Science*, pp. 342–345, doi:10.1007/978-3-642-04898-2_202, ISBN 978-3-642-04897-5
92. ^ [a][b][c][d][e] Andress, J. (2014). *The Basics of Information Security: Understanding the Fundamentals of InfoSec in Theory and Practice*. Syngress. p. 240. ISBN 9780128008126.
93. ^ Boritz, J. Efrim (2005). "IS Practitioners' Views on Core Concepts of Information Integrity". *International Journal of Accounting Information Systems*. Elsevier. **6** (4): 260–279. doi:10.1016/j.accinf.2005.07.001.
94. ^ Hryshko, I. (2020). "Unauthorized Occupation of Land and Unauthorized Construction: Concepts and Types of Tactical Means of Investigation". *International Humanitarian University Herald. Jurisprudence* (43): 180–184. doi:10.32841/2307-1745.2020.43.40. ISSN 2307-1745.
95. ^ Kim, Bonn-Oh (2000-09-21), "Referential Integrity for Database Design", *High-Performance Web Databases*, Auerbach Publications, pp. 427–434, doi:10.1201/9781420031560-34, ISBN 978-0-429-11600-1, retrieved 2021-05-29
96. ^ Pevnev, V. (2018). "Model Threats and Ensure the Integrity of Information". *Systems and Technologies*. **2** (56): 80–95. doi:10.32836/2521-6643-2018.2-56.6. ISSN 2521-6643.
97. ^ Fan, Lejun; Wang, Yuanzhuo; Cheng, Xueqi; Li, Jinming; Jin, Shuyuan (2013-02-26). "Privacy theft malware multi-process collaboration analysis". *Security and Communication Networks*. **8** (1): 51–67. doi:10.1002/sec.705. ISSN 1939-0114.
98. ^ "Completeness, Consistency, and Integrity of the Data Model". *Measuring Data Quality for Ongoing Improvement*. MK Series on Business Intelligence. Elsevier. 2013. pp. e11–e19. doi:10.1016/b978-0-12-397033-6.00030-4. ISBN 978-0-12-397033-6. Retrieved 2021-05-29.
99. ^ "Video from SPIE - the International Society for Optics and Photonics". dx.doi.org. doi:10.1117/12.2266326.5459349132001. Retrieved 2021-05-29.
100. ^ "Communication Skills Used by Information Systems Graduates". *Issues in Information Systems*. 2005. doi:10.48009/1_iis_2005_311-317. ISSN 1529-7314.
101. ^ "Outages of electric power supply resulting from cable failures Boston Edison Company system". 1980-07-01. doi:10.2172/5083196. OSTI 5083196. Retrieved 18 January 2022.
102. ^ Loukas, G.; Oke, G. (September 2010) [August 2009]. "Protection Against Denial of Service Attacks: A Survey" (PDF). *Comput. J.* **53** (7): 1020–1037. doi:10.1093/comjnl/bxp078. Archived from the original (PDF) on 2012-03-24. Retrieved 2015-08-28.
103. ^ "Be Able To Perform a Clinical Activity", *Definitions*, Qeios, 2020-02-02, doi:10.32388/dine5x, S2CID 241238722, retrieved 2021-05-29
104. ^ Ohta, Mai; Fujii, Takeo (May 2011). "Iterative cooperative sensing on shared primary spectrum for improving sensing ability". *2011 IEEE International Symposium on Dynamic Spectrum Access Networks (DySPAN)*. IEEE. pp. 623–627. doi:10.1109/dyspan.2011.5936257. ISBN 978-1-4577-0177-1. S2CID 15119653.
105. ^ *Information technology. Information security incident management*, BSI British Standards, doi:10.3403/30387743, retrieved 2021-05-29
106. ^ Blum, Dan (2020), "Identify and Align Security-Related Roles", *Rational Cybersecurity for Business*, Berkeley, CA: Apress, pp. 31–60, doi:10.1007/978-1-4842-5952-8_2, ISBN 978-1-4842-5951-1, S2CID 226626983, retrieved 2021-05-29
107. ^ McCarthy, C. (2006). "Digital Libraries: Security and Preservation Considerations". In Bidgoli, H. (ed.). *Handbook of Information Security, Threats, Vulnerabilities, Prevention, Detection, and Management*. Vol. 3. John Wiley & Sons. pp. 49–76. ISBN 9780470051214.
108. ^ *Information technology. Open systems interconnection. Security frameworks for open systems*, BSI British Standards, doi:10.3403/01110206u, retrieved 2021-05-29
109. ^ Christofori, Ralf (2014-01-01), "Thus could it have been", *Julio Rondo - O.k., Meta Memory*, Wilhelm Fink Verlag, doi:10.30965/9783846757673_003, ISBN 978-3-7705-5767-7, retrieved 2021-05-29
110. ^ Atkins, D. (May 2021). "Use of the Walnut Digital Signature Algorithm with CBOR Object Signing and Encryption (COSE)". doi:10.17487/rfc9021. S2CID 182252627. Retrieved 18 January 2022.
111. ^ Le May, I. (2003), "Structural Integrity in the Petrochemical Industry", *Comprehensive Structural Integrity*, Elsevier, pp. 125–149, doi:10.1016/b0-08-043749-4/01001-6, ISBN 978-0-08-043749-1, retrieved 2021-05-29
112. ^ Sodjahin, Amos; Champagne, Claudia; Coggins, Frank; Gillet, Roland (2017-01-11). "Leading or lagging indicators of risk? The informational content of extra-financial performance scores". *Journal of Asset Management*. **18** (5): 347–370. doi:10.1057/s41260-016-0039-y. ISSN 1470-8272. S2CID 157485290.
113. ^ Reynolds, E H (1995-07-22). "Folate has potential to cause harm". *BMJ*. **311** (6999): 257. doi:10.1136/bmj.311.6999.257. ISSN 0959-8138. PMC 2550299. PMID 7503870.
114. ^ Randall, Alan (2011), "Harm, risk, and threat", *Risk and Precaution*, Cambridge: Cambridge University Press, pp. 31–42, doi:10.1017/cbo9780511974557.003, ISBN 978-0-511-97455-7, retrieved 2021-05-29
115. ^ Grama, J.L. (2014). *Legal Issues in Information Security*. Jones & Bartlett Learning. p. 550. ISBN 9781284151046.
116. ^ Cannon, David L. (2016-03-04). "Audit Process". *CISA: Certified Information Systems Auditor Study Guide* (Fourth ed.). pp. 139–214. doi:10.1002/9781119419211.ch3. ISBN 9781119056249.
117. ^ *CISA Review Manual 2006*. Information Systems Audit and Control Association. 2006. p. 85. ISBN 978-1-933284-15-6.
118. ^ Kadlec, Jaroslav (2012-11-02). "Two-dimensional process modeling (2DPM)". *Business Process Management Journal*. **18** (6): 849–875. doi:10.1108/14637151211283320. ISSN 1463-7154.
119. ^ "All Countermeasures Have Some Value, But No Countermeasure Is Perfect", *Beyond Fear*, New York: Springer-Verlag, pp. 207–232, 2003, doi:10.1007/0-387-21712-6_14, ISBN 0-387-02620-7, retrieved 2021-05-29
120. ^ "Data breaches: Deloitte suffers serious hit while more details emerge about Equifax and Yahoo". *Computer Fraud & Security*. **2017** (10): 1–3. October 2017. doi:10.1016/s1361-3723(17)30086-6. ISSN 1361-3723.
121. ^ Spagnoletti, Paolo; Resca A. (2008). "The duality of Information Security Management: fighting against predictable and unpredictable threats". *Journal of Information System Security*. **4** (3): 46–62.
122. ^ Yusoff, Nor Hashim; Yusof, Mohd Radzuan (2009-08-04). "Managing HSE Risk in Harsh Environment". *All Days*. SPE. doi:10.2118/122545-ms.
123. ^ Baxter, Wesley (2010). *Sold out: how Ottawa's downtown business improvement areas have secured and valorized urban space* (Thesis). Carleton University. doi:10.22215/etd/2010-09016.
124. ^ de Souza, André; Lynch, Anthony (June 2012). "Does Mutual Fund Performance Vary over the Business Cycle?". Cambridge, MA. doi:10.3386/w18137.
125. ^ Kiountouzis, E.A.; Kokolakis, S.A. (1996-05-31). *Information systems security: facing the information society of the 21st century*. London: Chapman & Hall, Ltd. ISBN 978-0-412-78120-9.
126. ^ Newsome, B. (2013). *A Practical Introduction to Security and Risk Management*. SAGE Publications. p. 208. ISBN 9781483324852.
127. ^ [a][b] Whitman, M.E.; Mattord, H.J. (2016). *Management of Information Security* (5th ed.). Cengage Learning. p. 592. ISBN 9781305501256.
128. ^ "Hardware, Fabrics, Adhesives, and Other Theatrical Supplies", *Illustrated Theatre Production Guide*, Routledge, pp. 203–232, 2013-03-20, doi:10.4324/9780080958392-20, ISBN 978-0-08-095839-2, retrieved 2021-05-29
129. ^ Reason, James (2017-03-02), "Perceptions of Unsafe Acts", *The Human Contribution*, CRC Press, pp. 69–103, doi:10.1201/9781315239125-7, ISBN 978-1-315-23912-5, retrieved 2021-05-29
130. ^ "Information Security Procedures and Standards", *Information Security Policies, Procedures, and Standards*, Boca Raton, FL: Auerbach Publications, pp. 81–92, 2017-03-27, doi:10.1201/9781315372785-5, ISBN 978-1-315-37278-5, retrieved 2021-05-29

131. ^ Zhuang, Haifeng; Chen, Yu; Sheng, Xianfu; Hong, Lili; Gao, Ruilan; Zhuang, Xiaofen (25 June 2020). "Figure S1: Analysis of the prognostic impact of each single signature gene". PeerJ. **8**: e9437. doi:10.7717/peerj.9437/supp-1.
132. ^ Standaert, B.; Ethgen, O.; Emerson, R.A. (June 2012). "CO4 Cost-Effectiveness Analysis - Appropriate for All Situations?". Value in Health. **15** (4): A2. doi:10.1016/j.jval.2012.03.015. ISSN 1098-3015.
133. ^ "GRP canopies provide cost-effective over-door protection". Reinforced Plastics. **40** (11): 8. November 1996. doi:10.1016/s0034-3617(96)91328-4. ISSN 0034-3617.
134. ^ "Figure 2.3. Relative risk of being a low performer depending on personal circumstances (2012)". dx.doi.org. doi:10.1787/888933171410. Retrieved 2021-05-29.
135. ^ Stoneburner, Gary; Goguen, Alice; Feringa, Alexis (2002). "NIST SP 800-30 Risk Management Guide for Information Technology Systems". doi:10.6028/NIST.SP.800-30. Retrieved 18 January 2022.
136. ^ "May I Choose? Can I Choose? Oppression and Choice", A Theory of Freedom, Palgrave Macmillan, 2012, doi:10.1057/9781137295026.0007, ISBN 978-1-137-29502-6, retrieved 2021-05-29
137. ^ Parker, Donn B. (January 1994). "A Guide to Selecting and Implementing Security Controls". Information Systems Security. **3** (2): 75–86. doi:10.1080/10658989409342459. ISSN 1065-898X.
138. ^ Zoccali, Carmine; Mallamaci, Francesca; Tripepi, Giovanni (2007-09-25). "Guest Editor: Rajiv Agarwal: Cardiovascular Risk Profile Assessment and Medication Control Should Come First". Seminars in Dialysis. **20** (5): 405–408. doi:10.1111/j.1525-139x.2007.00317.x. ISSN 0894-0959. PMID 17897245. S2CID 33256127.
139. ^ Guide to the Implementation and Auditing of ISMS Controls based on ISO/IEC 27001. London: BSI British Standards. 2013-11-01. doi:10.3403/9780580829109. ISBN 978-0-580-82910-9.
140. ^ Johnson, L. (2015). Security Controls Evaluation, Testing, and Assessment Handbook. Syngress. p. 678. ISBN 9780128025642.
141. ^ Information technology. Security techniques. Mapping the revised editions of ISO/IEC 27001 and ISO/IEC 27002, BSI British Standards, doi:10.3403/30310928, retrieved 2021-05-29
142. ^ a b c "Administrative Controls", Occupational Ergonomics, CRC Press, pp. 443–666, 2003-03-26, doi:10.1201/9780203507933-6, ISBN 978-0-429-21155-3, retrieved 2021-05-29
143. ^ Chen, J.; Demers, E.A.; Lev, B. (June 2013). "How Time of Day Impacts on Business Conversations". doi:10.13007/141. Retrieved 18 January 2022.
144. ^ 44 U.S.C. § 3542(b)(1)
145. ^ "Appendix D", Information Security Policy Development for Compliance, Auerbach Publications, pp. 117–136, 2013-03-22, doi:10.1201/b13922-12, ISBN 978-1-4665-8058-9, retrieved 2021-05-29
146. ^ "Firewalls, Intrusion Detection Systems and Vulnerability Assessment: A Superior Conjunction?". Network Security. **2002** (9): 8–11. September 2002. doi:10.1016/s1353-4858(02)09009-8. ISSN 1353-4858.
147. ^ Ransome, J.; Misra, A. (2013). Core Software Security: Security at the Source. CRC Press. pp. 40–41. ISBN 9781466560956.
148. ^ Weik, Martin H. (2000), "least privilege principle", Computer Science and Communications Dictionary, p. 883, doi:10.1007/1-4020-0613-6_10052, ISBN 978-0-7923-8425-0
149. ^ Emir, Astra (September 2018). "19. Duties of Ex-employees". Law Trove. doi:10.1093/he/9780198814849.003.0019. ISBN 978-0-19-185251-0.
150. ^ Guide for Information Access Privileges to Health Information, ASTM International, doi:10.1520/e1986-09, retrieved 2021-05-29
151. ^ Drury, Bill (2009-01-01), "Physical environment", Control Techniques, Drives and Controls Handbook, Institution of Engineering and Technology, pp. 355–381, doi:10.1049/pbpo057e chb3, ISBN 978-1-84919-013-8, retrieved 2021-05-29
152. ^ Fire detection and fire alarms systems, BSI British Standards, doi:10.3403/30266863, retrieved 2021-05-29
153. ^ Silverman, Arnold B. (November 2001). "Employee exit interviews—An important but frequently overlooked procedure". JOM. **53** (11): 48. Bibcode:2001JOM....53k..48S. doi:10.1007/s11837-001-0195-4. ISSN 1047-4838. S2CID 137528079.
154. ^ "Many employee pharmacists should be able to benefit". The Pharmaceutical Journal. 2013. doi:10.1211/pj.2013.11124182. ISSN 2053-6186.
155. ^ "Segregation of Duties Control matrix". ISACA. 2008. Archived from the original on 3 July 2011. Retrieved 2008-09-30.
156. ^ "Residents Must Protect Their Private Information". JAMA. **279** (17): 1410B. 1998-05-06. doi:10.1001/jama.279.17.1410. ISSN 0098-7484.
157. ^ "Group Wisdom Support Systems: Aggregating the Insights of Many Through Information Technology". Issues in Information Systems. 2008. doi:10.48009/2_iis_2008_343-350. ISSN 1529-7314.
158. ^ "INTERDEPENDENCIES OF INFORMATION SYSTEMS", Lessons Learned: Critical Information Infrastructure Protection, IT Governance Publishing, pp. 34–37, 2018, doi:10.2307/j.ctt1xhr7hq.13, ISBN 978-1-84928-958-0, retrieved 2021-05-29
159. ^ "Managing Network Security", Network Perimeter Security, Auerbach Publications, pp. 17–66, 2003-10-27, doi:10.1201/9780203508046-3, ISBN 978-0-429-21157-7, retrieved 2021-05-29
160. ^ Kakareka, A. (2013). "Chapter 31: What is Vulnerability Assessment?". In Vacca, J.R. (ed.). Computer and Information Security Handbook (2nd ed.). Elsevier. pp. 541–552. ISBN 9780123946126.
161. ^ Duke, P. A.; Howard, I. P. (2012-08-17). "Processing vertical size disparities in distinct depth planes". Journal of Vision. **12** (8): 10. doi:10.1167/12.8.10. ISSN 1534-7362. PMID 22904355.
162. ^ "Security Onion Control Scripts". Applied Network Security Monitoring. Elsevier. 2014. pp. 451–456. doi:10.1016/b978-0-12-417208-1.09986-4. ISBN 978-0-12-417208-1. Retrieved 2021-05-29.
163. ^ "Metabolomics Provides Valuable Insight for the Study of Durum Wheat: A Review". dx.doi.org. doi:10.1021/acs.jafc.8b07097.s001. Retrieved 2021-05-29.
164. ^ "Overview", Information Security Policies, Procedures, and Standards, Auerbach Publications, 2001-12-20, doi:10.1201/9780849390326.ch1, ISBN 978-0-8493-1137-6, retrieved 2021-05-29
165. ^ Electrical protection relays. Information and requirements for all protection relays, BSI British Standards, doi:10.3403/bs142-1, retrieved 2021-05-29
166. ^ Dibattista, Joseph D.; Reimer, James D.; Stat, Michael; Masucci, Giovanni D.; Biondi, Piera; Brauwer, Maarten De; Bunce, Michael (6 February 2019). "Supplemental Information 4: List of all combined families in alphabetical order assigned in MEGAN vers. 5.11.3". PeerJ. **7**: e6379. doi:10.7717/peerj.6379/supp-4.
167. ^ Kim, Sung-Won (2006-03-31). "A Quantitative Analysis of Classification Classes and Classified Information Resources of Directory". Journal of Information Management. **37** (1): 83–103. doi:10.1633/jim.2006.37.1.083. ISSN 0254-3621.
168. ^ a b Bayuk, J. (2009). "Chapter 4: Information Classification". In Axelrod, C.W.; Bayuk, J.L.; Schutzer, D. (eds.). Enterprise Information Security and Privacy. Artech House. pp. 59–70. ISBN 9781596931916.
169. ^ "Welcome to the Information Age", Overload!, Hoboken, NJ, US: John Wiley & Sons, Inc., pp. 43–65, 2015-09-11, doi:10.1002/9781119200642.ch5, ISBN 978-1-119-20064-2, retrieved 2021-05-29
170. ^ Crooks, S. (2006). "102. Case Study: When Exposure Control Efforts Override Other Important Design Considerations". AIHce 2006. AIHA. doi:10.3320/1.2759009.
171. ^ "Business Model for Information Security (BMIS)". ISACA. Archived from the original on 26 January 2018. Retrieved 25 January 2018.
172. ^ McAuliffe, Leo (January 1987). "Top secret/trade secret: Accessing and safeguarding restricted information". Government Information Quarterly. **4** (1): 123–124. doi:10.1016/0740-624x(87)90068-2. ISSN 0740-624X.
173. ^ Iqbal, Javaid; Soroya, Saira Hanif; Mahmood, Khalid (2023-01-05). "Financial information security behavior in online banking". Information Development: 026666692211493. doi:10.1177/02666669221149346. ISSN 0266-6669. S2CID 255742685.
174. ^ Khairuddin, Ismail Mohd; Sidek, Shahrul Naim; Abdul Majeed, Anwar P.P.; Razman, Mohd Azraai Mohd; Puzi, Asmarani Ahmad; Yusof, Hazlina Md (25 February 2021). "Figure 7: Classification accuracy for each model for all features". PeerJ Computer Science. **7**: e379. doi:10.7717/peerj-cs.379/fig-7.
175. ^ "Asset Classification", Information Security Fundamentals, Auerbach Publications, pp. 327–356, 2013-10-16, doi:10.1201/b15573-18, ISBN 978-0-429-13028-1, retrieved 2021-06-01
176. ^ a b Almehmadi, Abdulaziz; El-Khatib, Khalil (2013). "Authorized! Access denied, unauthorized! Access granted". Proceedings of the 6th International Conference on Security of Information and Networks. Sin '13. New York, New York, US: ACM Press. pp. 363–367. doi:10.1145/2523514.2523612. ISBN 978-1-4503-2498-4. S2CID 17260474.
177. ^ a b Peiss, Kathy (2020), "The Country of the Mind Must Also Attack", Information Hunters, Oxford University Press, pp. 16–39, doi:10.1093/oso/9780190944612.003.0003, ISBN 978-0-19-094461-2, retrieved 2021-06-01
178. ^ Fugini, M.G.; Martella, G. (January 1988). "A petri-net model of access control mechanisms". Information Systems. **13** (1): 53–63. doi:10.1016/0306-4379(88)90026-9. ISSN 0306-4379.
179. ^ Information technology. Personal identification. ISO-compliant driving licence, BSI British Standards, doi:10.3403/30170670u, retrieved 2021-06-01
180. ^ Santos, Omar (2015). Ccna security 210-260 official cert guide. Cisco press. ISBN 978-1-58720-566-8. OCLC 951897116.
181. ^ "What is Assertion?", ASSERTION TRAINING, Abingdon, UK: Taylor & Francis, pp. 1–7, 1991, doi:10.4324/9780203169186_chapter_one, ISBN 978-0-203-28556-5, retrieved 2021-06-01
182. ^ Doe, John (1960). "Field Season In Illinois Begins May 2". Soil Horizons. **1** (2): 10. doi:10.2136/sh1960.2.0010. ISSN 2163-2812.
183. ^ Leech, M. (March 1996). "Username/Password Authentication for SOCKS V5". doi:10.17487/rfc1929. Retrieved 18 January 2022.
184. ^ Kirk, John; Wall, Christine (2011), "Teller, Seller, Union Activist: Class Formation and Changing Bank Worker Identities", Work and Identity, London: Palgrave Macmillan UK, pp. 124–148, doi:10.1057/9780230305625_6, ISBN 978-1-349-36871-6, retrieved 2021-06-01
185. ^ Dewi, Mila Nurmala (2020-12-23). "Perbandingan Kinerja Teller Kriya Dan Teller Organik Pt. Bank Syariah Mandiri". Nisbah: Jurnal Perbankan Syariah. **6** (2): 75. doi:10.30997/jn.v6i2.1932. ISSN 2528-6633. S2CID 234420571.
186. ^ Vile, John (2013), "License Checks", Encyclopedia of the Fourth Amendment, Washington DC: CQ Press, doi:10.4135/9781452234243.n462, ISBN 978-1-60426-589-7, retrieved 2021-06-01
187. ^ "He Said/She Said", My Ghost Has a Name, University of South Carolina Press, pp. 17–32, doi:10.2307/j.ctv6wgjjv.6, ISBN 978-1-61117-827-2, retrieved 2021-05-29
188. ^ Bacigalupo, Sonny A.; Dixon, Linda K.; Gubbins, Simon; Kucharski, Adam J.; Drewe, Julian A. (26 October 2020). "Supplemental Information 8: Methods used to monitor different types of contact". PeerJ. **8**: e10221. doi:10.7717/peerj.10221/supp-8.
189. ^ Igelnik, Boris M.; Zurada, Jacek (2013). Efficiency and scalability methods for computational intellect. Information Science Reference. ISBN 978-1-4666-3942-3. OCLC 833130899.
190. ^ "The Insurance Superbill Must Have Your Name as the Provider", Before You See Your First Client, Routledge, pp. 37–38, 2005-01-01, doi:10.4324/9780203020289-11, ISBN 978-0-203-02028-9, retrieved 2021-06-01
191. ^ Kissell, Joe. Take Control of Your Passwords. ISBN 978-1-4920-6638-5. OCLC 1029606129.
192. ^ "New smart Queensland driver license announced". Card Technology Today. **21** (7): 5. July 2009. doi:10.1016/s0965-2590(09)70126-4. ISSN 0965-2590.
193. ^ Lawrence Livermore National Laboratory. United States. Department of Energy. Office of Scientific and Technical Information (1995). A human engineering and ergonomic evaluation of the security access panel interface. United States. Dept. of Energy. OCLC 727181384.
194. ^ Lee, Paul (April 2017). "Prints charming: how fingerprints are trailblazing mainstream biometrics". Biometric Technology Today. **2017** (4): 8–11. doi:10.1016/s0969-4765(17)30074-7. ISSN 0969-4765.
195. ^ Landrock, Peter (2005), "Two-Factor Authentication", Encyclopedia of Cryptography and Security, p. 638, doi:10.1007/0-387-23483-7_443, ISBN 978-0-387-23473-1
196. ^ "Figure 1.5. Marriage remains the most common form of partnership among couples, 2000-07". dx.doi.org. doi:10.1787/888932392533. Retrieved 2021-06-01.
197. ^ Akpeninor, James Ohwofasa (2013). Modern Concepts of Security. Bloomington, IN: AuthorHouse. p. 135. ISBN 978-1-4817-8232-6. Retrieved 18 January 2018.
198. ^ Richards, G. (April 2012). "One-Time Password (OTP) Pre-Authentication". doi:10.17487/rfc6560.
199. ^ Schumacher, Dietmar (2016-04-03). "Surface geochemical exploration after 85 years: What has been accomplished and what more must be done". International Conference and Exhibition, Barcelona, Spain, 3-6 April 2016. SEG Global Meeting Abstracts. Society of Exploration Geophysicists and American Association of Petroleum Geologists. p. 100. doi:10.1190/ice2016-6522983.1.
200. ^ "Authorization And Approval Program", Internal Controls Policies and Procedures, Hoboken, NJ, US: John Wiley & Sons, Inc., pp. 69–72, 2015-10-23, doi:10.1002/9781119203964.ch10, ISBN 978-1-119-20396-4, retrieved 2021-06-01
201. ^ "What responses under what conditions?", Local Policies and the European Social Fund, Policy Press, pp. 81–102, 2019-10-02, doi:10.2307/j.ctvqc6hn1.12, ISBN 978-1-4473-4652-4, S2CID 241438707, retrieved 2021-06-01

202. ^ Cheng, Liang; Zhang, Yang; Han, Zhihui (June 2013). "Quantitatively Measure Access Control Mechanisms across Different Operating Systems". 2013 IEEE 7th International Conference on Software Security and Reliability. IEEE. pp. 50–59. doi:10.1109/sere.2013.12. ISBN 978-1-4799-0406-8. S2CID 13261344.
203. ^ a b Weik, Martin H. (2000), "discretionary access control", Computer Science and Communications Dictionary, p. 426, doi:10.1007/1-4020-0613-6_5225, ISBN 978-0-7923-8425-0
204. ^ "Individual Subunits of the Glutamate Transporter EAAC1 Homotrimer Function Independently of Each Other". dx.doi.org. doi:10.1021/bi050987n.s001. Retrieved 2021-06-01.
205. ^ Ellis Ormrod, Jeanne (2012). Essentials of educational psychology : big ideas to guide effective teaching. Pearson. ISBN 978-0-13-136727-2. OCLC 663953375.
206. ^ Belim, S. V.; Bogachenko, N. F.; Kabanov, A. N. (November 2018). "Severity Level of Permissions in Role-Based Access Control". 2018 Dynamics of Systems, Mechanisms and Machines (Dynamics). IEEE. pp. 1–5. arXiv:1812.11404. doi:10.1109/dynamics.2018.8601460. ISBN 978-1-5386-5941-0. S2CID 57189531.
207. ^ "Configuring TACACS and Extended TACACS", Securing and Controlling Cisco Routers, Auerbach Publications, 2002-05-15, doi:10.1201/9781420031454.ch11, ISBN 978-0-8493-1290-8, retrieved 2021-06-01
208. ^ "Developing Effective Security Policies", Risk Analysis and Security Countermeasure Selection, CRC Press, pp. 261–274, 2009-12-18, doi:10.1201/9781420078718-18, ISBN 978-0-429-24979-2, retrieved 2021-06-01
209. ^ "The Use of Audit Trails to Monitor Key Networks and Systems Should Remain Part of the Computer Security Material Weakness". www.treasury.gov. Retrieved 2017-10-06.
210. ^ "fixing-canadas-access-to-medicines-regime-what-you-need-to-know-about-bill-c398". Human Rights Documents online. doi:10.1163/2210-7975_hrd-9902-0152. Retrieved 2021-06-01.
211. ^ Salazar, Mary K. (January 2006). "Dealing with Uncertain Risks—When to Apply the Precautionary Principle". AAOHN Journal. **54** (1): 11–13. doi:10.1177/216507990605400102. ISSN 0891-0162. S2CID 87769508.
212. ^ "We Need to Know More About How the Government Censors Its Employees". Human Rights Documents Online. doi:10.1163/2210-7975_hrd-9970-2016117. Retrieved 2021-06-01.
213. ^ Pournelle, Jerry (2004-04-22), "1001 Computer Words You Need to Know", Oxford University Press, doi:10.1093/oso/9780195167757.003.0007, ISBN 978-0-19-516775-7, retrieved 2021-07-30 {{citation}}: Missing or empty |title= (help)
214. ^ Easttom, William (2021), "Elliptic Curve Cryptography", Modern Cryptography, Cham: Springer International Publishing, pp. 245–256, doi:10.1007/978-3-030-63115-4_11, ISBN 978-3-030-63114-7, S2CID 234106555, retrieved 2021-06-01
215. ^ Follman, Rebecca (2014-03-01). From Someone Who Has Been There: Information Seeking in Mentoring. IConference 2014 Proceedings (Thesis). iSchools. doi:10.9776/14322. hdl:1903/14292. ISBN 978-0-9884900-1-7.
216. ^ Weiss, Jason (2004), "Message Digests, Message Authentication Codes, and Digital Signatures", Java Cryptography Extensions, Elsevier, pp. 101–118, doi:10.1016/b978-012742751-5/50012-8, ISBN 978-0-12-742751-5, retrieved 2021-06-05
217. ^ Bider, D. (March 2018). "Use of RSA Keys with SHA-256 and SHA-512 in the Secure Shell (SSH) Protocol". doi:10.17487/rfc8332.
218. ^ Noh, Jaewon; Kim, Jeehyeong; Kwon, Giwon; Cho, Sunghyun (October 2016). "Secure key exchange scheme for WPA/WPA2-PSK using public key cryptography". 2016 IEEE International Conference on Consumer Electronics-Asia (ICCE-Asia). IEEE. pp. 1–4. doi:10.1109/icce-asia.2016.7804782. ISBN 978-1-5090-2743-9. S2CID 10595698.
219. ^ Van Buren, Roy F. (May 1990). "How you can use the data encryption standard to encrypt your files and data bases". ACM SIGSAC Review. **8** (2): 33–39. doi:10.1145/101126.101130. ISSN 0277-920X.
220. ^ Bonneau, Joseph (2016), "Why Buy when You Can Rent?", Financial Cryptography and Data Security, Lecture Notes in Computer Science, Berlin, Heidelberg: Springer Berlin Heidelberg, vol. 9604, pp. 19–26, doi:10.1007/978-3-662-53357-4_2, ISBN 978-3-662-53356-7, retrieved 2021-06-05
221. ^ Coleman, Heather; Andron, Jeff (2015-08-01), "What GIS Experts and Policy Professionals Need to Know about Using Marxan in Multiobjective Planning Processes", Ocean Solutions, Earth Solutions, Esri Press, doi:10.17128/9781589483651_2, ISBN 978-1-58948-365-1, retrieved 2021-06-05
222. ^ a b Landrock, Peter (2005), "Key Encryption Key", Encyclopedia of Cryptography and Security, pp. 326–327, doi:10.1007/0-387-23483-7_220, ISBN 978-0-387-23473-1
223. ^ Giri, Debasis; Barua, Prithayan; Srivastava, P. D.; Jana, Biswapati (2010), "A Cryptosystem for Encryption and Decryption of Long Confidential Messages", Information Security and Assurance, Communications in Computer and Information Science, vol. 76, Berlin, Heidelberg: Springer Berlin Heidelberg, pp. 86–96, Bibcode:2010isa..conf...86G, doi:10.1007/978-3-642-13365-7_9, ISBN 978-3-642-13364-0, retrieved 2021-06-05
224. ^ "Video from SPIE - the International Society for Optics and Photonics". dx.doi.org. doi:10.1117/12.2266326.5459349132001. Retrieved 2021-06-05.
225. ^ Vallabhaneni, S.R. (2008). Corporate Management, Governance, and Ethics Best Practices. John Wiley & Sons. p. 288. ISBN 9780470255803.
226. ^ Shon Harris (2003). All-in-one CISSP Certification Exam Guide (2nd ed.). Emeryville, California: McGraw-Hill/Osborne. ISBN 978-0-07-222966-0.
227. ^ Boncardo, Robert (2018-09-20). "Jean-Claude Milner's Mallarmé: Nothing Has Taken Place". Edinburgh University Press. **1**. doi:10.3366/edinburgh/9781474429528.003.0005. S2CID 172045429.
228. ^ "The Importance of Operational Due Diligence", Hedge Fund Operational Due Diligence, Hoboken, NJ, US: John Wiley & Sons, Inc., pp. 49–67, 2015-10-16, doi:10.1002/9781119197485.ch2, ISBN 978-1-119-19748-5, retrieved 2021-06-05
229. ^ Hall, Gaylord C. (March 1917). "Some Important Diagnostic Points the General Practioner [sic] Should Know About the Nose". Southern Medical Journal. **10** (3): 211. doi:10.1097/00007611-191703000-00007. ISSN 0038-4348.
230. ^ Renes, J. (1999). Landschappen van Maas en Peel: een toegepast historisch-geografisch onderzoek in het streekplangebied Noord- en Midden-Limburg. Eisma. ISBN 90-74252-84-2. OCLC 782897414.
231. ^ Thomas, Brook (2017-06-22). "Minding Previous Steps Taken". Oxford Scholarship Online. doi:10.1093/acprof:oso/9780190456368.003.0002. ISBN 978-0-19-045639-9.
232. ^ Lundgren, Regina E. (2018). Risk communication : a handbook for communicating environmental, safety, and health risks. Wiley. ISBN 978-1-119-45613-1. OCLC 1043389392.
233. ^ Jensen, Eric Talbot (2020-12-03), "Due Diligence in Cyber Activities", Due Diligence in the International Legal Order, Oxford University Press, pp. 252–270, doi:10.1093/oso/9780198869900.003.0015, ISBN 978-0-19-886990-0, retrieved 2021-06-05
234. ^ "The Duty of Care Risk Analysis Standard". DoCRA. Archived from the original on 2018-08-14. Retrieved 2018-08-15.
235. ^ Sutton, Adam; Cherney, Adrian; White, Rob (2008), "Evaluating crime prevention", Crime Prevention, Cambridge: Cambridge University Press, pp. 70–90, doi:10.1017/cbo9780511804601.006, ISBN 978-0-511-80460-1, retrieved 2021-06-05
236. ^ Check, Erika (2004-09-15). "FDA considers antidepressant risks for kids". Nature. doi:10.1038/news040913-15. ISSN 0028-0836.
237. ^ Auckland, Cressida (2017-08-16). "Protecting me from my Directive: Ensuring Appropriate Safeguards for Advance Directives in Dementia". Medical Law Review. **26** (1): 73–97. doi:10.1093/medlaw/fwx037. ISSN 0967-0742. PMID 28981694.
238. ^ Takach, George S. (2016), "Preparing for Breach Litigation", Data Breach Preparation and Response, Elsevier, pp. 217–230, doi:10.1016/b978-0-12-803451-4.00009-5, ISBN 978-0-12-803451-4, retrieved 2021-06-05
239. ^ Westby, J.R.; Allen, J.H. (August 2007). "Governing for Enterprise Security (GES) Implementation Guide" (PDF). Software Engineering Institute. Retrieved 25 January 2018.
240. ^ Fowler, Kevvie (2016), "Developing a Computer Security Incident Response Plan", Data Breach Preparation and Response, Elsevier, pp. 49–77, doi:10.1016/b978-0-12-803451-4.00003-4, ISBN 978-0-12-803451-4, retrieved 2021-06-05
241. ^ Bisogni, Fabio (2016). "Proving Limits of State Data Breach Notification Laws: Is a Federal Law the Most Adequate Solution?". Journal of Information Policy. **6**: 154–205. doi:10.5325/jinfopoli.6.2016.0154. JSTOR 10.5325/jinfopoli.6.2016.0154.
242. ^ "Understanding Plan for Every Part", Turbo Flow, Productivity Press, pp. 21–30, 2017-07-27, doi:10.1201/b10336-5, ISBN 978-0-429-24603-6, retrieved 2021-06-05
243. ^ a b Wills, Leonard (27 February 2019). "A Brief Guide to Handling a Cyber Incident". American Bar Association.
244. ^ Johnson, Leighton R. (2014), "Part 1. Incident Response Team", Computer Incident Response and Forensics Team Management, Elsevier, pp. 17–19, doi:10.1016/b978-1-59749-996-5.00038-8, ISBN 978-1-59749-996-5, retrieved 2021-06-05
245. ^ "Computer Incident Response and Forensics Team Management". Network Security. **2014** (2): 4. February 2014. doi:10.1016/s1353-4858(14)70018-2. ISSN 1353-4858.
246. ^ "Cybersecurity Threat Landscape and Future Trends", Cybersecurity, Routledge, pp. 304–343, 2015-04-16, doi:10.1201/b18335-12, ISBN 978-0-429-25639-4, retrieved 2021-06-05
247. ^ Information technology. Security techniques. Information security incident management, BSI British Standards, doi:10.3403/30268878u, retrieved 2021-06-05
248. ^ "Investigation of a Flow Step Clogging Incident: A Precautionary Note on the Use of THF in Commercial-Scale Continuous Process". dx.doi.org. doi:10.1021/acs.oprd.9b00366.s001. Retrieved 2021-06-05.
249. ^ Turner, Tim (2011-09-07), "Our Beginning: Team Members Who Began the Success Story", One Team on All Levels, Productivity Press, pp. 9–36, doi:10.4324/9781466500020-2, ISBN 978-0-429-25314-0, retrieved 2021-06-05
250. ^ Erlanger, Leon (2002). Defensive Strategies. PC Magazine. p. 70.
251. ^ "of Belgrade's main street. The event took place in absolute", Radical Street Performance, Routledge, pp. 81–83, 2013-11-05, doi:10.4324/9781315005140-28, ISBN 978-1-315-00514-0, retrieved 2021-06-05
252. ^ "Why Choice Matters So Much and What Can be Done to Preserve It". The Manipulation of Choice. Palgrave Macmillan. 2013. doi:10.1057/9781137313577.0010. ISBN 978-1-137-31357-7. Retrieved 2021-06-05.
253. ^ a b c "Computer Security Incident Handling Guide" (PDF). Nist.gov. 2012.
254. ^ Borgström, Pernilla; Strengbom, Joachim; Viketoft, Maria; Bommarco, Riccardo (4 April 2016). "Table S3: Results from linear-mixed models where non-signficant [sic] parameters have not been removed". PeerJ. **4**: e1867. doi:10.7717/peerj.1867/supp-3.
255. ^ Penfold, David (2000), "Selecting, Copying, Moving and Deleting Files and Directories", ECDL Module 2: Using the Computer and Managing Files, London: Springer London, pp. 86–94, doi:10.1007/978-1-4471-0491-9_6, ISBN 978-1-85233-443-7, retrieved 2021-06-05
256. ^ Gumus, Onur (2018). ASP. NET Core 2 Fundamentals : Build Cross-Platform Apps and Dynamic Web Services with This Server-side Web Application Framework. Packt Publishing Ltd. ISBN 978-1-78953-355-2. OCLC 1051139482.
257. ^ "Do the Students Understand What They Are Learning?", Trouble-shooting Your Teaching, Routledge, pp. 36–40, 2005-02-25, doi:10.4324/9780203416907-8, ISBN 978-0-203-41690-7, retrieved 2021-06-05
258. ^ "Where Are Films Restored, Where Do They Come From and Who Restores Them?", Film Restoration, Palgrave Macmillan, 2013, doi:10.1057/9781137328724.0006, ISBN 978-1-137-32872-4, retrieved 2021-06-05
259. ^ Liao, Qi; Li, Zhen; Striegel, Aaron (2011-01-24). "Could firewall rules be public - a game theoretical perspective". Security and Communication Networks. **5** (2): 197–210. doi:10.1002/sec.307. ISSN 1939-0114.
260. ^ Boeckman, Philip; Greenwald, David J.; Von Bismarck, Nilufer (2013). Twelfth annual institute on securities regulation in Europe : overcoming deal-making challenges in the current markets. Practising Law Institute. ISBN 978-1-4024-1932-4. OCLC 825824220.
261. ^ "Figure 1.8. Spending of social security has been growing, while self-financing has been falling". dx.doi.org. doi:10.1787/888932459242. Retrieved 2021-06-05.

262. ^ "Information Governance: The Crucial First Step", *Safeguarding Critical E-Documents*, Hoboken, NJ, US: John Wiley & Sons, Inc., pp. 13–24, 2015-09-19, doi:10.1002/9781119204909.ch2, ISBN 978-1-119-20490-9, retrieved 2021-06-05
263. ^ He, Ying (December 1, 2017). "Challenges of Information Security Incident Learning: An Industrial Case Study in a Chinese Healthcare Organization" (PDF). *Informatics for Health and Social Care*. **42** (4): 394–395. doi:10.1080/17538157.2016.1255629. PMID 28068150. S2CID 20139345.
264. ^ Kampfner, Roberto R. (1985). "Formal specification of information systems requirements". *Information Processing & Management*. **21** (5): 401–414. doi:10.1016/0306-4573(85)90086-x. ISSN 0306-4573.
265. ^ Jenner, H.A. (1995). *Assessment of ecotoxicological risks of element leaching from pulverized coal ashes*. s.n.] OCLC 905474381.
266. ^ "Desktop Computers: Software", *Practical Pathology Informatics*, New York: Springer-Verlag, pp. 51–82, 2006, doi:10.1007/0-387-28058-8_3, ISBN 0-387-28057-X, retrieved 2021-06-05
267. ^ Wilby, R.L.; Orr, H.G.; Hedger, M.; Forrow, D.; Blackmore, M. (December 2006). "Risks posed by climate change to the delivery of Water Framework Directive objectives in the UK". *Environment International*. **32** (8): 1043–1055. doi:10.1016/j.envint.2006.06.017. ISSN 0160-4120. PMID 16857260.
268. ^ Campbell, T. (2016). "Chapter 14: Secure Systems Development". *Practical Information Security Management: A Complete Guide to Planning and Implementation*. Apress. p. 218. ISBN 9781484216859.
269. ^ Koppelman, Kent L. (2011). *Understanding human differences : multicultural education for a diverse America*. Pearson/Allyn & Bacon. OCLC 1245910610.
270. ^ "POST-PROCESSING", *Simple Scene, Sensational Shot*, Routledge, pp. 128–147, 2013-04-12, doi:10.4324/9780240821351-9, ISBN 978-0-240-82135-1, retrieved 2021-06-05
271. ^ Kumar, Binay; Mahto, Tulsi; Kumari, Vinita; Ravi, Binod Kumar; Deepmala (2016). "Quackery: How It Can Prove Fatal Even in Apparently Simple Cases-A Case Report". *Medico-Legal Update*. **16** (2): 75. doi:10.5958/0974-1283.2016.00063.3. ISSN 0971-720X.
272. ^ Priest, Sally (2019-02-22). "Shared roles and responsibilities in flood risk management". *Journal of Flood Risk Management*. **12** (1): e12528. doi:10.1111/jfr3.12528. ISSN 1753-318X. S2CID 133789858.
273. ^ United States. Department of Energy. Office of Inspector General. Office of Scientific and Technical Information (2009). *Audit Report, "Fire Protection Deficiencies at Los Alamos National Laboratory."*. United States. Dept. of Energy. OCLC 727225166.
274. ^ Toms, Elaine G. (January 1992). "Managing change in libraries and information services; A systems approach". *Information Processing & Management*. **28** (2): 281–282. doi:10.1016/0306-4573(92)90052-2. ISSN 0306-4573.
275. ^ Abolhassan, Ferri (2003), "The Change Management Process Implemented at IDS Scheer", *Business Process Change Management*, Berlin, Heidelberg: Springer Berlin Heidelberg, pp. 15–22, doi:10.1007/978-3-540-24703-6_2, ISBN 978-3-642-05532-4, retrieved 2021-06-05
276. ^ Dawson, Chris (2020-07-01). *Leading Culture Change*. doi:10.1515/9780804774673. ISBN 9780804774673. S2CID 242348822.
277. ^ McCormick, Douglas P. (22 March 2016). *Family Inc. : using business principles to maximize your family's wealth*. John Wiley & Sons. ISBN 978-1-119-21976-7. OCLC 945632737.
278. ^ Schuler, Rainer (August 1995). "Some properties of sets tractable under every polynomial-time computable distribution". *Information Processing Letters*. **55** (4): 179–184. doi:10.1016/0020-0190(95)00108-o. ISSN 0020-0190.
279. ^ "Figure 12.2. Share of own-account workers who generally do not have more than one client" (Excel). dx.doi.org. doi:10.1787/888933881610. Retrieved 2021-06-05.
280. ^ "Multi-user file server for DOS LANs". *Computer Communications*. **10** (3): 153. June 1987. doi:10.1016/0140-3664(87)90353-7. ISSN 0140-3664.
281. ^ "Defining Organizational Change", *Organizational Change*, Oxford, UK: Wiley-Blackwell, pp. 21–51, 2011-04-19, doi:10.1002/9781444340372.ch1, ISBN 978-1-4443-4037-2, retrieved 2021-06-05
282. ^ Kirchmer, Mathias; Scheer, August-Wilhelm (2003), "Change Management — Key for Business Process Excellence", *Business Process Change Management*, Berlin, Heidelberg: Springer Berlin Heidelberg, pp. 1–14, doi:10.1007/978-3-540-24703-6_1, ISBN 978-3-642-05532-4, retrieved 2021-06-05
283. ^ More, Josh; Stieber, Anthony J.; Liu, Chris (2016), "Tier 2—Advanced Help Desk—Help Desk Supervisor", *Breaking Into Information Security*, Elsevier, pp. 111–113, doi:10.1016/b978-0-12-800783-9.00029-x, ISBN 978-0-12-800783-9, retrieved 2021-06-05
284. ^ "An Application of Bayesian Networks in Automated Scoring of Computerized Simulation Tasks", *Automated Scoring of Complex Tasks in Computer-Based Testing*, Routledge, pp. 212–264, 2006-04-04, doi:10.4324/9780415963572-10, ISBN 978-0-415-96357-2, retrieved 2021-06-05
285. ^ Kavanagh, Michael J. (June 1994). "Change, Change, Change". *Group & Organization Management*. **19** (2): 139–140. doi:10.1177/1059601194192001. ISSN 1059-6011. S2CID 144169263.
286. ^ Taylor, J. (2008). "Chapter 10: Understanding the Project Change Process". *Project Scheduling and Cost Control: Planning, Monitoring and Controlling the Baseline*. J. Ross Publishing. pp. 187–214. ISBN 9781932159110.
287. ^ "17. Innovation and Change: Can Anyone Do This?", *Backstage in a Bureaucracy*, University of Hawaii Press, pp. 87–96, 2017-12-31, doi:10.1515/9780824860936-019, ISBN 978-0-8248-6093-6, retrieved 2021-06-05
288. ^ Braun, Adam (3 February 2015). *Promise of a pencil : how an ordinary person can create extraordinary change*. Simon and Schuster. ISBN 978-1-4767-3063-9. OCLC 902912775.
289. ^ "Describing Within-Person Change Over Time", *Longitudinal Analysis*, Routledge, pp. 235–306, 2015-01-30, doi:10.4324/9781315744094-14, ISBN 978-1-315-74409-4, retrieved 2021-06-05
290. ^ Ingraham, Carolyn; Ban, Patricia W. (1984). *Legislating bureaucratic change : the Civil Service Reform Act of 1978*. State University of New York Press. ISBN 0-87395-886-1. OCLC 10300171.
291. ^ Wei, J. (2000-05-04). "Preliminary Change Request for the SNS 1.3 GeV-Compatible Ring". doi:10.2172/1157253. OSTI 1157253. Retrieved 18 January 2022.
292. ^ Chen Liang (May 2011). "Allocation priority management of agricultural water resources based on the theory of virtual water". *2011 International Conference on Business Management and Electronic Information*. Vol. 1. IEEE. pp. 644–647. doi:10.1109/icbmei.2011.5917018. ISBN 978-1-61284-108-3. S2CID 29137725.
293. ^ "Change risks and best practices in Business Change Management Unmanaged change risk leads to problems for change management", *Leading and Implementing Business Change Management*, Routledge, pp. 32–74, 2013-07-18, doi:10.4324/9780203073957-9, ISBN 978-0-203-07395-7, retrieved 2021-06-05
294. ^ Bragg, Steven M. (2016). *Accounting Best Practices*. Wiley. ISBN 978-1-118-41780-5. OCLC 946625204.
295. ^ "Successful change requires more than change management". *Human Resource Management International Digest*. **16** (7). 2008-10-17. doi:10.1108/hrmid.2008.04416gad.005. ISSN 0967-0734.
296. ^ "Planning for water resources under climate change", *Spatial Planning and Climate Change*, Routledge, pp. 287–313, 2010-09-13, doi:10.4324/9780203846537-20, ISBN 978-0-203-84653-7, retrieved 2021-06-05
297. ^ Rowan, John (January 1967). "Answering the computer back". *Management Decision*. **1** (1): 51–54. doi:10.1108/eb000776. ISSN 0025-1747.
298. ^ Biswas, Margaret R.; Biswas, Asit K. (February 1981). "Climatic change and food production". *Agriculture and Environment*. **5** (4): 332. doi:10.1016/0304-1131(81)90050-3. ISSN 0304-1131.
299. ^ Weik, Martin H. (2000), "backout", *Computer Science and Communications Dictionary*, p. 96, doi:10.1007/1-4020-0613-6_1259, ISBN 978-0-7923-8425-0
300. ^ "Editorial Advisory and Review Board", *Business and Sustainability: Concepts, Strategies and Changes, Critical Studies on Corporate Responsibility, Governance and Sustainability*, Emerald Group Publishing Limited, vol. 3, pp. xv–xvii, 2011-12-06, doi:10.1108/s2043-9059(2011)0000003005, ISBN 978-1-78052-438-2, retrieved 2021-06-05
301. ^ "Where a Mirage Has Once Been, Life Must Be", *New and Selected Poems*, University of South Carolina Press, p. 103, 2014, doi:10.2307/j.ctv6sj8d1.65, ISBN 978-1-61117-323-9, retrieved 2021-06-05
302. ^ Bell, Marvin (1983). "Two, When There Might Have Been Three". *The Antioch Review*. **41** (2): 209. doi:10.2307/4611230. JSTOR 4611230.
303. ^ "We can also make change". *Human Rights Documents Online*. doi:10.1163/2210-7975_hrd-0148-2015175. Retrieved 2021-06-05.
304. ^ Mazikana, Anthony Tapiwa (5 November 2020). "'Change Is the Law of Life. and Those Who Look only to the past or Present Are Certain to Miss the Future- John F. Kennedy' Assessing This Statement with References to Organizations in Zimbabwe Who Have Been Affected by Change". doi:10.2139/ssrn.3725707. S2CID 238964905.
305. ^ Ramanadham, V. V. (ed.). *Privatisation in the UK*. ISBN 978-0-429-19973-8. OCLC 1085890184.
306. ^ "More complex/realistic rheology must be implemented; Numerical convergence tests must be performed". 2020-09-22. doi:10.5194/gmd-2020-107-rc2. S2CID 241597573.
307. ^ Stone, Edward. *Edward C. Stone Collection*. OCLC 733102101.
308. ^ Lientz, B (2002), "Develop Your Improvement Implementation Plan", *Achieve Lasting Process Improvement*, Elsevier, pp. 151–171, doi:10.1016/b978-0-12-449984-3.50011-8, ISBN 978-0-12-449984-3, retrieved 2021-06-05
309. ^ Smeets, Peter (2009). *Expeditie agroparken : ontwerpend onderzoek naar metropolitane landbouw en duurzame ontwikkeling*. s.n.] ISBN 978-90-8585-515-6. OCLC 441821141.
310. ^ "Figure 1.3. About 50 percent of the Going for Growth recommendations have been implemented or are in process of implementation". dx.doi.org. doi:10.1787/888933323735. Retrieved 2021-06-05.
311. ^ Kekes, John (2019-02-21), "Must Justice Be Done at All Costs?", *Hard Questions*, Oxford University Press, pp. 98–126, doi:10.1093/oso/9780190919986.003.0005, ISBN 978-0-19-091998-6, retrieved 2021-06-05
312. ^ Forrester, Kellie (2014). *Macroeconomic implications of changes in the composition of the labor force*. University of California, Santa Barbara. ISBN 978-1-321-34938-2. OCLC 974418780.
313. ^ Choudhury, Gagan L.; Rappaport, Stephen S. (October 1981). "Demand assigned multiple access systems using collision type request channels". *ACM SIGCOMM Computer Communication Review*. **11** (4): 136–148. doi:10.1145/1013879.802667. ISSN 0146-4833.
314. ^ Crinson, Mark (2013). "'Certain Old and Lovely Things, Whose Signified Is Abstract, Out of Date": James Stirling and Nostalgia". *Change over Time*. **3** (1): 116–135. doi:10.1353/cot.2013.0000. ISSN 2153-0548. S2CID 144451363.
315. ^ Ahwidy, Mansour; Pemberton, Lyn (2016). "What Changes Need to be Made within the LNHS for Ehealth Systems to be Successfully Implemented?". *Proceedings of the International Conference on Information and Communication Technologies for Ageing Well and e-Health*. Scitepress. pp. 71–79. doi:10.5220/0005620400710079. ISBN 978-989-758-180-9.
316. ^ Mortimer, John (April 2010). *Paradise postponed*. Penguin Adult. ISBN 978-0-14-104952-6. OCLC 495596392.
317. ^ [a] [b] Cobey, Sarah; Larremore, Daniel B.; Grad, Yonatan H.; Lipsitch, Marc (2021). "Concerns about SARS-CoV-2 evolution should not hold back efforts to expand vaccination". *Nature Reviews Immunology*. **21** (5): 330–335. doi:10.1038/s41577-021-00544-9. PMC 8014893. PMID 33795856.
318. ^ Frampton, Michael (2014-12-26), "Processing Data with Map Reduce", *Big Data Made Easy*, Berkeley, CA: Apress, pp. 85–120, doi:10.1007/978-1-4842-0094-0_4, ISBN 978-1-4842-0095-7, retrieved 2021-06-05
319. ^ "Good study overall, but several procedures need fixing" (PDF). 2016-02-23. doi:10.5194/hess-2015-520-rc2. Retrieved 18 January 2022.
320. ^ Harrison, Kent; Craft, Walter M.; Hiller, Jack; McCluskey, Michael R. (July 1996). "Peer Review Coordinating Draft. Task Analysis for Conduct Intelligence Planning (Critical Combat Function 1): As Accomplished by a Battalion Task Force" (Document). DTIC ADA313949. {{cite document}}: Cite document requires |publisher= (help)
321. ^ itpi.org Archived December 10, 2013, at the Wayback Machine
322. ^ "book summary of The Visible Ops Handbook: Implementing ITIL in 4 Practical and Auditable Steps". wikisummaries.org. Retrieved 2016-06-22.
323. ^ Bigelow, Michelle (2020-09-23), "Change Control and Change Management", *Implementing Information Security in Healthcare*, HIMSS Publishing, pp. 203–214, doi:10.4324/9781003126294-17, ISBN 978-1-003-12629-4, S2CID 224866307, retrieved 2021-06-05
324. ^ *Business continuity management. Guidance on organization recovery following disruptive incidents*, BSI British Standards, doi:10.3403/30194308, retrieved 2021-06-05
325. ^ Hoanh, Chu Thai (1996). *Development of a computerized aid to integrated land use planning (cailup) at regional level in irrigated areas : a case study for the Quan Lo Phung Hiep region in the Mekong Delta, Vietnam*. ITC. ISBN 90-6164-120-9. OCLC 906763535.

326. ^ 1Hibberd, Gary (2015-09-11), "Developing a BCM Strategy in Line with Business Strategy", *The Definitive Handbook of Business Continuity Management*, Hoboken, NJ, US: John Wiley & Sons, Inc., pp. 23–30, doi:10.1002/9781119205883.ch2, ISBN 978-1-119-20588-3, retrieved 2021-06-05
327. ^ Hotchkiss, Stuart (2010). *Business Continuity Management: In Practice*. BCS Learning & Development Limited. ISBN 978-1-906124-72-4.[*page needed*]
328. ^ "Identifying Potential Failure Causes", *Systems Failure Analysis*, ASM International, pp. 25–33, 2009, doi:10.31399/asm.tb.sfa.t52780025, ISBN 978-1-62708-268-6, retrieved 2021-06-05
329. ^ Clemens, Jeffrey. *Risks to the returns to medical innovation : the case of myriad genetics*. OCLC 919958196.
330. ^ Goatcher, Genevieve (2013), "Maximum Acceptable Outage", *Encyclopedia of Crisis Management*, Thousand Oaks, CA: SAGE Publications, Inc., doi:10.4135/9781452275956.n204, ISBN 978-1-4522-2612-5, retrieved 2021-06-05
331. ^ "Segment Design Tradeoffs", *Software Radio Architecture*, New York, US: John Wiley & Sons, Inc., pp. 236–243, 2002-01-17, doi:10.1002/047121664x.ch6, ISBN 978-0-471-21664-3, retrieved 2021-06-05
332. ^ Blundell, S. (1998). "IN-EMERGENCY - integrated incident management, emergency healthcare and environmental monitoring in road networks". *IEE Seminar Using ITS in Public Transport and in Emergency Services*. Vol. 1998. IEE. p. 9. doi:10.1049/ic:19981090.
333. ^ King, Jonathan R. (January 1993). "Contingency Plans and Business Recovery". *Information Systems Management*. **10** (4): 56–59. doi:10.1080/10580539308906959. ISSN 1058-0530.
334. ^ Phillips, Brenda D.; Landahl, Mark (2021), "Strengthening and testing your business continuity plan", *Business Continuity Planning*, Elsevier, pp. 131–153, doi:10.1016/b978-0-12-813844-1.00001-4, ISBN 978-0-12-813844-1, S2CID 230582246, retrieved 2021-06-05
335. ^ Schnurr, Stephanie (2009), "The 'Other' Side of Leadership Discourse: Humour and the Performance of Relational Leadership Activities", *Leadership Discourse at Work*, London: Palgrave Macmillan UK, pp. 42–60, doi:10.1057/9780230594692_3, ISBN 978-1-349-30001-3, retrieved 2021-06-05
336. ^ *Specified time relays for industrial use*, BSI British Standards, doi:10.3403/02011580u, retrieved 2021-06-05
337. ^ "Sample Generic Plan and Procedure: Disaster Recovery Plan (DRP) for Operations/Data Center". *Workplace Violence*. Elsevier. 2010. pp. 253–270. doi:10.1016/b978-1-85617-698-9.00025-4. ISBN 978-1-85617-698-9. Retrieved 2021-06-05.
338. ^ "Information Technology Disaster Recovery Plan". *Disaster Planning for Libraries*. Chandos Information Professional Series. Elsevier. 2015. pp. 187–197. doi:10.1016/b978-1-84334-730-9.00019-3. ISBN 978-1-84334-730-9. Retrieved 2021-06-05.
339. ^ "The Disaster Recovery Plan". Sans Institute. Retrieved 7 February 2012.
340. ^ [a] [b] OECD (2016). "Figure 1.10. Regulations in non-manufacturing sector have significant impact on the manufacturing sector". *Economic Policy Reforms 2016: Going for Growth Interim Report*. Economic Policy Reforms. Paris: OECD Publishing. doi:10.1787/growth-2016-en. ISBN 9789264250079. Retrieved 2021-06-05.
341. ^ *Ahupua'a [electronic resource] : World Environmental and Water Resources Congress 2008, May 12-16, 2008, Honolulu, Hawai'i*. American Society of Civil Engineers. 2008. ISBN 978-0-7844-0976-3. OCLC 233033926.
342. ^ Great Britain. Parliament. House of Commons (2007). *Data protection [H.L.] A bill [as amended in standing committee d] intituled an act to make new provision for the regulation of the processing of information relating to individuals, including the obtaining, holding, use or disclosure of such information*. Proquest LLC. OCLC 877574826.
343. ^ "Data protection, access to personal information and privacy protection", *Government and Information Rights: The Law Relating to Access, Disclosure and their Regulation*, Bloomsbury Professional, 2019, doi:10.5040/9781784518998.chapter-002, ISBN 978-1-78451-896-7, S2CID 239376648, retrieved 2021-06-05
344. ^ Lehtonen, Lasse A. (2017-07-05), "Genetic Information and the Data Protection Directive of the European Union", *The Data Protection Directive and Medical Research Across Europe*, Routledge, pp. 103–112, doi:10.4324/9781315240350-8, ISBN 978-1-315-24035-0, retrieved 2021-06-05
345. ^ "Data Protection Act 1998". legislation.gov.uk. The National Archives. Retrieved 25 January 2018.
346. ^ "Computer Misuse Act 1990", *Criminal Law Statutes 2011-2012*, Routledge, pp. 114–118, 2013-06-17, doi:10.4324/9780203722763-42, ISBN 978-0-203-72276-3, retrieved 2021-06-05
347. ^ Dharmapala, Dhammika; Hines, James (December 2006). "Which Countries Become Tax Havens?". Cambridge, MA. doi:10.3386/w12802.
348. ^ "Figure 1.14. Participation rates have risen but labour force growth has slowed in several countries". dx.doi.org. doi:10.1787/888933367391. Retrieved 2021-06-05.
349. ^ "Computer Misuse Act 1990". legislation.gov.uk. The National Archives. Retrieved 25 January 2018.
350. ^ "Directive 2006/24/EC of the European Parliament and of the Council of 15 March 2006". EUR-Lex. European Union. 15 March 2006. Retrieved 25 January 2018.
351. ^ "Defamation, Student Records, and the Federal Family Education Rights and Privacy Act", *Higher Education Law*, Routledge, pp. 361–394, 2010-12-14, doi:10.4324/9780203846940-22, ISBN 978-0-203-84694-0, retrieved 2021-06-05
352. ^ [a] [b] "Alabama Schools Receive NCLB Grant To Improve Student Achievement". PsycEXTRA Dataset. 2004. doi:10.1037/e486682006-001. Retrieved 2021-06-05.
353. ^ Turner-Gottschang, Karen (1987). *China bound : a guide to academic life and work in the PRC : for the Committee on Scholarly Communication with the People's Republic of China*, National Academy of Sciences, American Council of Learned Societies, Social Science Research Council. National Academy Press. ISBN 0-309-56739-4. OCLC 326709779.
354. ^ Codified at 20 U.S.C. § 1232g, with implementing regulations in title 34, part 99 of the Code of Federal Regulations
355. ^ "Audit Booklet". *Information Technology Examination Handbook*. FFIEC. Retrieved 25 January 2018.
356. ^ Ray, Amy W. (2004), "Health Insurance Portability and Accountability Act (HIPAA)", *Encyclopedia of Health Care Management*, Thousand Oaks, CA: SAGE Publications, Inc., doi:10.4135/9781412950602.n369, ISBN 978-0-7619-2674-0, retrieved 2021-06-05
357. ^ "Public Law 104 - 191 - Health Insurance Portability and Accountability Act of 1996". U.S. Government Publishing Office. Retrieved 25 January 2018.
358. ^ "Public Law 106 - 102 - Gramm–Leach–Bliley Act of 1999" (PDF). U.S. Government Publishing Office. Retrieved 25 January 2018.
359. ^ Alase, Abayomi Oluwatosin (2016). *The impact of the Sarbanes-Oxley Act (SOX) on small-sized publicly traded companies and their communities* (Thesis). Northeastern University Library. doi:10.17760/d20204801.
360. ^ Solis, Lupita (2019). *Educational and Professional Trends of Chief Financial Officers* (Thesis). Portland State University Library. doi:10.15760/honors.763.
361. ^ "Public Law 107 - 204 - Sarbanes-Oxley Act of 2002". U.S. Government Publishing Office. Retrieved 25 January 2018.
362. ^ "Pci Dss Glossary, Abbreviations, and Acronyms", *Payment Card Industry Data Security Standard Handbook*, Hoboken, NJ, US: John Wiley & Sons, Inc., pp. 185–199, 2015-09-18, doi:10.1002/9781119197218.gloss, ISBN 978-1-119-19721-8, retrieved 2021-06-05
363. ^ "PCI Breakdown (Control Objectives and Associated Standards)", *Payment Card Industry Data Security Standard Handbook*, Hoboken, NJ, US: John Wiley & Sons, Inc., p. 61, 2015-09-18, doi:10.1002/9781119197218.part2, ISBN 978-1-119-19721-8, retrieved 2021-06-05
364. ^ Ravallion, Martin; Chen, Shaohua (August 2017). "Welfare-Consistent Global Poverty Measures". *Working Paper Series*. doi:10.3386/w23739. Retrieved 18 January 2022.
365. ^ "Payment Card Industry (PCI) Data Security Standard: Requirements and Security Assessment Procedures - Version 3.2" (PDF). Security Standards Council. April 2016. Retrieved 25 January 2018.
366. ^ "Security Breach Notification Laws". National Conference of State Legislatures. 12 April 2017. Retrieved 25 January 2018.
367. ^ Stein, Stuart G.; Schaberg, Richard A.; Biddle, Laura R., eds. (23 June 2015). *Financial institutions answer book, 2015 : law, governance, compliance*. Practising Law Institute. ISBN 978-1-4024-2405-2. OCLC 911952833.
368. ^ "Personal Information and Data Protection", *Protecting Personal Information*, Hart Publishing, 2019, doi:10.5040/9781509924882.ch-002, ISBN 978-1-5099-2485-1, S2CID 239275871, retrieved 2021-06-05
369. ^ Chapter 5. *An Act to support and promote electronic commerce by protecting personal information that is collected, used or disclosed in certain circumstances, by providing for the use of electronic means to communicate or record information or transactions and by amending the Canada Evidence Act, the Statutory Instruments Act and the Statute Revision Act*. Queen's Printer for Canada. 2000. OCLC 61417862.
370. ^ "Comments". *Statute Law Review*. **5** (1): 184–188. 1984. doi:10.1093/slr/5.1.184. ISSN 0144-3593.
371. ^ "Personal Information Protection and Electronic Documents Act" (PDF). Canadian Minister of Justice. Retrieved 25 January 2018.
372. ^ Werner, Martin (2011-05-11). "Privacy-protected communication for location-based services". *Security and Communication Networks*. **9** (2): 130–138. doi:10.1002/sec.330. ISSN 1939-0114.
373. ^ "Regulation for the Assurance of Confidentiality in Electronic Communications" (PDF). *Government Gazette of the Hellenic Republic*. Hellenic Authority for Communication Security and Privacy. 17 November 2011. Retrieved 25 January 2018.
374. ^ de Guise, Preston (2020-04-29), "Security, Privacy, Ethical, and Legal Considerations", *Data Protection*, Auerbach Publications, pp. 91–108, doi:10.1201/9780367463496-9, ISBN 978-0-367-46349-6, S2CID 219013948, retrieved 2021-06-05
375. ^ "Αριθμ. αποφ. 205/2013" (PDF). *Government Gazette of the Hellenic Republic*. Hellenic Authority for Communication Security and Privacy. 15 July 2013. Retrieved 25 January 2018.
376. ^ Andersson and Reimers, 2019, CYBER SECURITY EMPLOYMENT POLICY AND WORKPLACE DEMAND IN THE U.S. GOVERNMENT, EDULEARN19 Proceedings, Publication year: 2019 Pages: 7858-7866 https://library.iated.org/view/ANDERSON2019CYB
377. ^ "Definition of Security Culture". The Security Culture Framework. 9 April 2014.
378. ^ Roer, Kai; Petric, Gregor (2017). *The 2017 Security Culture Report - In depth insights into the human factor*. CLTRe North America, Inc. pp. 42–43. ISBN 978-1544933948.
379. ^ Akhtar, Salman, ed. (2018-03-21). *Good Feelings*. Routledge. doi:10.4324/9780429475313. ISBN 9780429475313.
380. ^ Anderson, D., Reimers, K. and Barretto, C. (March 2014). Post-Secondary Education Network Security: Results of Addressing the End-User Challenge.publication date Mar 11, 2014 publication description INTED2014 (International Technology, Education, and Development Conference)
381. ^ [a] [b] Schlienger, Thomas; Teufel, Stephanie (December 2003). "Information security culture - from analysis to change". *South African Computer Society (SAICSIT)*. **2003** (31): 46–52. hdl:10520/EJC27949.
382. ^ "IISP Skills Framework". Archived from the original on 2014-03-15. Retrieved 2014-04-27.
383. ^ "BSI-Standards". BSI. Archived from the original on 3 December 2013. Retrieved 29 November 2013.

Encryption, References

1. ^ [a] [b] [c] [d] [e] Kessler, Gary (November 17, 2006). "An Overview of Cryptography". Princeton University.
2. ^ [a] [b] [c] "History of Cryptography". Binance Academy. Archived from the original on 2020-04-26. Retrieved 2020-04-02.
3. ^ "Caesar Cipher in Cryptography". GeeksforGeeks. 2016-06-02. Retrieved 2020-04-02.
4. ^ "Wheel Cipher". www.monticello.org. Retrieved 2020-04-02.

5. ^ "M-94". www.cryptomuseum.com. Retrieved 2020-04-02.
6. ^ Hern, Alex (2014-11-14). "How did the Enigma machine work?". The Guardian. ISSN 0261-3077. Retrieved 2020-04-02.
7. ^ Unisys, Dr Glen E. Newton (2013-05-07). "The Evolution of Encryption". Wired. ISSN 1059-1028. Retrieved 2020-04-02.
8. ^ "Key Cryptography – an overview | ScienceDirect Topics". www.sciencedirect.com. Retrieved 2021-02-03.
9. ^ Stubbs, Rob. "Classification of Cryptographic Keys". www.cryptomathic.com. Retrieved 2021-02-03.
10. ^ "Chapter 3. Modular Arithmetic". www.doc.ic.ac.uk. Retrieved 2021-08-15.
11. ^ "Symmetric-key encryption software". Archived from the original on 2022-03-10. Retrieved 2022-02-15.
12. ^ Bellare, Mihir. "Public-Key Encryption in a Multi-user Setting: Security Proofs and Improvements." Springer Berlin Heidelberg, 2000. p. 1.
13. ^ "Public-Key Encryption – how GCHQ got there first!". gchq.gov.uk. Archived from the original on May 19, 2010.
14. ^ Goldreich, Oded. Foundations of Cryptography: Volume 2, Basic Applications. Vol. 2. Cambridge university press, 2004.
15. ^ Diffie, Whitfield; Hellman, Martin (1976), New directions in cryptography, vol. 22, IEEE transactions on Information Theory, pp. 644–654
16. ^ Kelly, Maria (December 7, 2009). "The RSA Algorithm: A Mathematical History of the Ubiquitous Cryptological Algorithm" (PDF). Swarthmore College Computer Society. Retrieved March 30, 2022.
17. ^ Prasetyo, Deny; Widianto, Eko Didik; Indasari, Ike Pratiwi (2019-09-06). "Short Message Service Encoding Using the Rivest-Shamir-Adleman Algorithm". Jurnal Online Informatika. 4 (1): 39. doi:10.15575/join.v4i1.264. ISSN 2527-9165.
18. ^ Kirk, Jeremy (April 29, 2010). "Symantec buys encryption specialist PGP for $300M". Computerworld.
19. ^ Robert Richardson, 2008 CSI Computer Crime and Security Survey at 19.i.cmpnet.com
20. ^ Keane, J. (13 January 2016). "Why stolen laptops still cause data breaches, and what's being done to stop them". PCWorld. IDG Communications, Inc. Retrieved 8 May 2018.
21. ^ Castricone, D.M. (2 February 2018). "Health Care Group News: $3.5 M OCR Settlement for Five Breaches Affecting Fewer Than 500 Patients Each". The National Law Review. National Law Forum LLC. Retrieved 8 May 2018.
22. ^ Bek, E. (19 May 2016). "Protect Your Company from Theft: Self Encrypting Drives". Western Digital Blog. Western Digital Corporation. Retrieved 8 May 2018.
23. ^ "DRM". Electronic Frontier Foundation.
24. ^ Fiber Optic Networks Vulnerable to Attack, Information Security Magazine, November 15, 2006, Sandra Kay Miller
25. ^ "Data Encryption in Transit Guideline | Information Security Office". security.berkeley.edu.
26. ^ "Welcome". Apple Support.
27. ^ Abood, Omar (July 2018). "A Survey on Cryptography Algorithms". International Journal of Scientific and Research Publications. 6: 495–516 – via ResearchGate.
28. ^ "Encryption methods: An overview". IONOS Digital Guide. Retrieved 2022-10-07.
29. ^ "Quantum computers vastly outperform supercomputers when it comes to energy efficiency". Physics World. 2020-05-01. Retrieved 2021-05-02.
30. ^ Sharma, Moolchand; Choudhary, Vikas; Bhatia, R. S.; Malik, Sahil; Raina, Anshuman; Khandelwal, Harshit (2021-04-03). "Leveraging the power of quantum computing for breaking RSA encryption". Cyber-Physical Systems. 7 (2): 73–92. doi:10.1080/23335777.2020.1811384. ISSN 2333-5777. S2CID 225312133.
31. ^ a b Solenov, Dmitry; Brieler, Jay; Scherrer, Jeffrey F. (2018). "The Potential of Quantum Computing and Machine Learning to Advance Clinical Research and Change the Practice of Medicine". Missouri Medicine. 115 (5): 463–467. ISSN 0026-6620. PMC 6205278. PMID 30385997.
32. ^ "Post-Quantum Cybersecurity Resources". www.nsa.gov. Archived from the original on 2021-01-18. Retrieved 2021-01-16.
33. ^ Yan Li; Nakul Sanjay Dhotre; Yasuhiro Ohara; Thomas M. Kroeger; Ethan L. Miller; Darrell D. E. Long. "Horus: Fine-Grained Encryption-Based Security for Large-Scale Storage" (PDF). www.ssrc.ucsc.edu. Discussion of encryption weaknesses for petabyte scale datasets.
34. ^ "The Padding Oracle Attack – why crypto is terrifying". Robert Heaton. Retrieved 2016-12-25.
35. ^ "Researchers crack open unusually advanced malware that hid for 5 years". Ars Technica. Retrieved 2016-12-25.
36. ^ "New cloud attack takes full control of virtual machines with little effort". Ars Technica. Retrieved 2016-12-25.
37. ^ Examples of data fragmentation technologies include Tahoe-LAFS and Storj.
38. ^ Burshteyn, Mike (2016-12-22). "What does 'Active Defense' mean?". CryptoMove. Retrieved 2016-12-25.[permanent dead link]
39. ^ CryptoMove Archived 2021-02-06 at the Wayback Machine is the first technology to continuously move, mutate, and re-encrypt ciphertext as a form of data protection.
40. ^ Catania, Simone. "The Modern Encryption Debate: What's at Stake?". CircleID.
41. ^ "What is a Trojan Virus – Malware Protection – Kaspersky Lab US".
42. ^ Kumar, Mohit (July 2019). "Kazakhstan Begins Intercepting HTTPS Internet Traffic Of All Citizens Forcefully". The Hacker News.
43. ^ Sheffer, Y.; Holz, R.; Saint-Andre, P. (February 2015). Summarizing Known Attacks on Transport Layer Security (TLS) and Datagram TLS (DTLS) (Report).
44. ^ Nikitin, Kirill; Barman, Ludovic; Lueks, Wouter; Underwood, Matthew; Hubaux, Jean-Pierre; Ford, Bryan (2019). "Reducing Metadata Leakage from Encrypted Files and Communication with PURBs" (PDF). Proceedings on Privacy Enhancing Technologies (PoPETS). 2019 (4): 6–33. arXiv:1806.03160. doi:10.2478/popets-2019-0056. S2CID 47011059.

Computer Security, References

1. ^ Schatz, Daniel; Bashroush, Rabih; Wall, Julie (2017). "Towards a More Representative Definition of Cyber Security". Journal of Digital Forensics, Security and Law. 12 (2). ISSN 1558-7215.
2. ^ "computer security | Definition & Facts | Britannica". www.britannica.com. Retrieved 12 July 2022.
3. ^ "Reliance spells end of road for ICT amateurs". The Australian. 7 May 2013.[dead link]
4. ^ Kianpour, Mazaher; Kowalski, Stewart; Øverby, Harald (2021). "Systematically Understanding Cybersecurity Economics: A Survey". Sustainability. 13 (24): 13677. doi:10.3390/su132413677.
5. ^ Stevens, Tim (11 June 2018). "Global Cybersecurity: New Directions in Theory and Methods" (PDF). Politics and Governance. 6 (2): 1–4. doi:10.17645/pag.v6i2.1569. Archived (PDF) from the original on 4 September 2019.
6. ^ a b Misa, Thomas J. (2016). "Computer Security Discourse at RAND, SDC, and NSA (1958-1970)". IEEE Annals of the History of Computing. 38 (4): 12–25. doi:10.1109/MAHC.2016.48. S2CID 17609542.
7. ^ A. J. Neumann, N. Statland and R. D. Webb (1977). "Post-processing audit tools and techniques" (PDF). nist.gov. US Department of Commerce, National Bureau of Standards. pp. 11-3–11-4. Archived (PDF) from the original on 10 October 2016. Retrieved 19 June 2020.
8. ^ Irwin, Luke (5 April 2018). "How NIST can protect the CIA triad, including the often overlooked 'I' – integrity". www.itgovernanceusa.com. Retrieved 16 January 2021.
9. ^ Perrin, Chad (30 June 2008). "The CIA Triad". techrepublic.com. Retrieved 31 May 2012.
10. ^ Stoneburner, G.; Hayden, C.; Feringa, A. (2004). Engineering Principles for Information Technology Security (PDF) (Report). csrc.nist.gov. doi:10.6028/NIST.SP.800-27rA. Archived (PDF) from the original on 12 October 2004. Note: this document has been superseded by later versions.
11. ^ Yost, Jeffrey R. (April 2015). "The Origin and Early History of the Computer Security Software Products Industry". IEEE Annals of the History of Computing. 37 (2): 46–58. doi:10.1109/MAHC.2015.21. ISSN 1934-1547. S2CID 18929482.
12. ^ Nakashima, Ellen (26 January 2008). "Bush Order Expands Network Monitoring: Intelligence Agencies to Track Intrusions". The Washington Post. Retrieved 8 February 2021.
13. ^ a b Nicole Perlroth (7 February 2021). "How the U.S. Lost to Hackers". The New York Times. Archived from the original on 28 December 2021. Retrieved 9 February 2021.
14. ^ "cve-website". www.cve.org. Retrieved 12 April 2023.
15. ^ "Computer Security and Mobile Security Challenges". researchgate.net. 3 December 2015. Archived from the original on 12 October 2016. Retrieved 4 August 2016.
16. ^ "Ghidra". Archived from the original on 15 August 2020. Retrieved 17 August 2020.
17. ^ Larabel, Michael (28 December 2017). "Syzbot: Google Continuously Fuzzing The Linux Kernel". www.phoronix.com/. Retrieved 25 March 2021.
18. ^ GOsafeonline (12 November 2014). "Distributed Denial of Service Attack". csa.gov.sg. Archived from the original on 6 August 2016. Retrieved 12 November 2014.
19. ^ Webroot (24 July 2018). "Multi-Vector Attacks Demand Multi-Vector Protection". MSSP Alert. Retrieved 11 May 2022.
20. ^ Millman, Renee (15 December 2017). "New polymorphic malware evades three-quarters of AV scanners". SC Magazine UK.
21. ^ "Identifying Phishing Attempts". Case. Archived from the original on 13 September 2015. Retrieved 4 July 2016.
22. ^ Lazarus, Ari (23 February 2018). "Phishers send fake invoices". Consumer Information. Retrieved 17 February 2020.
23. ^ a b "Email Security | Trellix". www.trellix.com. Retrieved 24 October 2022.
24. ^ Eilam, Eldad (2005). Reversing: secrets of reverse engineering. John Wiley & Sons. ISBN 978-0764574818.
25. ^ Arcos Sergio. "Social Engineering" (PDF). upc.edu. Archived (PDF) from the original on 3 December 2013. Retrieved 16 April 2019.
26. ^ Scannell, Kara (24 February 2016). "CEO email scam costs companies $2bn". Financial Times. No. 25 February 2016. Archived from the original on 23 June 2016. Retrieved 7 May 2016.
27. ^ "Bucks leak tax info of players, employees as result of email scam". Associated Press. 20 May 2016. Archived from the original on 20 May 2016. Retrieved 20 May 2016.
28. ^ "What is Spoofing? – Definition from Techopedia". techopedia.com. Archived from the original on 30 June 2016. Retrieved 16 January 2022.
29. ^ Butterfield, Andrew; Ngondi, Gerard Ekembe, eds. (21 January 2016). spoofing. doi:10.1093/acref/9780199688975.001.0001. ISBN 978-0199688975. Retrieved 8 October 2017. {{cite book}}: |journal= ignored (help)
30. ^ Marcel, Sébastien; Nixon, Mark; Li, Stan, eds. (2014). Handbook of Biometric Anti-Spoofing: Trusted Biometrics under Spoofing Attacks. Advances in Computer Vision and Pattern Recognition. London: Springer. doi:10.1007/978-1-4471-6524-8. ISBN 978-1447165248. ISSN 2191-6594. LCCN 2014942635. S2CID 27594864.
31. ^ "80 to 0 in Under 5 Seconds: Falsifying a Medical Patient's Vitals". www.trellix.com. Retrieved 9 February 2023.
32. ^ Gallagher, Sean (14 May 2014). "Photos of an NSA "upgrade" factory show Cisco router getting implant". Ars Technica. Archived from the original on 4 August 2014. Retrieved 3 August 2014.
33. ^ Bendovschi, Andreea (2015). "Cyber-Attacks – Trends, Patterns and Security Countermeasures". Procedia Economics and Finance. 28: 24–31. doi:10.1016/S2212-5671(15)01077-1.
34. ^ "Obfuscated Files or Information: HTML Smuggling, Sub-technique T1027.006 - Enterprise | MITRE ATT&CK®". attack.mitre.org. Retrieved 22 February 2023.

35. ^ Lim, Joo S., et al. "Exploring the Relationship between Organizational Culture and Information Security Culture." Australian Information Security Management Conference.
36. ^ K. Reimers, D. Andersson (2017) Post-Secondary Education Network Security: The End User Challenge and Evolving Threats, ICERI2017 Proceedings, pp. 1787–1796.
37. ^ "Verizon Data Breach Investigations Report 2020" (PDF). verizon.com. Archived (PDF) from the original on 19 May 2020. Retrieved 17 September 2021.
38. ^ a b c Schlienger, Thomas; Teufel, Stephanie (2003). "Information security culture-from analysis to change". South African Computer Journal. 31: 46–52.
39. ^ Lin, Tom C. W. (3 July 2017). "The New Market Manipulation". Emory Law Journal. 66: 1253. SSRN 2996896.
40. ^ Lin, Tom C. W. (2016). "Financial Weapons of War". Minnesota Law Review. SSRN 2765010.
41. ^ Lebo, Harlan (2000). The UCLA Internet Report: Surveying the Digital Future. World Internet Project. 1-55
42. ^ Pagliery, Jose (18 November 2014). "Hackers attacked the U.S. energy grid 79 times this year". CNN Money. Cable News Network. Archived from the original on 18 February 2015. Retrieved 16 April 2015.
43. ^ P. G. Neumann, "Computer Security in Aviation," presented at International Conference on Aviation Safety and Security in the 21st Century, White House Commission on Safety and Security, 1997.
44. ^ J. Zellan, Aviation Security. Hauppauge, NY: Nova Science, 2003, pp. 65–70.
45. ^ "Air Traffic Control Systems Vulnerabilities Could Make for Unfriendly Skies [Black Hat] – SecurityWeek.Com". 27 July 2012. Archived from the original on 8 February 2015.
46. ^ "Hacker Says He Can Break into Airplane Systems Using In-Flight Wi-Fi". NPR. 4 August 2014. Archived from the original on 8 February 2015. Retrieved 19 March 2020.
47. ^ Jim Finkle (4 August 2014). "Hacker says to show passenger jets at risk of cyber attack". Reuters. Archived from the original on 13 October 2015. Retrieved 21 November 2021.
48. ^ "Pan-European Network Services (PENS) – Eurocontrol.int". Archived from the original on 12 December 2016.
49. ^ "Centralised Services: NewPENS moves forward – Eurocontrol.int". 17 January 2016. Archived from the original on 19 March 2017.
50. ^ "NextGen Data Communication". FAA. Archived from the original on 13 March 2015. Retrieved 15 June 2017.
51. ^ "e-Passports | Homeland Security". www.dhs.gov. Retrieved 3 February 2023.
52. ^ "The Australian ePassport. Australian Government Department of Foreign Affairs and Trade website". Archived from the original on 9 January 2015. Retrieved 1 May 2023.
53. ^ a b "Is Your Watch Or Thermostat A Spy? Cybersecurity Firms Are On It". NPR. 6 August 2014. Archived from the original on 11 February 2015.
54. ^ Humana Inc. (15 November 2000). "Humana Web Site Named Best Interactive Site by eHealthcare Strategy & Trends; re LOUISVILLE, Ky., Nov. 15 PRNewswire". prnewswire.com.
55. ^ Kruse, CB; Smith, B; Vanderlinden, H; Nealand, A (21 July 2017). "Security Techniques for the Electronic Health Records". Journal of Medical Systems. 41 (8): 127. doi:10.1007/s10916-017-0778-4. PMC 5522514. PMID 28733949.
56. ^ Melvin Backman (18 September 2014). "Home Depot: 56 million cards exposed in breach". CNNMoney. Archived from the original on 18 December 2014.
57. ^ "Staples: Breach may have affected 1.16 million customers' cards". Fortune.com. 19 December 2014. Archived from the original on 21 December 2014. Retrieved 21 December 2014.
58. ^ "Target: 40 million credit cards compromised". CNN. 19 December 2013. Archived from the original on 1 December 2017. Retrieved 29 November 2017.
59. ^ Cowley, Stacy (2 October 2017). "2.5 Million More People Potentially Exposed in Equifax Breach". The New York Times. Archived from the original on 1 December 2017. Retrieved 29 November 2017.
60. ^ Jim Finkle (23 April 2014). "Exclusive: FBI warns healthcare sector vulnerable to cyber attacks". Reuters. Archived from the original on 4 June 2016. Retrieved 23 May 2016.
61. ^ Seals, Tara (6 November 2015). "Lack of Employee Security Training Plagues US Businesses". Infosecurity Magazine. Archived from the original on 9 November 2017. Retrieved 8 November 2017.
62. ^ Bright, Peter (15 February 2011). "Anonymous speaks: the inside story of the HBGary hack". Arstechnica.com. Archived from the original on 27 March 2011. Retrieved 29 March 2011.
63. ^ Anderson, Nate (9 February 2011). "How one man tracked down Anonymous – and paid a heavy price". Arstechnica.com. Archived from the original on 29 March 2011. Retrieved 29 March 2011.
64. ^ Palilery, Jose (24 December 2014). "What caused Sony hack: What we know now". CNN Money. Archived from the original on 4 January 2015. Retrieved 4 January 2015.
65. ^ James Cook (16 December 2014). "Sony Hackers Have Over 100 Terabytes Of Documents. Only Released 200 Gigabytes So Far". Business Insider. Archived from the original on 17 December 2014. Retrieved 18 December 2014.
66. ^ a b Timothy B. Lee (18 January 2015). "The next frontier of hacking: your car". Vox. Archived from the original on 17 March 2017.
67. ^ Tracking & Hacking: Security & Privacy Gaps Put American Drivers at Risk (PDF) (Report). 6 February 2015. Archived (PDF) from the original on 9 November 2016. Retrieved 4 November 2016.
68. ^ "Cybersecurity expert: It will take a 'major event' for companies to take this issue seriously". AOL.com. 5 January 2017. Archived from the original on 20 January 2017. Retrieved 22 January 2017.
69. ^ "The problem with self-driving cars: who controls the code?". The Guardian. 23 December 2015. Archived from the original on 16 March 2017. Retrieved 22 January 2017.
70. ^ Stephen Checkoway; Damon McCoy; Brian Kantor; Danny Anderson; Hovav Shacham; Stefan Savage; Karl Koscher; Alexei Czeskis; Franziska Roesner; Tadayoshi Kohno (2011). Comprehensive Experimental Analyses of Automotive Attack Surfaces (PDF). SEC'11 Proceedings of the 20th USENIX conference on Security. Berkeley, California, US: USENIX Association. p. 6. Archived (PDF) from the original on 21 February 2015.
71. ^ Greenberg, Andy (21 July 2015). "Hackers Remotely Kill a Jeep on the Highway – With Me in It". Wired. Archived from the original on 19 January 2017. Retrieved 22 January 2017.
72. ^ "Hackers take control of car, drive it into a ditch". The Independent. 22 July 2015. Archived from the original on 2 February 2017. Retrieved 22 January 2017.
73. ^ "Tesla fixes software bug that allowed Chinese hackers to control car remotely". The Telegraph. 21 September 2016. Archived from the original on 2 February 2017. Retrieved 22 January 2017.
74. ^ Kang, Cecilia (19 September 2016). "Self-Driving Cars Gain Powerful Ally: The Government". The New York Times. Archived from the original on 14 February 2017. Retrieved 22 January 2017.
75. ^ "Federal Automated Vehicles Policy" (PDF). Archived (PDF) from the original on 21 January 2017. Retrieved 22 January 2017.
76. ^ "Vehicle Cybersecurity | NHTSA". www.nhtsa.gov. Retrieved 25 November 2022.
77. ^ "Thales supplies smart driver license to 4 states in Mexico".
78. ^ "4 Companies Using RFID for Supply Chain Management". atlasRFIDstore. Retrieved 3 February 2023.
79. ^ "The Cutting Edge of RFID Technology and Applications for Manufacturing and Distribution".
80. ^ Rahman, Mohammad Anwar; Khadem, Mohammad Miftaur; Sarder, MD. "Application of RFID in Supply Chain System". CiteSeerX 10.1.1.397.7831.
81. ^ "Gary McKinnon profile: Autistic 'hacker' who started writing computer programs at 14". The Daily Telegraph. London. 23 January 2009. Archived from the original on 2 June 2010.
82. ^ "Gary McKinnon extradition ruling due by 16 October". BBC News. 6 September 2012. Archived from the original on 6 September 2012. Retrieved 25 September 2012.
83. ^ Law Lords Department (30 July 2008). "House of Lords – Mckinnon V Government of The United States of America and Another". Publications.parliament.uk. Archived from the original on 7 March 2009. Retrieved 30 January 2010. 15. ... alleged to total over $700,000
84. ^ "NSA Accessed Mexican President's Email" Archived 6 November 2015 at the Wayback Machine, 20 October 2013, Jens Glüsing, Laura Poitras, Marcel Rosenbach and Holger Stark, spiegel.de
85. ^ Sanders, Sam (4 June 2015). "Massive Data Breach Puts 4 Million Federal Employees' Records at Risk". NPR. Archived from the original on 5 June 2015. Retrieved 5 June 2015.
86. ^ Liptak, Kevin (4 June 2015). "U.S. government hacked; feds think China is the culprit". CNN. Archived from the original on 6 June 2015. Retrieved 5 June 2015.
87. ^ Sean Gallagher. "Encryption "would not have helped" at OPM, says DHS official". Archived from the original on 24 June 2017.
88. ^ Davis, Michelle R. (19 October 2015). "Schools Learn Lessons From Security Breaches". Education Week. Archived from the original on 10 June 2016. Retrieved 23 May 2016.
89. ^ "GE's Introduces ACUVision as a Single Panel Solution". www.securityinfowatch.com. Security Info Watch. 11 August 2005. Retrieved 24 September 2019.
90. ^ "Internet of Things Global Standards Initiative". ITU. Archived from the original on 26 June 2015. Retrieved 26 June 2015.
91. ^ Singh, Jatinder; Pasquier, Thomas; Bacon, Jean; Ko, Hajoon; Eyers, David (2015). "Twenty Cloud Security Considerations for Supporting the Internet of Things". IEEE Internet of Things Journal. 3 (3): 269–284. doi:10.1109/JIOT.2015.2460333. S2CID 4732406.
92. ^ Chris Clearfield. "Why The FTC Can't Regulate The Internet Of Things". Forbes. Archived from the original on 27 June 2015. Retrieved 26 June 2015.
93. ^ "Internet of Things: Science Fiction or Business Fact?" (PDF). Harvard Business Review. Archived (PDF) from the original on 17 March 2015. Retrieved 4 November 2016.
94. ^ Ovidiu Vermesan; Peter Friess. "Internet of Things: Converging Technologies for Smart Environments and Integrated Ecosystems" (PDF). River Publishers. Archived (PDF) from the original on 12 October 2016. Retrieved 4 November 2016.
95. ^ Christopher Clearfield "Rethinking Security for the Internet of Things" Harvard Business Review Blog, 26 June 2013 Archived 20 September 2013 at the Wayback Machine/
96. ^ "Hotel room burglars exploit critical flaw in electronic door locks". Ars Technica. 26 November 2012. Archived from the original on 14 May 2016. Retrieved 23 May 2016.
97. ^ "Hospital Medical Devices Used As Weapons in Cyberattacks". Dark Reading. 6 August 2015. Archived from the original on 29 May 2016. Retrieved 23 May 2016.
98. ^ Jeremy Kirk (17 October 2012). "Pacemaker hack can deliver deadly 830-volt jolt". Computerworld. Archived from the original on 4 June 2016. Retrieved 23 May 2016.
99. ^ "How Your Pacemaker Will Get Hacked". The Daily Beast. Kaiser Health News. 17 November 2014. Archived from the original on 20 May 2016. Retrieved 23 May 2016.
100. ^ Leetaru, Kalev. "Hacking Hospitals And Holding Hostages: Cybersecurity In 2016". Forbes. Archived from the original on 29 December 2016. Retrieved 29 December 2016.
101. ^ a b "Cyber-Angriffe: Krankenhäuser rücken ins Visier der Hacker". Wirtschafts Woche. 7 December 2016. Archived from the original on 29 December 2016. Retrieved 29 December 2016.
102. ^ "Hospitals keep getting attacked by ransomware – Here's why". Business Insider. Archived from the original on 29 December 2016. Retrieved 29 December 2016.
103. ^ "MedStar Hospitals Recovering After 'Ransomware' Hack". NBC News. 31 March 2016. Archived from the original on 29 December 2016. Retrieved 29 December 2016.
104. ^ Pauli, Darren. "US hospitals hacked with ancient exploits". The Register. Archived from the original on 16 November 2016. Retrieved 29 December 2016.
105. ^ Pauli, Darren. "Zombie OS lurches through Royal Melbourne Hospital spreading virus". The Register. Archived from the original on 29 December 2016. Retrieved 29 December 2016.
106. ^ "Hacked Lincolnshire hospital computer systems 'back up'". BBC News. 2 November 2016. Archived from the original on 29 December 2016. Retrieved 29 December 2016.
107. ^ "Lincolnshire operations cancelled after network attack". BBC News. 31 October 2016. Archived from the original on 29 December 2016. Retrieved 29 December 2016.
108. ^ "Legion cyber-attack: Next dump is sansad.nic.in, say hackers". The Indian Express. 12 December 2016. Archived from the original on 29 December 2016. Retrieved 29 December 2016.
109. ^ "Former New Hampshire Psychiatric Hospital Patient Accused Of Data Breach". CBS Boston. 27 December 2016. Archived from the original on 29 September 2017. Retrieved 29 December 2016.
110. ^ "Texas Hospital hacked, affects nearly 30,000 patient records". Healthcare IT News. 4 November 2016. Archived from the original on 29 December 2016. Retrieved 29 December 2016.
111. ^ Becker, Rachel (27 December 2016). "New cybersecurity guidelines for medical devices tackle evolving threats". The Verge. Archived from the original on 28 December 2016. Retrieved 29 December 2016.
112. ^ "Postmarket Management of Cybersecurity in Medical Devices" (PDF). Food and Drug Administration. 28 December 2016. Archived (PDF) from the original on 29 December 2016. Retrieved 29 December 2016.
113. ^ Brandt, Jaclyn (18 June 2018). "D.C. distributed energy proposal draws concerns of increased cybersecurity risks". Daily Energy Insider. Retrieved 4 July 2018.
114. ^ "Current Releases - The Open Mobile Alliance". openmobilealliance.org.
115. ^ Cashell, B., Jackson, W. D., Jickling, M., & Webel, B. (2004). The Economic Impact of Cyber-Attacks. Congressional Research Service, Government, and Finance Division. Washington DC: The Library of Congress.

116. ^ Gordon, Lawrence; Loeb, Martin (November 2002). "The Economics of Information Security Investment". ACM Transactions on Information and System Security. **5** (4): 438–457. doi:10.1145/581271.581274. S2CID 1500788.
117. ^ Han, Chen; Dongre, Rituja (2014). "Q&A. What Motivates Cyber-Attackers?". Technology Innovation Management Review. **4** (10): 40–42. doi:10.22215/timreview/838. ISSN 1927-0321.
118. ^ Chermick, Steven; Freilich, Joshua; Holt, Thomas (April 2017). "Exploring the Subculture of Ideologically Motivated Cyber-Attackers". Journal of Contemporary Criminal Justice. **33** (3): 212–233. doi:10.1177/1043986217699100. S2CID 152277480.
119. ^ Anderson, Ross (2020). Security engineering : a guide to building dependable distributed systems (3rd ed.). Indianapolis, IN. ISBN 978-1119642817. OCLC 1224516855.
120. ^ RFC 2828 Internet Security Glossary
121. ^ CNSS Instruction No. 4009 Archived 27 February 2012 at the Wayback Machine dated 26 April 2010
122. ^ "InfosecToday Glossary" (PDF). Archived (PDF) from the original on 20 November 2014.
123. ^ Definitions: IT Security Architecture Archived 15 March 2014 at the Wayback Machine. SecurityArchitecture.org, Jan 2006
124. ^ Jannsen, Cory. "Security Architecture". Techopedia. Janalta Interactive Inc. Archived from the original on 3 October 2014. Retrieved 9 October 2014.
125. ^ "How to Increase Cybersecurity Awareness". ISACA. Retrieved 25 February 2023.
126. ^ Woodie, Alex (9 May 2016). "Why ONI May Be Our Best Hope for Cyber Security Now". Archived from the original on 20 August 2016. Retrieved 13 July 2016.
127. ^ "Firms lose more to electronic than physical theft". Reuters. 18 October 2010. Archived from the original on 25 September 2015.
128. ^ Walkowski, Debbie (9 July 2019). "What Is The CIA Triad?". F5 Labs. Retrieved 25 February 2020.
129. ^ "Knowing Value of Data Assets is Crucial to Cybersecurity Risk Management | SecurityWeek.Com". www.securityweek.com. 3 December 2018. Retrieved 25 February 2020.
130. ^ Foreman, P: Vulnerability Management, p. 1. Taylor & Francis Group, 2010. ISBN 978-1439801505
131. ^ Academy, Cisco Networking (2018). CCNA Cybersecurity Operations Companion Guide. Cisco Press. ISBN 978-0135166246.
132. ^ Alan Calder and Geraint Williams (2014). PCI DSS: A Pocket Guide (3rd ed.). IT Governance Limited. ISBN 978-1849285544. network vulnerability scans at least quarterly and after any significant change in the network
133. ^ Harrison, J. (2003). "Formal verification at Intel". 18th Annual IEEE Symposium of Logic in Computer Science, 2003. Proceedings. pp. 45–54. doi:10.1109/LICS.2003.1210044. ISBN 978-0769518848. S2CID 44585546.
134. ^ Umrigar, Zerksis D.; Pitchumani, Vijay (1983). "Formal verification of a real-time hardware design". Proceeding DAC '83 Proceedings of the 20th Design Automation Conference. IEEE Press. pp. 221–227. ISBN 978-0818600265.
135. ^ "Abstract Formal Specification of the seL4/ARMv6 API" (PDF). Archived from the original (PDF) on 21 May 2015. Retrieved 19 May 2015.
136. ^ Christoph Baumann, Bernhard Beckert, Holger Blasum, and Thorsten Bormer Ingredients of Operating System Correctness? Lessons Learned in the Formal Verification of PikeOS Archived 19 July 2011 at the Wayback Machine
137. ^ "Getting it Right" Archived 4 May 2013 at the Wayback Machine by Jack Ganssle
138. ^ Treglia, J., & Delia, M. (2017). Cyber Security Inoculation. Presented at NYS Cyber Security Conference, Empire State Plaza Convention Center, Albany, NY, 3–4 June.
139. ^ Villasenor, John (2010). "The Hacker in Your Hardware: The Next Security Threat". Scientific American. **303** (2): 82–88. Bibcode:2010SciAm.303b..82V. doi:10.1038/scientificamerican0810-82. PMID 20684377.
140. ^ Waksman, Adam; Sethumadhavan, Simha (2010), "Tamper Evident Microprocessors" (PDF), Proceedings of the IEEE Symposium on Security and Privacy, Oakland, California, archived from the original (PDF) on 21 September 2013, retrieved 27 August 2019
141. ^ "Token-based authentication". SafeNet.com. Archived from the original on 20 March 2014. Retrieved 20 March 2014.
142. ^ "Lock and protect your Windows PC". TheWindowsClub.com. 10 February 2010. Archived from the original on 20 March 2014. Retrieved 20 March 2014.
143. ^ James Greene (2012). "Intel Trusted Execution Technology: White Paper" (PDF). Intel Corporation. Archived (PDF) from the original on 11 June 2014. Retrieved 18 December 2013.
144. ^ "SafeNet ProtectDrive 8.4". SCMagazine.com. 4 October 2008. Archived from the original on 20 March 2014. Retrieved 20 March 2014.
145. ^ "Secure Hard Drives: Lock Down Your Data". PCMag.com. 11 May 2009. Archived from the original on 21 June 2017.
146. ^ Souppaya, Murugiah P.; Scarfone, Karen (2013). "Guidelines for Managing the Security of Mobile Devices in the Enterprise". National Institute of Standards and Technology. Special Publication (NIST SP). Gaithersburg, MD. doi:10.6028/NIST.SP.800-124r1.
147. ^ "Forget IDs, use your phone as credentials". Fox Business Network. 4 November 2013. Archived from the original on 20 March 2014. Retrieved 20 March 2014.
148. ^ "Direct memory access protections for Mac computers". Apple. Retrieved 16 November 2022.
149. ^ "Using IOMMU for DMA Protection in UEFI Firmware" (PDF). Intel Corporation. Archived (PDF) from the original on 9 December 2021. Retrieved 16 November 2022.
150. ^ Babaei, Armin; Schiele, Gregor; Zohner, Michael (26 July 2022). "Reconfigurable Security Architecture (RESA) Based on PUF for FPGA-Based IoT Devices". Sensors. **22** (15): 5577. Bibcode:2022Senso..22.5577B. doi:10.3390/s22155577. ISSN 1424-8220. PMC 9331300. PMID 35898079.
151. ^ Hassija, Vikas; Chamola, Vinay; Gupta, Vatsal; Jain, Sarthak; Guizani, Nadra (15 April 2021). "A Survey on Supply Chain Security: Application Areas, Security Threats, and Solution Architectures". IEEE Internet of Things Journal. **8** (8): 6222–6246. doi:10.1109/JIOT.2020.3025775. ISSN 2327-4662. S2CID 226767829.
152. ^ Lipner, Steve (2015). "The Birth and Death of the Orange Book". IEEE Annals of the History of Computing. **37** (2): 19–31. doi:10.1109/MAHC.2015.27. S2CID 16625319.
153. ^ Kelly Jackson Higgins (18 November 2008). "Secure OS Gets Highest NSA Rating, Goes Commercial". Dark Reading. Archived from the original on 3 December 2013. Retrieved 1 December 2013.
154. ^ "Board or bored? Lockheed Martin gets into the COTS hardware biz". VITA Technologies Magazine. 10 December 2010. Archived from the original on 2 May 2012. Retrieved 9 March 2012.
155. ^ Sanghavi, Alok (21 May 2010). "What is formal verification?". EE Times_Asia.
156. ^ Ferraiolo, D.F. & Kuhn, D.R. (October 1992). "Role-Based Access Control" (PDF). 15th National Computer Security Conference: 554–563.
157. ^ Sandhu R, Coyne EJ, Feinstein HL, Youman CE (August 1996). "Role-Based Access Control Models" (PDF). IEEE Computer. **29** (2): 38–47. CiteSeerX 10.1.1.50.7649. doi:10.1109/2.485845. S2CID 1958270.
158. ^ Abreu, Vilmar; Santin, Altair O.; Viegas, Eduardo K.; Stihler, Maicon (2017). "A multi-domain role activation model". 2017 IEEE International Conference on Communications (ICC) (PDF). IEEE Press. pp. 1–6. doi:10.1109/ICC.2017.7997247. ISBN 978-1467389990. S2CID 6185138.
159. ^ A.C. O'Connor & R.J. Loomis (March 2002). Economic Analysis of Role-Based Access Control (PDF). Research Triangle Institute. p. 145.
160. ^ "Studies prove once again that users are the weakest link in the security chain". CSO Online. 22 January 2014. Retrieved 8 October 2018.
161. ^ "The Role of Human Error in Successful Security Attacks". IBM Security Intelligence. 2 September 2014. Retrieved 8 October 2018.
162. ^ "90% of security incidents trace back to PEBKAC and ID10T errors". Computerworld. 15 April 2015. Retrieved 8 October 2018.
163. ^ "Protect your online banking with 2FA". NZ Bankers Association. 7 October 2018. Retrieved 7 September 2019.
164. ^ "IBM Security Services 2014 Cyber Security Intelligence Index" (PDF). 2014. Retrieved 9 October 2020.[permanent dead link]
165. ^ Caldwell, Tracey (12 February 2013). "Risky business: why security awareness is crucial for employees". The Guardian. Retrieved 8 October 2018.
166. ^ "Developing a Security Culture". CPNI - Centre for the Protection of National Infrastructure. Archived from the original on 9 October 2018. Retrieved 8 October 2018.
167. ^ [a] [b] "Cyber Hygiene – ENISA". Retrieved 27 September 2018.
168. ^ [a] [b] Kaljulaid, Kersti (16 October 2017). "President of the Republic at the Aftenposten's Technology Conference". Retrieved 27 September 2018.
169. ^ Kuchler, Hannah (27 April 2015). "Security execs call on companies to improve 'cyber hygiene'". Financial Times. Archived from the original on 10 December 2022. Retrieved 27 September 2018.
170. ^ "From AI to Russia, Here's How Estonia's President Is Planning for the Future". WIRED. Retrieved 28 September 2018.
171. ^ "Professor Len Adleman explains how he coined the term "computer virus"". WeLiveSecurity. 1 November 2017. Retrieved 28 September 2018.
172. ^ "Statement of Dr. Vinton G. Cerf". www.jec.senate.gov. Retrieved 28 September 2018.
173. ^ Anna, Eshoo (22 May 2018). "H.R.3010 - 115th Congress (2017-2018): Promoting Good Cyber Hygiene Act of 2017". www.congress.gov. Retrieved 28 September 2018.
174. ^ "Analysis | The Cybersecurity 202: Agencies struggling with basic cybersecurity despite Trump's pledge to prioritize it". The Washington Post. Retrieved 28 September 2018.
175. ^ "Protected Voices". Federal Bureau of Investigation. Retrieved 28 September 2018.
176. ^ "The Leading Cloud Recruiting Software". iCIMS. Retrieved 13 March 2021.
177. ^ Wilcox, S. and Brown, B. (2005) 'Responding to Security Incidents – Sooner or Later Your Systems Will Be Compromised', Journal of Health Care Compliance, 7(2), pp. 41-48
178. ^ [a] [b] Jonathan Zittrain, 'The Future of The Internet', Penguin Books, 2008
179. ^ Information Security Archived 6 March 2016 at the Wayback Machine. United States Department of Defense, 1986
180. ^ "The TJX Companies, Inc. Victimized by Computer System Intrusion; Provides Information to Help Protect Customers" (Press release). The TJX Companies, Inc. 17 January 2007. Archived from the original on 27 September 2012. Retrieved 12 December 2009.
181. ^ Largest Customer Info Breach Grows Archived 28 September 2007 at the Wayback Machine. MyFox Twin Cities, 29 March 2007.
182. ^ "The Stuxnet Attack On Iran's Nuclear Plant Was 'Far More Dangerous' Than Previously Thought". Business Insider. 20 November 2013. Archived from the original on 9 May 2014.
183. ^ Reals, Tucker (24 September 2010). "Stuxnet Worm a U.S. Cyber-Attack on Iran Nukes?". CBS News. Archived from the original on 16 October 2013.
184. ^ Kim Zetter (17 February 2011). "Cyberwar Issues Likely to Be Addressed Only After a Catastrophe". Wired. Archived from the original on 18 February 2011. Retrieved 18 February 2011.
185. ^ Chris Carroll (18 October 2011). "Cone of silence surrounds U.S. cyberwarfare". Stars and Stripes. Archived from the original on 7 March 2012. Retrieved 30 October 2011.
186. ^ John Bumgarner (27 April 2010). "Computers as Weapons of War" (PDF). IO Journal. Archived from the original (PDF) on 19 December 2011. Retrieved 30 October 2011.
187. ^ Greenwald, Glenn (6 June 2013). "NSA collecting phone records of millions of Verizon customers daily". The Guardian. Archived from the original on 16 August 2013. Retrieved 16 August 2013. Exclusive: Top secret court order requiring Verizon to hand over all call data shows scale of domestic surveillance under Obama
188. ^ Seipel, Hubert. "Transcript: ARD interview with Edward Snowden". La Foundation Courage. Archived from the original on 14 July 2014. Retrieved 11 June 2014.
189. ^ Newman, Lily Hay (9 October 2013). "Can You Trust NIST?". IEEE Spectrum. Archived from the original on 1 February 2016.
190. ^ "NIST Removes Cryptography Algorithm from Random Number Generator Recommendations". National Institute of Standards and Technology. 21 April 2014.
191. ^ "New Snowden Leak: NSA Tapped Google, Yahoo Data Centers" Archived 9 July 2014 at the Wayback Machine, 31 October 2013, Lorenzo Franceschi-Bicchierai, mashable.com

192. ^ Michael Riley; Ben Elgin; Dune Lawrence; Carol Matlack (17 March 2014). "Target Missed Warnings in Epic Hack of Credit Card Data – Businessweek". Businessweek.com. Archived from the original on 27 January 2015.
193. ^ "Home Depot says 53 million emails stolen". CNET. CBS Interactive. 6 November 2014. Archived from the original on 9 December 2014.
194. ^ "Millions more Americans hit by government personnel data hack". Reuters. 9 July 2017. Archived from the original on 28 February 2017. Retrieved 25 February 2017.
195. ^ Barrett, Devlin (4 June 2015). "U.S. Suspects Hackers in China Breached About four (4) Million People's Records, Officials Say". The Wall Street Journal. Archived from the original on 4 June 2015.
196. ^ Risen, Tom (5 June 2015). "China Suspected in Theft of Federal Employee Records". U.S. News & World Report. Archived from the original on 6 June 2015.
197. ^ Zengerle, Patricia (19 July 2015). "Estimate of Americans hit by government personnel data hack skyrockets". Reuters. Archived from the original on 10 July 2015.
198. ^ Sanger, David (5 June 2015). "Hacking Linked to China Exposes Millions of U.S. Workers". The New York Times. Archived from the original on 5 June 2015.
199. ^ Mansfield-Devine, Steve (1 September 2015). "The Ashley Madison affair". Network Security. 2015 (9): 8–16. doi:10.1016/S1353-4858(15)30080-5.
200. ^ "Hackers Breached Colonial Pipeline Using Compromised Password".
201. ^ a b "Mikko Hypponen: Fighting viruses, defending the net". TED. Archived from the original on 16 January 2013.
202. ^ "Mikko Hypponen – Behind Enemy Lines". Hack in the Box Security Conference. Archived from the original on 25 November 2016.
203. ^ "Ensuring the Security of Federal Information Systems and Cyber Critical Infrastructure and Protecting the Privacy of Personally Identifiable Information". Government Accountability Office. Archived from the original on 19 November 2015. Retrieved 3 November 2015.
204. ^ King, Georgia (23 May 2018). "The Venn diagram between libertarians and crypto bros is so close it's basically a circle". Quartz.
205. ^ Kirby, Carrie (24 June 2011). "Former White House aide backs some Net regulation / Clarke says government, industry deserve 'F' in cyber security". The San Francisco Chronicle.
206. ^ McCarthy, Daniel (11 June 2018). "Privatizing Political Authority: Cybersecurity, Public-Private Partnerships, and the Reproduction of Liberal Political Order". Politics and Governance. 6 (2): 5–12. doi:10.17645/pag.v6i2.1335.
207. ^ "It's Time to Treat Cybersecurity as a Human Rights Issue". Human Rights Watch. 26 May 2020. Retrieved 26 May 2020.
208. ^ "FIRST Mission". FIRST. Retrieved 6 July 2018.
209. ^ "FIRST Members". FIRST. Retrieved 6 July 2018.
210. ^ "European council". Archived from the original on 3 December 2014.
211. ^ "MAAWG". Archived from the original on 23 September 2014.
212. ^ "MAAWG". Archived from the original on 17 October 2014.
213. ^ "Government of Canada Launches Canada's Cyber Security Strategy". Market Wired. 3 October 2010. Archived from the original on 2 November 2014. Retrieved 1 November 2014.
214. ^ a b "Canada's Cyber Security Strategy". Public Safety Canada. Government of Canada. Archived from the original on 2 November 2014. Retrieved 1 November 2014.
215. ^ a b c "Action Plan 2010–2015 for Canada's Cyber Security Strategy". Public Safety Canada. Government of Canada. Archived from the original on 2 November 2014. Retrieved 3 November 2014.
216. ^ "Cyber Incident Management Framework For Canada". Public Safety Canada. Government of Canada. Archived from the original on 2 November 2014. Retrieved 3 November 2014.
217. ^ "Action Plan 2010–2015 for Canada's Cyber Security Strategy". Public Safety Canada. Government of Canada. Archived from the original on 2 November 2014. Retrieved 1 November 2014.
218. ^ "Canadian Cyber Incident Response Centre". Public Safety Canada. Archived from the original on 8 October 2014. Retrieved 1 November 2014.
219. ^ "Cyber Security Bulletins". Public Safety Canada. Archived from the original on 8 October 2014. Retrieved 1 November 2014.
220. ^ "Report a Cyber Security Incident". Public Safety Canada. Government of Canada. Archived from the original on 11 November 2014. Retrieved 3 November 2014.
221. ^ "Government of Canada Launches Cyber Security Awareness Month With New Public Awareness Partnership". Market Wired. Government of Canada. 27 September 2012. Archived from the original on 3 November 2014. Retrieved 3 November 2014.
222. ^ "Cyber Security Cooperation Program". Public Safety Canada. Archived from the original on 2 November 2014. Retrieved 1 November 2014.
223. ^ "Cyber Security Cooperation Program". Public Safety Canada. 16 December 2015. Archived from the original on 2 November 2014.
224. ^ "GetCyberSafe". Get Cyber Safe. Government of Canada. Archived from the original on 11 November 2014. Retrieved 3 November 2014.
225. ^ "6.16 Internet security: National IT independence and China's cyber policy," in: Sebastian Heilmann, editor, ["China's Political System - Publications - About us - Mercator Institute for China Studies". Archived from the original on 23 March 2017. Retrieved 11 May 2017. China's Political System], Lanham, Boulder, New York, London: Rowman & Littlefield Publishers (2017) ISBN 978-1442277342
226. ^ "Need for proper structure of PPPs to address specific cyberspace risks". Archived from the original on 13 November 2017.
227. ^ "National Cyber Safety and Security Standards(NCSSS)-Home". www.ncdrc.res.in.
228. ^ "South Korea seeks global support in cyber attack probe". BBC Monitoring Asia Pacific. 7 March 2011.
229. ^ Kwanwoo Jun (23 September 2013). "Seoul Puts a Price on Cyberdefense". The Wall Street Journal. Dow Jones & Company, Inc. Archived from the original on 25 September 2013. Retrieved 24 September 2013.
230. ^ "Text of H.R.4962 as Introduced in House: International Cybercrime Reporting and Cooperation Act – U.S. Congress". OpenCongress. Archived from the original on 28 December 2010. Retrieved 25 September 2013.
231. ^ "Home | Homeland Security & Governmental Affairs Committee". www.hsgac.senate.gov. Archived from the original on 20 January 2012.
232. ^ "Biden Adviser On Cyber Threats And The New Executive Order To Combat Them". NPR.
233. ^ Executive Order on Improving the Nation's Cybersecurity (full text)
234. ^ "National Cyber Security Division". U.S. Department of Homeland Security. Archived from the original on 11 June 2008. Retrieved 14 June 2008.
235. ^ a b "FAQ: Cyber Security R&D Center". U.S. Department of Homeland Security S&T Directorate. Archived from the original on 6 October 2008. Retrieved 14 June 2008.
236. ^ AFP-JiJi, "U.S. boots up cybersecurity center", 31 October 2009.
237. ^ "Federal Bureau of Investigation – Priorities". Federal Bureau of Investigation. Archived from the original on 11 July 2016.
238. ^ "Internet Crime Complaint Center (IC3) – Home". Archived from the original on 20 November 2011.
239. ^ "Infragard, Official Site". Infragard. Archived from the original on 9 September 2010. Retrieved 10 September 2010.
240. ^ "Robert S. Mueller, III – InfraGard Interview at the 2005 InfraGard Conference". Infragard (Official Site) – "Media Room". Archived from the original on 17 June 2011. Retrieved 9 December 2009.
241. ^ "CCIPS". 25 March 2015. Archived from the original on 23 August 2006.
242. ^ "A Framework for a Vulnerability Disclosure Program for Online Systems". Cybersecurity Unit, Computer Crime & Intellectual Property Section Criminal Division U.S. Department of Justice. July 2017. Retrieved 9 July 2018.
243. ^ "Mission and Vision". www.cybercom.mil. Retrieved 20 June 2020.
244. ^ "Speech". Defense.gov. Archived from the original on 15 April 2010. Retrieved 10 July 2010.
245. ^ Shachtman, Noah. "Military's Cyber Commander Swears: "No Role" in Civilian Networks" Archived 6 November 2010 at the Wayback Machine, The Brookings Institution Archived 10 February 2006 at the Wayback Machine, 23 September 2010.
246. ^ "FCC Cybersecurity". FCC. Archived from the original on 27 May 2010. Retrieved 3 December 2014.
247. ^ "Cybersecurity for Medical Devices and Hospital Networks: FDA Safety Communication". Food and Drug Administration. Archived from the original on 28 May 2016. Retrieved 23 May 2016.
248. ^ "Automotive Cybersecurity – National Highway Traffic Safety Administration (NHTSA)". Archived from the original on 25 May 2016. Retrieved 23 May 2016.
249. ^ Air Traffic Control: FAA Needs a More Comprehensive Approach to Address Cybersecurity As Agency Transitions to NextGen (Report). U. S. Government Accountability Office. 14 April 2015. Archived from the original on 13 June 2016. Retrieved 23 May 2016.
250. ^ Aliya Sternstein (4 March 2016). "FAA Working on New Guidelines for Hack-Proof Planes". Nextgov. Archived from the original on 19 May 2016. Retrieved 23 May 2016.
251. ^ Bart Elias (18 June 2015). "Protecting Civil Aviation from Cyberattacks" (PDF). Archived (PDF) from the original on 17 October 2016. Retrieved 4 November 2016.
252. ^ Andersson and Reimers, 2019, CYBER SECURITY EMPLOYMENT POLICY AND WORKPLACE DEMAND IN THE U.S. GOVERNMENT, EDULEARN19 Proceedings, Publication year: 2019 Pages: 7858-7866 https://library.iated.org/view/ANDERSON2019CYB
253. ^ Verton, Dan (28 January 2004). "DHS launches national cyber alert system". Computerworld. IDG. Archived from the original on 31 August 2005. Retrieved 15 June 2008.
254. ^ Clayton, Mark (7 March 2011). "The new cyber arms race". The Christian Science Monitor. Archived from the original on 16 April 2015. Retrieved 16 April 2015.
255. ^ Nakashima, Ellen (13 September 2016). "Obama to be urged to split cyberwar command from NSA". The Washington Post. Archived from the original on 12 October 2016. Retrieved 15 June 2017.
256. ^ Overland, Indra (1 March 2019). "The geopolitics of renewable energy: Debunking four emerging myths". Energy Research & Social Science. 49: 36–40. doi:10.1016/j.erss.2018.10.018. ISSN 2214-6296.
257. ^ Maness, Ryan C.; Valeriano, Brandon (11 June 2018). "How We Stopped Worrying about Cyber Doom and Started Collecting Data". Politics and Governance. 6 (2): 49–60. doi:10.17645/pag.v6i2.1368. ISSN 2183-2463.
258. ^ Maness, Ryan C.; Valeriano, Brandon (25 March 2015). "The Impact of Cyber Conflict on International Interactions". Armed Forces & Society. 42 (2): 301–323. doi:10.1177/0095327x15572997. ISSN 0095-327X. S2CID 146145942.
259. ^ Bullard, Brittany (2016). Style and Statistics: The Art of Retail Analytics. Wiley. doi:10.1002/9781119271260.ch8. ISBN 978-1119270317.
260. ^ Oltsik, Jon (18 March 2016). "Cybersecurity Skills Shortage Impact on Cloud Computing". Network World. Archived from the original on 23 March 2016. Retrieved 23 March 2016.
261. ^ Robinson, Terry (30 May 2018). "Why is a Degree in Cyber Security one of the Best?". DegreeQuery.com. Archived from the original on 10 October 2021. Retrieved 10 October 2021.
262. ^ de Silva, Richard (11 October 2011). "Government vs. Commerce: The Cyber Security Industry and You (Part One)". Defence IQ. Archived from the original on 24 April 2014. Retrieved 24 April 2014.
263. ^ "Department of Computer Science". Archived from the original on 3 June 2013. Retrieved 30 April 2013.
264. ^ "About Cyber Security architect". cisa.gov. 1 August 2021. Retrieved 1 January 2022.
265. ^ Thomas, Jennifer (2 June 2021). "About Cyber Security Administrator (DPO)". cybersguards.com. Retrieved 4 January 2022.
266. ^ "How to become a Chief Information Security Officer (CISO)?". cybersecuritycareer.org. 1 August 2021. Retrieved 4 January 2022.
267. ^ "Data Protection Officers". ico.org.uk. January 2021.
268. ^ "Student Cybersecurity Resources". NICCS (US National Initiative for Cybercareers and Studies). Archived from the original on 5 November 2020.

269. ^ "Current Job Opportunities at DHS". U.S. Department of Homeland Security. Archived from the original on 2 May 2013. Retrieved 5 May 2013.
270. ^ "Cybersecurity Training & Exercises". U.S. Department of Homeland Security. 12 May 2010. Archived from the original on 7 January 2015. Retrieved 9 January 2015.
271. ^ "Cyber Security Awareness Free Training and Webcasts". MS-ISAC (Multi-State Information Sharing & Analysis Center). Archived from the original on 6 January 2015. Retrieved 9 January 2015.
272. ^ "DoD Approved 8570 Baseline Certifications". iase.disa.mil. Archived from the original on 21 October 2016. Retrieved 19 June 2017.
273. ^ "The UK Cyber Security Strategy: Report on Progress and Forward Plans December 2014" (PDF). United Kingdom Cabinet Office. Archived (PDF) from the original on 18 April 2018. Retrieved 20 August 2021.
274. ^ "Cyber skills for a vibrant and secure UK". GOV.UK.
275. ^ "Singapore Operational Technology (OT) Cybersecurity Competency Framework".
276. ^ "Confidentiality". Retrieved 31 October 2011.
277. ^ "Data Integrity". Archived from the original on 6 November 2011. Retrieved 31 October 2011.
278. ^ "Endpoint Security". 10 November 2010. Archived from the original on 16 March 2014. Retrieved 15 March 2014.

Physical Security, References

1. ^ "Chapter 1: Physical Security Challenges". Field Manual 3-19.30: Physical Security. Headquarters, United States Department of Army. 2001. Archived from the original on 2013-03-13.
2. ^ Garcia, Mary Lynn (2007). Design and Evaluation of Physical Protection Systems. Butterworth-Heinemann. pp. 1–11. ISBN 9780080554280. Archived from the original on 2013-09-21.
3. ^ "Chapter 2: The Systems Approach". Field Manual 3-19.30: Physical Security. Headquarters, United States Department of Army. 2001. Archived from the original on 2013-09-21.
4. ^ Anderson, Ross (2001). Security Engineering. Wiley. ISBN 978-0-471-38922-4.
5. ^ For a detailed discussion on natural surveillance and CPTED, see Fennelly, Lawrence J. (2012). Effective Physical Security. Butterworth-Heinemann. pp. 4–6. ISBN 9780124158924. Archived from the original on 2018-01-05.
6. ^ Task Committee; Structural Engineering Institute (1999). Structural Design for Physical Security. ASCE. ISBN 978-0-7844-0457-7. Archived from the original on 2018-01-05.
7. ^ Baker, Paul R. (2012). "Security Construction Projects". In Baker, Paul R.; Benny, Daniel J. (eds.). The Complete Guide to Physical Security. CRC Press. ISBN 9781420099638. Archived from the original on 2018-01-05.
8. ^ "Chapter 4: Protective Barriers". Field Manual 3-19.30: Physical Security. Headquarters, United States Department of Army. 2001. Archived from the original on 2013-03-13.
9. ^ Talbot, Julian & Jakeman, Miles (2011). Security Risk Management Body of Knowledge. John Wiley & Sons. pp. 72–73. ISBN 9781118211267. Archived from the original on 2018-01-05.
10. ^ Kovacich, Gerald L. & Halibozek, Edward P. (2003). The Manager's Handbook for Corporate Security: Establishing and Managing a Successful Assets Protection Program. Butterworth-Heinemann. pp. 192–193. ISBN 9780750674874. Archived from the original on 2018-01-05.
11. ^ "Use of LED Lighting for Security Purposes". silvaconsultants.com. Retrieved 2020-10-06.
12. ^ "Chapter 6: Electronic Security Systems". Field Manual 3-19.30: Physical Security. Headquarters, United States Department of Army. 2001. Archived from the original on 2013-03-13.
13. ^ Fennelly, Lawrence J. (2012). Effective Physical Security. Butterworth-Heinemann. pp. 345–346. ISBN 9780124158924. Archived from the original on 2013-09-21.
14. ^ "Evaluation of alternative policies to combat false emergency calls" (PDF). p. 238. Archived from the original (PDF) on 2012-11-01.
15. ^ "Evaluation of alternative policies to combat false emergency calls" (PDF). p. 233. Archived from the original (PDF) on 2012-11-01.
16. ^ "Evaluating the Use of Public Surveillance Cameras for Crime Control and Prevention" (PDF). Archived (PDF) from the original on 2012-12-01.
17. ^ Crowell, William P.; et al. (2011). "Intelligent Video Analytics". In Cole, Eric (ed.). Physical and Logical Security Convergence. Syngress. ISBN 9780080558783. Archived from the original on 2018-01-05.
18. ^ Dufour, Jean-Yves (2012). Intelligent Video Surveillance Systems. John Wiley & Sons. ISBN 9781118577868. Archived from the original on 2018-01-05.
19. ^ Caputo, Anthony C. (2010). Digital Video Surveillance and Security. Butterworth-Heinemann. ISBN 9780080961699. Archived from the original on 2013-09-29.
20. ^ Tyska, Louis A. & Fennelly, Lawrence J. (2000). Physical Security: 150 Things You Should Know. Butterworth-Heinemann. p. 3. ISBN 9780750672559. Archived from the original on 2018-01-05.
21. ^ "Chapter 7: Access Control". Field Manual 3-19.30: Physical Security. Headquarters, United States Department of Army. 2001. Archived from the original on 2007-05-10.
22. ^ Pearson, Robert (2011). "Chapter 1: Electronic Access Control". Electronic Security Systems: A Manager's Guide to Evaluating and Selecting System Solutions. Butterworth-Heinemann. ISBN 9780080494708. Archived from the original on 2018-01-05.
23. ^ Secure (2023) Fast Security Guard Service From security guards to event security. Retrieved 2023-08-07.
24. ^ Reid, Robert N. (2005). "Guards and guard forces". Facility Manager's Guide to Security: Protecting Your Assets. The Fairmont Press. ISBN 9780881734836. Archived from the original on 2018-01-05.

Wireless Security, References

1. ^ IEEE 802.11-1997 Information Technology- telecommunications And Information exchange Between Systems-Local And Metropolitan Area Networks-specific Requirements-part 11: Wireless Lan Medium Access Control (MAC) And Physical Layer (PHY) Specifications. 1997. doi:10.1109/IEEESTD.1997.85951. ISBN 978-0738130446.
2. ^ "Definition of WEP". PCMAG. Retrieved 2021-06-04.
3. ^ LinkedIn. "How Can You Secure a Wi-Fi Network With WPA2?". Lifewire. Retrieved 2021-06-04.
4. ^ a b "How to: Define Wireless Network Security Policies". Retrieved 2008-10-09.
5. ^ a b "Wireless Security Primer (Part II)". windowsecurity.com. 2003-04-23. Retrieved 2008-04-27.
6. ^ "Fitting the WLAN Security pieces together". pcworld.com. 2008-10-30. Retrieved 2008-10-30.
7. ^ "Security Vulnerabilities and Risks in Industrial Usage of Wireless Communication". IEEE ETFA 2014 – 19th IEEE International Conference on Emerging Technology and Factory Automation. Retrieved 2014-08-04.
8. ^ "Network Security Tips". Cisco. Retrieved 2011-04-19.
9. ^ "The Hidden Downside Of Wireless Networking". Retrieved 2010-10-28.
10. ^ "Top reasons why corporate WiFi clients connect to unauthorized networks". InfoSecurity. 2010-02-17. Retrieved 2010-03-22.
11. ^ Margaret Rouse. "Encryption". TechTarget. Retrieved 26 May 2015.
12. ^ Bradely Mitchell. "What is Ad-Hoc Mode in Wireless Networking?". about tech. Retrieved 26 May 2015.
13. ^ Browning, Dennis; Kessler, Gary (2009). "Bluetooth Hacking: A Case Study". Journal of Digital Forensics, Security and Law. doi:10.15394/jdfsl.2009.1058. ISSN 1558-7223.
14. ^ "SMAC 2.0 MAC Address Changer". klcconsulting.com. Retrieved 2008-03-17.
15. ^ Lisa Phifer. "The Caffe Latte Attack: How It Works – and How to Block It". wi-fiplanet.com. Retrieved 2008-03-21.
16. ^ "Caffe Latte with a Free Topping of Cracked WEP: Retrieving WEP Keys from Road-Warriors". Archived from the original on 2015-05-11. Retrieved 2008-03-21.
17. ^ Ramachandran, Vivek (2009-09-18). "Caffe Latte Attack". www.slideshare.net. Retrieved 2023-01-12.
18. ^ "Cafe Latte with a Free Topping of Cracked WEP - Retrieving WEP Keys From Road-Warriors". toorcon.org. 2009-04-24. Archived from the original on 2009-04-24. Retrieved 2023-01-12.
19. ^ "Official PCI Security Standards Council Site". PCI Security Standards Council.
20. ^ "PCI DSS Wireless Guidelines" (PDF). Retrieved 2009-07-16.
21. ^ a b Ou, George (March 2005). "The six dumbest ways to secure a wireless LAN". ZDNet.
22. ^ "What is a WEP key?". lirent.net. Retrieved 2008-03-11.
23. ^ e.g. "Weaknesses in the Key Scheduling Algorithm of RC4" by Fluhrer, Mantin and Shamir
24. ^ "FBI Teaches Lesson In How To Break Into Wi-Fi Networks". informationweek.com.
25. ^ "Analyzing the TJ Maxx Data Security Fiasco". New York State Society of CPAs.
26. ^ "PCI DSS 1.2".
27. ^ a b Beaver, Kevin; Davis, Peter T. (13 September 2005). Hacking Wireless Networks for Dummies. ISBN 978-0764597305.
28. ^ Robert McMillan. "Once thought safe, WPA Wi-Fi encryption is cracked". IDG. Retrieved 2008-11-06.
29. ^ Nate Anderson (2009). "One-minute WiFi crack puts further pressure on WPA". Ars Technica. Retrieved 2010-06-05.
30. ^ Kevin Beaver; Peter T. Davis; Devin K. Akin (2011). Hacking Wireless Networks For Dummies. p. 295. ISBN 978-1118084922.
31. ^ "Extensible Authentication Protocol Overview". TechNet. 11 September 2009. Retrieved 26 May 2015.
32. ^ "Extensible Authentication Protocol Overview". Microsoft TechNet. Retrieved 2008-10-02.
33. ^ Joshua Bardwell; Devin Akin (2005). CWNA Official Study Guide (Third ed.). McGraw-Hill. p. 435. ISBN 978-0072255386.
34. ^ George Ou. "Ultimate wireless security guide: A primer on Cisco EAP-FAST authentication". TechRepublic. Archived from the original on 2012-07-07. Retrieved 2008-10-02.
35. ^ "Wi-Fi Protected Access". Wi-Fi Alliance. Archived from the original on May 21, 2007. Retrieved 2008-02-06.
36. ^ "WiGLE – Wireless Geographic Logging Engine – Stats".
37. ^ "WPA2 Hole196 Vulnerability". 2019-01-28.
38. ^ "Secure Technology Alliance". Retrieved 23 April 2021.
39. ^ Etienne, Stefan (2019-02-22). "The best hardware security keys for two-factor authentication". The Verge. Retrieved 2021-06-03.

40. ^ "How to: Improve Wireless Security with Shielding". Retrieved 2008-10-09.
41. ^ "What is Kismet?". kismetwireless.net. Retrieved 2008-02-06.
42. ^ Khamish Malhotra; Stephen Gardner; Will Mepham. "A novel implementation of signature, encryption and authentication (SEA) protocol on mobile patient monitoring devices". IOS Press. Retrieved 2010-03-11.
43. ^ Briere, Danny; Hurley, Pat (2005). Wireless Networks, Hacks and Mods for Dummies. ISBN 978-0764595837.
44. ^ Jonathan Hassell (2003). RADIUS: Securing Public Access to Private Resources. O'Reilly Media. pp. 15–16. ISBN 978-0596003227.
45. ^ John Vollbrecht (2006). "The Beginnings and History of RADIUS" (PDF). Interlink Networks. Retrieved 2009-04-15.
46. ^ "Offene Netzwerke auch für Deutschland!". netzpolitik.org. 2006-09-15.

Social Engineering, References

1. ^ Anderson, Ross J. (2008). Security engineering: a guide to building dependable distributed systems (2 ed.). Indianapolis, IN: Wiley. p. 1040. ISBN 978-0-470-06852-6. Chapter 2, page 17
2. ^ "Social Engineering Defined". Security Through Education. Retrieved 3 October 2021.
3. ^ Jaco, K: "CSEPS Course Workbook" (2004), unit 3, Jaco Security Publishing.
4. ^ Kirdemir, Baris (2019). "HOSTILE INFLUENCE AND EMERGING COGNITIVE THREATS IN CYBERSPACE". Centre for Economics and Foreign Policy Studies.
5. ^ Hatfield, Joseph M (June 2019). "Virtuous human hacking: The ethics of social engineering in penetration-testing". Computers & Security. 83: 354–366. doi:10.1016/j.cose.2019.02.012. S2CID 86565713.
6. ^ The story of HP pretexting scandal with discussion is available at Davani, Faraz (14 August 2011). "HP Pretexting Scandal by Faraz Davani". Retrieved 15 August 2011 – via Scribd.
7. ^ "Pretexting: Your Personal Information Revealed", Federal Trade Commission
8. ^ "Chinese Espionage Campaign Compromises Forbes.com to Target US Defense, Financial Services Companies in Watering Hole Style Attack". invincea.com. 10 February 2015. Retrieved 23 February 2017.
9. ^ "Social Engineering, the USB Way". Light Reading Inc. 7 June 2006. Archived from the original on 13 July 2006. Retrieved 23 April 2014.
10. ^ "Archived copy" (PDF). Archived from the original (PDF) on 11 October 2007. Retrieved 2 March 2012.
11. ^ Conklin, Wm. Arthur; White, Greg; Cothren, Chuck; Davis, Roger; Williams, Dwayne (2015). Principles of Computer Security, Fourth Edition (Official Comptia Guide). New York: McGraw-Hill Education. pp. 193–194. ISBN 978-0071835978.
12. ^ Raywood, Dan (4 August 2016). "#BHUSA Dropped USB Experiment Detailed". info security. Retrieved 28 July 2017.
13. ^ Hafner, Katie (August 1995). "Kevin Mitnick, unplugged". Esquire. 124 (2): 80(9).
14. ^ Social Engineering: Manipulating the human. Scorpio Net Security Services. 16 May 2013. ISBN 9789351261827. Retrieved 11 April 2012.
15. ^ Niekerk, Brett van. "Mobile Devices and the Military: useful Tool or Significant Threat". Proceedings of the 4Th Workshop on Ict Uses in Warfare and the Safeguarding of Peace 2012 (Iwsp 2012) and Journal of Information Warfare. academia.edu. Retrieved 11 May 2013.
16. ^ "Social Engineering: Manipulating the human". YouTube. Retrieved 11 April 2012.
17. ^ "BsidesPDX Track 1 10/07/11 02:52PM, BsidesPDX Track 1 10/07/11 02:52PM BsidesPDX on USTREAM. Conference". Ustream.tv. 7 October 2011. Archived from the original on 4 August 2012. Retrieved 11 April 2012.
18. ^ "Automated Social Engineering". BrightTALK. 29 September 2011. Retrieved 11 April 2012.
19. ^ "Social Engineering a General Approach" (PDF). Informatica Economica journal. Retrieved 11 January 2015.
20. ^ "Cyber Crime". Hays. 7 November 2018. ISBN 9781839473036. Retrieved 11 January 2020.
21. ^ "Wired 12.02: Three Blind Phreaks". Wired. 14 June 1999. Retrieved 11 April 2012.
22. ^ "Social Engineering A Young Hacker's Tale" (PDF). 15 February 2013. Retrieved 13 January 2020.
23. ^ "43 Best Social Engineering Books of All Time". BookAuthority. Retrieved 22 January 2020.
24. ^ "Bens Book of the Month Review of Social Engineering The Science of Human Hacking". RSA Conference. 31 August 2018. Retrieved 22 January 2020.
25. ^ "Book Review: Social Engineering: The Science of Human Hacking". The Ethical Hacker Network. 26 July 2018. Retrieved 22 January 2020.
26. ^ Hadnagy, Christopher; Fincher, Michele (22 January 2020). "Phishing Dark Waters: The Offensive and Defensive Sides of Malicious E-mails". ISACA. Retrieved 22 January 2020.
27. ^ "WTVR:"Protect Your Kids from Online Threats"
28. ^ Larson, Selena (14 August 2017). "Hacker creates organization to unmask child predators". CNN. Retrieved 14 November 2019.
29. ^ Restatement 2d of Torts § 652C.
30. ^ "Congress outlaws pretexting". 109th Congress (2005–2006) H.R.4709 – Telephone Records and Privacy Protection Act of 2006. 2007.
31. ^ Mitnick, K (2002): "The Art of Deception", p. 103 Wiley Publishing Ltd: Indianapolis, Indiana; United States of America. ISBN 0-471-23712-4
32. ^ HP chairman: Use of pretexting 'embarrassing' Stephen Shankland, 8 September 2006 1:08 PM PDT CNET News.com
33. ^ "Calif. court drops charges against Dunn". CNET. 14 March 2007. Retrieved 11 April 2012.

Malware, References

1. ^ [a] [b] [c] [d] [e] Tahir, R. (2018). A study on malware and malware detection techniques. Archived 10 January 2023 at the Wayback Machine. International Journal of Education and Management Engineering, 8(2), 20.
2. ^ "An Undirected Attack Against Critical Infrastructure" (PDF). United States Computer Emergency Readiness Team(Us-cert.gov). Archived (PDF) from the original on 24 December 2016. Retrieved 28 September 2014.
3. ^ [a] [b] Cani, Andrea; Gaudesi, Marco; Sanchez, Ernesto; Squillero, Giovanni; Tonda, Alberto (24 March 2014). "Towards automated malware creation". Proceedings of the 29th Annual ACM Symposium on Applied Computing. SAC '14. New York, NY, USA: Association for Computing Machinery. pp. 157–160. doi:10.1145/2554850.2555157. ISBN 978-1-4503-2469-4. S2CID 14324560.
4. ^ Brewer, Ross (1 September 2016). "Ransomware attacks: detection, prevention and cure". Network Security. 2016 (9): 5–9. doi:10.1016/S1353-4858(16)30086-1. ISSN 1353-4858. Archived from the original on 10 April 2019. Retrieved 2 December 2021.
5. ^ Zhong, Fangtian; Chen, Zekai; Xu, Minghui; Zhang, Guoming; Yu, Dongxiao; Cheng, Xiuzhen (2022). "Malware-on-the-Brain: Illuminating Malware Byte Codes with Images for Malware Classification". IEEE Transactions on Computers. 72 (2): 438–451. arXiv:2108.04314. doi:10.1109/TC.2022.3160357. ISSN 0018-9340. S2CID 236965755. Archived from the original on 2 September 2022. Retrieved 2 September 2022.
6. ^ [a] [b] Kim, Jin-Young; Bu, Seok-Jun; Cho, Sung-Bae (1 September 2018). "Zero-day malware detection using transferred generative adversarial networks based on deep autoencoders". Information Sciences. 460–461: 83–102. doi:10.1016/j.ins.2018.04.092. ISSN 0020-0255. S2CID 51882216. Archived from the original on 23 June 2020. Retrieved 2 December 2021.
7. ^ Razak, Mohd Faizal Ab; Anuar, Nor Badrul; Salleh, Rosli; Firdaus, Ahmad (1 November 2016). "The rise of "malware": Bibliometric analysis of malware study". Journal of Network and Computer Applications. 75: 58–76. doi:10.1016/j.jnca.2016.08.022. Archived from the original on 26 June 2022. Retrieved 30 April 2022.
8. ^ [a] [b] Xiao, Fei; Sun, Yi; Du, Donggao; Li, Xuelei; Luo, Min (21 March 2020). "A Novel Malware Classification Method Based on Crucial Behavior". Mathematical Problems in Engineering. 2020: 1–12. doi:10.1155/2020/6804290. ISSN 1024-123X.
9. ^ Morgan, Steve (13 November 2020). "Cybercrime To Cost The World $10.5 Trillion Annually By 2025". Cybercrime magazine website. Cybersecurity ventures. Archived from the original on 5 March 2022. Retrieved 5 March 2022.
10. ^ Eder-Neuhauser, Peter; Zseby, Tanja; Fabini, Joachim (1 June 2019). "Malware propagation in smart grid networks: metrics, simulation and comparison of three malware types". Journal of Computer Virology and Hacking Techniques. 15 (2): 109–125. doi:10.1007/s11416-018-0325-y. ISSN 2263-8733. S2CID 255164530. Archived from the original on 27 February 2023. Retrieved 10 January 2023.
11. ^ John von Neumann, "Theory of Self-Reproducing Automata", Part 1: Transcripts of lectures given at the University of Illinois, December 1949, Editor: A. W. Burks, University of Illinois, USA, 1966.
12. ^ Fred Cohen, "Computer Viruses", PhD Thesis, University of Southern California, ASP Press, 1988.
13. ^ Young, Adam; Yung, Moti (2004). Malicious cryptography - exposing cryptovirology. Wiley. pp. 1–392. ISBN 978-0-7645-4975-5.
14. ^ "Boot sector virus repair". Antivirus.about.com. 10 June 2010. Archived from the original on 12 January 2011. Retrieved 27 August 2010.
15. ^ Avoine, Gildas; Pascal Junod; Philippe Oechslin (2007). Computer system security: basic concepts and solved exercises. EFPL Press. p. 20. ISBN 978-1-4200-4620-5. The first PC virus is credited to two brothers, Basit Farooq Alvi and Amjad Farooq Alvi, from Pakistan
16. ^ [a] [b] "USB devices spreading viruses". CNET. CBS Interactive. Archived from the original on 24 September 2015. Retrieved 18 February 2015.
17. ^ 2018 Data Breach Investigations Report (PDF) (Report) (11th ed.). Verizon. 2018. p. 18. Archived (PDF) from the original on 16 October 2021. Retrieved 26 September 2022.
18. ^ Fruhlinger, Josh (10 October 2018). "Top cybersecurity facts, figures and statistics for 2018". CSO Online. Archived from the original on 2 June 2019. Retrieved 20 January 2020.
19. ^ William A Hendric (4 September 2014). "Computer Virus history". The Register. Archived from the original on 10 May 2018. Retrieved 29 March 2015.
20. ^ "Cryptomining Worm MassMiner Exploits Multiple Vulnerabilities - Security Boulevard". Security Boulevard. 2 May 2018. Archived from the original on 9 May 2018. Retrieved 9 May 2018.
21. ^ "Beware of Word Document Viruses". us.norton.com. Archived from the original on 26 September 2017. Retrieved 25 September 2017.
22. ^ Tipton, Harold F. (26 December 2002). Information Security Management Handbook. CRC Press. ISBN 978-1-4200-7241-9. Archived from the original on 27 February 2023. Retrieved 16 November 2020.
23. ^ "Malware". FEDERAL TRADE COMMISSION- CONSUMER INFORMATION. Archived from the original on 20 March 2017. Retrieved 27 March 2014.
24. ^ Hernandez, Pedro. "Microsoft Vows to Combat Government Cyber-Spying". eWeek. Archived from the original on 23 January 2014. Retrieved 15 December 2013.
25. ^ "Malware Revolution: A Change in Target". March 2007. Archived from the original on 16 October 2008. Retrieved 26 August 2017.

26. ^ "Child Porn: Malware's Ultimate Evil". November 2009. Archived from the original on 22 October 2013. Retrieved 22 November 2010.
27. ^ PC World – Zombie PCs: Silent, Growing Threat Archived 27 July 2008 at the Wayback Machine.
28. ^ Kovacs, Eduard (27 February 2013). "MiniDuke Malware Used Against European Government Organizations". Softpedia. Archived from the original on 11 October 2016. Retrieved 27 February 2013.
29. ^ Claburn, Thomas (26 October 2022). "Ukrainian indicted by US govt on cybercrime charges". theregister.com. Archived from the original on 26 October 2022. Retrieved 27 October 2022. Those deploying Raccoon used phishing messages and other tricks to get the malware onto potentially millions of victims' computers worldwide. Once installed, the code provided access to login credentials and other data stored on the compromised system.
30. ^ "Raccoon Infostealer Disclosure". raccoon.ic3.gov. Archived from the original on 27 February 2023. Retrieved 27 October 2022.
31. ^ "Shamoon is latest malware to target energy sector". Archived from the original on 23 September 2015. Retrieved 18 February 2015.
32. ^ "Computer-killing malware used in Sony attack a wake-up call". Archived from the original on 7 December 2017. Retrieved 18 February 2015.
33. ^ [a] [b] [c] [d] [e] Molina-Coronado, Borja; Mori, Usue; Mendiburu, Alexander; Miguel-Alonso, Jose (1 January 2023). "Towards a fair comparison and realistic evaluation framework of android malware detectors based on static analysis and machine learning". Computers & Security. 124: 102996. arXiv:2205.12569. doi:10.1016/j.cose.2022.102996. ISSN 0167-4048. S2CID 252734950. Archived from the original on 10 January 2023. Retrieved 10 January 2023.
34. ^ "What are viruses, worms, and Trojan horses?". Indiana University. The Trustees of Indiana University. Archived from the original on 4 September 2016. Retrieved 23 February 2015.
35. ^ Peter Szor (3 February 2005). The Art of Computer Virus Research and Defense. Pearson Education. p. 204. ISBN 978-0-672-33390-3.
36. ^ "computer virus – Encyclopædia Britannica". Britannica.com. Archived from the original on 13 May 2013. Retrieved 28 April 2013.
37. ^ McDowell, Mindi. "Understanding Hidden Threats: Rootkits and Botnets". US-CERT. Archived from the original on 29 March 2017. Retrieved 6 February 2013.
38. ^ "The Meaning of 'Hack'". Catb.org. Archived from the original on 13 October 2016. Retrieved 15 April 2010.
39. ^ [a] [b] Gill, Harjeevan (21 June 2022). "Malware: Types, Analysis and Classifications". doi:10.31224/2423. Archived from the original on 10 January 2023. Retrieved 10 January 2023.
40. ^ Staff, SPIEGEL (29 December 2013). "Inside TAO: Documents Reveal Top NSA Hacking Unit". Spiegel Online. SPIEGEL. Archived from the original on 20 April 2017. Retrieved 23 January 2014.
41. ^ Edwards, John. "Top Zombie, Trojan Horse and Bot Threats". IT Security. Archived from the original on 9 February 2017. Retrieved 25 September 2007.
42. ^ Appelbaum, Jacob (29 December 2013). "Shopping for Spy Gear:Catalog Advertises NSA Toolbox". Spiegel Online. SPIEGEL. Archived from the original on 20 April 2017. Retrieved 29 December 2013.
43. ^ Landwehr, C. E; A. R Bull; J. P McDermott; W. S Choi (1993). A taxonomy of computer program security flaws, with examples (PDF). DTIC Document. Archived from the original on 8 April 2013. Retrieved 5 April 2012.
44. ^ "Trojan Horse: [coined By MIT-hacker-turned-NSA-spook Dan Edwards] N." Archived from the original on 5 July 2017. Retrieved 5 April 2012.
45. ^ "What is the difference between viruses, worms, and Trojan horses?". Symantec Corporation. Archived from the original on 13 February 2015. Retrieved 10 January 2009.
46. ^ "VIRUS-L/comp.virus Frequently Asked Questions (FAQ) v2.00 (Question B3: What is a Trojan Horse?)". 9 October 1995. Archived from the original on 24 September 2015. Retrieved 13 September 2012.
47. ^ "Proton Mac Trojan Has Apple Code Signing Signatures Sold to Customers for $50k". AppleInsider. 14 March 2017. Archived from the original on 19 October 2017. Retrieved 19 October 2017.
48. ^ "Non-Windows Malware". Betanews. 24 August 2017. Archived from the original on 20 October 2017. Retrieved 19 October 2017.
49. ^ "Trojan Dropper". MalwareBytes. 30 January 2020. Archived from the original on 31 October 2022. Retrieved 31 October 2022.
50. ^ Richardson, Ronny; North, Max (1 January 2017). "Ransomware: Evolution, Mitigation and Prevention". International Management Review. 13 (1): 10–21. Archived from the original on 5 October 2022. Retrieved 23 November 2019.
51. ^ Fruhlinger, Josh (1 August 2017). "The 5 biggest ransomware attacks of the last 5 years". CSO. Archived from the original on 24 March 2018. Retrieved 23 March 2018.
52. ^ "Another way Microsoft is disrupting the malware ecosystem". Archived from the original on 20 September 2015. Retrieved 18 February 2015.
53. ^ "Rise of Android Ransomware, research" (PDF). ESET. Archived (PDF) from the original on 19 October 2017. Retrieved 19 October 2017.
54. ^ "State of Malware, research" (PDF). Malwarebytes. Archived (PDF) from the original on 21 May 2017. Retrieved 19 October 2017.
55. ^ O'Kane, P., Sezer, S. and Carlin, D. (2018), Evolution of ransomware. IET Netw., 7: 321-327. https://doi.org/10.1049/iet-net.2017.0207
56. ^ [a] [b] Russinovich, Mark (31 October 2005). "Sony, Rootkits and Digital Rights Management Gone Too Far". Mark's Blog. Microsoft MSDN. Archived from the original on 2 June 2012. Retrieved 29 July 2009.
57. ^ "Rating the best anti-malware solutions". Arstechnica. 15 December 2009. Archived from the original on 2 February 2014. Retrieved 28 January 2014.
58. ^ [a] [b] [c] Kammerstetter, Markus; Platzer, Christian; Wondracek, Gilbert (16 October 2012). "Vanity, cracks and malware". Proceedings of the 2012 ACM conference on Computer and communications security. CCS '12. New York, NY, USA: Association for Computing Machinery. pp. 809–820. doi:10.1145/2382196.2382282. ISBN 978-1-4503-1651-4. S2CID 3423843.
59. ^ Casey, Henry T. (25 November 2015). "Latest adware disables antivirus software". Tom's Guide. Yahoo.com. Archived from the original on 27 November 2015. Retrieved 25 November 2015.
60. ^ "Peer To Peer Information". NORTH CAROLINA STATE UNIVERSITY. Archived from the original on 2 July 2015. Retrieved 25 March 2011.
61. ^ [a] [b] Singh, Jagsir; Singh, Jaswinder (1 September 2018). "Challenge of Malware Analysis: Malware obfuscation Techniques". International Journal of Information Security Science. 7 (3): 100–110. Archived from the original on 10 January 2023. Retrieved 10 January 2023.
62. ^ [a] [b] The Four Most Common Evasive Techniques Used by Malware Archived 29 May 2021 at the Wayback Machine. 27 April 2015.
63. ^ Kirat, Dhilung; Vigna, Giovanni; Kruegel, Christopher (2014). Barecloud: bare-metal analysis-based evasive malware detection. ACM. pp. 287–301. ISBN 978-1-931971-15-7. Archived from the original on 1 August 2019. Retrieved 28 November 2018.
Freely accessible at: "Barecloud: bare-metal analysis-based evasive malware detection" (PDF). Archived from the original (PDF) on 4 March 2016. Retrieved 28 November 2018.
64. ^ Young, Adam; Yung, Moti (1997). "Deniable Password Snatching: On the Possibility of Evasive Electronic Espionage". Symp. on Security and Privacy. IEEE. pp. 224–235. ISBN 0-8186-7828-3.
65. ^ Cabaj, Krzysztof; Caviglione, Luca; Mazurczyk, Wojciech; Wendzel, Steffen; Woodward, Alan; Zander, Sebastian (May 2018). "The New Threats of Information Hiding: The Road Ahead". IT Professional. 20 (3): 31–39. arXiv:1801.00694. doi:10.1109/MITP.2018.032501746. S2CID 22328658.
66. ^ Sudhakar; Kumar, Sushil (14 January 2020). "An emerging threat Fileless malware: a survey and research challenges". Cybersecurity. 3 (1): 1. doi:10.1186/s42400-019-0043-x. ISSN 2523-3246. S2CID 257111442.
67. ^ "Penn State WebAccess Secure Login". webaccess.psu.edu. doi:10.1145/3365001. S2CID 219884145. Archived from the original on 8 March 2021. Retrieved 29 February 2020.
68. ^ "Malware Dynamic Analysis Evasion Techniques: A Survey". ResearchGate. Archived from the original on 14 April 2021. Retrieved 29 February 2020.
69. ^ Nemeth, Zoltan L. (2015). "Modern binary attacks and defences in the windows environment — Fighting against microsoft EMET in seven rounds". 2015 IEEE 13th International Symposium on Intelligent Systems and Informatics (SISY). pp. 275–280. doi:10.1109/SISY.2015.7325394. ISBN 978-1-4673-9388-1. S2CID 18914754.
70. ^ "Global Web Browser... Security Trends" (PDF). Kaspersky lab. November 2012. Archived (PDF) from the original on 2 February 2013. Retrieved 17 January 2013.
71. ^ Rashid, Fahmida Y. (27 November 2012). "Updated Browsers Still Vulnerable to Attack if Plugins Are Outdated". pcmag.com. Archived from the original on 9 April 2016. Retrieved 17 January 2013.
72. ^ Danchev, Dancho (18 August 2011). "Kaspersky: 12 different vulnerabilities detected on every PC". pcmag.com. Archived from the original on 5 July 2014. Retrieved 17 January 2013.
73. ^ "Adobe Security bulletins and advisories". Adobe.com. Archived from the original on 15 November 2013. Retrieved 19 January 2013.
74. ^ Rubenking, Neil J. "Secunia Personal Software Inspector 3.0 Review & Rating". PCMag.com. Archived from the original on 16 January 2013. Retrieved 19 January 2013.
75. ^ Morales, Jose Andre; Al-Bataineh, Areej; Xu, Shouhuai; Sandhu, Ravi (2010). Jajodia, Sushil; Zhou, Jianying (eds.). "Analyzing and Exploiting Network Behaviors of Malware". Security and Privacy in Communication Networks. Lecture Notes of the Institute for Computer Sciences, Social Informatics and Telecommunications Engineering. Berlin, Heidelberg: Springer. 50: 20–34. doi:10.1007/978-3-642-16161-2_2. ISBN 978-3-642-16161-2. Archived from the original on 2 December 2021. Retrieved 2 December 2021.
76. ^ Felt, Adrienne Porter; Chin, Erika; Hanna, Steve; Song, Dawn; Wagner, David (17 October 2011). "Android permissions demystified". Proceedings of the 18th ACM conference on Computer and communications security. CCS '11. New York, NY, USA: Association for Computing Machinery. pp. 627–638. doi:10.1145/2046707.2046779. ISBN 978-1-4503-0948-6. S2CID 895039.
77. ^ Wu, Sha; Liu, Jiajia (May 2019). "Overprivileged Permission Detection for Android Applications". ICC 2019 - 2019 IEEE International Conference on Communications (ICC). pp. 1–6. doi:10.1109/ICC.2019.8761572. ISBN 978-1-5386-8088-9. S2CID 198168673. Archived from the original on 21 January 2022. Retrieved 1 January 2022.
78. ^ "Malware, viruses, worms, Trojan horses and spyware". list.ercacinnican.tk. Archived from the original on 5 February 2021. Retrieved 14 November 2020.
79. ^ Mutch, John; Anderson, Brian (2011), Mutch, John; Anderson, Brian (eds.), "The Hard and Soft Cost of Apathy", Preventing Good People from doing Bad Things: Implementing Least Privilege, Berkeley, CA: Apress, pp. 163–175, doi:10.1007/978-1-4302-3922-2_10, ISBN 978-1-4302-3922-2, archived from the original on 27 February 2023, retrieved 2 December 2021
80. ^ Singh, Vaishali; Pandey, S. K. (2021). Rathore, Vijay Singh; Dey, Nilanjan; Piuri, Vincenzo; Babo, Rosalina; Polkowski, Zdzislaw; Tavares, João Manuel R. S. (eds.). "Revisiting Cloud Security Attacks: Credential Attack". Rising Threats in Expert Applications and Solutions. Advances in Intelligent Systems and Computing. Singapore: Springer. 1187: 339–350. doi:10.1007/978-981-15-6014-9_39. ISBN 978-981-15-6014-9. S2CID 224940546. Archived from the original on 4 March 2022. Retrieved 2 December 2021.
81. ^ "LNCS 3786 – Key Factors Influencing Worm Infection", U. Kanlayasiri, 2006, web (PDF): SL40-PDF Archived 27 February 2023 at the Wayback Machine.
82. ^ Cohen, Jason (28 August 2020). "Windows Computers Account for 83% of All Malware Attacks in Q1 2020". PCMag Australia. Archived from the original on 2 December 2021. Retrieved 2 December 2021.
83. ^ Wagner, Neal; Şahin, Cem Ş.; Winterrose, Michael; Riordan, James; Pena, Jaime; Hanson, Diana; Streilein, William W. (December 2016). "Towards automated cyber decision support: A case study on network segmentation for security". 2016 IEEE Symposium Series on Computational Intelligence (SSCI). pp. 1–10. doi:10.1109/SSCI.2016.7849908. ISBN 978-1-5090-4240-1. S2CID 9065830. Archived from the original on 2 December 2021. Retrieved 1 January 2022.
84. ^ Hemberg, Erik; Zipkin, Joseph R.; Skowyra, Richard W.; Wagner, Neal; O'Reilly, Una-May (6 July 2018). "Adversarial co-evolution of attack and defense in a segmented computer network environment". Proceedings of the Genetic and Evolutionary Computation Conference Companion. GECCO '18. New York, NY, USA: Association for Computing Machinery. pp. 1648–1655. doi:10.1145/3205651.3208287. ISBN 978-1-4503-5764-7. S2CID 51603533.
85. ^ "Malicious Software Removal Tool". Microsoft. Archived from the original on 21 June 2012. Retrieved 21 June 2012.
86. ^ [a] [b] Rubenking, Neil J. (8 January 2014). "The Best Free Antivirus for 2014". pcmag.com. Archived from the original on 30 August 2017. Retrieved 4 September 2017.
87. ^ "Free antivirus profiles in 2018". antivirusgratis.org. Archived from the original on 10 August 2018. Retrieved 13 February 2020.
88. ^ "Quickly identify malware running on your PC". techadvisor.co.uk. Archived from the original on 2 September 2018. Retrieved 2 September 2018.
89. ^ "How Antivirus Software Works?". Archived from the original on 12 January 2017. Retrieved 16 October 2015.
90. ^ [a] [b] Souppaya, Murugiah; Scarfone, Karen (July 2013). "Guide to Malware Incident Prevention and Handling for Desktops and Laptops". National Institute of Standards and Technology. doi:10.6028/nist.sp.800-83r1.
91. ^ Al-Saleh, Mohammed Ibrahim; Espinoza, Antonio M.; Crandall, Jedediah R. (2013). "Antivirus performance characterisation: system-wide view". IET Information Security. 7 (2): 126–133. doi:10.1049/iet-ifs.2012.0192. ISSN 1751-8717.

92. ^ M. Guri, G. Kedma, A. Kachlon and Y. Elovici, "AirHopper: Bridging the air-gap between isolated networks and mobile phones using radio frequencies," *Malicious and Unwanted Software: The Americas (MALWARE), 2014 9th International Conference on,* Fajardo, PR, 2014, pp. 58-67.
93. ^ M. Guri, M. Monitz, Y. Mirski and Y. Elovici, "BitWhisper: Covert Signaling Channel between Air-Gapped Computers Using Thermal Manipulations," *2015 IEEE 28th Computer Security Foundations Symposium,* Verona, 2015, pp. 276-289.
94. ^ GSMem: Data Exfiltration from Air-Gapped Computers over GSM Frequencies. Mordechai Guri, Assaf Kachlon, Ofer Hasson, Gabi Kedma, Yisroel Mirsky, and Yuval Elovici, *Ben-Gurion University of the Negev; USENIX Security Symposium 2015*
95. ^ Hanspach, Michael; Goetz, Michael; Daidakulov, Andrey; Elovici, Yuval (2016). "Fansmitter: Acoustic Data Exfiltration from (Speakerless) Air-Gapped Computers". arXiv:1606.05915 [cs.CR].

Security Testing, References

1. ^ M Martellini, & Malizia, A. (2017). Cyber and chemical, biological, radiological, nuclear, explosives challenges : threats and counter efforts. Springer.
2. ^ "Introduction to Information Security" US-CERT https://www.us-cert.gov/security-publications/introduction-information-security
3. ^ [a] [b] [c] A, Madhu (2017-12-04). "The Six Principles of Security Testing | Trigent Vantage". Retrieved 2022-08-28.
4. ^ "Container Security Verification Standard". GitHub. 20 July 2022.
5. ^ "Infrastructure as Code Security - OWASP Cheat Sheet Series".
6. ^ "OWASP DevSecOps Guideline - v-0.2 | OWASP Foundation".
7. ^ "Component Analysis | OWASP Foundation".

Cryptography, References

1. ^ Liddell, Henry George; Scott, Robert; Jones, Henry Stuart; McKenzie, Roderick (1984). A Greek-English Lexicon. Oxford University Press.
2. ^ Rivest, Ronald L. (1990). "Cryptography". In J. Van Leeuwen (ed.). Handbook of Theoretical Computer Science. Vol. 1. Elsevier.
3. ^ Bellare, Mihir; Rogaway, Phillip (21 September 2005). "Introduction". Introduction to Modern Cryptography. p. 10.
4. ^ Sadkhan, Sattar B. (December 2013). "Key note lecture multidisciplinary in cryptology and information security". 2013 International Conference on Electrical Communication, Computer, Power, and Control Engineering (ICECCPCE). pp. 1–2. doi:10.1109/ICECCPCE.2013.6998773. ISBN 978-1-4799-5633-3. S2CID 22378547. Archived from the original on 27 August 2022. Retrieved 20 September 2022.
5. ^ [a] [b] [c] [d] [e] [f] [g] Menezes, A.J.; van Oorschot, P.C.; Vanstone, S.A. (1997). Handbook of Applied Cryptography. Taylor & Francis. ISBN 978-0-8493-8523-0.
6. ^ [a] [b] Biggs, Norman (2008). Codes: An introduction to Information Communication and Cryptography. Springer. p. 171.
7. ^ [a] [b] "Overview per country". Crypto Law Survey. February 2013. Archived from the original on 1 January 2013. Retrieved 26 March 2015.
8. ^ [a] [b] "UK Data Encryption Disclosure Law Takes Effect". PC World. 1 October 2007. Archived from the original on 20 January 2012. Retrieved 26 March 2015.
9. ^ [a] [b] [c] [d] Ranger, Steve (24 March 2015). "The undercover war on your internet secrets: How online surveillance cracked our trust in the web". TechRepublic. Archived from the original on 12 June 2016. Retrieved 12 June 2016.
10. ^ [a] [b] Doctorow, Cory (2 May 2007). "Digg users revolt over AACS key". Boing Boing. Archived from the original on 12 May 2015. Retrieved 26 March 2015.
11. ^ Whalen, Terence (1994). "The Code for Gold: Edgar Allan Poe and Cryptography". Representations. University of California Press. 46 (46): 35–57. doi:10.2307/2928778. JSTOR 2928778.
12. ^ Rosenheim, Shawn (1997). The Cryptographic Imagination: Secret Writing from Edgar Poe to the Internet. Johns Hopkins University Press. p. 20. ISBN 978-0801853319.
13. ^ [a] [b] [c] [d] Kahn, David (1967). The Codebreakers. ISBN 978-0-684-83130-5.
14. ^ "An Introduction to Modern Cryptosystems". Archived from the original on 17 November 2015. Retrieved 12 October 2015.
15. ^ Sharbaf, M.S. (1 November 2011). "Quantum cryptography: An emerging technology in network security". 2011 IEEE International Conference on Technologies for Homeland Security (HST). pp. 13–19. doi:10.1109/THS.2011.6107841. ISBN 978-1-4577-1376-7. S2CID 17915038.
16. ^ "cryptology | Britannica". www.britannica.com. Archived from the original on 10 July 2022. Retrieved 22 June 2022.
17. ^ Oded Goldreich, Foundations of Cryptography, Volume 1: Basic Tools, Cambridge University Press, 2001, ISBN 0-521-79172-3
18. ^ "Cryptology (definition)". Merriam-Webster's Collegiate Dictionary (11th ed.). Merriam-Webster. Retrieved 26 March 2015.
19. ^ Shirey, Rob (May 2000). "Internet Security Glossary". Internet Engineering Task Force. doi:10.17487/RFC2828. RFC 2828. Archived from the original on 18 April 2015. Retrieved 26 March 2015.
20. ^ Military.com (13 May 2021). "What's a Cryptologic Linguist?". Military.com. Retrieved 17 July 2023.
21. ^ Benson, Cummings, Greaves, ed. (January 1988). Linguistics in a Systemic Perspective. John Benjamins Publishing Company. p. 38. ISBN 9789027278760.
22. ^ Saltzman, Benjamin A. (1 October 2018). "Vt hkskdlxt: Early Medieval Cryptography, Textual Errors, and Scribal Agency". Speculum. 93 (4): 975–1009. doi:10.1086/698861. ISSN 0038-7134. S2CID 165362817. Archived from the original on 26 February 2022. Retrieved 26 February 2022.
23. ^ Iashchenko, V.V. (2002). Cryptography: an introduction. AMS Bookstore. p. 6. ISBN 978-0-8218-2986-8.
24. ^ electricpulp.com. "CODES – Encyclopaedia Iranica". www.iranicaonline.org. Archived from the original on 5 March 2017. Retrieved 4 March 2017.
25. ^ Kahn, David (1996). The Codebreakers: The Comprehensive History of Secret Communication from Ancient Times to the Internet. Simon and Schuster. ISBN 978-1439103555. Archived from the original on 1 July 2023. Retrieved 16 October 2020.
26. ^ Broemeling, Lyle D. (1 November 2011). "An Account of Early Statistical Inference in Arab Cryptology". The American Statistician. 65 (4): 255–257. doi:10.1198/tas.2011.10191. S2CID 123537702.
27. ^ [a] [b] Singh, Simon (2000). The Code Book. New York: Anchor Books. pp. 14–20. ISBN 978-0-385-49532-5.
28. ^ [a] [b] Al-Kadi, Ibrahim A. (April 1992). "The origins of cryptology: The Arab contributions". Cryptologia. 16 (2): 97–126. doi:10.1080/0161-119291866801.
29. ^ Schrödel, Tobias (October 2008). "Breaking Short Vigenère Ciphers". Cryptologia. 32 (4): 334–337. doi:10.1080/01611190802336097. S2CID 21812933.
30. ^ Hakim, Joy (1995). A History of US: War, Peace and all that Jazz. New York: Oxford University Press. ISBN 978-0-19-509514-2.
31. ^ Gannon, James (2001). Stealing Secrets, Telling Lies: How Spies and Codebreakers Helped Shape the Twentieth Century. Washington, D.C.: Brassey's. ISBN 978-1-57488-367-1.
32. ^ "The Legacy of DES - Schneier on Security". www.schneier.com. Archived from the original on 23 February 2022. Retrieved 26 January 2022.
33. ^ [a] [b] [c] Diffie, Whitfield; Hellman, Martin (November 1976). "New Directions in Cryptography" (PDF). IEEE Transactions on Information Theory. IT-22 (6): 644–654. CiteSeerX 10.1.1.37.9720. doi:10.1109/tit.1976.1055638. Archived (PDF) from the original on 3 December 2017. Retrieved 16 November 2015.
34. ^ Singh, Simon (1999). The Code Book: The Science of Secrecy From Ancient Egypt To Quantum Cryptography (First Anchor Books ed.). New York: Anchor Books. pp. 278. ISBN 978-0-385-49532-5.
35. ^ Cryptography: Theory and Practice, Third Edition (Discrete Mathematics and Its Applications), 2005, by Douglas R. Stinson, Chapman and Hall/CRC
36. ^ Blaze, Matt; Diffie, Whitfield; Rivest, Ronald L.; Schneier, Bruce; Shimomura, Tsutomu; Thompson, Eric; Wiener, Michael (January 1996). "Minimal key lengths for symmetric ciphers to provide adequate commercial security". Fortify. Archived from the original on 24 September 2015. Retrieved 26 March 2015.
37. ^ Diffie, W.; Hellman, M. (1 September 2006). "New directions in cryptography". IEEE Transactions on Information Theory. 22 (6): 644–654. doi:10.1109/TIT.1976.1055638. Archived from the original on 19 April 2022. Retrieved 19 April 2022.
38. ^ "FIPS PUB 197: The official Advanced Encryption Standard" (PDF). Computer Security Resource Center. National Institute of Standards and Technology. Archived from the original (PDF) on 7 April 2015. Retrieved 26 March 2015.
39. ^ "NCUA letter to credit unions" (PDF). National Credit Union Administration. July 2004. Archived (PDF) from the original on 12 September 2014. Retrieved 26 March 2015.
40. ^ Finney, Hal; Thayer, Rodney L.; Donnerhacke, Lutz; Callas, Jon (November 1998). "Open PGP Message Format". Internet Engineering Task Force. doi:10.17487/RFC2440. RFC 2440. Archived from the original on 15 March 2015. Retrieved 26 March 2015.
41. ^ Golen, Pawel (19 July 2002). "SSH". WindowSecurity. Archived from the original on 29 October 2009. Retrieved 26 March 2015.
42. ^ [a] [b] Schneier, Bruce (1996). Applied Cryptography (2nd ed.). Wiley. ISBN 978-0-471-11709-4.
43. ^ Paar, Christof (2009). Understanding cryptography : a textbook for students and practitioners. Jan Pelzl. Berlin: Springer. p. 123. ISBN 978-3-642-04101-3. OCLC 567365751.
44. ^ Bernstein, Daniel J.; Lange, Tanja (14 September 2017). "Post-quantum cryptography". Nature. 549 (7671): 188–194. Bibcode:2017Natur.549..188B. doi:10.1038/nature23461. ISSN 0028-0836. PMID 28905891. S2CID 4446249. Archived from the original on 10 July 2022. Retrieved 26 August 2022.
45. ^ [a] [b] "Notices". Federal Register. 72 (212). 2 November 2007.
   "Archived copy" (PDF). Archived from the original on 28 February 2008. Retrieved 27 January 2009.
46. ^ [a] [b] "NIST Selects Winner of Secure Hash Algorithm (SHA-3) Competition". NIST. National Institute of Standards and Technology. 2 October 2012. Archived from the original on 2 April 2015. Retrieved 26 March 2015.
47. ^ Diffie, Whitfield; Hellman, Martin (8 June 1976). "Multi-user cryptographic techniques". AFIPS Proceedings. 45: 109–112. doi:10.1145/1499799.1499815. S2CID 13210741.
48. ^ Ralph Merkle was working on similar ideas at the time and encountered publication delays, and Hellman has suggested that the term used should be Diffie–Hellman–Merkle asymmetric key cryptography.
49. ^ Kahn, David (Fall 1979). "Cryptology Goes Public". Foreign Affairs. 58 (1): 141–159. doi:10.2307/20040343. JSTOR 20040343.
50. ^ "Using Client-Certificate based authentication with NGINX on Ubuntu". SSLTrust. Archived from the original on 26 August 2019. Retrieved 13 June 2019.
51. ^ Rivest, Ronald L.; Shamir, A.; Adleman, L. (1978). "A Method for Obtaining Digital Signatures and Public-Key Cryptosystems". Communications of the ACM. 21 (2): 120–126. CiteSeerX 10.1.1.607.2677. doi:10.1145/359340.359342. S2CID 2873616.
   "Archived copy" (PDF). Archived from the original (PDF) on 16 November 2001. Retrieved 20 April 2006.
   Previously released as an MIT "Technical Memo" in April 1977, and published in Martin Gardner's Scientific American Mathematical recreations column
52. ^ [a] [b] Wayner, Peter (24 December 1997). "British Document Outlines Early Encryption Discovery". The New York Times. Archived from the original on 27 June 2017. Retrieved 26 March 2015.

53. ^ *Cocks, Clifford (20 November 1973). "A Note on 'Non-Secret Encryption'" (PDF). CESG Research Report. Archived (PDF) from the original on 27 July 2011. Retrieved 22 July 2009.*
54. ^ *Singh, Simon (1999). The Code Book. Doubleday. pp. 279–292. ISBN 9780385495318.*
55. ^ *Shannon, Claude; Weaver, Warren (1963). The Mathematical Theory of Communication. University of Illinois Press. ISBN 978-0-252-72548-7.*
56. ^ *"An Example of a Man-in-the-middle Attack Against Server Authenticated SSL-sessions" (PDF). Archived (PDF) from the original on 3 June 2016. Retrieved 13 October 2015.*
57. ^ *Junod, Pascal (2001). "On the Complexity of Matsui's Attack". Selected Areas in Cryptography (PDF). Lecture Notes in Computer Science. Vol. 2259. pp. 199–211. doi:10.1007/3-540-45537-X_16. ISBN 978-3-540-43066-7.*
58. ^ *Song, Dawn; Wagner, David A.; Tian, Xuqing (2001). "Timing Analysis of Keystrokes and Timing Attacks on SSH" (PDF). Tenth USENIX Security Symposium.*
59. ^ *Brands, S. (1994). "Untraceable Off-line Cash in Wallet with Observers". Advances in Cryptology — CRYPTO' 93. Lecture Notes in Computer Science. Vol. 773. pp. 302–318. doi:10.1007/3-540-48329-2_26. ISBN 978-3-540-57766-9. Archived from the original on 26 July 2011.*
60. ^ *Babai, László (1985). "Trading group theory for randomness". Proceedings of the seventeenth annual ACM symposium on Theory of computing - STOC '85. pp. 421–429. CiteSeerX 10.1.1.130.3397. doi:10.1145/22145.22192. ISBN 978-0-89791-151-1. S2CID 17981195.*
61. ^ *Goldwasser, S.; Micali, S.; Rackoff, C. (1989). "The Knowledge Complexity of Interactive Proof Systems". SIAM Journal on Computing. **18** (1): 186–208. CiteSeerX 10.1.1.397.4002. doi:10.1137/0218012.*
62. ^ *Blakley, G. (June 1979). "Safeguarding cryptographic keys". Proceedings of AFIPS 1979. **48**: 313–317.*
63. ^ *Shamir, A. (1979). "How to share a secret". Communications of the ACM. **22** (11): 612–613. doi:10.1145/359168.359176. S2CID 16321225.*
64. ^ *Gunathilake, Nilupulee A.; Al-Dubai, Ahmed; Buchana, William J. (2 November 2020). "Recent Advances and Trends in Lightweight Cryptography for IoT Security". 2020 16th International Conference on Network and Service Management (CNSM). Izmir, Turkey: IEEE. pp. 1–5. doi:10.23919/CNSM50824.2020.9269083. ISBN 978-3-903176-31-7. S2CID 227277538. Archived from the original on 24 April 2021. Retrieved 24 April 2021.*
65. ^ *Thakor, Vishal A.; Razzaque, Mohammad Abdur; Khandaker, Muhammad R. A. (2021). "Lightweight Cryptography Algorithms for Resource-Constrained IoT Devices: A Review, Comparison and Research Opportunities". IEEE Access. **9**: 28177–28193. doi:10.1109/ACCESS.2021.3052867. ISSN 2169-3536. S2CID 232042514.*
66. ^ *Cohen, Fred (1995). "2.4 - Applications of Cryptography". all.net. Archived from the original on 24 August 1999. Retrieved 21 December 2021.*
67. ^ *"4 Common Encryption Methods to Shield Sensitive Data From Prying Eyes". GetApp. Archived from the original on 14 May 2022. Retrieved 14 May 2022.*
68. ^ *a b c d e Chamberlain, Austin (12 March 2017). "Applications of Cryptography | UCL Risky Business". blogs.ucl.ac.uk. Archived from the original on 26 February 2018. Retrieved 21 December 2021.*
69. ^ *"6.5.1 What Are the Cryptographic Policies of Some Countries?". RSA Laboratories. Archived from the original on 16 April 2015. Retrieved 26 March 2015.*
70. ^ *Rosenoer, Jonathan (1995). "Cryptography & Speech". CyberLaw. "Archived copy". Archived from the original on 1 December 2005. Retrieved 23 June 2006.*
71. ^ *"Case Closed on Zimmermann PGP Investigation". IEEE Computer Society's Technical Committee on Security and Privacy. 14 February 1996. Archived from the original on 11 June 2010. Retrieved 26 March 2015.*
72. ^ *a b c Levy, Steven (2001). Crypto: How the Code Rebels Beat the Government – Saving Privacy in the Digital Age. Penguin Books. p. 56. ISBN 978-0-14-024432-8. OCLC 244148644.*
73. ^ *"Bernstein v USDOJ". Electronic Privacy Information Center. United States Court of Appeals for the Ninth Circuit. 6 May 1999. Archived from the original on 13 August 2009. Retrieved 26 March 2015.*
74. ^ *"Dual-use List – Category 5 – Part 2 – "Information Security"" (PDF). Wassenaar Arrangement. Archived from the original on 26 September 2018. Retrieved 26 March 2015.*
75. ^ *".4 United States Cryptography Export/Import Laws". RSA Laboratories. Archived from the original on 31 March 2015. Retrieved 26 March 2015.*
76. ^ *Schneier, Bruce (15 June 2000). "The Data Encryption Standard (DES)". Crypto-Gram. Archived from the original on 2 January 2010. Retrieved 26 March 2015.*
77. ^ *Coppersmith, D. (May 1994). "The Data Encryption Standard (DES) and its strength against attacks" (PDF). IBM Journal of Research and Development. **38** (3): 243–250. doi:10.1147/rd.383.0243. Archived from the original on 4 March 2016. Retrieved 26 March 2015.*
78. ^ *Biham, E.; Shamir, A. (1991). "Differential cryptanalysis of DES-like cryptosystems". Journal of Cryptology. **4** (1): 3–72. doi:10.1007/bf00630563. S2CID 206783462.*
79. ^ *"The Digital Millennium Copyright Act of 1998" (PDF). United States Copyright Office. Archived (PDF) from the original on 8 August 2007. Retrieved 26 March 2015.*
80. ^ *Ferguson, Niels (15 August 2001). "Censorship in action: why I don't publish my HDCP results". Archived from the original on 1 December 2001. Retrieved 16 February 2009.*
81. ^ *Schneier, Bruce (6 August 2001). "Arrest of Computer Researcher Is Arrest of First Amendment Rights". InternetWeek. Archived from the original on 7 March 2017. Retrieved 7 March 2017.*
82. ^ *Williams, Christopher (11 August 2009). "Two convicted for refusal to decrypt data". The Register. Archived from the original on 17 March 2015. Retrieved 26 March 2015.*
83. ^ *Williams, Christopher (24 November 2009). "UK jails schizophrenic for refusal to decrypt files". The Register. Archived from the original on 26 March 2015. Retrieved 26 March 2015.*
84. ^ *Ingold, John (4 January 2012). "Password case reframes Fifth Amendment rights in context of digital world". The Denver Post. Archived from the original on 2 April 2015. Retrieved 26 March 2015.*
85. ^ *Leyden, John (13 July 2011). "US court test for rights not to hand over crypto keys". The Register. Archived from the original on 24 October 2014. Retrieved 26 March 2015.*
86. ^ *"Order Granting Application under the All Writs Act Requiring Defendant Fricosu to Assist in the Execution of Previously Issued Search Warrants" (PDF). United States District Court for the District of Colorado. Archived (PDF) from the original on 9 June 2021. Retrieved 26 March 2015.*

Electronic Authentication, References

1. ^ *The Office of the Government Chief Information Officer. "What is e-Authentication?". The Government of the Hong Kong Special Administrative Region of the People's Republic of China. Archived from the original on 22 December 2015. Retrieved 1 November 2015.*
2. ^ *a b c d Balbas, Luis. "Digital Authentication - Factors, Mechanisms and Schemes". Cryptomathic. Retrieved 9 January 2017.*
3. ^ *McMahon, Mary. "What is E-Authentication?". wiseGEEK. Retrieved 2 November 2015.*
4. ^ *a b Turner, Dawn M. "Digital Authentication - the Basics". Cryptomathic. Retrieved 9 January 2017.*
5. ^ *Burr, W. E.; Dodson, D. F.; Newton, E. M.; Perlner, R. A.; Polk, W. T.; Gupta, S.; Nabbus, E. A. (2011). "Electronic authentication guideline". doi:10.6028/NIST.SP.800-63-1.*
6. ^ *Schneier, Bruce. "The Failure of Two-Factor Authentication". Schneier on Security. Retrieved 2 November 2015.*
7. ^ *Office of the Government Chief Information Officer. "Passwords and PINs based Authentication". The Government of the Hong Kong Special Administrative Region of the People's Republic of China. Archived from the original on May 31, 2015. Retrieved 2 November 2015.*
8. ^ *Office of the Government Chief Information Officer. "Public-Key Authentication". The Government of the Hong Kong Special Administrative Region of the People's Republic of China. Archived from the original on May 31, 2015. Retrieved 3 November 2015.*
9. ^ *Office of the Government Chief Information Officer. "Symmetric-key Authentication". The Government of the Hong Kong Special Administrative Region of the People's Republic of China. Archived from the original on July 9, 2015. Retrieved 3 November 2015.*
10. ^ *Office of the Government Chief Information Officer. "SMS based Authentication". The Government of the Hong Kong Special Administrative Region of the People's Republic of China. Archived from the original on August 27, 2015. Retrieved 3 November 2015.*
11. ^ *Office of the Government Chief Information Officer. "Biometric Authentication". The Government of the Hong Kong Special Administrative Region of the People's Republic of China. Archived from the original on January 8, 2015. Retrieved 3 November 2015.*
12. ^ *Andriamilanto, Nampoina; Allard, Tristan (2021). "BrFAST: A Tool to Select Browser Fingerprinting Attributes for Web Authentication According to a Usability-Security Trade-off" (PDF). Companion Proceedings of the Web Conference 2021. pp. 701–704. doi:10.1145/3442442.3458610. ISBN 978-1-4503-8313-4. S2CID 233296722.*
13. ^ *Burr, W. E.; Dodson, D. F.; Polk, W. T. (2006). "Electronic authentication guideline". doi:10.6028/NIST.SP.800-63v1.0.2.*
14. ^ *Turner, Dawn M. "Understanding Non-Repudiation of Origin and Non-Repudiation of Emission". Cryptomathic. Retrieved 9 January 2017.*
15. ^ *"E-Authentication Risk Assessment for Electronic Prescriptions for Controlled Substances" (PDF). Retrieved 3 November 2015.*
16. ^ *Radack, Shirley. "ELECTRONIC AUTHENTICATION: GUIDANCE FOR SELECTING SECURE TECHNIQUES". Archived from the original on September 15, 2015. Retrieved 3 November 2015.*
17. ^ *a b c Bolten, Joshua. "Memorandum: E-Authentication Guideline for Federal Agencies" (PDF). Executive Office of the President, Office of Management and Budget (OMB). Retrieved 9 January 2017.*
18. ^ *Radack, Shirley. "ELECTRONIC AUTHENTICATION: GUIDANCE FOR SELECTING SECURE TECHNIQUES". National Institute of Standards and Technology. Archived from the original on September 15, 2015. Retrieved 3 November 2015.*
19. ^ *McCarthy, Shawn. "E-authentication: What IT managers will be focusing on over the next 18 months". GCN. Retrieved 2 November 2015.*
20. ^ *"Whole of Government Information and Communications Technology".*
21. ^ Breaking Barriers to eGovernment (Draft Deliverable 1b), eGovernment unit, European Commission, August 2006. See table 1
22. ^ An overview of International Initiatives in the field of Electronic Authentication Archived 2011-07-22 at the Wayback Machine, Japan PKI Forum, June 2, 2005.
23. ^ Australia Archived 2012-02-12 at the Wayback Machine, Canada Archived 2008-03-05 at the Wayback Machine, US (M04-04).
24. ^ *"Draft NIST Special Publication 800-63-3: Digital Authentication Guideline". National Institute of Standards and Technology, USA. Retrieved 9 January 2017.*
25. ^ *Turner, Dawn. "Understanding eIDAS". Cryptomathic. Retrieved 12 April 2016.*
26. ^ *"Regulation (EU) No 910/2014 of the European Parliament and of the Council of 23 July 2014 on electronic identification and trust services for electronic transactions in the internal market and repealing Directive 1999/93/EC". EUR-Lex. The European Parliament and the Council of the European Union. Retrieved 18 March 2016.*
27. ^ *"Постановление Правительства РФ от 28 ноября 2011 г. N 977 "О федеральной государственной информационной системе "Единая система идентификации и аутентификации в инфраструктуре, обеспечивающей информационно-технологическое взаимодействие информационных систем, используемых для предоставления государственных и муниципальных услуг в электронной форме"".*
28. ^ *Margaret, Rouse. "mobile authentication definition". SearchSecurity.com. Retrieved 3 November 2015.*
29. ^ *Government of India Department of Electronics and Information Technology Ministry of Communications and Information Technology. "e-Pramaan: Framework for e-Authentication" (PDF). Retrieved 3 November 2015.*
30. ^ *Tolentino, Jamie (16 March 2015). "How to Increase App Security Through Mobile Phone Authentication". TNW news. Retrieved 3 November 2015.*
31. ^ *Ford, Matthew (23 Feb 2005). "Identity Authentication and 'E-Commerce'". Warwick, Journal of Information Law & Technology. Retrieved 3 November 2015.*
32. ^ *Sawma, Victor. "A New Methodology for Deriving Effective Countermeasures Design Models". School of Information Technology and Engineering, University of Ottawa. CiteSeerX 10.1.1.100.1216.*

33. ^ Walker, Heather. "How eIDAS affects the USA". Cryptomathic. Retrieved 9 January 2017.

Public Key Infrastructure, References

1. ^ Chien, Hung-Yu (2021-08-19). "Dynamic Public Key Certificates with Forward Secrecy". Electronics. **10** (16): 2009. doi:10.3390/electronics10162009. ISSN 2079-9292.
2. ^ Fruhlinger, Josh (29 May 2020). "What is PKI? And how it secures just about everything online". CSOOnline. Retrieved 26 August 2021.
3. ^ "Internet X.509 Public Key Infrastructure Certificate Policy and Certification Practices Framework". IETF. Retrieved 26 August 2020.
4. ^ "Public Key Infrastructure". MSDN. Retrieved 26 March 2015.
5. ^ "Using Client-Certificate based authentication with NGINX on Ubuntu - SSLTrust". SSLTrust. Retrieved 13 June 2019.
6. ^ Adams, Carlisle; Lloyd, Steve (2003). Understanding PKI: concepts, standards, and deployment considerations. Addison-Wesley Professional. pp. 11–15. ISBN 978-0-672-32391-1.
7. ^ Trček, Denis (2006). Managing information systems security and privacy. Birkhauser. p. 69. ISBN 978-3-540-28103-0.
8. ^ [a] [b] Vacca, Jhn R. (2004). Public key infrastructure: building trusted applications and Web services. CRC Press. p. 8. ISBN 978-0-8493-0822-2.
9. ^ Viega, John; et al. (2002). Network Security with OpenSSL. O'Reilly Media. pp. 61–62. ISBN 978-0-596-00270-1.
10. ^ McKinley, Barton (January 17, 2001). "The ABCs of PKI: Decrypting the complex task of setting up a public key infrastructure". Network World. Archived from the original on May 29, 2012.
11. ^ Al-Janabi, Sufyan T. Faraj; et al. (2012). "Combining Mediated and Identity-Based Cryptography for Securing Email". In Ariwa, Ezendu; et al. (eds.). Digital Enterprise and Information Systems: International Conference, Deis, [...] Proceedings. Springer. pp. 2–3. ISBN 9783642226021.
12. ^ "Mike Meyers CompTIA Security+ Certification Passport", by T. J. Samuelle, p. 137.
13. ^ Henry, William (4 March 2016). "Trusted Third Party Service".
14. ^ Smith, Dickinson & Seamons 2020, p. 1.
15. ^ [a] [b] Sheffer, Saint-Andre & Fossati 2022, 7.5. Certificate Revocation.
16. ^ Chung et al. 2018, p. 3.
17. ^ Smith, Dickinson & Seamons 2020, p. 10.
18. ^ Larisch et al. 2017, p. 542.
19. ^ Smith, Dickinson & Seamons 2020, p. 1-2.
20. ^ "Counting SSL certificates". 13 May 2015.
21. ^ "CA:Symantec Issues". Mozilla Wiki. Retrieved 10 January 2020.
22. ^ "Chrome's Plan to Distrust Symantec Certificates". Google security blog. Retrieved 10 January 2020.
23. ^ "JDK-8215012 : Release Note: Distrust TLS Server Certificates Anchored by Symantec Root CAs". Java Bug Database. Retrieved 10 January 2020.
24. ^ Single Sign-On Technology for SAP Enterprises: What does SAP have to say? "Single Sign-On Technology for SAP Enterprises: What does SAP have to say? | May 2010 | SECUDE AG". Archived from the original on 2011-07-16. Retrieved 2010-05-25.
25. ^ Ed Gerck, Overview of Certification Systems: x.509, CA, PGP and SKIP, in The Black Hat Briefings '99, http://www.securitytechnet.com/resource/rsc-center/presentation/black/vegas99/certover.pdf and http://mcwg.org/mcg-mirror/cert.htm Archived 2008-09-05 at the Wayback Machine
26. ^ Gonzalez, Eloi. "Simple Public Key Infrastructure" (PDF).
27. ^ "Decentralized Identifiers (DIDs)". World Wide Web Consortium. 9 December 2019. Archived from the original on 14 May 2020. Retrieved 16 June 2020.
28. ^ "Decentralized Public Key Infrastructure" (PDF). weboftrust.info. 23 December 2015. Retrieved 23 June 2020.
29. ^ Ellis, James H. (January 1970). "The Possibility of Secure Non-Secret Digital Encryption" (PDF). Archived from the original (PDF) on 2014-10-30.
30. ^ Stephen Wilson, December 2005, "The importance of PKI today" Archived 2010-11-22 at the Wayback Machine, China Communications, Retrieved on 2010-12-13
31. ^ Mark Gasson, Martin Meints, Kevin Warwick (2005), D3.2: A study on PKI and biometrics, FIDIS deliverable (3)2, July 2005
32. ^ "xipki/xipki · GitHub". Github.com. Retrieved 2016-10-17.
33. ^ Sullivan, Nick (10 July 2014). "Introducing CFSSL - Cloudflare's PKI toolkit". CloudFlare's Blog. CloudFlare. Retrieved 18 April 2018.
34. ^ "cloudflare/cfssl · GitHub". Github.com. Retrieved 18 April 2018.
35. ^ "hashicorp/vault · GitHub". Github.com. Retrieved 18 April 2018.
36. ^ "Should We Abandon Digital Certificates, Or Learn to Use Them Effectively?". Forbes.
37. ^ "HTTP/2 Frequently Asked Questions". HTTP/2 wiki – via Github.
38. ^ "Root Certificate vs Intermediate Certificates". About SSL. Retrieved 2022-05-02.
39. ^ "Fraudulent Digital Certificates could allow spoofing". Microsoft Security Advisory. Microsoft. March 23, 2011. Retrieved 2011-03-24.

Certificate Authority, References

1. ^ Chien, Hung-Yu (2021-08-19). "Dynamic Public Key Certificates with Forward Secrecy". Electronics. **10** (16): 2009. doi:10.3390/electronics10162009. ISSN 2079-9292.
2. ^ "What is a certificate authority (CA)?".
3. ^ Villanueva, John Carl. "How do Digital Certificates Work - An Overview". www.jscape.com. Retrieved 2021-09-05.
4. ^ "Mozilla Included CA Certificate List — Mozilla". Mozilla.org. Archived from the original on 2013-08-04. Retrieved 2014-06-11.
5. ^ "EMV CA". EMV Certificate Authority Worldwide. 2 October 2010. Retrieved February 17, 2019.
6. ^ Zakir Durumeric; James Kasten; Michael Bailey; J. Alex Halderman (12 September 2013). "Analysis of the HTTPS Certificate Ecosystem" (PDF). The Internet Measurement Conference. SIGCOMM. Archived (PDF) from the original on 22 December 2013. Retrieved 20 December 2013.
7. ^ "What is an SSL Certificate?". Archived from the original on 2015-11-03. Retrieved 2022-03-19.
8. ^ "webtrust". webtrust. Archived from the original on 2013-08-18. Retrieved 2013-03-02.
9. ^ Kirk Hall (April 2013). "Standards and Industry Regulations Applicable to Certification Authorities" (PDF). Trend Micro. Archived (PDF) from the original on 2016-03-04. Retrieved 2014-06-11.
10. ^ "CA:IncludedCAs - MozillaWiki". wiki.mozilla.org. Archived from the original on 2017-03-25. Retrieved 2017-03-18.
11. ^ "List of available trusted root certificates in macOS High Sierra". Apple Support. Retrieved 2020-08-24.
12. ^ "Microsoft Included CA Certificate List". ccadb-public.secure.force.com. Retrieved 2020-08-24.
13. ^ "Security with HTTPS and SSL". developer.android.com. Archived from the original on 2017-07-08. Retrieved 2017-06-09.
14. ^ "Let's Encrypt: Delivering SSL/TLS Everywhere" (Press release). Let's Encrypt. Archived from the original on 2014-11-18. Retrieved 2014-11-20.
15. ^ "About". Let's Encrypt. Archived from the original on 2015-06-10. Retrieved 2015-06-07.
16. ^ "Counting SSL certificates - Netcraft". news.netcraft.com. 13 May 2015. Archived from the original on 2015-05-16.
17. ^ "DigiCert - World's Largest High-Assurance Certificate Authority | Netcraft". trends.netcraft.com.
18. ^ "Usage statistics of SSL certificate authorities for websites, April 2023 - W3Techs". w3techs.com.
19. ^ "Archived copy" (PDF). Archived (PDF) from the original on 2015-03-23. Retrieved 2015-03-20.
20. ^ "CA/Forbidden or Problematic Practices - MozillaWiki". wiki.mozilla.org. Archived from the original on 2017-07-21. Retrieved 2017-07-06.
21. ^ "SSL FAQ - Frequently Asked Questions - Rapid SSL". www.rapidssl.com. Archived from the original on 2015-02-06.
22. ^ Zusman, Mike (2009). Criminal charges are not pursued: Hacking PKI (PDF). DEF CON 17. Las Vegas. Archived (PDF) from the original on 2013-04-15.
23. ^ "A Finnish man created this simple email account - and received Microsoft's security certificate". tivi.fi. Archived from the original on 2015-08-08.
24. ^ "Responsibilities of Certificate Authority". Archived from the original on 2015-02-12. Retrieved 2015-02-12.
25. ^ "Network World". 17 January 2000.
26. ^ Applied Cryptography and Network Security: Second International Conference, ACNS 2004, Yellow Mountain, China, June 8-11, 2004. Proceedings. Springer. June 2004. ISBN 9783540222170.
27. ^ The Shortcut Guide to Managing Certificate Lifecycles. Realtimepublishers.com. 2006. ISBN 9781931491594.
28. ^ "Electronic Signatures and Records" (PDF). Archived (PDF) from the original on 2016-03-04. Retrieved 2014-08-28.
29. ^ "Certificate transparency". Archived from the original on 2013-11-01. Retrieved 2013-11-03.
30. ^ Laurie, Ben; Langley, Adam; Kasper, Emilia (June 2013). "Certificate transparency". Internet Engineering Task Force. doi:10.17487/RFC6962. Archived from the original on 2013-11-22. Retrieved 2013-11-03.
31. ^ Smith, Dickinson & Seamons 2020, p. 1.
32. ^ [a] [b] Sheffer, Saint-Andre & Fossati 2022, 7.5. Certificate Revocation.
33. ^ Chung et al. 2018, p. 3.
34. ^ Smith, Dickinson & Seamons 2020, p. 10.
35. ^ Larisch et al. 2017, p. 542.
36. ^ Smith, Dickinson & Seamons 2020, p. 1-2.

37. ^ "Multivendor power council formed to address digital certificate issues". Network World. February 14, 2013. Archived from the original on July 28, 2013.
38. ^ "Major Certificate Authorities Unite In The Name Of SSL Security". Dark Reading. February 14, 2013. Archived from the original on April 10, 2013.
39. ^ "CA/Browser Forum Founder". Archived from the original on 2014-08-23. Retrieved 2014-08-23.
40. ^ "CA/Browser Forum". Archived from the original on 2013-05-12. Retrieved 2013-04-23.
41. ^ Wilson, Wilson. "CA/Browser Forum History" (PDF). DigiCert. Archived (PDF) from the original on 2013-05-12. Retrieved 2013-04-23.
42. ^ "Baseline Requirements". CAB Forum. Archived from the original on 7 January 2014. Retrieved 14 April 2017.
43. ^ "Mozilla Root Store Policy". Mozilla. Archived from the original on 15 April 2017. Retrieved 14 April 2017.
44. ^ "Apple Root Certificate Program". Apple. Archived from the original on 20 March 2017. Retrieved 14 April 2017.
45. ^ "CA-2001-04". Cert.org. Archived from the original on 2013-11-02. Retrieved 2014-06-11.
46. ^ Microsoft, Inc. (2007-02-21). "Microsoft Security Bulletin MS01-017: Erroneous VeriSign-Issued Digital Certificates Pose Spoofing Hazard". Archived from the original on 2011-10-26. Retrieved 2011-11-09.
47. ^ Seltzer, Larry. "SSL Certificate Vendor Sells Mozilla.com CSSL Certificate to Some Guy". eWeek. Retrieved 5 December 2021.
48. ^ Bright, Peter (28 March 2011). "Independent Iranian hacker claims responsibility for Comodo hack". Ars Technica. Archived from the original on 29 August 2011. Retrieved 2011-09-01.
49. ^ Bright, Peter (2011-08-30). "Another fraudulent certificate raises the same old questions about certificate authorities". Ars Technica. Archived from the original on 2011-09-12. Retrieved 2011-09-01.
50. ^ Leyden, John (2011-09-06). "Inside 'Operation Black Tulip': DigiNotar hack analysed". The Register. Archived from the original on 2017-07-03.
51. ^ "Trustwave issued a man-in-the-middle certificate". The H Security. 2012-02-07. Archived from the original on 2012-03-13. Retrieved 2012-03-14.
52. ^ Osborne, Charlie. "Symantec sacks staff for issuing unauthorized Google certificates - ZDNet". zdnet.com. Archived from the original on 2016-10-02.
53. ^ "Unauthorized Google Digital Certificates Discovered". linkedin.com. 12 August 2014.
54. ^ "In the Wake of Unauthorized Certificate Issuance by the Indian CA NIC, can Government CAs Still be Considered "Trusted Third Parties"?". casecurity.org. 24 July 2014. Archived from the original on 3 October 2016.

Vulnerability, References

1. ^ "Vulnerability Management Life Cycle | NPCR | CDC". www.cdc.gov. 2019-03-12. Retrieved 2020-07-04.
2. ^ Ding, Aaron Yi; De Jesus, Gianluca Limon; Janssen, Marijn (2019). "Ethical hacking for boosting IoT vulnerability management". Proceedings of the Eighth International Conference on Telecommunications and Remote Sensing. Ictrs '19. Rhodes, Greece: ACM Press. pp. 49–55. arXiv:1909.11166. doi:10.1145/3357767.3357774. ISBN 978-1-4503-7669-3. S2CID 202676146.
3. ^ [a][b] ISO/IEC, "Information technology -- Security techniques-Information security risk management" ISO/IEC FIDIS 27005:2008
4. ^ British Standard Institute, Information technology -- Security techniques -- Management of the information and communications technology security -- Part 1: Concepts and models for information and communications technology security management BS ISO/IEC 13335-1-2004
5. ^ [a][b] Internet Engineering Task Force RFC 4949 Internet Security Glossary, Version 2
6. ^ "CNSS Instruction No. 4009" (PDF). 26 April 2010. Archived from the original (PDF) on 2013-06-28.
7. ^ "FISMApedia". fismapedia.org.
8. ^ "Term:Vulnerability". fismapedia.org.
9. ^ NIST SP 800-30 Risk Management Guide for Information Technology Systems
10. ^ "Glossary". europa.eu.
11. ^ Technical Standard Risk Taxonomy ISBN 1-931624-77-1 Document Number: C081 Published by The Open Group, January 2009.
12. ^ [a][b] "An Introduction to Factor Analysis of Information Risk (FAIR)", Risk Management Insight LLC, November 2006 Archived 2014-11-18 at the Wayback Machine;
13. ^ Matt Bishop and Dave Bailey. A Critical Analysis of Vulnerability Taxonomies. Technical Report CSE-96-11, Department of Computer Science at the University of California at Davis, September 1996
14. ^ Schou, Corey (1996). Handbook of INFOSEC Terms, Version 2.0. CD-ROM (Idaho State University & Information Systems Security Organization)
15. ^ NIATEC Glossary
16. ^ ISACA THE RISK IT FRAMEWORK (registration required) Archived July 5, 2010, at the Wayback Machine
17. ^ [a][b] Wright, Joe; Harmening, Jim (2009). "15". In Vacca, John (ed.). Computer and Information Security Handbook. Morgan Kaufmann Publications. Elsevier Inc. p. 257. ISBN 978-0-12-374354-1.
18. ^ [a][b][c][d][e] Kakareka, Almantas (2009). "23". In Vacca, John (ed.). Computer and Information Security Handbook. Morgan Kaufmann Publications. Elsevier Inc. p. 393. ISBN 978-0-12-374354-1.
19. ^ Krsul, Ivan (April 15, 1997). Technical Report CSD-TR-97-026. The COAST Laboratory Department of Computer Sciences, Purdue University. CiteSeerX 10.1.1.26.5435.
20. ^ Pauli, Darren (16 January 2017). "Just give up: 123456 is still the world's most popular password". The Register. Retrieved 2017-01-17.
21. ^ "The Six Dumbest Ideas in Computer Security". ranum.com.
22. ^ "The Web Application Security Consortium / Web Application Security Statistics". webappsec.org.
23. ^ Ross Anderson. Why Cryptosystems Fail. Technical report, University Computer Laboratory, Cam- bridge, January 1994.
24. ^ Neil Schlager. When Technology Fails: Significant Technological Disasters, Accidents, and Failures of the Twentieth Century. Gale Research Inc., 1994.
25. ^ Hacking: The Art of Exploitation Second Edition
26. ^ Kiountouzis, E. A.; Kokolakis, S. A. (31 May 1996). Information systems security: facing the information society of the 21st century. London: Chapman & Hall, Ltd. ISBN 0-412-78120-4.
27. ^ [a][b] Rasmussen, Jeremy (February 12, 2018). "Best Practices for Cybersecurity: Stay Cyber SMART". Tech Decisions. Retrieved September 18, 2020.
28. ^ "What is a vulnerability? - Knowledgebase - ICTEA". www.ictea.com. Retrieved 2021-04-03.
29. ^ Bavisi, Sanjay (2009). "22". In Vacca, John (ed.). Computer and Information Security Handbook. Morgan Kaufmann Publications. Elsevier Inc. p. 375. ISBN 978-0-12-374354-1.
30. ^ "The new era of vulnerability disclosure - a brief chat with HD Moore". The Tech Herald. Archived from the original on 2010-08-26. Retrieved 2010-08-24.
31. ^ Betz, Chris (11 Jan 2015). "A Call for Better Coordinated Vulnerability Disclosure - MSRC - Site Home - TechNet Blogs". blogs.technet.com. Retrieved 12 January 2015.
32. ^ "Wiz launches open database to track cloud vulnerabilities". SearchSecurity. Retrieved 2022-07-20.
33. ^ Barth, Bradley (2022-06-08). "Centralized database will help standardize bug disclosure for the cloud". www.scmagazine.com. Retrieved 2022-07-20.
34. ^ Vijayan, Jai (2022-06-28). "New Vulnerability Database Catalogs Cloud Security Issues". Dark Reading. Retrieved 2022-07-20.
35. ^ "Category:Vulnerability". owasp.org.
36. ^ David Harley (10 March 2015). "Operating System Vulnerabilities, Exploits and Insecurity". Retrieved 15 January 2019.
37. ^ Most laptops vulnerable to attack via peripheral devices. http://www.sciencedaily.com/releases/2019/02/190225192119.htm Source: University of Cambridge]
38. ^ Exploiting Network Printers. Institute for IT-Security, Ruhr University Bochum
39. ^ [1] Archived October 21, 2007, at the Wayback Machine
40. ^ "Jesse Ruderman » Race conditions in security dialogs". squarefree.com.
41. ^ "lcamtuf's blog". lcamtuf.blogspot.com. 16 August 2010.
42. ^ "Warning Fatigue". freedom-to-tinker.com. 22 October 2003.

Computer Network, References

1. ^ Sterling, Christopher H., ed. (2008). Military Communications: From Ancient Times to the 21st Century. ABC-Clio. p. 399. ISBN 978-1-85109-737-1.
2. ^ Haigh, Thomas; Ceruzzi, Paul E. (14 September 2021). A New History of Modern Computing. MIT Press. pp. 87–89. ISBN 978-0262542906.
3. ^ Ulmann, Bernd (August 19, 2014). AN/FSQ-7: the computer that shaped the Cold War. De Gruyter. ISBN 978-3-486-85670-5.
4. ^ Corbató, F. J.; et al. (1963). The Compatible Time-Sharing System A Programmer's Guide] (PDF). MIT Press. ISBN 978-0-262-03008-3. Archived (PDF) from the original on 2012-05-27. Retrieved 2020-05-26. Shortly after the first paper on time-shared computers by C. Strachey at the June 1959 UNESCO Information Processing conference, H. M. Teager and J. McCarthy at MIT delivered an unpublished paper "Time-shared Program Testing" at the August 1959 ACM Meeting.
5. ^ "Computer Pioneers - Christopher Strachey". history.computer.org. Archived from the original on 2019-05-15. Retrieved 2020-01-23.
6. ^ "Reminiscences on the Theory of Time-Sharing". jmc.stanford.edu. Archived from the original on 2020-04-28. Retrieved 2020-01-23.
7. ^ "Computer - Time-sharing and minicomputers". Encyclopedia Britannica. Archived from the original on 2015-01-02. Retrieved 2020-01-23.
8. ^ Gillies, James M.; Gillies, James; Gillies, James and Cailliau Robert; Cailliau, R. (2000). How the Web was Born: The Story of the World Wide Web. Oxford University Press. pp. 13. ISBN 978-0-19-286207-5.
9. ^ Kitova, O. "Kitov Anatoliy Ivanovich. Russian Virtual Computer Museum". computer-museum.ru. Translated by Alexander Nitusov. Archived from the original on 2023-02-04. Retrieved 2021-10-11.
10. ^ Peters, Benjamin (25 March 2016). How Not to Network a Nation: The Uneasy History of the Soviet Internet. MIT Press. ISBN 978-0262034180.
11. ^ Isaacson, Walter (2014). The Innovators: How a Group of Hackers, Geniuses, and Geeks Created the Digital Revolution. Simon and Schuster. pp. 237–246. ISBN 9781476708690. Archived from the original on 2023-02-04. Retrieved 2021-06-04.
12. ^ "NIHF Inductee Paul Baran, Who Invented Packet Switching". National Inventors Hall of Fame. Archived from the original on 2022-02-12. Retrieved 2022-02-12.
13. ^ "NIHF Inductee Donald Davies, Who Invented Packet Switching". National Inventors Hall of Fame. Archived from the original on 2022-02-12. Retrieved 2022-02-12.

14. ^ a b Roberts, Lawrence G. (November 1978). "The evolution of packet switching" (PDF). Proceedings of the IEEE. 66 (11): 1307–13. doi:10.1109/PROC.1978.11141. S2CID 26876676. Archived (PDF) from the original on 2023-02-04. Retrieved 2022-02-12. Both Paul Baran and Donald Davies in their original papers anticipated the use of T1 trunks
15. ^ Cambell-Kelly, Martin (1987). "Data Communications at the National Physical Laboratory (1965-1975)". Annals of the History of Computing. 9 (3/4): 221–247. doi:10.1109/MAHC.1987.10023. S2CID 8172150. Transmission of packets of data over the high-speed lines
16. ^ Guardian Staff (2013-06-25). "Internet pioneers airbrushed from history". The Guardian. ISSN 0261-3077. Archived from the original on 2020-01-01. Retrieved 2020-07-31. This was the first digital local network in the world to use packet switching and high-speed links.
17. ^ Chris Sutton. "Internet Began 35 Years Ago at UCLA with First Message Ever Sent Between Two Computers". UCLA. Archived from the original on 2008-03-08.
18. ^ Gillies, James; Cailliau, Robert (2000). How the Web was Born: The Story of the World Wide Web. Oxford University Press. p. 25. ISBN 0192862073.
19. ^ C. Hempstead; W. Worthington (2005). Encyclopedia of 20th-Century Technology. Routledge. ISBN 9781135455514. Archived from the original on 2023-02-04. Retrieved 2017-10-01.
20. ^ Alarcia, G.; Herrera, S. (1974). "C.T.N.E.'s PACKET SWITCHING NETWORK. ITS APPLICATIONS". Proceedings of 2nd ICCC 74. pp. 163–170. Archived from the original on 2021-04-14.
21. ^ Cuenca, L. (1980). "A public packet switching data communications network: eight years of operating experience". Conference Record of ICC 80. IEEE. pp. 39.3.1–39.3.5. Archived from the original on 2021-04-14.
22. ^ Lavandera, Luis (1980). "ARCHITECTURE, PROTOCOLS AND PERFORMANCE OF RETD". Conference Record of ICC 80. IEEE. pp. 28.4.1–28.4.5. Archived from the original on 2021-04-14.
23. ^ Council, National Research; Sciences, Division on Engineering and Physical; Board, Computer Science and Telecommunications; Applications, Commission on Physical Sciences, Mathematics, and; Committee, NII 2000 Steering (1998-02-05). The Unpredictable Certainty: White Papers. National Academies Press. ISBN 978-0-309-17414-5. Archived from the original on 2023-02-04. Retrieved 2021-03-08.
24. ^ Bennett, Richard (September 2009). "Designed for Change: End-to-End Arguments, Internet Innovation, and the Net Neutrality Debate" (PDF). Information Technology and Innovation Foundation. p. 11. Archived from the original (PDF) on 2019-08-29. Retrieved 2017-09-11.
25. ^ Kirstein, P.T. (1999). "Early experiences with the Arpanet and Internet in the United Kingdom". IEEE Annals of the History of Computing. 21 (1): 38–44. doi:10.1109/85.759368. S2CID 1558618.
26. ^ Kirstein, Peter T. (2009). "The early history of packet switching in the UK". IEEE Communications Magazine. 47 (2): 18–26. doi:10.1109/MCOM.2009.4785372. S2CID 34735326.
27. ^ Robert M. Metcalfe; David R. Boggs (July 1976). "Ethernet: Distributed Packet Switching for Local Computer Networks". Communications of the ACM. 19 (5): 395–404. doi:10.1145/360248.360253. S2CID 429216.
28. ^ Cerf, Vinton; dalal, Yogen; Sunshine, Carl (December 1974). Specification of Internet Transmission Control Protocol. IETF. doi:10.17487/RFC0675. RFC 675.
29. ^ Pelkey, James L. (2007). "6.9 - Metcalfe Joins the Systems Development Division of Xerox 1975-1978". Entrepreneurial Capitalism and Innovation: A History of Computer Communications, 1968-1988. Archived from the original on 2023-02-04. Retrieved 2019-09-05.
30. ^ a b Spurgeon, Charles E. (2000). Ethernet The Definitive Guide. O'Reilly & Associates. ISBN 1-56592-660-9.
31. ^ "Introduction to Ethernet Technologies". www.wband.com. WideBand Products. Archived from the original on 2018-04-10. Retrieved 2018-04-09.
32. ^ Pelkey, James L. (2007). "Yogen Dalal". Entrepreneurial Capitalism and Innovation: A History of Computer Communications, 1968-1988. Retrieved 2023-05-07.
33. ^ a b D. Andersen; H. Balakrishnan; M. Kaashoek; R. Morris (October 2001), Resilient Overlay Networks, Association for Computing Machinery, archived from the original on 2011-11-24, retrieved 2011-11-12
34. ^ "End System Multicast". project web site. Carnegie Mellon University. Archived from the original on 2005-02-21. Retrieved 2013-05-25.
35. ^ a b Meyers, Mike (2012). CompTIA Network+ exam guide : (Exam N10-005) (5th ed.). New York: McGraw-Hill. ISBN 9780071789226. OCLC 748332969.
36. ^ A. Hooke (September 2000), Interplanetary Internet (PDF), Third Annual International Symposium on Advanced Radio Technologies, archived from the original (PDF) on 2012-01-13, retrieved 2011-11-12
37. ^ "Bergen Linux User Group's CPIP Implementation". Blug.linux.no. Archived from the original on 2014-02-15. Retrieved 2014-03-01.
38. ^ Bradley Mitchell. "bridge – network bridges". About.com. Archived from the original on 2008-03-28.
39. ^ "Define switch". webopedia. September 1996. Archived from the original on 2008-04-08. Retrieved 2008-04-08.
40. ^ Tanenbaum, Andrew S. (2003). Computer Networks (4th ed.). Prentice Hall.
41. ^ IEEE Standard for Local and Metropolitan Area Networks--Port-Based Network Access Control. February 2020. 7.1.3 Connectivity to unauthenticated systems. doi:10.1109/IEEESTD.2020.9018454. ISBN 978-1-5044-6440-6. Archived from the original on 2023-02-04. Retrieved 2022-05-09. {{cite book}}: |journal= ignored (help)
42. ^ IEEE Standard for Information Technology--Telecommunications and Information Exchange between Systems - Local and Metropolitan Area Networks--Specific Requirements - Part 11: Wireless LAN Medium Access Control (MAC) and Physical Layer (PHY) Specifications. February 2021. 4.2.5 Interaction with other IEEE 802 layers. doi:10.1109/IEEESTD.2021.9363693. ISBN 978-1-5044-7283-8. Archived from the original on 2022-05-17. Retrieved 2022-05-09. {{cite book}}: |journal= ignored (help)
43. ^ Martin, Thomas. "Design Principles for DSL-Based Access Solutions" (PDF). Archived from the original (PDF) on 2011-07-22.
44. ^ Paetsch, Michael (1993). The evolution of mobile communications in the US and Europe: Regulation, technology, and markets. Boston, London: Artech House. ISBN 978-0-8900-6688-1.
45. ^ Bush, S. F. (2010). Nanoscale Communication Networks. Artech House. ISBN 978-1-60807-003-9.
46. ^ Margaret Rouse. "personal area network (PAN)". TechTarget. Archived from the original on 2023-02-04. Retrieved 2011-01-29.
47. ^ "New global standard for fully networked home". ITU-T Newslog. ITU. 2008-12-12. Archived from the original on 2009-02-21. Retrieved 2011-11-12.
48. ^ "IEEE P802.3ba 40Gb/s and 100Gb/s Ethernet Task Force". IEEE 802.3 ETHERNET WORKING GROUP. Archived from the original on 2011-11-20. Retrieved 2011-11-12.
49. ^ "IEEE 802.20 Mission and Project Scope". IEEE 802.20 — Mobile Broadband Wireless Access (MBWA). Retrieved 2011-11-12.
50. ^ "Maps". The Opto Project. Archived from the original on 2005-01-15.
51. ^ Mansfield-Devine, Steve (December 2009). "Darknets". Computer Fraud & Security. 2009 (12): 4–6. doi:10.1016/S1361-3723(09)70150-2.
52. ^ Wood, Jessica (2010). "The Darknet: A Digital Copyright Revolution" (PDF). Richmond Journal of Law and Technology. 16 (4). Archived (PDF) from the original on 2012-04-15. Retrieved 2011-10-25.
53. ^ Klensin, J. (October 2008). Simple Mail Transfer Protocol. doi:10.17487/RFC5321. RFC 5321.
54. ^ Mockapetris, P. (November 1987). Domain names – Implementation and Specification. doi:10.17487/RFC1035. RFC 1035.
55. ^ Peterson, L.L.; Davie, B.S. (2011). Computer Networks: A Systems Approach (5th ed.). Elsevier. p. 372. ISBN 978-0-1238-5060-7.
56. ^ ITU-D Study Group 2 (June 2006). Teletraffic Engineering Handbook (PDF). Archived from the original (PDF) on 2007-01-11.
57. ^ Telecommunications Magazine Online Archived 2011-02-08 at the Wayback Machine, Americas January 2003, Issue Highlights, Online Exclusive: Broadband Access Maximum Performance, Retrieved on February 13, 2005.
58. ^ "State Transition Diagrams". Archived from the original on 2003-10-15. Retrieved 2003-07-13.
59. ^ "Definitions: Resilience". ResiliNets Research Initiative. Archived from the original on 2020-11-06. Retrieved 2011-11-12.
60. ^ Simmonds, A; Sandilands, P; van Ekert, L (2004). "An Ontology for Network Security Attacks". Applied Computing. Lecture Notes in Computer Science. Vol. 3285. pp. 317–323. doi:10.1007/978-3-540-30176-9_41. ISBN 978-3-540-23659-7. S2CID 2204780.
61. ^ a b "Is the U.S. Turning Into a Surveillance Society?". American Civil Liberties Union. Archived from the original on 2017-03-14. Retrieved 2009-03-13.
62. ^ Jay Stanley; Barry Steinhardt (January 2003). "Bigger Monster, Weaker Chains: The Growth of an American Surveillance Society" (PDF). American Civil Liberties Union. Archived (PDF) from the original on 2022-10-09. Retrieved 2009-03-13.
63. ^ Emil Protalinski (2012-04-07). "Anonymous hacks UK government sites over 'draconian surveillance'". ZDNet. Archived from the original on 2013-04-03. Retrieved 12 March 2013.
64. ^ James Ball (2012-04-20). "Hacktivists in the frontline battle for the internet". The Guardian. Archived from the original on 2018-03-14. Retrieved 2012-06-17.
65. ^ a b Rosen, E.; Rekhter, Y. (March 1999). BGP/MPLS VPNs. doi:10.17487/RFC2547. RFC 2547.

Cloud Computing, References

1. ^ Ray, Partha Pratim (2018). "An Introduction to Dew Computing: Definition, Concept and Implications - IEEE Journals & Magazine". IEEE Access. 6: 723–737. doi:10.1109/ACCESS.2017.2775042. S2CID 3324933. Archived from the original on 2021-02-10. Retrieved 2021-02-12.
2. ^ Montazerolghaem, Ahmadreza; Yaghmaee, Mohammad Hossein; Leon-Garcia, Alberto (September 2020). "Green Cloud Multimedia Networking: NFV/SDN Based Energy-Efficient Resource Allocation". IEEE Transactions on Green Communications and Networking. 4 (3): 873–889. doi:10.1109/TGCN.2020.2982821. ISSN 2473-2400. S2CID 216188024. Archived from the original on 2020-12-09. Retrieved 2020-12-06.
3. ^ Wray, Jared (2014-02-27). "Where's The Rub: Cloud Computing's Hidden Costs". Forbes. Archived from the original on 2014-07-14. Retrieved 2014-07-14.
4. ^ a b c d e f g h i Mell, Peter; Timothy Grance (September 2011). The NIST Definition of Cloud Computing (Technical report). National Institute of Standards and Technology: U.S. Department of Commerce. doi:10.6028/NIST.SP.800-145. Special publication 800-145.
5. ^ White, J. E. (1971). "Network Specifications for Remote Job Entry and Remote Job Output Retrieval at UCSB". tools.ietf.org. doi:10.17487/RFC0105. Archived from the original on 2016-03-30. Retrieved 2016-03-21.
6. ^ Levy, Steven (April 1994). "Bill and Andy's Excellent Adventure II" Archived 2015-10-02 at the Wayback Machine. Wired.
7. ^ Mosco, Vincent (2015). To the Cloud: Big Data in a Turbulent World. Taylor & Francis. p. 15. ISBN 9781317250388.
8. ^ "Announcing Amazon Elastic Compute Cloud (Amazon EC2) – beta". 24 August 2006. Archived from the original on 13 August 2014. Retrieved 31 May 2014.
9. ^ Qian, Ling; Lou, Zhigou; Du, Yujian; Gou, Leitao. "Cloud Computing: An Overview". Retrieved 19 April 2021.
10. ^ "Windows Azure General Availability". The Official Microsoft Blog. Microsoft. 2010-02-01. Archived from the original on 2014-05-11. Retrieved 2015-05-03.
11. ^ "Announcing General Availability of AWS Outposts". Amazon Web Services, Inc. Archived from the original on 2021-01-21. Retrieved 2021-02-04.
12. ^ "Remote work helps Zoom grow 169% in one year, posting $328.2M in Q1 revenue". TechCrunch. Archived from the original on 2023-01-17. Retrieved 2021-04-27.
13. ^ "What is Cloud Computing?". Amazon Web Services. 2013-03-19. Archived from the original on 2013-03-22. Retrieved 2013-03-20.
14. ^ Baburajan, Rajani (2011-08-24). "The Rising Cloud Storage Market Opportunity Strengthens Vendors". It.tmcnet.com. Archived from the original on 2012-06-17. Retrieved 2011-12-02.
15. ^ Oestreich, Ken (2010-11-15). "Converged Infrastructure". CTO Forum. Thectoforum.com. Archived from the original on 2012-01-13. Retrieved 2011-12-02.

16. ^ Simpson, Ted; Jason Novak, *Hands on Virtual Computing*, 2017, ISBN 1337515744, p. 451. Archived 2023-01-17 at the Wayback Machine
17. ^ *"Recession Is Good For Cloud Computing – Microsoft Agrees". CloudAve. 2009-02-12. Archived from the original on 2010-08-14. Retrieved 2010-08-22.*
18. ^ *a b c d "Defining 'Cloud Services' and "Cloud Computing"". IDC. 2008-09-23. Archived from the original on 2010-07-22. Retrieved 2010-08-22.*
19. ^ *"State of the Art | e-FISCAL project". www.efiscal.eu. Archived from the original on 2013-01-27. Retrieved 2012-04-19.*
20. ^ *Farber, Dan (2008-06-25). "The new geek chic: Data centers". CNET News. Archived from the original on 2013-11-04. Retrieved 2010-08-22.*
21. ^ *"Jeff Bezos' Risky Bet". Business Week. Archived from the original on 2012-06-27. Retrieved 2008-08-21.*
22. ^ *He, Sijin; Guo, L.; Guo, Y.; Ghanem, M. (June 2012). "Improving Resource Utilisation in the Cloud Environment Using Multivariate Probabilistic Models". 2012 IEEE Fifth International Conference on Cloud Computing. 2012 2012 IEEE 5th International Conference on Cloud Computing (CLOUD). pp. 574–581. doi:10.1109/CLOUD.2012.66. ISBN 978-1-4673-2892-0. S2CID 15374752.*
23. ^ He, Qiang, et al. "Formulating Cost-Effective Monitoring Strategies for Service-based Systems." (2013): 1–1.
24. ^ *King, Rachael (2008-08-04). "Cloud Computing: Small Companies Take Flight". Bloomberg BusinessWeek. Archived from the original on 2010-08-07. Retrieved 2010-08-22.*
25. ^ *a b Mao, Ming; M. Humphrey (2012). "A Performance Study on the VM Startup Time in the Cloud". 2012 IEEE Fifth International Conference on Cloud Computing. p. 423. doi:10.1109/CLOUD.2012.103. ISBN 978-1-4673-2892-0. S2CID 1285357.*
26. ^ *Bruneo, Dario; Distefano, Salvatore; Longo, Francesco; Puliafito, Antonio; Scarpa, Marco (2013). "Workload-Based Software Rejuvenation in Cloud Systems". IEEE Transactions on Computers. **62** (6): 1072–1085. doi:10.1109/TC.2013.30. S2CID 23981532.*
27. ^ *Kuperberg, Michael; Herbst, Nikolas; Kistowski, Joakim Von; Reussner, Ralf (2011). "Defining and Measuring Cloud Elasticity". KIT Software Quality Departement. doi:10.5445/IR/1000023476. Archived from the original on 6 April 2013. Retrieved 13 August 2011.*
28. ^ *"Economies of Cloud Scale Infrastructure". Cloud Slam 2011. Archived from the original on 2021-10-27. Retrieved 13 May 2011.*
29. ^ *He, Sijin; L. Guo; Y. Guo; C. Wu; M. Ghanem (March 2012). "Elastic Application Container: A Lightweight Approach for Cloud Resource Provisioning". 2012 IEEE 26th International Conference on Advanced Information Networking and Applications. 2012 IEEE 26th International Conference on Advanced Information Networking and Applications (AINA). pp. 15–22. doi:10.1109/AINA.2012.74. ISBN 978-1-4673-0714-7. S2CID 4863927.*
30. ^ *Marston, Sean; Li, Zhi; Bandyopadhyay, Subhajyoti; Zhang, Juheng; Ghalsasi, Anand (2011-04-01). "Cloud computing – The business perspective". Decision Support Systems. **51** (1): 176–189. doi:10.1016/j.dss.2010.12.006.*
31. ^ Why Cloud computing scalability matters for business growth Archived 2021-07-09 at the Wayback Machine, Symphony Solutions, 2021
32. ^ *Nouri, Seyed; Han, Li; Srikumar, Venugopal; Wenxia, Guo; MingYun, He; Wenhong, Tian (2019). "Autonomic decentralized elasticity based on a reinforcement learning controller for cloud applications". Future Generation Computer Systems. **94**: 765–780. doi:10.1016/j.future.2018.11.049. S2CID 59284268.*
33. ^ *Mills, Elinor (2009-01-27). "Cloud computing security forecast: Clear skies". CNET News. Archived from the original on 2020-01-28. Retrieved 2019-09-19.*
34. ^ *a b Marko, Kurt; Bigelow, Stephen J. (10 Nov 2022). "The pros and cons of cloud computing explained". TechTarget.*
35. ^ *Bratton, Benjamin H. (2015). The stack: on software and sovereignty. Software studies. Cambridge, Mass. London: MIT press. ISBN 978-0-262-02957-5.*
36. ^ *Bridle, James (2019). New dark age: technology and the end of the future. Verso.*
37. ^ *Shurma, Ramesh (8 Mar 2023). "The Hidden Costs Of Cloud Migration". Forbes.*
38. ^ *Duan, Yucong; Fu, Guohua; Zhou, Nianjun; Sun, Xiaobing; Narendra, Nanjangud; Hu, Bo (2015). "Everything as a Service (XaaS) on the Cloud: Origins, Current and Future Trends". 2015 IEEE 8th International Conference on Cloud Computing. IEEE. pp. 621–628. doi:10.1109/CLOUD.2015.88. ISBN 978-1-4673-7287-9. S2CID 8201466.*
39. ^ *Amies, Alex; Sluiman, Harm; Tong, Qiang Guo; Liu, Guo Ning (July 2012). "Infrastructure as a Service Cloud Concepts". Developing and Hosting Applications on the Cloud. IBM Press. ISBN 978-0-13-306684-5. Archived from the original on 2012-09-15. Retrieved 2012-07-19.*
40. ^ *Nelson, Michael R. (2009). "The Cloud, the Crowd, and Public Policy". Issues in Science and Technology. **25** (4): 71–76. JSTOR 43314918. Archived from the original on 2022-09-10. Retrieved 2022-09-10.*
41. ^ *Boniface, M.; et al. (2010). Platform-as-a-Service Architecture for Real-Time Quality of Service Management in Clouds. 5th International Conference on Internet and Web Applications and Services (ICIW). Barcelona, Spain: IEEE. pp. 155–160. doi:10.1109/ICIW.2010.91.*
42. ^ *"Integration Platform as a Service (iPaaS)". Gartner IT Glossary. Gartner. Archived from the original on 2015-07-29. Retrieved 2015-07-20.*
43. ^ *Gartner; Massimo Pezzini; Paolo Malinverno; Eric Thoo. "Gartner Reference Model for Integration PaaS". Archived from the original on 1 July 2013. Retrieved 16 January 2013.*
44. ^ *Loraine Lawson (3 April 2015). "IT Business Edge". Archived from the original on 7 July 2015. Retrieved 6 July 2015.*
45. ^ *Enterprise CIO Forum; Gabriel Lowy. "The Value of Data Platform-as-a-Service (dPaaS)". Archived from the original on 19 April 2015. Retrieved 6 July 2015.*
46. ^ *"Definition of: SaaS". PC Magazine Encyclopedia. Ziff Davis. Archived from the original on 14 July 2014. Retrieved 14 May 2014.*
47. ^ *Hamdaqa, Mohammad. A Reference Model for Developing Cloud Applications (PDF). Archived (PDF) from the original on 2012-10-05. Retrieved 2012-05-23.*
48. ^ *Chou, Timothy. Introduction to Cloud Computing: Business & Technology. Archived from the original on 2016-05-05. Retrieved 2017-09-09.*
49. ^ *"HVD: the cloud's silver lining" (PDF). Intrinsic Technology. Archived from the original (PDF) on 2 October 2012. Retrieved 30 August 2012.*
50. ^ *Sun, Yunchuan; Zhang, Junsheng; Xiong, Yongping; Zhu, Guangyu (2014-07-01). "Data Security and Privacy in Cloud Computing". International Journal of Distributed Sensor Networks. **10** (7): 190903. doi:10.1155/2014/190903. ISSN 1550-1477. S2CID 13213544.*
51. ^ *"Use OneDrive with Office". support.microsoft.com. Archived from the original on 2022-10-15. Retrieved 2022-10-15.*
52. ^ *Carney, Michael (2013-06-24). "AnyPresence partners with Heroku to beef up its enterprise mBaaS offering". PandoDaily. Archived from the original on 2013-06-27. Retrieved 24 June 2013.*
53. ^ *Alex Williams (11 October 2012). "Kii Cloud Opens Doors For Mobile Developer Platform With 25 Million End Users". TechCrunch. Archived from the original on 15 October 2012. Retrieved 16 October 2012.*
54. ^ *Aaron Tan (30 September 2012). "FatFractal ups the ante in backend-as-a-service market". Techgoondu.com. Archived from the original on 10 October 2012. Retrieved 16 October 2012.*
55. ^ *Dan Rowinski (9 November 2011). "Mobile Backend As A Service Parse Raises $5.5 Million in Series A Funding". ReadWrite. Archived from the original on 1 November 2012. Retrieved 23 October 2012.*
56. ^ *Pankaj Mishra (7 January 2014). "MobStac Raises $2 Million in Series B To Help Brands Leverage Mobile Commerce". TechCrunch. Archived from the original on 15 May 2014. Retrieved 22 May 2014.*
57. ^ *"built.io Is Building an Enterprise MBaas Platform for IoT". programmableweb. 2014-03-03. Archived from the original on 2014-03-06. Retrieved 3 March 2014.*
58. ^ *a b Miller, Ron (24 Nov 2015). "AWS Lambda Makes Serverless Applications A Reality". TechCrunch. Archived from the original on 23 May 2019. Retrieved 10 July 2016.*
59. ^ *"bliki: Serverless". martinfowler.com. Archived from the original on 2018-05-05. Retrieved 2018-05-04.*
60. ^ *Sbarski, Peter (2017-05-04). Serverless Architectures on AWS: With examples using AWS Lambda (1st ed.). Manning Publications. ISBN 9781617293825.*
61. ^ *"Self-Run Private Cloud Computing Solution – GovConnection". govconnection.com. 2014. Archived from the original on April 6, 2014. Retrieved April 15, 2014.*
62. ^ *"Private Clouds Take Shape – Services – Business services – Informationweek". 2012-09-09. Archived from the original on 2012-09-09.*
63. ^ *Haff, Gordon (2009-01-27). "Just don't call them private clouds". CNET News. Archived from the original on 2014-12-27. Retrieved 2010-08-22.*
64. ^ *"There's No Such Thing As A Private Cloud – Cloud-computing -". 2013-01-26. Archived from the original on 2013-01-26.*
65. ^ *Rouse, Margaret. "What is public cloud?". Definition from Whatis.com. Archived from the original on 16 October 2014. Retrieved 12 October 2014.*
66. ^ *"FastConnect | Oracle Cloud Infrastructure". cloud.oracle.com. Archived from the original on 2017-11-15. Retrieved 2017-11-15.*
67. ^ *Schmidt, Rainer; Möhring, Michael; Keller, Barbara (2017). "Customer Relationship Management in a Public Cloud environment - Key influencing factors for European enterprises". HICSS. Proceedings of the 50th Hawaii International Conference on System Sciences (2017). doi:10.24251/HICSS.2017.513. hdl:10125/41673. ISBN 9780998133102.*
68. ^ *"What is hybrid cloud? - Definition from WhatIs.com". SearchCloudComputing. Archived from the original on 2019-07-16. Retrieved 2019-08-10.*
69. ^ *Butler, Brandon (2017-10-17). "What is hybrid cloud computing? The benefits of mixing private and public cloud services". Network World. Archived from the original on 2019-08-11. Retrieved 2019-08-11.*
70. ^ *"Mind the Gap: Here Comes Hybrid Cloud – Thomas Bittman". Thomas Bittman. 24 September 2012. Archived from the original on 17 April 2015. Retrieved 22 April 2015.*
71. ^ *"Business Intelligence Takes to Cloud for Small Businesses". CIO.com. 2014-06-04. Archived from the original on 2014-06-07. Retrieved 2014-06-04.*
72. ^ *Désiré Athow (24 August 2014). "Hybrid cloud: is it right for your business?". TechRadar. Archived from the original on 7 July 2017. Retrieved 22 April 2015.*
73. ^ Metzler, Jim; Taylor, Steve. (2010-08-23) "Cloud computing: Reality vs. fiction" Archived 2013-06-19 at the Wayback Machine, Network World.
74. ^ Rouse, Margaret. "Definition: Cloudbursting" Archived 2013-03-19 at the Wayback Machine, May 2011. SearchCloudComputing.com.
75. ^ *"How Cloudbursting "Rightsizes" the Data Center". 2012-06-22. Archived from the original on 2016-10-19. Retrieved 2016-10-19.*
76. ^ *Cunsolo, Vincenzo D.; Distefano, Salvatore; Puliafito, Antonio; Scarpa, Marco (2009). "Volunteer Computing and Desktop Cloud: The Cloud@Home Paradigm". 2009 Eighth IEEE International Symposium on Network Computing and Applications. pp. 134–139. doi:10.1109/NCA.2009.41. S2CID 15848602.*
77. ^ *Rouse, Margaret. "What is a multi-cloud strategy". SearchCloudApplications. Archived from the original on 5 July 2014. Retrieved 3 July 2014.*
78. ^ *King, Rachel. "Pivotal's head of products: We're moving to a multi-cloud world". ZDnet. Archived from the original on 4 July 2014. Retrieved 3 July 2014.*
79. ^ Multcloud manage multiple cloud accounts Archived 2023-01-17 at the Wayback Machine. Retrieved on 06 August 2014
80. ^ *Gall, Richard (2018-05-16). "Polycloud: a better alternative to cloud agnosticism". Packt Hub. Archived from the original on 2019-11-11. Retrieved 2019-11-11.*
81. ^ *Roh, Lucas (31 August 2016). "Is the Cloud Finally Ready for Big Data?". dataconomy.com. Archived from the original on 30 January 2018. Retrieved 29 January 2018.*
82. ^ *Yang, C.; Huang, Q.; Li, Z.; Liu, K.; Hu, F. (2017). "Big Data and cloud computing: innovation opportunities and challenges". International Journal of Digital Earth. **10** (1): 13–53. Bibcode:2017IJDE...10...13Y. doi:10.1080/17538947.2016.1239771. S2CID 8053067.*
83. ^ *Netto, M.; Calheiros, R.; Rodrigues, E.; Cunha, R.; Buyya, R. (2018). "HPC Cloud for Scientific and Business Applications: Taxonomy, Vision, and Research Challenges". ACM Computing Surveys. **51** (1): 8:1–8:29. arXiv:1710.08731. doi:10.1145/3150224. S2CID 3604131.*
84. ^ *Eadline, Douglas. "Moving HPC to the Cloud". Admin Magazine. Archived from the original on 30 March 2019. Retrieved 30 March 2019.*
85. ^ *"Penguin Computing On Demand (POD)". Archived from the original on 9 March 2018. Retrieved 23 January 2018.*
86. ^ *Niccolai, James (11 August 2009). "Penguin Puts High-performance Computing in the Cloud". PCWorld. IDG Consumer & SMB. Archived from the original on 19 August 2016. Retrieved 6 June 2016.*
87. ^ *"HPC in AWS". Archived from the original on 1 December 2017. Retrieved 23 January 2018.*
88. ^ *"Building GrepTheWeb in the Cloud, Part 1: Cloud Architectures". Developer.amazonwebservices.com. Archived from the original on 5 May 2009. Retrieved 22 August 2010.*
89. ^ *a b c Ryan, Mark D. "Cloud Computing Privacy Concerns on Our Doorstep". cacm.acm.org. Archived from the original on 2021-12-28. Retrieved 2021-05-21.*

90. ^ Indu, I.; Anand, P.M. Rubesh; Bhaskar, Vidhyacharan (August 1, 2018). "Identity and access management in cloud environment: Mechanisms and challenges". *Engineering Science and Technology*. **21** (4): 574–588. doi:10.1016/j.jestch.2018.05.010. Archived from the original on December 28, 2021. Retrieved July 29, 2020 – via www.sciencedirect.com.
91. ^ a b "Google Drive, Dropbox, Box and iCloud Reach the Top 5 Cloud Storage Security Breaches List". psg.hitachi-solutions.com. Archived from the original on 2015-11-23. Retrieved 2015-11-22.
92. ^ Maltais, Michelle (26 April 2012). "Who owns your stuff in the cloud?". *Los Angeles Times*. Archived from the original on 2013-01-20. Retrieved 2012-12-14.
93. ^ "Security of virtualization, cloud computing divides IT and security pros". Network World. 2010-02-22. Archived from the original on 2014-07-02. Retrieved 2010-08-22.
94. ^ "The Bumpy Road to Private Clouds". 2010-12-20. Archived from the original on 2014-10-15. Retrieved 8 October 2014.
95. ^ "IDC Forecasts Worldwide "Whole Cloud" Spending to Reach $1.3 Trillion by 2025". Idc.com. 2021-09-14. Archived from the original on 2022-07-29. Retrieved 2022-07-30.
96. ^ "Gartner Forecasts Worldwide Public Cloud End-User Spending to Reach Nearly $500 Billion in 2022". Archived from the original on 2022-07-25. Retrieved 2022-07-25.
97. ^ "Cloud's trillion-dollar prize is up for grabs". McKinsey. Archived from the original on 2022-07-25. Retrieved 2022-07-30.
98. ^ "Gartner Says More Than Half of Enterprise IT Spending in Key Market Segments Will Shift to the Cloud by 2025". Archived from the original on 2022-07-25. Retrieved 2022-07-25.
99. ^ a b c HAMDAQA, Mohammad (2012). Cloud Computing Uncovered: A Research Landscape (PDF). Elsevier Press. pp. 41–85. ISBN 978-0-12-396535-6. Archived (PDF) from the original on 2013-06-19. Retrieved 2013-03-19.
100. ^ "Distributed Application Architecture" (PDF). Sun Microsystem. Archived (PDF) from the original on 2011-04-06. Retrieved 2009-06-16.
101. ^ Vaquero, Luis M.; Rodero-Merino, Luis; Caceres, Juan; Lindner, Maik (December 2008). "It's probable that you've misunderstood 'Cloud Computing' until now". *Sigcomm Comput. Commun. Rev. TechPluto*. **39** (1): 50–55. doi:10.1145/1496091.1496100. S2CID 207171174.
102. ^ Danielson, Krissi (2008-03-26). "Distinguishing Cloud Computing from Utility Computing". Ebizq.net. Archived from the original on 2017-11-10. Retrieved 2010-08-22.

Computer Access Control, References

1. ^ Dieter Gollmann. *Computer Security*, 3rd ed. Wiley Publishing, 2011, p. 387, bottom
2. ^ Marcon, A. L.; Olivo Santin, A.; Stihler, M.; Bachtold, J., "A UCONabc Resilient Authorization Evaluation for Cloud Computing," *Parallel and Distributed Systems, IEEE Transactions on*, vol. 25, no. 2, pp. 457–467, Feb. 2014 doi:10.1109/TPDS.2013.113, bottom
3. ^ "Definition of: clipping level". PC Magazine.
4. ^ Jin, Xin, Ram Krishnan, and Ravi Sandhu. "A unified attribute-based access control model covering dac, mac and rbac." *Data and Applications Security and Privacy XXVI*. Springer Berlin Heidelberg, 2012. 41–55.
5. ^ Hu, Vincent C.; Ferraiolo, David; Kuhn, Rick; Schnitzer, Adam; Sandlin, Kenneth; Miller, Robert; Scarfone, Karen. "Guide to Attribute Based Access Control (ABAC) Definition and Considerations" (PDF).
6. ^ eXtensible Access Control Markup Language (XACML) V3.0 approved as an OASIS Standard, eXtensible Access Control Markup Language (XACML) V3.0 approved as an OASIS Standard.
7. ^ Ferreira, Ana; Chadwick, David; Farinha, Pedro; Correia, Ricardo; Zao, Gansen; Chiro, Rui; Antunes, Luis (2009). "How to Securely Break into RBAC: The BTG-RBAC Model". *Computer Security Applications Conference (ACSAC)*. IEEE. pp. 23–31. doi:10.1109/ACSAC.2009.12.
8. ^ Brucker, Achim D.; Petritsch, Helmut (2009). "Extending Access Control Models with Break-glass.". *ACM symposium on access control models and technologies (SACMAT)*. ACM Press. pp. 197–206. doi:10.1145/1542207.1542239.
9. ^ Ballard, Ella Deon (2013). "Identity Management Guide: Managing Identity and Authorization Policies for Linux-Based Infrastructures". Red Hat. Retrieved 2014-01-06. Any PAM service can be identified as to the host-based access control (HBAC) system in IdM.

Honey Token, References

1. ^ Honeytokens and honeypots for web ID and IH
2. ^ White Paper: "Honeypot, Honeynet, Honeytoken: Terminological issues"
3. ^ DLP and honeytokens
4. ^ IDS: RES: Protocol Anomaly Detection IDS – Honeypots
5. ^ Has my mailing list been stolen? | Plynt Security Testing Learning Center
6. ^ "Why Honeytokens Are the Future of Intrusion Detection". The Hacker News. Retrieved 2023-08-16.

Network Security, References

1. ^ "What is Network Security? Poda myre". Forcepoint. 2018-08-09. Retrieved 2020-12-05.
2. ^ A Role-Based Trusted Network Provides Pervasive Security and Compliance - interview with Jayshree Ullal, senior VP of Cisco
3. ^ Macfarlane, Richard; Buchanan, William; Ekonomou, Elias; Uthmani, Omair; Fan, Lu; Lo, Owen (2012). "Formal security policy implementations in network firewalls". *Computers & Security*. **31** (2): 253–270. doi:10.1016/j.cose.2011.10.003.
4. ^ Rana, Shrikant (2021-12-01). *The Learning Zone 8: A Textbook for Computer Science*. Shrikant Rana. ISBN 978-93-5593-008-8.
5. ^ Dave Dittrich, *Network monitoring/Intrusion Detection Systems (IDS)* Archived 2006-08-27 at the Wayback Machine, University of Washington.
6. ^ "Dark Reading: Automating Breach Detection For The Way Security Professionals Think". October 1, 2015.
7. ^ "What is a honeypot? How it protects against cyber attacks". SearchSecurity. Retrieved 2021-03-04.
8. ^ "Honeypots, Honeynets". Honeypots.net. 2007-05-26. Retrieved 2011-12-09.
9. ^ Wright, Joe; Jim Harmening (2009) "15" Computer and Information Security Handbook Morgan Kaufmann Publications Elsevier Inc p. 257
10. ^ "BIG-IP logout page" (PDF). Cnss.gov. 1970-01-01. Archived from the original (PDF) on 2012-02-27. Retrieved 2018-09-24.

Data Backup, References

1. ^ "back•up". *The American Heritage Dictionary of the English Language*. Houghton Mifflin Harcourt. 2018. Retrieved 9 May 2018.
2. ^ S. Nelson (2011). "Chapter 1: Introduction to Backup and Recovery". *Pro Data Backup and Recovery*. Apress. pp. 1–16. ISBN 978-1-4302-2663-5. Retrieved 8 May 2018.
3. ^ Cougias, D.J.; Heiberger, E.L.; Koop, K. (2003). "Chapter 1: What's a Disaster Without a Recovery?". *The Backup Book: Disaster Recovery from Desktop to Data Center*. Network Frontiers. pp. 1–14. ISBN 0-9729039-0-9.
4. ^ a b c Joe Kissell (2007). *Take Control of Mac OS X Backups* (PDF) (Version 2.0 ed.). Ithaca, NY: TidBITS Electronic Publishing. pp. 18–20 ("The Archive", meaning information repository, including versioning), 24 (client-server), 82–83 (archive file), 112–114 (Off-site storage backup rotation scheme), 126–141 (old Retrospect terminology and GUI—still used in Windows variant), 165 (client-server), 128 (subvolume—later renamed Favorite Folder in Macintosh variant). ISBN 978-0-9759503-0-2. Retrieved 17 May 2019.
5. ^ Terry Sullivan (11 January 2018). "A Beginner's Guide to Backing Up Photos". *The New York Times*. a hard drive ... an established company ... declared bankruptcy ... where many ... had ...
6. ^ McMahon, Mary (1 April 2019). "What Is an Information Repository?". wiseGEEK. Conjecture Corporation. Retrieved 8 May 2019. In the sense of an approach to data management, an information repository is a secondary storage space for data.
7. ^ "Five key questions to ask about your backup solution". sysgen.ca. 23 March 2014. Does your company have a low tolerance to longer "data access outages" and/or would you like to minimize the time your company may be without its data?. Archived from the original on 4 March 2016. Retrieved 23 September 2015.
8. ^ "Incremental Backup". Tech-FAQ. Independent Media. 13 June 2005. Archived from the original on 21 June 2016. Retrieved 10 March 2006.
9. ^ Pond, James (31 August 2013). "How Time Machine Works its Magic". Apple OSX and Time Machine Tips. baligu.com. File System Event Store, Hard Links. Retrieved 19 May 2019.
10. ^ a b Behzad Behtash (6 May 2010). "Why Continuous Data Protection's Getting More Practical". Disaster recovery/business continuity. InformationWeek. Retrieved 12 November 2011. A true CDP approach should capture all data writes, thus continuously backing up data and eliminating backup windows.... CDP is the gold standard—the most comprehensive and advanced data protection. But "near CDP" technologies can deliver enough protection for many companies with less complexity and cost. For example, snapshots can provide a reasonable near-CDP-level of protection for file shares, letting users directly access data on the file share at regular intervals—say, every half-hour or 15 minutes. That's certainly a higher level of protection than tape-based or disk-based nightly backups and may be all you need.
11. ^ a b "Continuous data protection (CDP) explained: True CDP vs near-CDP". ComputerWeekly.com. TechTarget. July 2010. Retrieved 22 June 2019. ... copies data from a source to a target. True CDP does this every time a change is made, while so-called near-CDP does this at pre-set time intervals. Near-CDP is effectively the same as snapshotting....True CDP systems record every write and copy them to the target where all changes are stored in a log. [new paragraph] By contrast, near-CDP/snapshot systems copy files in a straightforward manner but require applications to be quiesced and made ready for backup, either via the application's backup mode or using, for example, Microsoft's Volume Shadow Copy Services (VSS).
12. ^ Pond, James (31 August 2013). "How Time Machine Works its Magic". Apple OSX and Time Machine Tips. Baligu.com (as mirrored after James Pond died in 2013). Retrieved 10 July 2019. The File System Event Store is a hidden log that OSX keeps on each HFS+ formatted disk/partition of changes made to the data on it. It doesn't list every file that's changed, but each directory (folder) that's had anything changed inside it.
13. ^ de Guise, P. (2009). *Enterprise Systems Backup and Recovery: A Corporate Insurance Policy*. CRC Press. pp. 285–287. ISBN 978-1-4200-7639-4.

14. ^ Wu, Victor (4 March 2017). "EMC RecoverPoint for Virtual Machine Overview". Victor Virtual. WuChiKin. Retrieved 22 June 2019. *The splitter splits out the Write IOs to the VMDK/RDM of a VM and sends a copy to the production VMDK and also to the RecoverPoint for VMs cluster.*
15. ^ "Zerto or Veeam?". RES-Q Services. March 2017. Retrieved 7 July 2019. *Zerto doesn't use snapshot technology like Veeam. Instead, Zerto deploys small virtual machines on its physical hosts. These Zerto VMs capture the data as it is written to the host and then send a copy of that data to the replication site.....However, Veeam has the advantage of being able to more efficiently capture and store data for long-term retention needs. There is also a significant pricing difference, with Veeam being cheaper than Zerto.*
16. ^ "Agent Related". CloudEndure.com. 2019. What does the CloudEndure Agent do?. Retrieved 3 July 2019. *The CloudEndure Agent performs an initial block-level read of the content of any volume attached to the server and replicates it to the Replication Server. The Agent then acts as an OS-level read filter to capture writes and synchronizes any block level modifications to the CloudEndure Replication Server, ensuring near-zero RPO.*
17. ^ Gardner, Steve (9 December 2004). "Disk to Disk Backup versus Tape – War or Truce?". Engenio. Peaceful coexistence. Archived from the original on 7 February 2005. Retrieved 26 May 2019.
18. ^ a b c "Digital Data Storage Outlook 2017" (PDF). Spectra. Spectra Logic. 2017. p. 7(Solid-State), 10(Magnetic Disk), 14(Tape), 17(Optical). Retrieved 11 July 2018.
19. ^ a b c Tom Coughlin (29 June 2014). "Keeping Data for a Long Time". Forbes. para. Magnetic Tapes(popular formats, storage life), para. Hard Disk Drives(active archive), para. First consider flash memory in archiving(... may not have good media archive life). Retrieved 19 April 2018.
20. ^ a b c d Jacobi, John L. (29 February 2016). "Hard-core data preservation: The best media and methods for archiving your data". PC World. sec. External Hard Drives(on the shelf, magnetic properties, mechanical stresses, vulnerable to shocks), Tape, Online storage. Retrieved 19 April 2018.
21. ^ "Ramp Load/Unload Technology in Hard Disk Drives" (PDF). HGST. Western Digital. November 2007. p. 3(sec. Enhanced Shock Tolerance). Retrieved 29 June 2018.
22. ^ "Toshiba Portable Hard Drive (Canvio® 3.0)". Toshiba Data Dynamics Singapore. Toshiba Data Dynamics Pte Ltd. 2018. sec. Overview(Internal shock sensor and ramp loading technology). Retrieved 16 June 2018.
23. ^ a b "Iomega Drop Guard™ Technology" (PDF). Hard Drive Storage Solutions. Iomega Corp. 20 September 2010. pp. 2(What is Drop Shock Technology?, What is Drop Guard Technology? (... features special internal cushioning .... 40% above the industry average)), 3(*NOTE). Retrieved 12 July 2018.
24. ^ a b John Burek (15 May 2018). "The Best Rugged Hard Drives and SSDs". PC Magazine. Ziff Davis. What Exactly Makes a Drive Rugged?(When a drive is encased ... you're mostly at the mercy of the drive vendor to tell you the rated maximum drop distance for the drive). Retrieved 4 August 2018.
25. ^ Justin Krajeski; Kimber Streams (20 March 2017). "The Best Portable Hard Drive". The New York Times. Archived from the original on 31 March 2017. Retrieved 4 August 2018.
26. ^ "Best Long-Term Data Archive Solutions". Iron Mountain. Iron Mountain Inc. 2018. sec. More Reliable(average mean time between failure ... rates, best practice for migrating data). Retrieved 19 April 2018.
27. ^ Kissell, Joe (2011). Take Control of Backing Up Your Mac. Ithaca NY: TidBITS Publishing Inc. p. 41(Deduplication). ISBN 978-1-61542-394-1. Retrieved 17 September 2019.
28. ^ "Symantec Shows Backup Exec a Little Dedupe Love; Lays out Source Side Deduplication Roadmap – DCIG". DCIG. 7 July 2009. Archived from the original on 4 March 2016. Retrieved 26 February 2016.
29. ^ "Veritas NetBackup™ Deduplication Guide". Veritas. Veritas Technologies LLC. 2016. Retrieved 26 July 2018.
30. ^ S. Wan; Q. Cao; C. Xie (2014). "Optical storage: An emerging option in long-term digital preservation". Frontiers of Optoelectronics. 7 (4): 486–492. doi:10.1007/s12200-014-0442-2. S2CID 60816607.
31. ^ Q. Zhang; Z. Xia; Y.-B. Cheng; M. Gu (2018). "High-capacity optical long data memory based on enhanced Young's modulus in nanoplasmonic hybrid glass composites". Nature Communications. 9 (1): 1183. Bibcode:2018NatCo...9.1183Z. doi:10.1038/s41467-018-03589-y. PMC 5864957. PMID 29568055.
32. ^ Bärwaldt, Erik (2014). "Full Control » Linux Magazine". Linux Magazine.
33. ^ "5. Conditions That Affect CDs and DVDs • CLIR". CLIR.
34. ^ Gérard Poirier; Foued Berahou (3 March 2008). "Journal de 20 Heures". Institut national de l'audiovisuel. approximately minute 30 of the TV news broadcast. Retrieved 3 March 2008.
35. ^ "Archival Gold CD-R "300 Year Disc" Binder of 10 Discs with Scratch Armor Surface". Delkin Devices. Delkin Devices Inc. Archived from the original on 27 September 2013.
36. ^ "Optical Disc Archive Generation 2" (PDF). Optical Disc Archive. Sony. April 2016. p. 12(World's First 8-Channel Optical Drive Unit). Retrieved 15 August 2019.
37. ^ R. Micheloni; P. Olivo (2017). "Solid-State Drives (SSDs)". Proceedings of the IEEE. 105 (9): 1586–88. doi:10.1109/JPROC.2017.2727228.
38. ^ "Remote Backup". EMC Glossary. Dell, Inc. Retrieved 8 May 2018. *Effective remote backup requires that production data be regularly backed up to a location far enough away from the primary location so that both locations would not be affected by the same disruptive event.*
39. ^ Stackpole, B.; Hanrion, P. (2007). Software Deployment, Updating, and Patching. CRC Press. pp. 164–165. ISBN 978-1-4200-1329-0. Retrieved 8 May 2018.
40. ^ Gnanasundaram, S.; Shrivastava, A., eds. (2012). Information Storage and Management: Storing, Managing, and Protecting Digital Information in Classic, Virtualized, and Cloud Environments. John Wiley and Sons. p. 255. ISBN 978-1-118-23696-3. Retrieved 8 May 2018.
41. ^ Lee (25 January 2017). "What to backup – a critical look at your data". Irontree Blog. Irontree Internet Services CC. Retrieved 8 May 2018.
42. ^ Preston, W.C. (2007). Backup & Recovery: Inexpensive Backup Solutions for Open Systems. O'Reilly Media, Inc. pp. 111–114. ISBN 978-0-596-55504-7. Retrieved 8 May 2018.
43. ^ Preston, W.C. (1999). Unix Backup & Recovery. O'Reilly Media, Inc. pp. 73–91. ISBN 978-1-56592-642-4. Retrieved 8 May 2018.
44. ^ "NILFS Home". NILFS Continuous Snapshotting System. NILFS Community. 2019. Retrieved 22 August 2019.
45. ^ a b Cougias, D.J.; Heiberger, E.L.; Koop, K. (2003). "Chapter 11: Open file backup for databases". The Backup Book: Disaster Recovery from Desktop to Data Center. Network Frontiers. pp. 356–360. ISBN 0-9729039-0-9.
46. ^ Liotine, M. (2003). Mission-critical Network Planning. Artech House. p. 244. ISBN 978-1-58053-559-5. Retrieved 8 May 2018.
47. ^ de Guise, P. (2009). Enterprise Systems Backup and Recovery: A Corporate Insurance Policy. CRC Press. pp. 50–54. ISBN 978-1-4200-7639-4.
48. ^ "Open File Backup Software for Windows". Handy Backup. Novosoft LLC. 8 November 2018. Retrieved 29 November 2018.
49. ^ Reitshamer, Stefan (5 July 2017). "Troubleshooting backing up open/locked files on Windows". Arq Blog. Haystack Software. *Stefan Reitshamer is the principal developer of Arq.* Retrieved 29 November 2018.
50. ^ Boss, Nina (10 December 1997). "Oracle Tips Session #3: Oracle Backups". www.wisc.edu. University of Wisconsin. Archived from the original on 2 March 2007. Retrieved 1 December 2018.
51. ^ "What is ARCHIVE-LOG and NO-ARCHIVE-LOG mode in Oracle and the advantages & disadvantages of these modes?". Arcserve Backup. Arcserve. 27 September 2018. Retrieved 29 November 2018.
52. ^ Grešovnik, Igor (April 2016). "Preparation of Bootable Media and Images". Archived from the original on 25 April 2016. Retrieved 21 April 2016.
53. ^ Tridgell, Andrew; Mackerras, Paul; Davison, Wayne. "rsync(1) - Linux man page". linux.die.net.
54. ^ "Archive maintenance". Code42 Support. 2023.
55. ^ Pond, James (2 June 2012). "12. Should I delete old backups? If so, How?". Time Machine. baligu.com. Green box, Gray box. Retrieved 21 June 2019.
56. ^ Kissell, Joe (12 March 2019). "The Best Online Cloud Backup Service". wirecutter. The New York Times. Next, there's file retention. Retrieved 21 June 2019.
57. ^ a b c D. Cherry (2015). Securing SQL Server: Protecting Your Database from Attackers. Syngress. pp. 306–308. ISBN 978-0-12-801375-5. Retrieved 8 May 2018.
58. ^ Backups tapes a backdoor for identity thieves Archived 5 April 2016 at the Wayback Machine (28 April 2004). Retrieved 10 March 2007
59. ^ a b c Preston, W.C. (2007). Backup & Recovery: Inexpensive Backup Solutions for Open Systems. O'Reilly Media, Inc. pp. 219–220. ISBN 978-0-596-55504-7. Retrieved 8 May 2018.
60. ^ "Recovery Point Objective (Definition)". ARL Risky Thinking. Albion Research Ltd. 2007. Retrieved 4 August 2019.
61. ^ "Recovery Time Objective (Definition)". ARL Risky Thinking. Albion Research Ltd. 2007. Retrieved 4 August 2019.
62. ^ a b Little, D.B. (2003). "Chapter 2: Business Requirements of Backup Systems". Implementing Backup and Recovery: The Readiness Guide for the Enterprise. John Wiley and Sons. pp. 17–30. ISBN 978-0-471-48081-5. Retrieved 8 May 2018.
63. ^ "How do the "verify" and "write checksums to media" processes work and why are they necessary?". Veritas Support. Veritas.com. 15 October 2015. Write checksums to media. Retrieved 16 September 2019.
64. ^ HIPAA Advisory Archived 11 April 2007 at the Wayback Machine. Retrieved 10 March 2007

Cloud Computing Security, References

Incident Detection, Handling, and Response in the Cloud

1. ^ a b c d Haghighat, Mohammad; Zonouz, Saman; Abdel-Mottaleb, Mohamed (November 2015). "CloudID: Trustworthy cloud-based and cross-enterprise biometric identification". Expert Systems with Applications. 42 (21): 7905–7916. doi:10.1016/j.eswa.2015.06.025.
2. ^ a b Srinivasan, Madhan Kumar; Sarukesi, K.; Rodrigues, Paul; Manoj, M. Sai; Revathy, P. (2012). "State-of-the-art cloud computing security taxonomies". Proceedings of the International Conference on Advances in Computing, Communications and Informatics - ICACCI '12. pp. 470–476. doi:10.1145/2345396.2345474. ISBN 978-1-4503-1196-0. S2CID 18507025.
3. ^ "Swamp Computing a.k.a. Cloud Computing". Web Security Journal. 2009-12-28. Retrieved 2010-01-25.
4. ^ "Cloud Controls Matrix v4" (xlsx). Cloud Security Alliance. 15 March 2021. Retrieved 21 May 2021.
5. ^ a b "Shared Security Responsibility Model". Navigating GDPR Compliance on AWS. AWS. December 2020. Retrieved 21 May 2021.
6. ^ a b Tozzi, C. (24 September 2020). "Avoiding the Pitfalls of the Shared Responsibility Model for Cloud Security". Pal Alto Blog. Palo Alto Networks. Retrieved 21 May 2021.
7. ^ "Top Threats to Cloud Computing v1.0" (PDF). Cloud Security Alliance. March 2010. Retrieved 2020-09-19.
8. ^ Winkler, Vic. "Cloud Computing: Virtual Cloud Security Concerns". Technet Magazine, Microsoft. Retrieved 12 February 2012.
9. ^ Hickey, Kathleen (18 March 2010). "Dark Cloud: Study finds security risks in virtualization". Government Security News. Retrieved 12 February 2012.
10. ^ Winkler, Joachim R. (2011). Securing the Cloud: Cloud Computer Security Techniques and Tactics. Elsevier. p. 59. ISBN 978-1-59749-592-9.
11. ^ Andress, J. (2014). Deterrent Control - an overview | ScienceDirect Topics. Retrieved October 14, 2021, from https://www.sciencedirect.com/topics/computer-science/deterrent-control
12. ^ Virtue, T., & Rainey, J. (2015). Preventative Control - an overview | ScienceDirect Topics. Retrieved October 13, 2021, from https://www.sciencedirect.com/topics/computer-science/preventative-control
13. ^ Marturano, G. (2020b, December 4). Detective Security Controls. Retrieved December 1, 2021, from https://lifars.com/2020/12/detective-security-controls/
14. ^ Walkowski, D. (2019, August 22). What are Security Controls? Retrieved December 1, 2021, from https://www.f5.com/labs/articles/education/what-are-security-controls
15. ^ www.guidepointsecurity.com https://www.guidepointsecurity.com/education-center/cloud-security-architecture/. Retrieved 2021-12-06. {{cite web}}: Missing or empty |title= (help)
16. ^ "Gartner: Seven cloud-computing security risks". InfoWorld. 2008-07-02. Retrieved 2010-01-25.

17. ^ "Top Threats to Cloud Computing Plus: Industry Insights". Cloud Security Alliance. 2017-10-20. Retrieved 2018-10-20.
18. ^ "What is a CASB (Cloud Access Security Broker)?". CipherCloud. Archived from the original on 2018-08-31. Retrieved 2018-08-30.
19. ^ Thangasamy, Veeraiyah (2017). "Journal of Applied Technology and Innovation" (PDF). 1: 97.
20. ^ "Identity Management in the Cloud". Information Week. 2013-10-25. Retrieved 2013-06-05.
21. ^ Guarda, Teresa; Orozco, Walter; Augusto, Maria Fernanda; Morillo, Giovanna; Navarrete, Silvia Arévalo; Pinto, Filipe Mota (2016). "Penetration Testing on Virtual Environments". Proceedings of the 4th International Conference on Information and Network Security - ICINS '16. pp. 9–12. doi:10.1145/3026724.3026728. ISBN 978-1-4503-4796-9. S2CID 14414621.
22. ^ Tang, Jun; Cui, Yong; Li, Qi; Ren, Kui; Liu, Jiangchuan; Buyya, Rajkumar (28 July 2016). "Ensuring Security and Privacy Preservation for Cloud Data Services". ACM Computing Surveys. 49 (1): 1–39. doi:10.1145/2906153. S2CID 11126705.
23. ^ "Confidentiality, Integrity and Availability - The CIA Triad". CertMike. 2018-08-04. Retrieved 2021-11-27.
24. ^ Tabrizchi, Hamed; Kuchaki Rafsanjani, Marjan (2020-12-01). "A survey on security challenges in cloud computing: issues, threats, and solutions". The Journal of Supercomputing. 76 (12): 9493–9532. doi:10.1007/s11227-020-03213-1. ISSN 1573-0484. S2CID 255070071.
25. ^ Carroll, Mariana; van der Merwe, Alta; Kotzé, Paula (August 2011). "Secure cloud computing: Benefits, risks and controls". 2011 Information Security for South Africa. pp. 1–9. CiteSeerX 10.1.1.232.2868. doi:10.1109/ISSA.2011.6027519. ISBN 978-1-4577-1481-8. S2CID 6208118.
26. ^ a b Svantesson, Dan; Clarke, Roger (July 2010). "Privacy and consumer risks in cloud computing". Computer Law & Security Review. 26 (4): 391–397. doi:10.1016/j.clsr.2010.05.005. hdl:1885/57037. S2CID 62515390.
27. ^ a b c Grobauer, Bernd; Walloschek, Tobias; Stocker, Elmar (March 2011). "Understanding Cloud Computing Vulnerabilities". IEEE Security Privacy. 9 (2): 50–57. doi:10.1109/MSP.2010.115. S2CID 1156866.
28. ^ Rukavitsyn, Andrey N.; Borisenko, Konstantin A.; Holod, Ivan I.; Shorov, Andrey V. (2017). "The method of ensuring confidentiality and integrity data in cloud computing". 2017 XX IEEE International Conference on Soft Computing and Measurements (SCM). pp. 272–274. doi:10.1109/SCM.2017.7970558. ISBN 978-1-5386-1810-3. S2CID 40593182.
29. ^ Yao, Huiping; Shin, Dongwan (2013). "Towards preventing QR code based attacks on android phone using security warnings". Proceedings of the 8th ACM SIGSAC symposium on Information, computer and communications security - ASIA CCS '13. p. 341. doi:10.1145/2484313.2484357. ISBN 9781450317672. S2CID 1851039.
30. ^ Iqbal, Salman; Mat Kiah, Miss Laiha; Dhaghighi, Babak; Hussain, Muzammil; Khan, Suleman; Khan, Muhammad Khurram; Raymond Choo, Kim-Kwang (October 2016). "On cloud security attacks: A taxonomy and intrusion detection and prevention as a service". Journal of Network and Computer Applications. 74: 98–120. doi:10.1016/j.jnca.2016.08.016.
31. ^ Alashhab, Ziyad R.; Anbar, Mohammed; Singh, Manmeet Mahinderjit; Leau, Yu-Beng; Al-Sai, Zaher Ali; Abu Alhayja'a, Sami (March 2021). "Impact of coronavirus pandemic crisis on technologies and cloud computing applications". Journal of Electronic Science and Technology. 19 (1): 100059. doi:10.1016/j.jnlest.2020.100059.
32. ^ Xu, Shengmin; Yuan, Jiaming; Xu, Guowen; Li, Yingjiu; Liu, Ximeng; Zhang, Yinghui; Ying, Zuobin (October 2020). "Efficient ciphertext-policy attribute-based encryption with blackbox traceability". Information Sciences. 538: 19–38. doi:10.1016/j.ins.2020.05.115. S2CID 224845384.
33. ^ Bethencourt, John; Sahai, Amit; Waters, Brent (May 2007). "Ciphertext-Policy Attribute-Based Encryption" (PDF). 2007 IEEE Symposium on Security and Privacy (SP '07). 2007 IEEE Symposium on Security and Privacy (SP '07). pp. 321–334. doi:10.1109/SP.2007.11. ISBN 978-0-7695-2848-9. S2CID 6282684.
34. ^ Wang, Changji; Luo, Jianfa (2013). "An Efficient Key-Policy Attribute-Based Encryption Scheme with Constant Ciphertext Length". Mathematical Problems in Engineering. 2013: 1–7. doi:10.1155/2013/810969. S2CID 55470802.
35. ^ Wang, Chang-Ji; Luo, Jian-Fa (November 2012). "A Key-policy Attribute-based Encryption Scheme with Constant Size Ciphertext". 2012 Eighth International Conference on Computational Intelligence and Security. pp. 447–451. doi:10.1109/CIS.2012.106. ISBN 978-1-4673-4725-9. S2CID 1116590.
36. ^ Bethencourt, John; Sahai, Amit; Waters, Brent (May 2007). "Ciphertext-Policy Attribute-Based Encryption" (PDF). 2007 IEEE Symposium on Security and Privacy (SP '07). 2007 IEEE Symposium on Security and Privacy (SP '07). pp. 321–334. doi:10.1109/SP.2007.11. ISBN 978-0-7695-2848-9. S2CID 6282684.
37. ^ Armknecht, Frederik; Katzenbeisser, Stefan; Peter, Andreas (2012). "Shift-Type Homomorphic Encryption and Its Application to Fully Homomorphic Encryption" (PDF). Progress in Cryptology - AFRICACRYPT 2012. Lecture Notes in Computer Science. Vol. 7374. pp. 234–251. doi:10.1007/978-3-642-31410-0_15. ISBN 978-3-642-31409-4.
38. ^ Zhao, Feng; Li, Chao; Liu, Chun Feng (2014). "A cloud computing security solution based on fully homomorphic encryption". 16th International Conference on Advanced Communication Technology. pp. 485–488. doi:10.1109/icact.2014.6779008. ISBN 978-89-968650-3-2. S2CID 20678842.
39. ^ Wang, Qian; He, Meiqi; Du, Minxin; Chow, Sherman S. M.; Lai, Russell W. F.; Zou, Qin (1 May 2018). "Searchable Encryption over Feature-Rich Data". IEEE Transactions on Dependable and Secure Computing. 15 (3): 496–510. doi:10.1109/TDSC.2016.2593444. S2CID 13708908.
40. ^ Naveed, Muhammad; Prabhakaran, Manoj; Gunter, Carl A. (2014). "Dynamic Searchable Encryption via Blind Storage". 2014 IEEE Symposium on Security and Privacy. pp. 639–654. doi:10.1109/SP.2014.47. ISBN 978-1-4799-4686-0. S2CID 10910918.
41. ^ Sahayini, T (2016). "Enhancing the security of modern ICT systems with multimodal biometric cryptosystem and continuous user authentication". International Journal of Information and Computer Security. 8 (1): 55. doi:10.1504/IJICS.2016.075310.
42. ^ "Managing legal risks arising from cloud computing". DLA Piper. 29 August 2014. Retrieved 2014-11-22.
43. ^ "It's Time to Explore the Benefits of Cloud-Based Disaster Recovery". Dell.com. Archived from the original on 2012-05-15. Retrieved 2012-03-26.
44. ^ Winkler, Joachim R. (2011). Securing the Cloud: Cloud Computer Security Techniques and Tactics. Elsevier. pp. 65, 68, 72, 81, 218–219, 231, 240. ISBN 978-1-59749-592-9.
45. ^ Adams, Richard (2013). "The emergence of cloud storage and the need for a new digital forensic process model" (PDF). In Ruan, Keyun (ed.). Cybercrime and Cloud Forensics: Applications for Investigation Processes. Information Science Reference. pp. 79–104. ISBN 978-1-4666-2662-1.

IT Risk Management, References

1. ^ a b c "ISACA THE RISK IT FRAMEWORK (registration required)" (PDF). Archived from the original (PDF) on 2010-07-05. Retrieved 2010-12-14.
2. ^ a b c Enisa Risk management, Risk assessment inventory, page 46
3. ^ a b c d e f Katsicas, Sokratis K. (2009). "35". In Vacca, John (ed.). Computer and Information Security Handbook. Morgan Kaufmann Publications. Elsevier Inc. p. 605. ISBN 978-0-12-374354-1.
4. ^ "Risk is a combination of the likelihood of an occurrence of a hazardous event or exposure(s) and the severity of injury or ill health that can be caused by the event or exposure(s)" (OHSAS 18001:2007).
5. ^ a b c Caballero, Albert (2009). "14". In Vacca, John (ed.). Computer and Information Security Handbook. Morgan Kaufmann Publications. Elsevier Inc. p. 232. ISBN 978-0-12-374354-1.
6. ^ ISACA (2006). CISA Review Manual 2006. Information Systems Audit and Control Association. p. 85. ISBN 978-1-933284-15-6.
7. ^ a b c d e f g h i j k Feringa, Alexis; Goguen, Alice; Stoneburner, Gary (1 July 2002). "Risk Management Guide for Information Technology Systems". doi:10.6028/NIST.SP.800-30 – via csrc.nist.gov.
8. ^ a b "Glossary of Terms". www.niatec.iri.isu.edu.
9. ^ The Risk IT Framework by ISACA, ISBN 978-1-60420-111-6
10. ^ a b The Risk IT Practitioner Guide, Appendix 3 ISACA ISBN 978-1-60420-116-1 (registration required)
11. ^ Standard of Good Practice by Information Security Forum (ISF) Section SM3.4 Information risk analysis methodologies
12. ^ a b c d ISO/IEC, "Information technology -- Security techniques-Information security risk management" ISO/IEC FIDIS 27005:2008
13. ^ a b ISO/IEC 27001
14. ^ a b Official (ISC)2 Guide to CISSP CBK. Risk Management: Auerbach Publications. 2007. p. 1065.
15. ^ "CNN article about a class action settlement for a Veteran Affair stolen laptop". Archived from the original on 2012-01-21. Retrieved 2010-12-20.
16. ^ a b "An Introduction to Factor Analysis of Information Risk" (FAIR), Risk Management Insight LLC, November 2006 Archived 2014-11-18 at the Wayback Machine;
17. ^ Spring, J.; Kern, S.; Summers, A. (2015-05-01). "Global adversarial capability modeling". 2015 APWG Symposium on Electronic Crime Research (ECrime). pp. 1–21. doi:10.1109/ECRIME.2015.7120797. ISBN 978-1-4799-8909-6. S2CID 24580989.
18. ^ British Standard Institute "ISMSs-Part 3: Guidelines for information security risk management" BS 7799-3:2006
19. ^ Costas Lambrinoudakisa, Stefanos Gritzalisa, Petros Hatzopoulosb, Athanasios N. Yannacopoulosb, Sokratis Katsikasa, "A formal model for pricing information systems insurance contracts", Computer Standards & Interfaces - Volume 27, Issue 5, June 2005, Pages 521-532 doi:10.1016/j.csi.2005.01.010
20. ^ "Risk Reduction Overview". rro.sourceforge.net.
21. ^ a b c Gulick, Jessica; Fahlsing, Jim; Rossman, Hart; Scholl, Matthew; Stine, Kevin; Kissel, Richard (16 October 2008). "Security Considerations in the System Development Life Cycle". doi:10.6028/NIST.SP.800-64r2 – via csrc.nist.gov.
22. ^ "Wiki Content Now Available at Spaces". wiki.internet2.edu.
23. ^ "Inventory of Risk Management / Risk Assessment Methods". www.enisa.europa.eu.
24. ^ "Inventory of Risk Management / Risk Assessment Methods and Tools". www.enisa.europa.eu.
25. ^ "CLUSIF | Bienvenue". Archived from the original on 2010-10-26. Retrieved 2010-12-14.
26. ^ http://itriskinstitute.com/
27. ^ Technical Standard Risk Taxonomy ISBN 1-931624-77-1 Document Number: C081 Published by The Open Group, January 2009.
28. ^ "Build Security In - US-CERT". www.us-cert.gov.
29. ^ "Threat Sketch: A Start-up Grows Up in the Innovation Quarter". Innovation Quarter Hub. 2016-10-05. Retrieved 2016-11-15.
30. ^ "Triad Entrepreneurs Share Business Ideas on Startup Weekend". TWC News. Retrieved 2016-11-15.